Bridled POWER

New Zealand Government under MMP

Sir Geoffrey Palmer
Dr Matthew Palmer

Auckland
OXFORD UNIVERSITY PRESS
Oxford Melbourne New York

OXFORD UNIVERSITY PRESS NEW ZEALAND

Oxford New York
Athens Auckland Bangkok Bombay
Calcutta Cape Town Dar es Salaam Delhi
Florence Hong Kong Istanbul Karachi
Kuala Lumpur Madras Melbourne
Mexico City Nairobi Paris Port Moresby
Singapore Taipei Tokyo Toronto

and associated companies in
Berlin Ibadan

First edition published 1979
Second edition published 1987
Third edition published 1997

0 19558326 4

Edited by Anna Rogers
Typeset by Egan-Reid Limited
Printed through Bookpac Production Services
Published by Oxford University Press,
540 Great South Road, Greenlane,
PO Box 11-149, Auckland, New Zealand

Contents

Preface

In 1979 Geoffrey Palmer wrote a book called *Unbridled Power?*, which was important in terms of the intellectual origins of this volume. But the content was so different as to raise the question of whether it was about the same nation. In constitutional terms, New Zealand is now a different nation.

In 1987 a second edition of *Unbridled Power* appeared, when the author was then a busy minister of the Crown in a government that produced many changes to the policies and laws of New Zealand. That book reflected some of the experience of being in the crucible of political fire. It concluded with the thought that the unclimbed peaks of constitutional reform in New Zealand were the adoption of a Bill of Rights and a mixed-member proportional (MMP) electoral system of the type recommended by the 1986 Royal Commission. Both these measures have now come to pass in one form or another.

When Geoffrey Palmer became Prime Minister of New Zealand some thought the book ought to be renamed 'Unbridled Power and how to get it'. Yet political power is ephemeral and it soon passed. It was not an experience that changed the author's views on the nature and dangers of executive power. His basic convictions about the defects of New Zealand's system of government remained and were articulated in his 1992 book, *New Zealand's Constitution in Crisis: Reforming our Political System*, designed to influence the debate and to promote MMP.

One of the purposes of the first edition of *Unbridled Power?* was to provide a simple text about the New Zealand system of government as might be read by Matthew Palmer, who was then a secondary school student. In 1993 the latter completed three years of analysing and comparing the Westminster and United States constitutional systems for his doctorate at the Yale Law School, 'Constitutional Design and Law: The Political Economy of Cabinet and Congressional Government'. He then returned to work in the New Zealand Treasury. His study and experience convinced him that New Zealand's old constitution and first-past-the-post electoral system were part of a dangerously streamlined constitutional design that overvalued governmental efficiency at the expense of democratic representation.

Geoffrey Palmer is currently a partner in the public law firm of Chen & Palmer. Matthew Palmer is currently Deputy Secretary for Justice, in charge of the Public Law Group in the Ministry of Justice. The opinions expressed in this book are a mixture of the personal opinions of the two authors and *do not* represent the views of the Ministry of Justice or the New Zealand Government. We wish to express our gratitude to Mai Chen, Sue Cole, Andrew Hawke, Rachel Schmidt, Heather Toebes, and Nicola White, who have provided helpful suggestions and comments.

The primary purpose of this edition of the book is to provide easily read outlines for the New Zealand citizen who wishes to understand the system of New Zealand government on the threshold of MMP. How does it work? Where do the responsibilities lie? Who can be held to account and for what? How can citizens participate in the democratic processes of making policy, law, and expenditure decisions? Who can they complain to?

Massive numbers of changes have been made to the system of government in New Zealand since *Unbridled Power?* first appeared. Little is untouched and each chapter of this book has required substantial revision. In some areas changes have been fundamental. There has been a revolution with the adoption of MMP, as well as the growth in the Treaty of Waitangi jurisprudence, the enactment of the Constitution Act 1986 and the New Zealand Bill of Rights Act 1990, and the reform of the state sector accountability and financial management regimes through the State-Owned Enterprises Act 1986, the State Sector Act 1988, the Public Finance Act 1989, and the Fiscal Responsibility Act 1994. Furthermore, the international trends in law, technology, culture, and commerce, which influence New Zealand in so many ways, are now more obvious. New Zealand's constitutional system is now much less streamlined. With MMP, in particular, New Zealand government is less skewed in favour of efficiency of decision-making and more encouraging of democratic representation and dialogue. Hence we have decided to call this book *Bridled Power*.

New Zealand may now have fashioned its own uniquely New Zealand system of government, but it will continue to evolve and change. There are uncertainties, as illustrated by the debates about the future of the right of appeal to the Privy Council, about the appropriate place of the Treaty of Waitangi, and about whether New Zealand should become a republic. For a constitution to work properly, people need to understand it. This book is designed to be a guide to the modern New Zealand constitution and government in the age of MMP. It offers a stimulus to public debate which, after all, underlies any democratic constitution. *Bridled*

Power also offers some ideas about the future. And what form that takes will depend ultimately on what sort of society New Zealanders believe they live in.

Geoffrey Palmer
Matthew Palmer
25 August 1996

part one

government

1 The Changing System of New Zealand Government

INTRODUCTION

A constitution is the system or body of fundamental principles under which a nation is constituted or governed; it sets up the framework for government itself. The nature of New Zealand's constitution has been fundamental to the way in which governments have behaved in the past. It has been an important influence on New Zealand's society, culture, economy, and history while, in turn, being influenced by them. Improvement in New Zealand's constitutional ground rules can lead to widespread improvement in the quality of government decisions and in the well-being of our society. Now, more than ever, we should heed the late Professor Quentin-Baxter's words:[1]

> A constitution is a human habitation. Like a city, it may preserve its life and beauty through centuries of change. It may, on the other hand, become either a glorious ruin from which life has departed, or a dilapidated slum that no longer knows the great tradition of its builders. Constitutions, like ancient buildings, need the care and protection of an Historic Places Trust, to draw attention to weaknesses in the fabric, and to suggest how present needs can be met without sacrificing the inspiration of the past. They also need an enlightened and interested general public, with a strong collective feeling about the difference between a folly and a landmark of enduring significance.

Our primary purpose in undertaking the substantial revisions necessary to *Unbridled Power?* is to inform and educate New Zealanders in a straightforward, accessible manner, about the ground rules of the New Zealand system of government, particularly as they are undergoing fundamental changes brought by the transition to an MMP (mixed-member proportional) electoral system. Constitutions do not stand still—they develop over time. The three editions of

---

[1] R.Q. Quentin-Baxter, 'The Governor-General's Constitutional Discretions: An Essay towards a Redefinition', 10 *Victoria University of Wellington Law Review*, 1980, p.313.

Unbridled Power? have seen many dramatic changes in New Zealand's constitution but none have been so far-reaching as the changes flowing from the change of the electoral system from first-past-the-post (FPP) to MMP.

It is too early to identify all the constitutional changes that accompany MMP. We, however, feel that, as a result of MMP, government in New Zealand will be more democratic and more accountable than before. New Zealand's constitution under FPP offered the most streamlined executive decision-making machine in the democratic world—once elected to government a political party could do what it liked for the next three years. MMP changes that fundamentally. Hence we have called this book *Bridled Power*. In it we provide informed speculation about the nature of MMP-related changes while covering the significant features of New Zealand's constitution and government.[2]

NEW ZEALAND'S CHANGING CONSTITUTION

In 1852 the Imperial Parliament at Westminster conferred on New Zealand an elaborate and extensive constitutional structure. The New Zealand Constitution Act 1852 was 'An act to grant a Representative Constitution to the Colony of New Zealand'. The act was much amended over the years, as New Zealand progressed from self-government to dominion status and gradually acquired the status of a completely independent nation.

To a substantial extent New Zealand has been in charge of its own rules of government since 1857, although the New Zealand Parliament was clearly legally subordinate to the Parliament of the United Kingdom until 1947, when New Zealand secured full control with the passing by the New Zealand Parliament of the Statute of Westminster Adoption Act (and the enactment by the United Kingdom Parliament, at New Zealand's request, of the New Zealand Constitution

---

[2] For readers who want to go into the issues raised in this book in greater depth, or from different perspectives, the following recent publications may assist: Cabinet Office, *Cabinet Office Manual*, Wellington, 1996; J. Boston, S. Levine, E. McLeay, & N. Roberts, *New Zealand under MMP*, Auckland University Press with Bridget Williams Books, Auckland, 1996; Electoral Commission, *Everything You Need to Know about Voting Under MMP: New Zealand's Electoral System*, GP Publications, Wellington, 1996; State Services Commission, *Working Under Proportional Representation: A Reference for the Public Service*, Wellington, 1995; M. Chen & G. Palmer, *Public Law in New Zealand: Materials, Commentary and Questions*, Oxford University Press, Auckland, 1993; P. Joseph, *Constitutional and Administrative Law in New Zealand*, Law Book Company, Sydney, 1993; D. McGee, *Parliamentary Practice in New Zealand*, GP Publications, Wellington, 1994; E.M. McLeay, *The Cabinet and Political Power in New Zealand*, Oxford University Press, Auckland, 1995; A. McRobie (ed.), *Taking It to the People?: The New Zealand Electoral Referendum Debate*, Hazard Press, Christchurch, 1993; R. Mulgan, *Politics in New Zealand*, Auckland University Press, Auckland, 1994; G. Palmer, *New Zealand's Constitution in Crisis: Reforming Our Political System*, John McIndoe, Dunedin, 1992.

Amendment Act). Curiously, it took New Zealand from 1931, when the Statute of Westminster was passed by the United Kingdom Parliament, until 1947 to cut the constitutional apron string. Other oddities remained even longer. The United Kingdom could still make law for New Zealand by the request and consent of the New Zealand Parliament until that power was removed by the Constitution Act 1986. Finally and completely, the New Zealand constitution was 'patriated' to New Zealand.

Otherwise, the constitutional history of New Zealand from 1852 until 1986 was largely a whittling away of the 1852 act until all that was left at the end were twelve provisions where once there had been eighty-two. These provisions gave no clue as to the structure of government in New Zealand or how power was exercised. The old Constitution Act was a relic, harmless, but also useless.

It is very doubtful whether this strange relic would have changed quickly had it not been for a constitutional crisis in 1984. In July 1984, immediately after the Labour Government was elected, a serious constitutional event occurred. It arose from the unwillingness of the outgoing National Prime Minister, Sir Robert Muldoon, to recommend to the Governor-General urgent financial measures concerning devaluation of the currency which those who would form the incoming government saw as essential. Under New Zealand law then, there was real doubt whether, in law, an opposition party which had won a general election could immediately form a government and take responsibility for the measures. In the event, a grave situation was narrowly averted.

The crisis exposed major uncertainties in New Zealand's constitutional law. Clear practical rules to enable a swift transfer of power were needed, so the government decided to set up an expert committee of officials to examine the issue and make recommendations. The terms of reference dealt not only with the transfer of power problem but also required the committee to make a general review of New Zealand's constitutional provisions with the object of putting the most important into one enactment. The result was a report that formed the basis for the Constitution Act 1986,[3] which was passed by the New Zealand Parliament with unanimous support. Even though it contains nothing radical, it represented a new constitutional beginning. To the public it passed without fanfare. Only eight submissions were received by the select committee of Parliament which scrutinised the bill.

NEW ZEALAND'S WESTMINSTER CONSTITUTION—UNTIL MMP

Most nations have a document called a constitution that lays down the framework

[3] Report of an Officials Committee, *Constitutional Reform*, Department of Justice, Wellington, February 1986.

of government and sets many of the rules. The Constitution Act 1986 contains less detail and coverage than most similar documents elsewhere.

The purpose of the act, as stated in its long title, is: '. . . to reform the constitutional law of New Zealand, to bring together in one enactment certain provisions of constitutional significance, and to provide that the New Zealand Constitution Act 1852 of the Parliament of the United Kingdom shall cease to have effect as part of the law of New Zealand.' To that end, it sets out in law a few key rules, which we will meet throughout this book, regarding four sets of key constitutional institutions:

- The Sovereign: the Queen and her representative the Governor-General;
- The executive: ministers of the Crown and parliamentary under-secretaries and public servants;
- The legislature: the House of Representatives, Parliament;
- The judiciary: judges.

One of the significant features of the Constitution Act 1986 is that it brings together in one enactment the most important constitutional provisions scattered around the statute books. The fragmentary nature of New Zealand's statutory constitutional law made it largely inaccessible. Much of it was obscure. Some of it was still in terms more appropriate for a colony than for a sovereign state. The 1986 act brings together the principal pieces of statutory constitutional law in a coherent whole, so that we now have a law containing much of what modern constitutions generally include. The act is, however, still only a basic guide to the composition and powers of even the key institutions of government. Most of the detail as to how they actually work is to be found elsewhere.

New Zealand's 'constitution', in the widest sense, is also to be found in other documents (such as legislation enacted in the United Kingdom and New Zealand, in prerogative instruments made by the Queen as Queen of New Zealand, and in judgments of the courts), in broader constitutional principles and ideas, and in day-to-day practice of participants in the constitutional system. The Governor-General, Parliament, political parties, caucus, Cabinet, the public service, other agencies, and the courts make up the institutions of the New Zealand Government. The web of relationships between them determines, in large measure, how we are governed.

The relationship between these units is complex. They all have different functions, and their responsibilities frequently overlap. The division between formal legal powers and the actual exercise of political power adds to the confusion. For example, no one doubts that Cabinet is a vital actor in our system of government, yet it is almost unknown to the common law and to statute. In law it is no more than an informal committee that operates according to a series of conventions that the law will probably not enforce. Constitutional conventions are customs or practices that politicians and commentators generally acknowledge to be effective rules. Parliamentary sovereignty, ministerial responsibility, and the Governor-General's exercise of power are all important constitutional conventions.

In 1867 Walter Bagehot described the Westminster system of government in a way that is still relevant:[4]

> The efficient secret of the English Constitution may be described as the close union, the nearly complete fusion, of the executive and legislative power. No doubt by the traditional theory, as it exists in all the books, the goodness of our Constitution consists in the entire separation of the legislative and executive authorities, but in truth its merit consists in their singular approximation. The connecting link is the Cabinet. By that new word we mean a committee of the legislative body selected to be the executive body. . . . a cabinet is a combining committee—a *hyphen* which joins, a buckle which fastens the legislative part of the State to the executive part of the State. In its origin it belongs to the one, in its functions it belongs to the other.

One way to make sense of the component parts of the New Zealand Westminster constitution, under the single-party majority governments that ruled before MMP, is understood by examining a simplifying diagram, such as Figure 1.1 below.

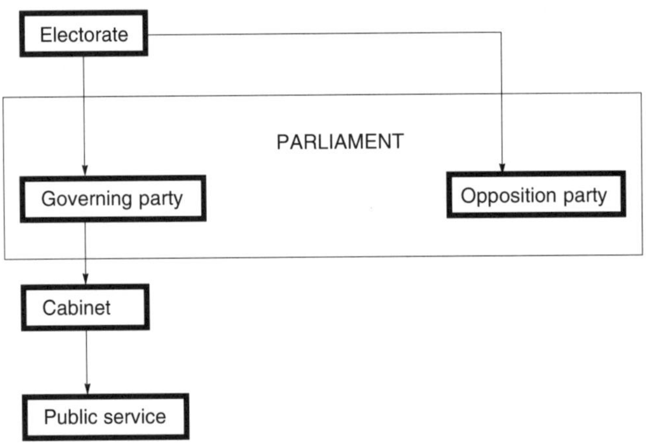

Figure 1.1: Single-party majority government under FPP

The key series of relationships in New Zealand's Westminster system of single-party majority government, the norm before MMP, are those between the electorate, the governing party, the Cabinet, and the public service. This series of relationships is sustained by several key characteristics of the Westminster constitution:

---

[4] W. Bagehot, *The English Constitution*, London, 1945, p.12.

- *A single political party is elected to government.* The central democratic element in our government is the election of members of Parliament (MPs). Elections must be held at least every three years and they may be held more frequently. The country is divided into electorates, each represented by an MP. Until 1996, there were ninety-nine MPs. They were elected under a first-past-the-post electoral system (FPP), which contained a systematic bias in favour of a single party obtaining a majority of parliamentary seats, thereby electing it to government. Single-party majority governments are still possible under MMP, but much less likely.
- *The governing party selects the Cabinet from among its own MPs.* Because a single party has a majority in Parliament, and therefore the 'confidence' of the House of Representatives, it can appoint its own leader as Prime Minister and its own members to run the government as Cabinet ministers. In a National Party Government the leader selects colleagues to hold ministerial office. In a Labour Party Government, the Labour MPs (the caucus) elect the Cabinet ministers by secret ballot, then the Prime Minister allocates the portfolios.
- *The governing party acts as one unit.* There are strong pressures on all MPs in a single governing party (the caucus) to be very disciplined in following whatever decision the Cabinet as a whole makes. This is because of the comparatively small size of the New Zealand Parliament in international terms and because Cabinet dominates the government caucus through seniority, experience, and numbers.
- *The governing party dominates Parliament, which can make any law it wishes.* The constitutional doctrine of parliamentary sovereignty gives Parliament virtually unlimited political power. With some uncertain limitations around the edges, Parliament can 'make or unmake' any law it wishes.[5] Since a single party controls a majority of parliamentary votes, the modern New Zealand Parliament has been highly unlikely to pass legislation or approve measures that were unacceptable to the Cabinet or even not to accept the government's proposals. There have been qualifications to this rule. Sometimes on matters of conscience, such as abortion, homosexual law reform, or capital punishment, MPs voted according to their own personal views and not according to party policy. And the members of the government caucus could, and sometimes did, stop the Cabinet from pursuing a certain course. In theory, the MPs could combine to turn a government out by passing a motion of no confidence in it or by denying it funds to continue. Under the domination of a two-party system, where party discipline was exceedingly strict, as it has been in New Zealand from 1935 until 1993, this possibility was remote and theoretical.

---

5 A.V. Dicey, *Introduction to the Study of the Law of the Constitution*, 10th ed., Macmillan, London, 1959, pp.406–11.

- *The Cabinet runs the government through the public service.* The public service is the machinery of government. What government does is done largely by public servants: collecting taxes, paying social welfare benefits, and performing the countless number of tasks that citizens demand of modern government. The Cabinet directs the public service, largely as a result of the constitutional 'conventions', or practices, of individual ministerial responsibility and collective Cabinet responsibility. Public servants must be politically neutral but must otherwise serve the incumbent minister and Cabinet to the best of their professional ability.

Two institutions that do not figure in the key series of relationships examined in Figure 1.1 are the courts and the opposition parties in Parliament. Both are important to the constitution. The opposition parties (usually one main opposition party, under FPP) represent the governing party's competition in the next election. As examined further in Part III, they use all the procedures of Parliament, including parliamentary questions, select committee investigations, and parliamentary debate, to scrutinise and criticise vigorously the actions of the government. The courts are independent of the other institutions and judge the actions of all other institutions against the law. The courts provide authoritative interpretations of the laws where disputes arise. Their function is to provide fair, impartially administered justice according to law. In the end, however, the power of the courts and the opposition parties under a single-party majority government is dominated by the key institutions, notably the governing party and its Cabinet. The opposition parties have always held a minority of seats in an FPP Parliament and so could not enforce their criticisms of the government. The courts can only apply the law and through its dominance of Parliament the government can change the law.

Similarly, there are a variety of other institutions, practices, laws, and conventions that have restrained the exercise of power by the governing party and its Cabinet in New Zealand's Westminster system before MMP. Each chapter in Part IV of this book concerns a significant aspect of restraint on government:

- *Local government* plays an important role in exercising power over a variety of aspects of New Zealand life. But its role is governed by the laws passed by the national Parliament.
- *Public opinion* indicates the electoral chances of a governing party. But an election can seem a long time away and is rarely won or lost on a single issue. Official information is usually available to the general public, media, and lobbyists, under the Official Information Act. It helps to ensure that the reasons for government decisions cannot be easily hidden.
- *Avenues for complaint* exist in growing multitudes of independent offices: the Ombudsmen, the Privacy Commissioner, the Human Rights Commission, the Race Relations Conciliator, the Parliamentary Commissioner for the

Environment. But these bodies have mostly advisory roles with limited compulsory powers over government.

- *The New Zealand Bill of Rights Act 1990* now provides the courts with a set of independent basic standards of conduct against which the government can be judged, as do the principles of administrative law. But these standards can be overridden by laws passed by Parliament.
- *The Treaty of Waitangi* is an increasingly fruitful source of claims to the Waitangi Tribunal and lawsuits against the government. But its effectiveness depends to a large extent on the inclusion of references to the treaty in laws passed by Parliament.
- *International law* is of growing importance to international relations and commerce in the modern world. Although its effectiveness depends on the government's willingness to accede to a treaty or to accept an international judgment, in many instances the New Zealand Government has no practical choice but to accept the internationally agreed standard.

UNBRIDLED POWER UNDER FPP

Criticism of the unbridled power of the Cabinet and governing party in New Zealand's constitution under FPP has been at the heart of the earlier editions of this book (and the political career of author Geoffrey Palmer). The combined effect of the above restraints on government is increasingly significant in practice, as evidenced by the revisions since this book was first published in 1979. Yet New Zealand's Westminster constitution before MMP still had at its heart an extraordinarily streamlined decision-making machine. The governing party and its Cabinet directly dominated two of the three branches of government—the executive and legislature—and could overrule the third—the judiciary.

A concentration of power in one group or one person always presents dangers. Where power is divided between several groups, such dangers will be reduced. A short example will illustrate the point. A ruler with absolute power may do all of the following things: (a) pass a law that makes shop-lifting an offence punishable by death; (b) direct the police force to apprehend only shop-lifters; (c) adjudicate on all cases of shop-lifting to decide who is guilty of it; and (d) execute offenders. Such a ruler would be carrying out three functions: legislative, executive and judicial. Many advantages flow from dividing up power between different sections of government. The famous English legal writer William Blackstone wrote in 1765: 'In all tyrannical governments, the supreme magistracy, or the right both of *making and enforcing* the laws is vested in one and the same man, or one and the same body of men; and wherever these two powers are united together, there can be no public liberty.'[6]

---

[6] W. Blackstone, *Commentaries on the Laws of England,* reprint of 1st ed., Dawsons of Pall Mall, London, 1966, Vol. 1, p.142.

Practically, we cannot have either complete separation or complete fusion of powers. Some coordination of the various policies and administration in government as a whole is necessary; it would be impossible with complete separation of powers. Complete fusion, on the other hand, would tend to make control of the government by the people impossible and would tend to produce tyrannical government. The trick is to get sufficient coordination but not so much as becomes oppressive and unresponsive to the wishes of the public. Governmental power can be rendered less oppressive by dividing it up between various branches. And government can be made responsive by subjecting it to popular control in the form of elections.

As set out in the Constitution Act 1986, our system has three separate branches of government that correspond in a very rough and ready way to the legislative (Parliament), the executive (the Governor-General, Cabinet and the public service), and the judicial (the courts). The functions of New Zealand's three main branches of government are not identical with the functions their names suggest; the powers have overlapped and been amalgamated. Nonetheless, the theory of the separation of powers provides a useful touchstone in finding the location of powers in the New Zealand Government and judging the propriety of the arrangement. If any one of them carried out all three tasks, as in the example above, we would live under an autocracy.

The central feature of the old New Zealand system of government was a concentration of power in the central government. The distribution of power within that government resulted in effective power being located in a fusion of the legislature and executive—the governing party and its Cabinet. The dominance by Cabinet meant that the New Zealand system had been characterised as amounting to 'executive paradise'.[7] The predominance of the executive, when combined with the way in which Parliament, political parties, pressure groups, the media, and the public interact in the debating and making of policy decisions, produced a low level of public confidence in New Zealand's system of government. The performance of the system, and the public attitude to it, must be regarded as factors that caused the MMP referendum to carry.

The primary restraint on the executive's power was that the governing party faced the electorate at least once every three years. This was an important sanction, which made the system democratic and the government accountable to the people.[8] Limited parliamentary terms are a key feature of the Westminster system, which has been copied (and modified) around the world. And New Zealanders

7 L. Zines, *Constitutional Change in the Commonwealth*, Cambridge University Press, Cambridge, 1991, p.47.

8 R.G. Mulgan, 'Review Article: Palmer, Parliament and the Constitution', 32 *Political Science*, pp.171, 173; L. Cleveland, *The Politics of Utopia: New Zealand and its Government*, Methuen, Wellington, 1979, pp.10–11, 19–21.

traditionally seemed to want strong government with clear parliamentary majorities to act decisively in response to public demands.

From the early 1980s, however, successive Labour and National Governments used the power of the Westminster system to enact radical policies that were either contrary to their announced intentions in their election manifestos or at least not mentioned in them. The perceived difference between parties' electoral promises and their actions in government may have played an important role in persuading the public to vote for MMP in an attempt to tame the old system. They wanted their opinions to be taken into account.

Furthermore, many saw some results of the electoral system itself as unfair. The Royal Commission on the Electoral System found that 'since 1954 all Governments have been elected with the support of fewer than half the voters'.[9] Even in the landslide election of 1990, the National Party did not secure 50 per cent of the valid votes cast. In 1978 and 1981, Labour won more votes across New Zealand than National, but National's were better spread in marginal seats, so National had the majority and formed the government.

Whatever the political causes, the public's diagnosis, in referenda in 1992 and 1993, was of a terminal constitutional condition and the prescription was a change in the electoral system to a form of proportional representation—MMP.

MMP AND ITS LIKELY EFFECTS

A referendum conducted in conjunction with the general election in 1993 ushered in a new system of voting for parliamentary elections, a system known as MMP. In a special referendum in 1992, in which 55 per cent of eligible voters voted, 85 per cent of voters were in favour of a change to the voting system and, of four system options, 70 per cent were in favour of MMP. With the 1993 general election there was a binding referendum, in which 85 per cent of eligible voters voted, where 54 per cent voted for MMP and 46 per cent voted for the existing FPP system.[10]

Although MMP is simply a change in the voting system it has wider effects on the performance of the entire New Zealand system of government. It is likely to slow the system down and make it less friendly to executive power. It is likely to increase the distinction between the executive and Parliament. It will also revitalise Parliament.

Electoral change in New Zealand arrived not as an immediate reaction to the performance of the old constitutional system but from a 1986 Report of the

---

9 Report of the Royal Commission on the Electoral System, *Towards a Better Democracy*, Wellington, December 1986, p.14.

10 S. Levine & N. Roberts, 'The New Zealand General Election and Electoral Referendum of 1993', 46(1) *Political Science*, 1993, pp.40, 64.

Royal Commission on the Electoral System, *Towards a Better Democracy*. The logic of that report was founded firmly on the performance of the electoral system itself rather than upon the wider constitutional and structural issues emphasised above. Until this report there had been no serious official analysis of the basic principles of the electoral system; it was simply assumed that FPP was the system. The report's principal recommendation was to adopt a different voting system.[11] The commissioners recommended that the existing FPP or plurality system be replaced by an MMP system. Germany's system is the closest to the one recommended. Under proportional representation, seats in Parliament are allocated in relation to each party's share of the popular vote.

When the 1993 referendum was carried in favour of MMP, a new Electoral Act 1993 came into force, providing for the procedures for holding MMP elections. This is explained further in Chapter 2. Broadly, there are 120 MPs of which five represent Maori electorates, sixty represent general electorates, and fifty-five are chosen from the 'party lists'. Each voter has two votes. One vote, the constituency vote, is for an MP to represent the voter's electorate (general or Maori). The candidate with the most votes in an electorate will win a seat in Parliament. The other vote, the list vote, will be for a political party. Each party will receive the total number of seats in Parliament that corresponds to the proportion of the list votes it receives, if it is above 5 per cent (and taking into account the number of constituency seats its candidates win). The overall effect is that parties' strengths in Parliament will reflect the percentage of list votes they receive.

The change in the electoral system is so fundamental to New Zealand's constitution because it makes it much more unlikely that one political party will get a majority of seats in Parliament. Every list vote will count towards a voter's preferred party getting seats in Parliament. Under the FPP system, only votes in a few marginal electorates, where the result was close, affected the overall outcome of an election. Political science studies show that the FPP system had a distinct bias to producing only two viable political parties.[12] Moving to a form of proportional representation, even a modified form such as MMP, makes room for more viable political parties. When there are more than two political parties, it is unlikely that one will receive a majority of votes and therefore a majority of seats in Parliament. That could still occur—there could be a single-party majority government—but it is more likely that, to form a government, several parties will have to cooperate in some way: either by forming a government and sharing Cabinet positions together (a coalition government) or by one party agreeing generally to support another in government but not taking part in Cabinet (a minority government). In fact, since coalitions could be majority or minority governments and a minority

11 Report of the Royal Commission on the Electoral System.

12 E.g., R. Taagepera & M. Shugart, *Seats and Votes: The Effects and Determinants of Electoral Systems*, Yale University Press, New Haven, 1989.

government could be formed by one party or several parties, there are a variety of possibilities. The process of forming a government is outlined further in Chapter 2.

Once a single party no longer controls Cabinet and Parliament, the way in which governmental power is exercised changes throughout the system. Although the way in which MMP will work and how it will alter the working of the system cannot be confidently asserted at the time of writing, a number of tendencies can be discerned and they are presented throughout this book. We highlight some of the more significant implications here.

Before either a coalition or a minority government is formed, however, it is likely that the Governor-General will have more power under MMP. Without a single party having a majority in Parliament, the Governor-General may have more effective discretion than in the past in exercising the 'reserve powers' of the Sovereign in deciding who to ask to form a government and in dealing with requests for dissolutions of Parliament, although the powers are subservient to those of the House of Representatives in determining the identity of the government. The time taken to form a government may also be lengthy, perhaps as long as several months, as parties negotiate over the basis on which a government will run. During that period a caretaker government will be in place and controversial decisions will be avoided.

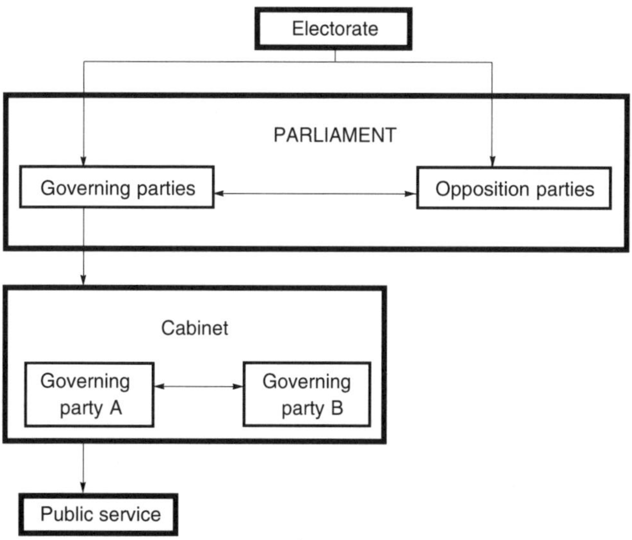

Figure 1.2: Minority and coalition governments under MMP

Compared with FPP, MMP encourages the formation of minority and coalition governments rather than single-party majority governments. The key changes likely to occur under minority or coalition governments compared with single-party majority governments include:

- *Parliament and opposition parties will determine the continued existence of a minority government.* If they have a majority, the opposition parties will be able to topple a minority governing party from office through a vote of no confidence in Parliament. Whether this happens will depend on the strength of individual parties, whether a new government could be formed without an election, the attitude of particular parties and their voters to the policies of the government, and whether particular parties see advantage in having another election.
- *There will be less pressure on Cabinet ministers to agree publicly with coalition Cabinet decisions.* The convention of public unanimity between ministers in a coalition Cabinet will no longer be reinforced by the fact that they all belong to the same political party.
- *The role of the Prime Minister and senior officials in coordinating ministers and officials will be more difficult in a coalition Cabinet.* Cooperation between ministers and between public servants serving different ministers is essential for the smooth running of executive government. Where ministers are from different parties and trust between ministers is diminished, there may be more explicit pressure inhibiting that cooperation. This will make the role of the Prime Minister and senior public servants more important in ensuring that government processes continue to function.
- *Public servants will face more direct pressure from opposition politicians.* Public servants are likely to have to brief opposition MPs more often, in the process of consulting opposition parties over government policies, especially under a minority government. Furthermore, public servants will not be able to rely on a minority governing party in Parliament or on select committees to protect them from constitutionally inappropriate questioning by opposition MPs.
- *Ministers may tend to make decisions within their portfolios without reference to a coalition Cabinet.* It is always difficult to know when a matter needs to go to Cabinet and when an individual minister can deal with it. In a coalition Cabinet there may be increased incentives to avoid collective Cabinet decision-making. It may also be tempting for individual ministers to circumvent a minority Cabinet by negotiating with opposition parties.
- *Regulations will tend to be used to avoid the need for legislation under a minority government.* Since a minority government needs other parties' support to pass legislation but not to pass regulations, it will tend to favour implementing policies by regulation. This will, in turn, increase the importance of the mechanisms used to scrutinise regulations.

- *Parliament and opposition parties will determine whether particular minority government policies will be implemented through legislation and possibly whether particular individual ministers will resign.* Each minority government policy that needs legislation will require the votes of one or more opposition parties to be passed through Parliament. This will entail much negotiation between parties. Opposition parties may also be able to force individual ministers to resign more easily. All this will mean that Parliament will be much more important than before. Parliamentary debate is likely to be meaningful as parties and the public listen to speeches to gauge whether a particular piece of legislation will be passed, defeated, or modified.
- *Legislation that is not supported by a minority government, and sometimes a coalition government, may be passed.* Opposition parties will be able to combine to pass a member's bill (formerly a private member's bill) even if a minority government opposes it. If a coalition agreement allows, the same may even occur under a coalition government.
- *Select committees of Parliament will be more important to the passage of legislation and the scrutiny of government through select committee investigations.* A minority governing party will not have a majority on select committees and can expect to face more searching scrutiny of its legislation in select committees and, potentially, embarrassing investigations by select committees. The increased number of MPs is also likely to assist the effectiveness of select committees under coalition governments.
- *There will be pressure to increase the resources available to Parliament, select committees, and political parties.* Opposition parties are likely to push for increased quality and quantity of expert advice that is independent of the government.
- *The judiciary may take up an increased policy-making role.* Increased use of regulations may lead to more challenges to regulatory power in the courts. If legislative wording that results from compromise between parties in Parliament or coalition partners in Cabinet is unclear or ambiguous, policy decisions will effectively be left to the courts. If legislation proves more difficult to pass under a minority or coalition government, courts may be under more pressure to take up an increased policy-making role.
- *There may be more meaningful public debate over government policy.* The public nature of debate and increased interparty negotiation, in a coalition Cabinet or a minority government Parliament, is likely to slow down the process of legislating and may increase the extent to which public consultation affects government policy. The key factor will be the need to build consensus.

In broad terms, MMP in New Zealand is likely to make the executive less dominant. Government power will be less concentrated and more separated. In some other countries, notably the United States, people tend to regard government as a necessary evil that should use and be given the least possible powers. New Zealand, almost since its European beginnings, did not follow that view. To New Zealanders, the government was a friend. It did for them things that they wanted done. The streamlined system of government decision-making made it internationally remarkable how easy it was for the New Zealand Government to do things, even if individuals' rights and freedoms sometimes got in the way. Since 1984 the role of government in New Zealand society has retreated somewhat. The speed, suddenness, and completeness of those policy shifts have also been internationally remarkable.

MMP does not mean that government will be impossible or will not take place. There will always be a government; that is one of the constitutional necessities of our system. And the basic structures and processes of Westminster government originally evolved in an era, before the dominance of the two-party system, which was more similar to relationships under MMP than FPP. Traditional mechanisms such as the vote of confidence, individual ministerial responsibility, and the power of Parliament make more sense in a multi-party than in a two-party system. In some ways, the new system will make more difference to the politicians and the political process than it will to the machinery of government itself. It may, however, be harder for one element of government to get its own way. In policy terms, MMP may mean that it is more difficult to change policy, but once it is in place a change is likely to be more enduring. MMP probably means that policy is more contestable, lobbying will be more common, and there will be greater public debate over government policy. To change major policies may require the development of a consensus. It seems to us that to slow down New Zealand's decision-making process and to introduce more public dialogue is no bad thing.

A MODIFIED PROCESS FOR MAKING DECISIONS?

How does government make decisions? The mechanisms tend to be extremely complex and the pattern of decision-making differs markedly from one kind of decision to another, depending upon the type of decision, the importance of the issue, and the interests at stake. The remainder of this chapter will outline, in simplified form, some of the more important stages of government decision-making, and speculate about the likely effects of the change to MMP.

Members of a political party tend to agree on their broad approach to public affairs. At conferences they discuss what policies to adopt. At election time they present to the public manifestos containing, often quite specifically, the measures they will adopt if they are elected to office. Many ideas that end up in the law or as part of government policy come from political parties. These tend to be the most important proposals in terms of scope. Under MMP, though, policies will be subject to more interparty negotiation and hence compromise. This is most likely to occur at the time of government decision-making on individual policies. It is likely, however, that parties will negotiate over key policies before or after an election in order to signal the nature of the government they form. Under MMP, specific election manifesto commitments are less likely to be made; parties will tend to rely more on projecting their political philosophy and identity through a general image.

Pressure groups, such as the Manufacturers Federation, Federated Farmers, the insurance companies, or the trade union movement, also urge changes that will help their members and oppose those against their interests. This lobbying, and the number of lobby groups, can be expected to increase under MMP since there will be more potential pressure points through which to propose or oppose policy change.

In terms of numbers of policies, many proposals emanate from the public service—the officials of government—in liaison with ministers. Public servants, who are responsible for administering the various statutes and schemes that make up the programmes of the New Zealand Government, can see defects in administration and are in a strong position to suggest changes. Almost all government policies in the past have been subject to scrutiny by public servants who advise ministers accordingly. Under a minority government, however, member's bills could be passed by Parliament without such scrutiny or advice. The constitutional role of the public servants is to advise the minister in charge of their department and to carry out his or her orders. Public servants tend to control much of the detail of policies, subject to the supervision of Cabinet ministers. Compared with ministers, they have at their disposal the power of information.

Whether a policy proposal comes from a member of the public, a pressure group, a party manifesto, or elsewhere, the minister concerned is a key figure in any decision to adopt or reject initiatives. The minister receives from the department a report on the idea that indicates weaknesses in the proposal, poses alternatives, and comments on practicability.

The cockpit of the decision-making system is Cabinet itself. This is likely to continue under MMP, although the decisions made by Cabinet under a minority government will no longer be so determinative of the end result. Cabinet meets regularly on Mondays, forty-eight weeks of the year, and very occasionally at other times. Cabinet and its committees will consider some 2500 submissions in a year as well as oral items that are not necessarily the subject of papers. At a typical meeting, Cabinet itself will make thirty decisions. Submissions or reports to Cabinet committees are presented by ministers but are usually written by public servants in the name of their minister. Few major items of government policy are settled without the approval of Cabinet or a Cabinet committee. Cabinet rules provide that particular departments must advise on proposals with implications for their area of expertise. For instance, all proposals involving government expenditure are examined by Treasury before being decided on by Cabinet or the relevant Cabinet committee. Officials committees are often used by ministers to ensure that the quality of advice in Cabinet papers is sound and that all relevant consultation has been undertaken. There may be pressure for greater institutionalisation of such procedures in a coalition Cabinet where ministers of different parties will want to ensure that their department knows about proposals and has commented on them.

Once a week while Parliament is in session all MPs of each party meet to discuss tactics and policy in confidence. This meeting is called 'caucus'. After a Cabinet decision has been reached upon a proposal it may be discussed in the government caucus. Caucus proceedings are secret. In the past, both major parties have had a standing system of caucus committees to deal with particular topics and to help a minister who refers a policy proposal to it for discussion. Under a coalition government, of course, no single party will encompass the whole government and so will not be able to determine government policy unilaterally. Consultation with several government caucuses may be necessary. Occasionally, in the past, backbench MPs have revolted against the policy decided by their Cabinet. It has not happened often because Cabinet ministers usually make up between a third and a half of the numbers in the caucus and they are the most experienced members. If such a revolt were to occur in a caucus of a governing party under a coalition government, it could threaten the stability of the government itself, since it could veto an agreement between coalition partners in Cabinet. The role of caucuses under MMP is likely to evolve in ways not yet easily foreseeable.

If a proposal requires legislation for its implementation, a bill is drafted by parliamentary counsel, legally trained specialists who draft laws on behalf of the government. No government bill can be drafted unless the Cabinet Legislation Committee has so ordered. The committee and Cabinet will approve the bill when it has been drafted. Usually a group of officials works with the parliamentary counsel in producing the bill, providing detailed instructions on policy and ironing out problems. Then the bill is approved by the government caucus before being introduced into the House of Representatives by the minister responsible for it. Under a minority government, though, members' bills that have not been through any such process may be passed. This raises questions about how members' bills should be drafted and what official involvement should occur.

In Parliament, the legislative process for making laws in New Zealand was revised in 1996. It is now transparent in the sense that the content of the law proposed can be read and absorbed by MPs and the interested public before it is debated and passed. Furthermore, there is plenty of opportunity for public input into the content of the law while it is travelling through its stages in Parliament. The process for a bill to become an act is as follows:

First reading
No debate

Second reading
Main debate in House of Representatives

Select committee
Study and public submission
Report presented to Clerk of the House

Report back to House
Debate in the House on
the select committee's report

Committee of the Whole House
Clause by clause debate

Third reading
Final debate

Royal Assent
Bill is passed—becomes an act

Figure 1.3: How a bill becomes law

It may take months, and even longer, for a bill to travel through the parliamentary process and become law. But it is also possible to pass laws very quickly where Parliament is of a mind to do so. Virtually all bills are sent to select committees where the public can make submissions on them. Frequently, select committees alter bills in important ways as a result of submissions.

When a bill is reported back to the House from the select committee, there is a debate on the committee's report and there is a written report on what the committee did. In this way, interested people can have some appreciation of the thinking of the committee as well as the amendments that it proposes.

Sometimes the process is not the same as set out above. Under standing orders, a bill can be introduced during an adjournment if the Business Committee established by the House of Representatives agrees. Government or members' bills may be introduced in this way. Such a bill is considered to have been read a first time on the day the Business Committee agrees to its introduction. It then automatically goes to a select committee.

The Business Committee is important in the legislative process in another way. It can limit the time of debates for each legislative stage where there is near unanimity on that course being adopted. Furthermore, it can decide that the Committee of the Whole House stage be omitted altogether.

Sometimes, where the House agrees, there may be very little debate at all. Where there is agreement, the leave of the House can be taken to abridge the procedures set out above. It is important, however, that proper scrutiny be given to proposed law so that, even where there is political agreement, it can be carefully examined and thought about before it has the force of law.

Once a law is passed it often has to be administered or implemented in some way. The relevant minister and public servants in the relevant department are usually in charge of ensuring that actions which need to take place under a statute do occur. Sometimes regulations will need to be passed—secondary legislation—in order to fill in the detail of a statute. Although regulations must also go through the Cabinet processes and be scrutinised by the Regulations Review Committee of Parliament, they are much more under the control of the relevant minister and department than is the passage of higher policy and legislation.

Finally, actions under statute, including the making of regulations, can be challenged in the courts as inconsistent with the wording of the statute. The already increasing recourse to such administrative law actions is likely to become even more common under MMP, where the wording of statutes is the subject of compromise and hence unclear. In the past, if the government has disagreed with a court's interpretation, it has always been able to use its majority in Parliament to overturn that interpretation.

SUMMARY

In broad outlines, this chapter provides an overview of how the structures and processes of New Zealand government work. Its essential elements are simple; complexity arises from the way it works in relation to particular issues. Government can be highly intricate and convoluted, depending on the issue to be determined and the political contention the issue generates. MMP adds new, and more complicated dynamics to government structures and processes, but because these allow more points of view to be heard, developed, and considered in the process of governing, our democracy will be enhanced.

2 Elections and Forming a Government

INTRODUCTION

We elect representatives to govern. Elections are fundamental to our constitution since they provide its basic democratic element. The whole of our system of government can be understood as a way of channelling communication between the voters and the decision-makers. The fact that voters vote checks the behaviour of their representatives. Only by competitive election can the identity of the main decision-makers be changed. Elections are so important to our constitution that the only laws which cannot be changed by a majority vote in Parliament are six provisions in the Electoral Act 1993, relating to elections—to amend them requires a 75 per cent majority in Parliament or a majority in a national referendum. Not even the Constitution Act 1986 or the New Zealand Bill of Rights Act 1990 requires such procedures.

In a democratic country such as New Zealand there can be no doubt about whether the majority should rule. The question is what kind of majority should rule (and what constraints on the rulers there should be). We have long had the FPP (or 'plurality') electoral system, which has almost always resulted in a single party forming the government and controlling a majority of seats in Parliament, even though they did not usually get a majority of votes. Under MMP, the number of seats a party gets in Parliament reflects the percentage of votes it gets overall. We can expect to have governments formed by more than one party and by parties without a majority in Parliament. The process of forming a government will itself become more complicated.

VOTING

The Electoral Act 1993 says who can vote. In general, to be able to vote you must be:

- over eighteen years old;

and you must be either:

- on or qualified to be on the electoral roll; or
- a member of the armed forces out of New Zealand;

and, you must be either

- a New Zealand citizen who has lived continuously in New Zealand for at least a year at some time and who has been in New Zealand at some time in the last three years; or
- a permanent resident of New Zealand who has lived continuously in New Zealand for at least a year at some time and who has been in New Zealand at some time in the last twelve months;

and you cannot be:

- currently in a mental hospital for over three years; or
- currently in prison for a term of over three years; or
- convicted of a corrupt electoral practice within the last three years.

If you satisfy these requirements but cannot vote at a polling booth on election day for a number of reasons, you can cast a special vote (the reasons are: you are not on the roll, you are out of New Zealand, you are too ill to vote, you have religious objections, or it is otherwise not practical without hardship or serious inconvenience).

By international standards, the percentage of eligible voters who actually vote in New Zealand is high. The percentage of eligible voters who vote has consistently exceeded 85 per cent for twenty years. In the United States voter turnout over 50 per cent is usually reached only in nationwide presidential elections. In New Zealand, unlike Australia, it is not compulsory to vote, although everyone is legally required to register as an elector with a registrar of electors (through New Zealand Post).

Voting under MMP has one main difference compared with voting under FPP. Under FPP you had one vote, for a party representative in your electorate. Under MMP you have two votes: one for a representative in your electorate and the other for a party list of representatives put up by each party. It is the party list vote that primarily determines parties' overall strengths in Parliament.

THE DEATH OF FPP

It is not always appreciated how recently FPP voting in single-member electorates was developed. In early English elections for Parliament, voting was all done in public; there was no secret ballot. If necessary, heads were counted. Indeed there was little discussion in Britain about the electoral system until the right to vote was extended, beginning with the first Reform Act in 1832. At that time, as a recent history of proportional representation in Britain observes, 'over five-sixths of United Kingdom returned two members each. In England proper there [were] only five single member constituencies.'[1] New Zealand has had a two-party system since the 1890s (although there was a transitional phase between 1911 and 1931). Until 1903, however, there were multi-member constituencies and between 1908 and 1911 a second ballot procedure was used.

FPP was the essence of simplicity. In each of ninety-nine electorates, political parties selected one candidate for election to Parliament. There were two main political parties in New Zealand: Labour and National. During the election campaign (usually lasting about three months), each party would try to convince voters to make them the government by voting for their candidate in each electorate. In this way, parties provided the link between popular consent and representative government, actively encouraging the inactive portion of the population to think about public issues and to take part in elections.

In each electorate, the candidate with the most votes won the seat. If there were only two candidates the winner needed more than 50 per cent of the votes cast to win. But there were often candidates from four or more parties. The candidate with most votes may not have had as many votes as all his or her opponents combined, although the candidate with the most votes still won. So results were frequently reached where the elected candidate had a minority of the valid votes cast, say 30–40 per cent, while together the three other candidates received 60–70 per cent between them, although none received as many votes as the elected candidate.

The outcome of the contest was that one party controlled the power of government in the country. Results were almost always decisive. Either a party controlled all the power of government or none of it. One of the few 'laws' of political science is that the FPP system has a bias toward the existence of two parties.[2] Consequently, one party would have a majority of seats in Parliament. If a voter wanted a say in which party formed the government, there was little point in voting for a third party because only one of the two main parties had a realistic chance of doing this. Furthermore, it was only votes in the 'marginal' seats, where the fight between the two main parties was close, that would matter and that parties would heed. The outcome of the contests in 'safe' seats, where most people would vote for Labour or for National, was virtually assured.

---

1 J. Hart, *Proportional Representation—Critics of the British Electoral System 1820–1945*, Oxford University Press, Oxford, 1992, pp.9–10.

2 R. Taagepera & M. Shugart, *Seats and Votes: The Effects and Determinants of Electoral Systems*, Yale University Press, New Haven, 1989.

Between 1957 and 1960 Labour enjoyed a majority of only one over National in Parliament, but Labour ran the government and National had no part in it. It was a similar situation for National between 1981 and 1984. And in both 1978 and 1981 Labour secured a few more votes than National but many fewer seats in Parliament. The FPP 'winner takes all' electoral system, and the contest between the parties, have been the dominating features in determining the nature of our government for the last sixty years.

The effect of the FPP system in New Zealand can be seen by a comparison between votes cast in favour of political parties and seats secured in Parliament, as shown in Table 2.1. The difference in percentage points shown in the third column is a measure of the extent to which a party is over- (+) or under- (-) represented in Parliament compared with their share of the vote.

A number of points emerge from the figures. The FPP system discriminated in favour of the party winning most votes in a two-party race and in favour of the two main parties where there was a significant third party vote. A New Zealand government has not received over 50 per cent of the votes cast in an election since 1951. The highest percentage of votes won by a government was 48.4 per cent by Labour in 1972 and the lowest 35 per cent by National in 1993.

In 1972 and 1975 the difference in voter support for National and Labour was 6.8 per cent and 7.7 per cent respectively. Yet on both occasions those differences produced a disparity of more than 26 percentage points in seats gained. Quite small changes in the level of relative support produced a landslide in parliamentary seats. In 1978, however, both major parties were supported by the voters nearly equally, but there was a disparity of 10 percentage points in seats secured. In 1978 and 1993, a third party obtained more than 50 per cent of the votes obtained by each of the two main parties yet received 2 per cent of the total seats in Parliament compared with their 46 per cent and 51 per cent each. Until 1993, the support for minor parties fluctuated between 10 per cent and 22 per cent over the period but the highest representation enjoyed by third parties in any of those Parliaments has been two seats. The effect of FPP was clearly to make political life hard for third parties. The minority of people who supported such parties did not have their views directly represented in Parliament.

Public criticism of the basic fairness of the FPP system was increased by the representation in Parliament of third parties from 1978 on. There was dissatisfaction, too, with aspects of the mechanics of the electoral system. A legal case followed the 1978 election—the ticks and crosses controversy canvassed in earlier editions of this book.[3] In 1985 the Labour Government established a Royal Commission on the Electoral System with extensive terms of reference:

---

3 *Re Hunua Petition* [1979] 1 *NZLR* 25, *Wybrow* v. *Chief Electoral Officer* [1980] 1 *NZLR* 162.

Table 2.1: Votes and seats 1972–93

Party	*% votes*	*% seats*	*Difference*
1972 Election			
Labour	48.4	63.2	+14.8
National	41.5	36.8	-4.7
Social Credit	6.7	0.0	-6.7
Values	2.0	0.0	-2.0
Others	1.5	0.0	-1.5
1975 Election			
Labour	39.7	36.8	-2.9
National	47.4	63.2	+15.8
Social Credit	7.4	0.0	-7.4
Values	5.2	0.0	-5.2
Others	0.2	0.0	-0.2
1978 Election			
Labour	40.4	44.6	+4.2
National	39.8	54.4	+14.6
Social Credit	16.1	1.1	-15.0
Values	2.4	0.0	-2.4
Others	1.3	0.0	-1.3
1981 Election			
Labour	39.0	46.7	+7.7
National	38.8	51.1	+12.3
Social Credit	20.7	2.2	-18.5
Values	0.2	0.0	-0.2
Others	1.4	0.0	-1.4
1984 Election			
Labour	43.0	59.0	+16.0
National	35.9	39.0	+3.1
New Zealand Party	12.3	0.0	-12.3
Social Credit	7.6	2.1	-5.5
Values	0.2	0.0	-0.2
Others	1.1	0.0	-1.1
1987 Election			
Labour	48.0	59.8	+11.8
National	44.0	40.2	-3.8
Democrats	5.7	0.0	-5.7
Mana Motuhake	0.5	0.0	-0.5
Others	1.8	0.0	-1.8
1990 Election			
Labour	35.1	29.9	-5.2
National	47.8	69.1	+21.3
Green	6.9	0.0	-6.8
NewLabour	5.2	1.0	-4.2
Democrat	1.7	0.0	-1.7
Others	3.4	0.0	-2.8

1993 Election			
Labour	34.7	45.5	+10.8
National	35.0	50.5	+15.5
Alliance	18.2	2.0	-16.2
New Zealand First	8.4	2.0	-6.4
Others	3.7	0.0	-3.7

. . . to receive representations upon, inquire into, investigate, and report upon the following matters:

1 Whether any changes to the law and practice governing the conduct of Parliamentary elections are necessary or desirable:

2 Whether the existing system of Parliamentary representation (whereby in respect of each electoral district the candidate with the highest number of votes is elected as the Member of Parliament for that district) should continue or whether all or a specified number or proportion of Members of Parliament should be elected under an alternative system or alternative systems, such as proportional representation or preferential voting:

3 Whether the number of Members of Parliament should be increased, and, if so, how many additional Members of Parliament there should be:

4 Whether the existing formulae and procedures for determining the number and boundaries of electoral districts should be changed, and, in particular, —

(a) Whether the redistribution of electoral districts should be based on total population or adult population

(b) Whether the allowance of five percent by which the population of an electoral district may vary from the quota should be changed

(c) Whether the membership and functions of the Representation Commission and the time limits and procedures governing its functions should be changed

(d) The feasibility of some form of appeal from decisions of the Representation Commission.

5 The nature and basis of Maori representation in Parliament:

6 The term of Parliament:

7 To what extent referenda should be used to determine controversial issues, the appropriateness of provisions governing the conduct of referenda, and whether referenda should be legislatively binding:

8 Whether the present limits on election expenses are appropriate and whether any limits on such expenses should be extended to political parties and to the amount of individual or total donations candidates or parties receive and whether such expenses should be defrayed wholly or in part by State grants and the conditions, if any, which should apply to such grants:

9 Any other question relating to the electoral system which you may see fit to inquire into, investigate, and report upon.[4]

4 Report of the Royal Commission on the Electoral System, *Towards a Better Democracy*, Wellington, December 1986, pp.xiii–xiv.

The commission was chaired by the Hon. Justice Wallace, a judge of the High Court (and later Chair of the Electoral Commission) and comprised: Dr J.H. Darwin, the former Government Statistician; Professor Sir Kenneth Keith of Victoria University, a constitutional lawyer (now a judge of the Court of Appeal); Professor Richard Mulgan, then Professor of Political Studies at Otago University; and Mrs Whetumarama Wereta, a research officer. The commission's report was tabled in Parliament in December 1986 and produced a blueprint for radical change to the New Zealand electoral system.

WHAT IS AN MMP ELECTION?

The Royal Commission examined many different types of electoral system, which were analysed in terms of a set of criteria drawn up by the commission:

- Fairness between political parties;
- Effective representation of minority and special interest groups;
- Effective Maori representation;
- Political integration;
- Effective representation of constituents;
- Effective voter participation;
- Effective government;
- Effective Parliament;
- Effective parties;
- Legitimacy.

The commission stated at the outset that: 'No voting system can fully meet the ideal standards set by the criteria . . .. The best voting system for any country will be one which provides the most satisfactory overall balance between them, taking account of that country's history and current circumstances.'[5] The commission rejected the purer forms of proportional representation and recommended MMP as the best voting system for New Zealand on the basis of the criteria above. As discussed in Chapter 1, MMP was adopted through two referenda. As enacted into law, the system varies from what the commission recommended; for the sake of clarity, only what was enacted is discussed here.

Under MMP, each voter has two votes—one for a party list vote and one for a constituency MP (the 'constituency' vote). There are 120 members of Parliament. They are elected as follows:

- *Sixty constituency MPs* are elected on the same basis as under FPP, where the candidate with the most constituency votes represents that constituency and

[5] *Ibid.*, p.11.

wins a seat in Parliament. The new electorates, however, are larger and contain more people because there are fewer of them. As noted below, the boundaries of these seats are set, as before, by the independent Representation Commission. If the population grows, the number of constituency MPs will also grow, although the total number of MPs will stay at 120.

- *Five Maori MPs* are elected from the Maori roll. Despite the Royal Commission's recommendation that the Maori seats be abolished, they have been retained. A Maori option enrolment exercise was carried out in 1994 and further Maori options will be held every five years, starting in 1997–98. Under the 1994 option, about 50 per cent of Maori chose the general roll and 50 per cent the Maori roll. This means that New Zealand is currently divided into five Maori seats under MMP compared with the four that had existed since the Maori seats were established in 1867.
- *Fifty-five party list MPs* are elected from party lists. The idea is to ensure that the overall percentage of parliamentary seats each party gets (including constituency seats) is in proportion to the overall percentage of party list votes that party gets. Party list MPs will be elected from ordered lists of candidates nominated by each registered political party before election day. The ballot paper is divided into two parts: the right-hand side shows the constituency candidates in alphabetical order and the left-hand side shows the names of the parties contesting the party list votes, opposite the appropriate constituency candidate if there is one. Once the constituency winners are known, parties receive a 'top-up' of party list seats, allocated by a statistical method, so as to achieve overall proportionality. The idea is that a party securing, say, 40 per cent of the vote would secure 40 per cent of the seats in Parliament. *It is the party list vote, not the constituency vote, that determines the overall number of seats a party gets.*

To avoid the proliferation of minor parties, a threshold applies. In order to get any party list seats, a party will have to have more than 5 per cent of all party list votes or have won at least one constituency seat. This is a substantial hurdle to overcome—5 per cent amounts to about 120,000 votes. Also, a party could receive more constituency seats than its proportion of the party list votes entitles it to, in which case the total number of MPs will be higher by that amount and that party will be overrepresented in Parliament. Finally, if the total population increases so that the number of constituency MPs increases, the number of party list MPs will fall so that there is still only a total of 120 MPs.

HOW IS AN MMP ELECTION ADMINISTERED?

There is a lot of machinery behind running elections. The Chief Electoral Office, returning officers, the Electoral Enrolment Centre, registrars of electors, the

Representation Commission, and the Electoral Commission all have important roles to play.

Electorate boundaries are set by the Representation Commission. The boundaries of the electorates (currently sixty general electorates and five Maori electorates) are settled by the Representation Commission, which comprises:

- the Surveyor-General
- the Government Statistician
- the Chief Electoral Officer
- the chairman of the Local Government Commission (who does not vote)
- a nominee of the government
- a nominee of the opposition
- a seventh member appointed to be chairman and chosen by the other six or a majority of them;

and in setting the boundaries of the Maori seats:

- the Chief Executive of Te Puni Kokiri
- a Maori nominee of the government
- a Maori nominee of the opposition.

The Representation Commission is not partial to any political party and the Electoral Act 1993 gives politicians no ability to interfere with the apportionment arrived at by the commission.

The first MMP boundaries were set in 1995. The next boundaries will be set after the Maori electoral option following the 1996 census and then after each census (every five years) after that. The number of general constituency seats in Parliament is determined by a formula similar to that used under FPP. The general population of the South Island revealed by the census (not including those associated with the Maori electoral roll) is divided by sixteen to give the population size of each South Island electorate. That population size is used to determine the number of electorates in the North Island and the number of Maori electorates. That method of drawing boundaries has a number of results. The South Island can never have fewer than sixteen parliamentary seats, even if its population declines relative to that of the North Island. Yet a vote in the South Island is not worth more than one in the North. The North Island simply receives more seats in Parliament as its population increases. Also, since 1995, the number of Maori seats is set on the same basis as general seats.

The Representation Commission then determines the boundaries of the individual electorates themselves. They publish draft boundaries (with reasons for them) for public inspection. They must consider objections, publish summaries of them, and consider counter-objections before determining final boundaries. In setting the boundaries the commission must consider:

- existing electoral boundaries;
- community of interest (including, in relation to Maori seats, community of interest among members of Maori tribes);
- facilities for communications;
- topographical features; and
- projected population changes.

The total population in each electorate has to be within five per cent of the electorate population size set as already outlined. Although the electorates are drawn up on the basis of total population, they vary quite markedly in the number of actual voters on the roll. Total population and numbers of eligible voters do not coincide very closely. By the standards of many overseas democracies, the tolerances for the total population are low and result in drastic redrawing of boundaries after every census.

The current New Zealand electorate system's dedication to equality of electorates' total population every five years in a country with difficult terrain produces considerable disruptions for politicians, political parties, and communities. In the past, a lot of political attention has been paid to electorate boundaries since they directly affected the relative political chances of the two main parties. Under MMP, however, while boundaries are still important to individual electorates and MPs, the overall number of seats each party receives depends on the party list votes, not the constituency votes.

The electoral rolls are compiled by the Chief Registrar of Electors, the Chief Executive of New Zealand Post Ltd, according to the Electoral Act 1993, who acts through the Electoral Enrolment Centre and acts under the direction of the Minister of Justice. The Chief Registrar appoints a registrar of electors for each electorate to be in charge of compiling and keeping the electoral roll for that electorate.

The Electoral Commission, another independent body established by the Electoral Act 1993, is chaired by a judge (the first incumbent was Justice Wallace, who chaired the 1986 Royal Commission). Its other members are the Secretary for Justice, the Chief Judge of the Maori Land Court, and a chief executive of the commission. Its principal functions are:

- to register political parties and their logos;
- to supervise political parties' financial disclosure of donations and filing of election expenses;
- to promote public awareness of electoral matters through, for instance, education and information programmes;
- to consider and report on electoral matters referred to it by the Minister of Justice or the House of Representatives; and

- to supervise the allocation of broadcasting time to political parties for election campaigns.

The Chief Electoral Officer looks after the running of elections. The Chief Electoral Officer is currently an employee of the Ministry of Justice but has independent statutory duties and functions. He or she directs the returning officers in each electorate who operate the polling booths and are in charge of counting votes and announcing the results. The Chief Electoral Officer also receives the party lists of candidates for party list seats that each party puts up and calculates how many candidates from each party list are elected.

Some commentators have pointed out that the Chief Electoral Officer is a public servant and therefore potentially subject to ministerial direction. On the other hand, it is important that there is enough pressure on officials to ensure that elections are run efficiently. After the first MMP election the government is likely to review how the bodies just mentioned should be organised and whether some of them should be amalgamated. The Royal Commission on the Electoral System recommended that a single Electoral Commission should be responsible for carrying into effect electoral law, including enrolment of voters and the conduct of elections.

HOW IS AN MMP GOVERNMENT FORMED?

According to the Constitution Act 1986, a general election has to be held every three years, although a Prime Minister can advise the Governor-General to call a snap election at any time. This is the same under MMP as under FPP. Snap elections have been unusual in New Zealand—the only two in modern times were in 1951 and 1984. Under MMP, however, it is likely that there will be more elections outside the regular three-yearly cycle. This is because of the likelihood of coalition or minority government. As we explain further in Chapter 4, a government must have the confidence of Parliament. If it loses a vote of confidence then it must resign and there may well be a new election. Under FPP, single-party majority governments were assured of winning confidence votes. Under MMP, however, a minority government could easily lose a confidence vote if the opposition parties decide to bring down the government. A coalition government could lose a vote of confidence if one of the coalition partners decides to withdraw from the coalition. And even if neither of these events occur, a Prime Minister of a coalition or minority government may be more tempted to call a snap election for electoral advantage, or as a result of interparty bargaining, under MMP than under FPP.

But although New Zealand will probably have more frequent elections under MMP, this does not necessarily mean that changes in government will happen more often. Since 1953 the average life expectancy of a German government under a very similar system to MMP has been 10.3 years; from 1949 to 1994 in New Zealand under FPP it has been 6.4 years.[6]

Under FPP, forming a government was usually very straightforward. Since one party always had a majority of seats, it would form the government by being sworn into office by the Governor-General. There were two main sources of complication in forming a government under FPP, both of which will become more important under MMP. In 1981 and 1993 it was not clear on election night that one party did have a majority of seats. In both cases it took ten days, while special votes were counted, for this to become clear. Under MMP, it is also possible that special votes may affect the composition of Parliament. The period of uncertainty may, however, be much longer under MMP, as parties negotiate over who is to form a government. The other complication in forming a government under FPP was highlighted after the 1984 election when a constitutional crisis arose over when a new government can be sworn in, and what the incumbent government can do in the meantime. This caretaker government situation is also likely to be more frequent and last longer under MMP while parties negotiate over who is to form a government.

After an MMP election, or when a government is defeated by a vote of confidence, it is likely that no party will have a majority of votes or, therefore, a majority of seats. For instance, if the 1993 election results had occurred under an MMP system, National would have got forty-four seats, Labour forty-three, the Alliance twenty-three, and New Zealand First ten. This is illustrated in Table 2.2. (This is not necessarily what would have happened if the 1993 election had been held under MMP rules, since voters may have voted differently.)

Table 2.2: The 1993 election results under MMP

Party	*Votes No*	*%*	*FPP Seats*	*%*	*MMP Seats*	*%*
National	673,892	35.0	50	50.5	44	36.7
Labour	666,800	34.7	45	45.5	43	35.8
Alliance	350,063	18.2	2	2.0	23	19.2
New Zealand First	161,481	8.4	2	2.0	10	8.3
Others	70,560	3.7	0	0.0	0	0.0
TOTAL	1,922,696	100%	99	100%	120	100%

In this situation, it is not clear who would form the new government. This is where the Governor-General potentially has an important role, as the representative

[6] K. Jackson, 'What are the Future Shapes of Government in New Zealand and How will They Affect the Decision-Making Process?', Paper to Seminar on *MMP: Managing the Political/Public Sector Interface*, 23–24 March 1994, Wellington, p.15.

of the Queen in New Zealand. Under the Letters Patent Constituting the Office of Governor-General of New Zealand made by the Queen in 1983, the Governor-General appoints the Prime Minister and other ministers. The Governor-General must invite someone to form a government, but who? Should the leader of the National Party, as the incumbent Prime Minister and the leader of the largest party in the House, have the first chance to form a government? If the leader of the National Party, as Prime Minister, advised the Governor-General to invite him or her to try to form a government, would the Governor-General be bound to accept that advice or should the leaders of the other parties be consulted to see where their preferences lie? The Alliance would be in a strong position to secure concessions from both major parties but New Zealand First would not, in itself, provide enough parliamentary votes to give either National or Labour a majority. If the Prime Minister said that no Government could be formed and advised the Governor-General that another general election should be held immediately, would the Governor-General be obliged to take that advice or could he or she require the House to meet and see whether a government could be formed?

The problem comes from the relationship between two different constitutional conventions. The Governor-General is obliged to act on the advice of his or her Prime Minister, yet the Prime Minister's party must have the confidence of Parliament in order to be in government. In the situation outlined above, it is not clear who has the confidence of Parliament. It will be necessary to make judgements on the relative strengths of the parties in Parliament and to discuss matters with the various party leaders. There are very few guidelines or precedents in New Zealand, but two things are plain. As the next chapter shows, the current Governor-General, Sir Michael Hardie Boys, has made it clear how he will exercise these powers; and the House of Representatives itself is the most important element in determining the identity of the government.

The political leaders will have to show responsibility and restraint. Negotiations between the political parties will be crucial to determining which party or parties have the confidence of Parliament in forming a government. This topic is explored further in Chapter 3.

CARETAKER, COALITION, AND MINORITY GOVERNMENTS

The period during which a coalition is formed could last for a long time. Yet government must continue during this period—taxes must be collected, welfare services must be provided, and all the multifarious tasks of government attended to. While a new government is being formed, the old government continues in office as a 'caretaker' government. In the past, such governments have lasted only ten days or so when there has been a change in power after an election. But in 1984, even this short period caused questioning about the ground rules for a caretaker government and gave New Zealand all the ingredients of a first-class constitutional crisis.

The results on election night in 1984 made it clear that the National Government had been defeated by the Labour opposition, but the final official results were some days away under the rules allowing for special votes. New Zealand was then in the throes of a financial crisis. The Reserve Bank had suspended all foreign exchange dealings to stop the flow of money out of the country. Officials had briefed the outgoing government that an immediate response by way of a devaluation was required. Yet Sir Robert Muldoon, the outgoing National Prime Minister, at first refused to act. Later he said on television that he would not devalue as long as he was Minister of Finance. In response to the reporter's suggestion that there was little sense in not letting the government-elect make the decision, Sir Robert said that he hoped to give the incoming Prime Minister some instruction in the realities of government over the next day or two.

Sir Robert saw himself as still in charge. Legally he was; he was still Prime Minister and Minister of Finance and would remain so until the Governor-General accepted his resignation or dismissed him. Over the next ten days the Muldoon Government was the lawful government. Its actions were, however, considered to be limited by certain constitutional conventions. The most important of these is that the outgoing government must not undertake any action that will embarrass the incoming government. That rule was generally understood. The question was whether constitutional convention required the outgoing government to act at the direction of the incoming government on a major policy issue. The situation was resolved three days after the election when Sir Robert wrote to the Prime Minister-elect saying he would act on the decisions of the incoming government in relation to the currency crisis.

As explained in Chapter 1, the legal root of this crisis was resolved permanently by the Constitution Act 1986 clarifying who could be ministers and when government could change. Critical to resolving the crisis at the time was a press statement by the Attorney-General, the Hon. J.K. McLay, in which he formulated the conventions to which outgoing governments were subject . He put the essentials like this:

> 1. that it [the outgoing government] will undertake no new policy initiatives.
> 2. that it will act on the advice of the incoming government on any matter of such great constitutional, economic or other significance that cannot be delayed until the new government formally takes office—even if the outgoing government disagrees with the course of action proposed.[7]

[7] J.K. McLay, press statement, 17 July 1984.

The 1996 *Cabinet Office Manual* has made it plain what the caretaker conventions are. There are two.

> 2.36 There are two arms to the convention. The first deals with the situation in which it is clear who will form the next government, but they have not yet taken office. Following the 1984 general election it was recognised that in that situation the outgoing government:
> - should undertake no new policy initiatives and
> - should act on the advice of the incoming government on any matter proposed.
>
> 2.38 The second arm of the convention was tested after the 1993 general election, and deals with the situation in which it is not clear who will form the next government. This situation could arise after a general election, or if a government falls part way through the term of Parliament. In 1993 the government refrained from making significant decisions where possible. If urgent decisions were needed, consideration was given to temporary or holding arrangements which did not commit the government in the longer term. Where temporary arrangements were not possible, decisions were taken only after consultation with other party leaders. All approaches to the leaders of other political parties were cleared in advance with the Prime Minister or Cabinet.

Under MMP, the question of what a caretaker government can and cannot do, and should and should not do, is even more important. In some European countries caretaker governments may have to function for several months while parties undertake complicated and detailed negotiations over who will form a government and what policies they will pursue. If this is a period when a Budget has to be put together, the task is even more complicated. In New Zealand, section 19 of the Constitution Act 1986 requires that Parliament is called together approximately two months after an election. If a government has been formed by then, this requirement is likely to test its support. If a government has not been formed, it will put pressure on resolution of negotiations through parliamentary votes. And section 6 of the act, designed to avoid crises like that described above, provides that a minister may stay in office for twenty-eight days after ceasing to be an MP. If several ministers are defeated and there are lengthy periods of caretaker government, this provision will need to be revised or provision made for new temporary ministers to be appointed.

Parties can be expected to negotiate over a number of different matters when forming a government. First, what policies will the government pursue? What is the bottom line of each party that would cause them to bring down the government over economic policy, foreign policy, social policy? Which policy positions of which parties can other parties live with? Second, who will get what ministerial portfolios? Who will be the Prime Minister, the Deputy Prime Minister, the

Minister of Finance, the Speaker, the Leader of the House? In addition, parties may be concerned about who will be on, and who will chair, Cabinet committees and select committees of Parliament. Coalition partners will draw up a formal agreement which will, no doubt, be made public.

Overseas experience suggests that policies and portfolios are the two most important sets of issues to be negotiated. Some parties overseas reach very detailed agreements about policies, running to hundreds of pages, prescribing what will and will not be done. Other agreements are based on a few core principles. In allocating portfolios in a coalition government, parties in most other countries will agree on who will be the Prime Minister and which parties will fill which portfolios. Usually the Prime Minister is the leader of the largest coalition partner and the leader of the next largest partner is the Deputy Prime Minister. It is then up to each party to decide who will be appointed to its portfolios. Parties formed around particular issue areas are usually most concerned to gain the portfolio associated with that issue and will agree to form a coalition in return for that. For instance, a Green party might seek the Conservation or Environment portfolios and a Maori party might seek the Maori Affairs or Treaty Negotiations portfolios. Finance is usually a key portfolio, sometimes held by the party that does not hold the Prime Ministership.

Finally, a key decision for parties is whether they wish to be part of a government. The difference is whether the party will be part of Cabinet decision-making. If a party wants to take part directly in governing the country, it may be happy to form a minority government or take part in a coalition. If, however, a party does not wish to be a partner with another party in government and cannot get support of other parties to form a minority government itself, it may support another party as a minority government. An agreement to support another party as a minority government is similar to a coalition agreement, but the supporting party will not take part in government and will outline the basis for its support and the conditions that would cause it to withdraw support. A coalition agreement or promised support for a minority government could be negotiated before an election and the relevant parties would campaign on that basis. This is particularly likely when an arrangement already exists before the election. Alternatively, negotiations could occur after an election. The parliamentary strength, policy preferences of each party, and negotiating process will determine whether a coalition or minority government is formed. It will also determine whether one or more parties take part in either form of government. As Figure 2.1 illustrates, there are four possible basic forms of government under MMP, apart from the transitional caretaker government.

Figure 2.1: Types of government

	Single-party	**Multi-party**
Minority in Parliament	Minority government	Multi-party minority government
Majority in Parliament	Single-party majority (FPP) government	Coalition government

part two

executive government

3 The Monarchy: Will New Zealand Become a Republic?

INTRODUCTION

Section 2 of the Constitution Act 1986 provides that:

(1) The sovereign in right of New Zealand is the Head of State of New Zealand, and shall be known by the royal style and titles proclaimed from time to time.

(2) The Governor-General appointed by the sovereign is the sovereign's representative in New Zealand.

The act goes on to state that the royal powers can be exercised by the Governor-General on behalf of the Sovereign or by the Sovereign in person.

Because we have a sovereign, our constitution is in the form of a monarchy. Under New Zealand law, the Queen is the Queen of New Zealand, whatever else she is monarch over; the Royal Titles Act 1974 says so. The authority of the Crown remains important from both a legal and a political point of view. Almost all of the Sovereign's powers are in fact exercised by the Queen's New Zealand ministers, who therefore inherit a tradition of strong, continuous government.

It is an important feature of our government that particular administrations may come and go, but the monarchy goes on forever. This means that any administration is not the embodiment of the state, but merely its agent. The advantage of this arrangement becomes obvious if our situation is compared with that in the United States. There the President is both the chief executive and the head of state for ceremonial and diplomatic purposes. On occasions, under such an arrangement, it becomes easy to confuse criticism of a president's policies with lack of patriotism on the part of the critics. During the Vietnam War the inability to distinguish the two caused considerable difficulty. In New Zealand such problems do not arise so easily. Here it is much more difficult to say that criticism of the policies of a particular government amounts to disloyal and unpatriotic conduct.

The Governor-General is appointed by the Queen on the advice of the government, usually for a term of five years. Opposition parties have usually been consulted about the nomination and this is likely to be regarded as more important under MMP. Sir Paul Reeves, who was appointed in 1985, was the first Maori to hold the office of Governor-General. Dame Catherine Tizard, appointed in 1990, was the first woman.

The office of Governor-General had a major constitutional facelift in 1983 when new Letters Patent were issued constituting the office of Governor-General.[1] The previous letters dated from 1917 and, with the accompanying royal instructions, were obsolete even to the point of giving a misleading impression as to the extent of the Governor-General's powers. The instructions said that the Governor-General could reject the advice of ministers 'if he shall see sufficient cause to dissent'. That was an inaccurate statement of the power in 1917 and was never used; it is omitted from the 1983 document. In all but the most extreme situations, the Governor-General acts on the advice of his or her responsible ministers.

In 1983, Parliament passed the Constitutional Provisions Bill, which became three separate acts: the Royal Powers Act 1983, clarifying the law relating to the exercise of royal powers and providing for a Regent acting for an incapacitated Sovereign; the Administrator's Powers Act 1983 to tidy up the law concerning the administrator (usually the Chief Justice) who performs the duties of the Governor-General when the latter is absent from New Zealand; the Acts Interpretation Amendment Act 1983 updating references to the Governor-General in the new modern form provided for in the Letters Patent.

The opposition was fully consulted and agreed to the changes, which were designed to remove the last vestiges of colonial status from the office. The Letters Patent were executed under the Seal of New Zealand and counter-signed by the Prime Minister, so that, for the first time, the office is constituted under the prerogative in right of New Zealand alone. In that sense the office has been 'patriated'—brought home.[2]

THE FUNCTIONS OF THE QUEEN AND THE GOVERNOR-GENERAL

The Governor-General in New Zealand (and the Queen when she is here) performs three main sets of functions—ceremonial, symbolic and constitutional.

Ceremony

The Queen or the Governor-General acts as head of state and many of the duties involved are ceremonial. He or she officiates at the opening of Parliament, conducts

1 S/R 1983/225 *Letters Patent Constituting the Office of Governor-General of New Zealand.*

2 F.M. Brookfield, 'The Reconstituted Office of Governor-General', *New Zealand Law Journal,* 1985, p.257.

investitures and receives the credentials of diplomats accredited to New Zealand. The Governor-General is also Commander-in-Chief of the New Zealand armed forces. He or she is the embodiment of the Crown to which they give their loyalty.

Symbolism

In the opinion of a former Governor-General, Sir Denis Blundell, the symbolic function was the most important.[3] Sir Denis was the first resident New Zealander appointed Governor-General and he dispensed with the traditional plumed hat because he thought it was unsuitable for this country. There was, he wrote, considerable ignorance and certainly misunderstanding by people as to the office of Governor-General and where it fitted into the New Zealand way of life.[4] This role is to embody the values of the nation; it is above party and politics. It involves travelling to all sorts of functions throughout New Zealand making speeches, holding numerous receptions at Government House, and generally meeting and greeting as broad a cross-section of the New Zealand community as possible.

Constitutionalism

The constitutional functions of the Sovereign and the Governor-General include:

- formally appointing and dismissing ministers and governments;
- dissolving and proroguing Parliament;
- being part of the legislative process by assenting to bills;
- providing appropriation messages to Parliament for the expenditure of public money;
- formally appointing and dismissing Court of Appeal and High Court judges and senior officials of state;
- exercising the royal prerogative of mercy and pardon; and
- presiding over meetings of the Executive Council.

The Governor-General presides over the Executive Council each week when he or she is in Wellington. Ministers attend the meeting, where the main business is to sign into law regulations previously agreed to by Cabinet and to make other orders-in-council. The Executive Council is the body through which Cabinet gives its collective advice to the Governor-General. Reasonably frequently there are discussions at Executive Council or information is exchanged between the Governor-General and ministers. On a few occasions, there are very detailed and lengthy discussions. For example, the way in which Waitangi Day would be commemorated and the part the Governor-General would play would be a subject for discussion.

---

3 D. Blundell, 'Some Reflections Upon the Office of Governor-General in New Zealand', 10 *Victoria University of Wellington Law Review*, 1980, p.198.

4 *Ibid.*

In theory, all these are great legal powers. In practice they are, by constitutional convention and democratic principle, exercised on the advice of ministers. Because of this, generally speaking, it cannot be said that the Governor-General in New Zealand takes a significant role in the decision-making of government. To a limited extent, however, the relationship between the Queen and her ministers works both ways. In 1867 the British writer Walter Bagehot noted that the monarch had three rights: the right to be consulted, the right to encourage, the right to warn.[5] Sir John Marshall, one of the longest serving ministers in the history of New Zealand, summed up the position in 1977 as follows:[6]

> Today even the Governor-General's rights to be consulted, to encourage and to warn are not exercised in any formal or regular way. The Prime Minister does not report regularly to the Governor-General as the British Prime Minister reports to the Queen. In 20 years as a Minister, I seldom attended at Government House for consultation, even less for encouragement and never for warning. Even when I was Prime Minister, the consultations with the Governor-General were infrequent, although our relationship, socially and on state occasions, was cordial. . . . In my experience, the Governor-General has always acted on the advice of his Ministers.

Since that time things have changed somewhat so that the Governor-General is kept fully informed. The 1983 New Zealand Letters Patent explicitly state that 'Our Ministers of the Crown in New Zealand shall keep Our Governor-General fully informed concerning the general conduct of the Government of Our said Realm, so far as they are responsible therefor, and shall furnish Our Governor-General with such information as he may request with respect to any particular matter relating to the Government of Our said Realm.'[7]

People tend either to think the office of Governor-General is of little significance, which is wrong, or that it represents a substantial check on the excesses of executive government, which is also wrong.

THE RESERVE POWERS AND MMP

In some extreme cases a Governor-General is entitled to act on his or her own, not on the advice of responsible ministers. These are known as the reserve powers.

Constitutional lawyers have long been interested in these powers. It is a contentious and uncertain area. In New Zealand, no significant event in modern times has involved the exercise of the reserve powers, but they may be needed more under MMP.

5 W.L. Bagehot, *The English Constitution*, London, 1973, p.111.

6 J. Marshall, 'The Power of Dissolution as Defined and Exercised in New Zealand', 58 *Parliamentarian*, 1977, p.13.

7 *Letters Patent Constituting the Office of Governor-General of New Zealand*, at XVI.

The term 'reserve powers' is perhaps misleading. One of the difficulties with the area is that the legal powers and the way in which they are exercised under constitutional convention diverge. The law appears to give the Governor-General power to do things which, by convention, he or she does on the advice of ministers. There are four generally accepted reserve powers in Westminster governments:

- to appoint a Prime Minister;
- to dismiss a Prime Minister;
- to refuse to dissolve Parliament; and
- in limited instances, to force a dissolution.

Difficulties arise when the Governor-General is required to make an independent judgement about matters where it would be impossible, imprudent or unfair to rely on the advice of ministers.

The very detailed and elegant essay of the late Professor Robert Quentin-Baxter on the reserve powers published in 1986 is one of the best pieces of writing in New Zealand constitutional law. After a meticulous consideration of the precedents, Professor Quentin-Baxter concluded:[8]

> The Prime Minister shares with the Governor-General the responsibility of ensuring that the Crown is never without ministerial advisers; and that, except where Parliament is dissolved in preparation for a general election, ministers must be those who have the confidence of Parliament. If the Governor-General believes that a change of ministers may become necessary, and that he has therefore a duty to inform himself about the parliamentary situation, he may, with the Prime Minister's knowledge, consult other members of Parliament, whether or not supporters of the present government, receiving in confidence information and opinions offered upon that basis, but not expressing views or intentions other than those of which the Prime Minister has notice.
>
> A Prime Minister has a duty to tender his resignation if the government of which he is the leader loses its parliamentary majority in a general election; or if he is no longer the leader of the government party or coalition; or if, after being commissioned to form a government, he fails to obtain the confidence of Parliament. In other circumstances, a Prime Minister who has lost the confidence of Parliament has a duty either to tender his resignation or to advise a dissolution of Parliament.
>
> The bond of mutual confidence between the Governor-General and the Prime Minister requires that each should bring to the attention of the other any circumstance which he believes may lead to a departure from constitutional principle, or to a situation of crisis or emergency; and that each should inform the other of any development in his

8 R.Q. Quentin-Baxter, 'The Governor-General's Constitutional Discretions: An Essay Towards a Redefinition', 10 *Victoria University of Wellington Law Review*, 1980, pp.289, 314–15.

> knowledge or assessment of the position. The Prime Minister has a duty to ensure that information available to the government is at the Governor-General's disposal.
>
> If the Governor-General is of the opinion that a course of action, proposed by the government and opposed by segments of public and parliamentary opinion, raises a question of constitutional principle and is not merely a matter of policy to be determined from time to time by the government in power; that the proposed course of action was not, before the most recent general election, a normal or foreseeable consequence of the present government's assumption of office; and that these considerations are not outweighed by the present or pending emergency; he may so inform the Prime Minister. In that case, it shall be the duty of the Prime Minister either to defer or modify the proposed course of action in conformity with the Governor-General's opinion, or to tender his resignation, or to advise a dissolution of Parliament.
>
> When the Prime Minister has occasion to tender advice to the Queen in relation to the appointment or tenure of a Governor-General, he shall bear in mind the need to afford the Sovereign ample time for consideration before signifying her pleasure. In principle, a new Governor-General should assume the duties of his office not less than [four] weeks, nor more than [eight] weeks, from the day on which his predecessor relinquished office.

A survey of the existing state of the law and convention on the reserve powers shows that, even before MMP, there are substantial areas of vagueness and uncertainty. Because MMP will probably increase the use of the reserve powers, what, if anything, needs to be done to clarify or further define these powers?

A useful recent analysis of the situation has been carried out by Caroline Morris in 'The Governor-General, the Reserve Power, Parliament and MMP: A New Era'. Her conclusion is as follows:[9]

> If the Governor-General is required to use the reserve powers more often, it is vital that they be credible and effective. Credibility and effectiveness can only come, it has been submitted, by the powers being exercised according to clear guidelines, soundly based in principle. These principles are those of Crown neutrality and democracy, meaning that the Governor-General should not only exercise her powers impartially but that she should also be seen to do so; and that the reserve powers should be exercised with reference to the renewed vitality of Parliament it is predicted that MMP will bring.
>
> An analysis of the reserve powers of the Governor-General in the new context of an MMP Parliament, concludes with three new possible conventions which may guide

9 25 *Victoria University of Wellington Law Review*, 1995, pp.345, 371. For a somewhat different account of the powers of the Governor-General, see Dr Andrew Stockley, 'The Governor-General and MMP', *New Zealand Law Journal*, 1986, p.13.

the exercise of the reserve powers, practices which are found in principle and buttressed by precedent. These suggested guidelines can be stated thus:

(i) **Power to refuse a request for a dissolution of Parliament before the summoning of Parliament:** the Governor-General should refuse the request and instead call Parliament as soon as practicable so that it may resolve any necessary constitutional issues.

(ii) **Power to appoint a Prime Minister:** The Governor-General should appoint that person who seems best able to hold the confidence of the House of Representatives. That person should be identified after party political negotiations and, once identified, the Governor-General should satisfy herself that this is indeed the case by consultation with the appropriate parties.

(iii) **Power to refuse a request for a dissolution of Parliament when Parliament is in session:** Parliament should not be dissolved if an alternative government exists in the House. The Governor-General should request that party leaders make clear their intended parliamentary alliances (preferably in writing) in order to determine whether this possible alternative government exists. If no such government is evidenced, the dissolution request should be acceded to.

The final question in this examination of the reserve powers and their underlying understandings is whether they should be codified or not. Codification has been posited as the solution for the sometimes uncertain nature of the reserve powers. Yet an analysis of various attempts to codify the reserve powers shows that these attempts provide little certainty or guidance for the Head of State in reserve power decisions. Moreover, judicial interpretation of these statutes also furnishes little elaboration on how the general discretion conferred on the Head of State is to be effected. Further, there remains the concern, acknowledged by the judiciary themselves, that such matters are not appropriate for judicial scrutiny. Codification would thus appear to serve little purpose. It also brings with it an 'ossifying' effect that prevents these conventions from developing and adapting to the political arena wherein they must operate.

To conclude, should the possible conventions outlined and suggested in this paper evolve into true conventions in future years, there must be an even greater sea-change to New Zealand's constitution before we can consider the drastic step of codification an attractive option.

MMP has arrived in New Zealand without any attempt to codify the reserve powers, and with no parliamentary understanding expressed about their exercise. As outlined in Chapter 2, the prime issue facing the Governor-General after an MMP election is who to call upon to form a government. Although it might develop, the New Zealand constitution does not require a vote of confidence in

Parliament to signal who has the confidence of Parliament, as happens in Germany and some other countries, before being sworn into office. There are, however, precedents from overseas concerning the role of the Governor-General, especially in Australia and Canada. In particular, the dismissal of the Whitlam Government in Australia in 1975 focused much attention on the powers of the Governor-General there.

The Governor-General will decide when to take a personal initiative and when to hold back. Apart from the Prime Minister, independent seasoned advisers, including the Solicitor-General, the Clerk of the Executive Council, the Speaker and, if necessary, independent constitutional authorities, are available to help but fine judgements may be called for. In the end, however, Parliament will decide upon the identity of the government.

In the run-up to MMP there was some speculation about the uncertainties that might be caused by exercise of the Governor-General's powers. In 1996 a new Governor-General took office. Sir Michael Hardie Boys had been a Judge of the Court of Appeal and was well versed in constitutional niceties. In May 1996 he made an important public statement about how he would exercise the powers of the office after the first MMP election. In a long and elegant speech, he reached the following conclusions which he summarised himself as follows:[10]

> The formation of a government is a political decision and must be arrived at by politicians.
>
> My task as Governor-General is to ascertain where the support of the House lies. In an unclear situation, that may require me to communicate with the leaders of all the parties represented in the new Parliament.
>
> Once political parties have reached an adequate accommodation, and a government is able to be formed or confirmed, I expect that the parties will make that clear by appropriate public announcements of their intentions. At that point it may be necessary for me to talk again with some party leaders. I would then expect to have sufficient information to be able to appoint a new Prime Minister, if that were required.
>
> Throughout this period of negotiation, the incumbent Prime Minister will remain in office, governing in accordance with the caretaker convention.

The second feature of Parliaments elected under MMP involving the Governor-General revolves around the question of dissolution. Governments may be defeated in Parliament. Certainly defeat on specific measures is likely to become more common. The question of what amounts to a question of confidence under

---

[10] Rt Hon. Sir Michael Hardie Boys, Speech to the Annual Dinner of the Institute of International Affairs, Wellington, 24 May 1996, p.10.

Parliament's standing orders and Speaker's rulings may raise many more practical issues than they have in the past because a government could actually fall on such votes. The automatic dissolution of Parliament that occurs under New Zealand law every three years in order for an election to be held may prevent problems arising which could occur if the term were longer.

The real nub of the issue in New Zealand comes when a Prime Minister asks for a dissolution because he or she feels that an election will be better than eking out the term in the House. The situation may be different, depending on whether the request comes from a Prime Minister with majority or minority support in the House. There is a good deal of controversy about what amounts to a sufficient reason to grant dissolutions in such situations. The current understanding in Westminster governments seems to be that a request to the Governor-General for a dissolution from a Prime Minister with majority support should be granted, as it was by Sir David Beattie to Sir Robert Muldoon, in 1984. There is little doubt, however, that the Governor-General exercises personal judgement when granting or refusing early dissolutions in the same way as when appointing or dismissing a Prime Minister. Before exercising the power to dissolve on the advice of a Prime Minister with only minority support in the Parliament, the Governor-General should probably consult with other parliamentary party leaders.

There are few situations in which a Governor-General in New Zealand could be called upon to exercise an independent judgement. It has never happened in modern times but is more likely to do so under MMP. If such a situation does occur, it will be necessary for the Governor-General to be seen as the neutral custodian of the public interest.

THE REPUBLICAN DEBATE IN NEW ZEALAND

During the 1990s there has been a vigorous debate across the Tasman over whether Australia should become a republic. The debate had been led by the Hon. Paul Keating, an ardent advocate of republicanism, when he was Prime Minister of Australia, and the issue remains alive despite the defeat of the Keating administration in 1996. The issue has always had a higher profile in Australia than in New Zealand; the issue took on particular urgency following the 1975 dismissal of Prime Minister Gough Whitlam by the Governor-General Sir John Kerr. Whitlam enjoyed the confidence of the House of Representatives, although the upper House, the Senate, would not agree to his Budget. The circumstances of that dismissal are fiercely debated in Australian political life to this day and they stirred up the republican debate.

Although there is undoubtedly a higher level of support for the constitutional monarchy in New Zealand than in Australia, the irony is that the change to a republic would be much easier to achieve here because of the structure of the respective constitutions. Section 128 of the Australian Constitution Act requires constitutional changes to be carried by a referendum which secures not only majority support of all the electors voting but also a majority of the electors in the majority of the states. This provision makes the Australian Constitution notoriously difficult to amend. In theory, the change in New Zealand could be accomplished by a statute passed by a simple majority in Parliament, although it could be strongly argued that such a profound constitutional change should be the result of a majority decision by electors at a referendum.

The level of public support in Australia for moving to a republic continues to be high. Serious official studies have been carried out investigating the legal, constitutional, and political issues. A Republic Advisory Committee set up to look at the options reported in 1993.[11] The Australian Government then studied the issues and, on 7 June 1995, announced an official policy that called for a new Head of State to be called the President of the Commonwealth of Australia. The President would be appointed by a two-thirds majority of a joint sitting of the two Houses of the Federal Parliament. The President's functions would essentially be those now performed by the Governor-General. The Labour Government had planned to hold a referendum on the issue in 1998 or 1999.[12] The succeeding Howard administration has stated its commitment to a constitutional convention to consider the issue. Just when the proposed changes will be put to electors is not clear at the time of writing. But it seems inevitable that, at some point, Australia will become a republic with a President who will have powers hardly distinguishable from those of the existing Governor-General.

Will the developments in Australia influence changes here? Although republican sentiment in New Zealand has never been as strong as in Australia, it does exist, and there has been a tendency to think that if Australia moves, then New Zealand will too, eventually. In 1994 this drift towards republicanism received a powerful boost when the Prime Minister, the Rt Hon. Jim Bolger, advocated republicanism for New Zealand in a series of speeches. In a parliamentary speech in March that year the Prime Minister said that the big constitutional question facing New Zealand:[13]

> . . . revolves around the role of our Governor-General. Is New Zealand to continue to have an appointed Governor-General as our Head of State, or should we move to an elected President? That is not an easy question, and our neighbour Australia is grappling with the issue right now. It is my view—it is a personal view not the Government's view—that the momentum for change will gather as we identify more with our Asia–

[11] *Report of the Republic Advisory Committee, An Australian Republic—the Options*, 2 vols, Government Printer, Canberra, 1993.

[12] Hon. Paul J. Keating, 'An Australian Republic: the Way Forward', Speech, Canberra, 1995.

[13] 539 *New Zealand Parliamentary Debates*, p.121, 8 March 1994.

> Pacific region of the world and as our direct links to Britain decline. But the big reason will be that we want to be independent New Zealanders. This will not happen because of any lack of affection or love for our Queen in London, but because the tide of history is moving in one direction. MMP could prove to be the catalyst, given the possible greater role for the Head of State as we form Governments under MMP.

In subsequent speeches the same year the Prime Minister developed the issues further. He pointed out that the options for choosing the head of state seemed either to be a general vote of all electors or by an electoral college. It was also important, he said, to determine the exact role and authority of an elected head of state.[14] After initial political discussion following these speeches, debate on republicanism has been more muted. But the issue is likely to be important in New Zealand in the next few years.

Both political and constitutional arguments are involved in the republican debate and it is important to understand the differences between these. The political arguments in favour of change revolve around nationhood: a hereditary monarch who reigns over the United Kingdom should not also be the Queen of New Zealand, where she does not live and from which she is physically far removed. An egalitarian country, it is said, ought not to have as its head of state a wealthy British aristocrat. It is a symbol of our government that conveys false messages about what New Zealand stands for and the values it holds. It also imperils this country's sense of independence in the eyes of other nations and New Zealanders' self-respect in their own sense of nationhood. These are arguments about New Zealand's national identity. They are linked with arguments that, in an egalitarian country, the principle of heredity should play no part in the selection of people for public office. The people should choose the head of the state.

Even at the political level, however, these arguments encounter some difficulties. Political neutrality in a head of state in a Westminster government is a vital advantage of a monarchy, given the discretions that head may be called upon to exercise in a narrow range of situations. Election of a head of state will not ensure political neutrality, rather the reverse. The incentives resulting from the holding of elective office are quite different from those affecting a hereditary head of state. Imagine, for example, how a president would campaign for re-election. Furthermore, the personal power of the Queen and her Governor-General is exceedingly limited. Confining the power of an elected head of state may not prove easy since he or she would have some form of democratic mandate. Ideally, the head of state should be above and beyond politics, a symbol of national unity that transcends the government of the day.

However strong the case for making New Zealand a republic may be in political

---

[14] Rt Hon. J.B. Bolger, Speech to the Newspaper Publishers Association Annual Conference, 16 March 1994.

terms, and it does not seem overwhelming, there are many legal and constitutional fish-hooks to be dealt with in bringing such a change about; it is a formidable legal and constitutional undertaking. These difficulties need to be weighed against the political arguments. Such a move should be preceded by a thorough and authoritative study that deals with all the technical legal issues as well as the political arguments.

The legal powers of the Crown are exercised on the advice of constitutionally responsible ministers. Remove the monarch and it may be necessary to dismantle the entire structure to find a stable substitute. This is not a simple undertaking. As Lord Cooke has put it: 'Let there be no mincing of words. A revolution it would be—and not necessarily only within such dictionary definitions as "a great upheaval" or "radical change in government". Arguably it would also be illegal.'[15] There is no such thing as minimalist change in this area. We cannot simply replace the Queen with a President. The legal powers of that person would be awesome and unacceptable unless a careful study were done to define and confine the powers. The key issues would be how the new head of state would be chosen and what powers the office would enjoy.

15 Sir Robin Cooke, 'The Suggested Revolution Against the Crown', in *Essays on the Constitution*, ed. P.A. Joseph, Brookers, Wellington, 1995, p.30.

4 The Prime Minister, Cabinet, and Ministerial Responsibility

The Prime Minister and Cabinet are at the pinnacle of political power in New Zealand's Westminster system of government. This will continue under MMP, even though Parliament is likely to be more important than in the past. Cabinet and the Prime Minister direct the executive branch of government. The way in which they work is based on a complex mixture of personalities, politics, and constitutional conventions such as the doctrines of ministerial responsibility.[1]

THE ROLE OF THE PRIME MINISTER

The first task that faces any analyst of prime ministerial power in New Zealand is to determine the nature and functions of the office. Those functions are not defined anywhere, they tend to be flexible, and, at the same time, they tend to be excessively broad.[2] No job description exists for the most powerful post in the land. The *Cabinet Office Manual* offers this insight: 'The Prime Minister is the head of the government. There is no statutory provision which establishes the office of Prime Minister, or which defines its role.'[3]

In New Zealand now there needs to be some clear understanding of what the Prime Minister is supposed to do. We tend to accept some impressionistic understanding of what Prime Ministers are supposed to do elsewhere, without stopping to see if such descriptions fit our own constitutional needs. Under MMP

---

1 For useful material on the topics in this chapter see E.M. McLeay, *The Cabinet and Political Power in New Zealand*, Oxford University Press, Auckland, 1995; and M.S.R. Palmer, 'Collective Cabinet decision-making in New Zealand', in *Cabinet Ministers and Parliamentary Government*, eds. K.A. Shepsle & M. Laver, Cambridge University Press, New York, 1994.

2 The two most useful sources we have found to be K.J. Scott, *The New Zealand Constitution*, Oxford University Press, Oxford, 1962, pp.94–136; R. Alley, 'The Powers of the Prime Minister', in *New Zealand Politics in Perspective*, ed. H. Gold, 3rd ed., Longman Paul, Auckland, 1992, p.174.

3 Cabinet Office, *Cabinet Office Manual*, Wellington, 1996, para 2.5.

the role is changing and evolving in new directions. The power of the Prime Minister may have diminished under MMP, but the importance of the role has not. It may now be more difficult for a Prime Minister to have his or her own way in government, but the Prime Minister remains a key part of the effective functioning of government.

Rodney Brazier's observation in an article in the *Modern Law Review* applies in New Zealand: '[t]he office of Prime Minister amounts to what each individual is able and willing to make of it.'[4] No two governments will ever work in the same way; because of temperament, aptitudes, and interests of its members, including the Prime Minister, no two administrations are ever the same.

It is difficult to communicate the flavour and the demands of the office of Prime Minister because these look quite different from the outside than from the inside. The Prime Minister is the Queen's first minister. Some older writers used to talk about the Prime Minister being *primus inter pares* or first among equals. Although that description has some constitutional attraction, it overlooks the development of the office in the mass media age.

In the minds of the public the Prime Minister is much more than a first among equals—he or she is regarded as being in charge of the government, as the boss. The political reality of that view does resonate through the system and give the Prime Minister added leverage, but it does not negate the collective nature of Cabinet decision-making. The media will often now pick up on a story that the Prime Minister's view has not prevailed or has been defeated on an issue. This sort of reporting in recent years has changed the perception from the outside, but it has not changed the reality of Cabinet government on the inside.

The task of political leadership in government is one of political management—of caucus, of Cabinet, of Parliament, of public opinion. It requires the resolution of conflicting points of view as harmoniously as possible. The art of government is, in many ways, the art of crisis management. And no one can be sure where the next issues will come from. Only the most difficult issues have to be dealt with by the leadership. Above all, leadership requires ability in political salesmanship and communication of the highest order.

Much of the Prime Minister's power will always depend upon personality and temperament. Some people like teamwork; some find the delegation of decisions uncongenial and want to have a hand in as many as possible. Legend in Wellington and Professor Keith Sinclair's biography suggest that Walter Nash was the latter sort of Prime Minister. David Lange, on the other hand, preferred to adopt a chairman of the board style. Sir Robert Muldoon was, in the words of a member

4 R. Brazier, 'The Downfall of Margaret Thatcher', 54 *Modern Law Review*, 1991, pp. 471, 487.

of his Cabinet, the Hon. Hugh Templeton, 'a prime minister who liked to dictate and dominate . . .'[5]

Since the style and nature of the Prime Ministership differed greatly from one incumbent to another under FPP, it will be fascinating to observe the changes that MMP will bring to the nature and functions of the office. In particular, one of the Prime Minister's greatest tasks will be forming and maintaining a coalition or gathering support for a minority government and keeping it together. Under a coalition government, especially, the Prime Minister's role of chairing Cabinet is different compared with MMP—from chairing a body composed by the government party to chairing a multi-party body. The Prime Minister is likely to come from the largest party in the coalition, but this is not necessarily the case.

A number of factors contribute to the power of a Prime Minister in New Zealand:

The Prime Minister can call an election. The Prime Minister can advise the Governor-General to dissolve the House of Representatives at any time and hold a general election. Such a step was taken before the normal election time in 1951 and again in 1984, and, in the more uncertain environment under MMP, it is likely to happen more frequently. It might be expected that the Prime Minister would discuss such a step with at least some of his or her colleagues, if not the whole Cabinet. This weapon becomes a crucial card to play in negotiations with other parties—whether in coalition or minority governments. All parties will have a vital interest in the timing of an election since their political standing at that time will affect their future representation in Parliament.

The Prime Minister is a party leader. An important feature of a New Zealand Prime Minister's power, and also that of a deputy, is that both are party leaders. They are elected by caucus to be leader and deputy. This has been true in both Labour and National. That fact gives the leadership authority not only in caucus but with the wider party organisation. In a coalition government, though, the minor party leader will probably not be Prime Minister but may hold another portfolio, perhaps Deputy Prime Minister or Minister of Finance. Both the leader and deputy leader of a political party, because of their offices, play an important role in that party organisation. Party political leadership is an important factor that distinguishes the leader and deputy leader from other senior politicians and, when in government, from other ministers. Public servants tend to recognise this fact and ensure that the leader or deputy is consulted where politically sensitive matters are concerned. Obviously, with a coalition government, where the Prime Minister and Deputy Prime Minister may come from different parties, the problems of political leadership and coordination will be greatly complicated.

5 H. Templeton, *All Honourable Men: Inside the Muldoon Cabinet 1975–1984*, Auckland University Press, Auckland, 1995, p.233.

The Prime Minister appoints ministers. The Prime Minister's right to appoint other ministers can also be regarded as a source of strength. In a single-party National Government the Prime Minister selects the ministers and allocates the portfolios. With Labour, caucus elects the members of Cabinet but the Prime Minister allocates the portfolios. In both parties, however, experience and representational considerations have been effective limits on who got into Cabinet. In 1975 Prime Minister Muldoon had only thirty members of Parliament with parliamentary experience from whom to select a Cabinet of twenty people and provide a Speaker, Chairman of Committees, and two whips. This may continue to be a problem with the formation of minority governments but, in coalition parties, Cabinet positions may become more exclusive. In either case, Cabinet selection is generally likely still to be governed by the internal rules of each party that forms a Cabinet and is still likely to be heavily influenced by experience and ability as well as a number of factors such as representation of gender, race, age, geography, and professional background. Overseas experience, however, suggests that the allocation of portfolios between parties in a coalition government is likely to be a core subject of the intricate negotiations that go into its formation. Parties concerned primarily with a particular sector, such as environmental, Maori or rural issues, are likely to want the portfolios most connected with those issues.

The Prime Minister sacks ministers. The right to dismiss a minister might be regarded as a potentially greater source of prime ministerial power. It is a right which has been exercised rarely in modern New Zealand politics, although there have been a few more examples in recent years. The idea of team solidarity is important in New Zealand's Cabinet. Under MMP, the Prime Minister's capacity to sack ministers is likely to be complicated by the fact that, in a coalition, the candidate for sacking may not be of the Prime Minister's own party. This will also, no doubt, be a matter of intense political negotiation.

The Prime Minister chairs and speaks for the Cabinet and caucus. The leader of a party (or, in his or her absence, the deputy) chairs and speaks for caucus as well as, when Prime Minister, Cabinet. This is a position of critical importance. The ability to determine the agenda and to sum up the decisions of Cabinet and caucus gives the Prime Minister considerable power. He or she needs a subtle understanding of what individual Cabinet and caucus members want and would be prepared to tolerate. And the fact that the Prime Minister makes public announcements cements and reinforces his or her leadership in the people's minds. The Prime Minister's ability to command media attention, through major press conferences, is a most important source of his or her power; the public regards the Prime Minister as the chief spokesperson of the government on all important issues.

The Prime Minister maintains and coordinates the government. The Prime Minister owes his or her position to the continued existence of the government he or she leads. More than other ministers and politicians, the Prime Minister has a particular concern for issues and events that affect the general health of the government. His or her opinion will carry weight on all issues, whereas individual ministers will tend to be regarded as at their most authoritative when dealing with matters within their own portfolios. Sir Keith Holyoake put it this way: 'The Prime Minister must maintain a fatherly oversight over the progress of his Cabinet colleagues, particularly in their work of implementing policy.'[6] The task of coordinating a coalition government of different parties who compete for votes yet work together in governing is particularly difficult. It may be necessary to adopt new and different processes for achieving cohesion and for keeping ministers in line. The leaders of the coalition parties in a government will need to have frequent consultations and good relationships with one another. In times of political adversity, there will be considerable strains.

The Prime Minister is in charge of the Security Intelligence Service. The Prime Minister is always Minister in Charge of the Security Intelligence Service (SIS) and the other intelligence services. In that capacity he or she is empowered by statute to issue warrants allowing the SIS to tap telephones and to issue interception warrants in relation to any communication not otherwise lawfully obtainable. The SIS has the awe-inspiring power of being able to investigate terrorism, subversion, and espionage, concepts which are but vaguely defined.

Finally, it is still worth pausing to note a source of power linked with the administration of Sir Robert Muldoon. From 1975 to 1984 Sir Robert held the portfolio of Minister of Finance. This minister is an important person in any government because he or she is concerned with all questions of expenditure and economics. Economic and fiscal policy lies at the heart of government policy in New Zealand. So the Minister of Finance, who presides over this financial machinery, is a pivotal figure; when he or she is also the Prime Minister, the concentration of power in one individual is overwhelming and undesirable. It is unlikely to be tolerated by other parties in a coalition or minority government.

The Deputy Prime Minister. We should perhaps also say a word about this position. As has been pointed out already, his or her authority flows from direct election by caucus. When the Prime Minister is out of New Zealand the Deputy Prime Minister is acting Prime Minister, and there are a number of other tasks that the deputy must perform. No doubt the division of labour differs greatly from administration to administration, depending on the personality and attributes of the incumbents.

In a coalition government, the Deputy Prime Minister is likely to be the leader of a different party from the Prime Minister. The job of deputy leader of a party, and hence Deputy Prime Minister in a single-party government, is one of admin-

---

6 K.J. Holyoake, 'The Task of the Prime Minister', in *Readings in New Zealand Government*, eds. L. Cleveland & A.D. Robinson, Reed Education, Wellington, 1972, p.73.

istrative coordination and sorting out problems. The problems can be both big and small but there are many of them and sometimes they are not easily solved. Success in the job is measured by what does not go wrong but could have. It requires ranging over portfolio areas, depending on where the problems are. But it is a job better done without the accompaniment of much publicity. When that stage is reached, the problem is better handed over to the Prime Minister. Ministers or caucus members who have political, personal, health, or other problems must be seen and talked to. Some of these difficulties can be time-consuming and complicated; their solution often requires some ingenuity.

THE PRIME MINISTER'S OFFICE AND DEPARTMENT

The main instrument available to the Prime Minister in coordinating the government is the Department of the Prime Minister and Cabinet.

Coordination requires the development of harmonious relations between ministers who must work together. Often there are personality clashes that do not make it easy. There are also a number of departments and committees of officials with different responsibilities and their activities frequently require coordination.

The Prime Minister has to keep in touch with the thinking of key elements in the community including, for example, Maoridom, the health and education communities, the manufacturing and agricultural industries, and the finance sector. The policy framework of the government is critical to all those groups. The Prime Minister needs continuous feedback on what they think about what is happening, and what adjustments they think should be made. The Prime Minister needs a number of people to act as his or her ears and eyes, reporting on the views of key sectors of the economy and society. Time needs to be put aside for regular briefing by advisers on these issues.

There was no separate Prime Minister's Department within the New Zealand government until after the 1975 election and, when it was formed, it was small. It became clear after many of the governmental reforms carried out by the Fourth Labour Government that further changes were needed because coordination of the advice systems was breaking down. When Geoffrey Palmer became Prime Minister in 1989 he immediately instituted a review of the office by the Chairman of the State Services Commission, Mr Don Hunn, and a retired former Secretary to the Treasury, Mr Henry Lang. They were invited 'To review the structure of the Prime Minister's Office and Cabinet Office with the objectives of improving the co-ordination of the conduct of Government business and improving the quality of the advice available to the Prime Minister and the Government, particularly in the economic and social areas.'[7]

7 H. Lang & D. Hunn, *Review of the Prime Minister's Office and Cabinet Office*, Wellington, 1989, Annex A.

The report, which stressed the Prime Minister's role as minister for coordination, found that the existing machinery was inadequate for such a role. The reviewers also said '[t]he opportunity should now be taken to draw a clear line between the political and the bureaucratic elements in the support system for the Prime Minister and Cabinet so that the structure and its operation are transparent: both of these elements are essential to the effectiveness of the system and both must be of the highest quality, but they should, as far as practicable, be kept separate and be seen to be so.'[8]

The review found that the passing of the State Sector Act and the Public Finance Act had had a substantial effect on the operations of the public service and that a gap had developed 'at the heart of the machinery of government'.[9] The coordinating functions of Treasury and the State Services Commission had been substantially reduced, with the result that Cabinet and its committees, while still responsible for coordinating the efforts of the government system, had had their ability impaired 'by the failure to receive high quality, fully tested and co-ordinated advice on some major policy issues'.[10]

The review recommended that a single department should be established which combined the Cabinet Office with the advisory side of the Prime Minister's Office. The purpose of this was to ensure that professional advice and coordination of the government machinery would function under a single chief executive. That person was also to be responsible for coordinating the intelligence function of the Prime Minister. The review also recommended that a separate Prime Minister's Office should carry out the political advice function, liaising with political parties as well as carrying out administrative and ceremonial functions. It recommended that the advisory and coordinating functions in the new department be substantially strengthened, with an increase of policy advisory staff from eight to twenty. The purposes of this recommendation were:[11]

> [T]o provide the group with sufficient quality and quantity of staff, first, to assure the Prime Minister that the departments whose duty it is to provide the detailed advice are in fact doing so to the required quality standard; second, to test that advice to ensure it addresses all the appropriate issues and offers viable, sensible solutions; and third, to insist on adequate co-ordination and co-operation in cases where issues cross departmental boundaries (as virtually all the major issues do).

The recommended structure is set out in Figure 4.1. The essence was to divide the political function from the policy coordination and advice function.

---

8 *Ibid*, p.4.
9 *Ibid*, p.5.
10 *Ibid*, p.5.
11 *Ibid*, pp.7, 8–9.

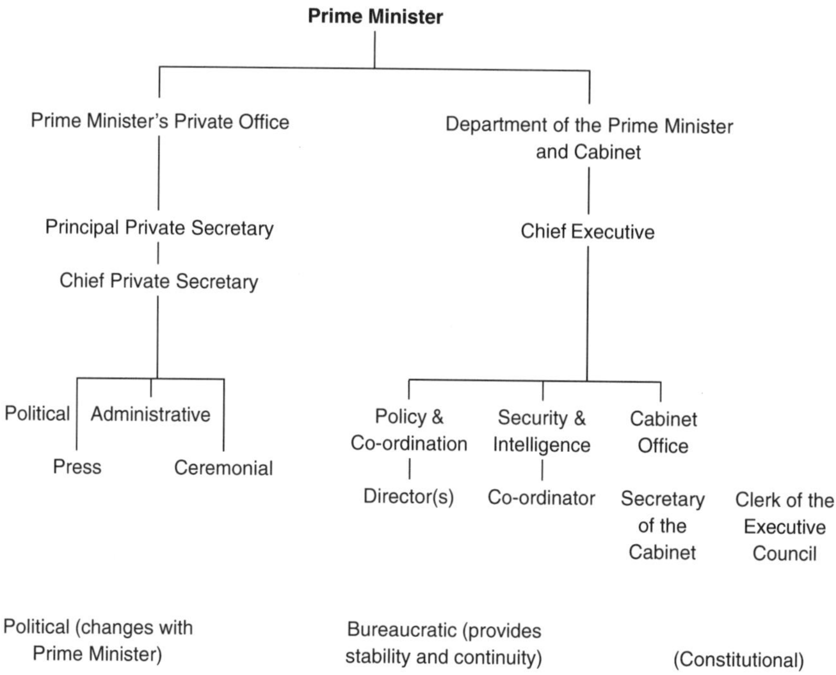

Figure 4.1: Recommended structure for Prime Minister's Office

These recommendations were rapidly implemented by Cabinet decision. The Leader of the Opposition agreed with the changes but asked for a review of the services available to him. The same team carried out that second review, which recommended some increases in staff, to which the government agreed.

The organisational structure was preserved by the National Prime Minister in substantially the same shape. The Rt Hon. Jim Bolger added a communications coordination unit, which he has put into the department; it is separate from the press office, which remains in the private office. Mr Bolger has merged the advisory and analytical groups and added an enterprise development emphasis. They preserve, however, the important feature that the bureaucratic advice comes from the public service, separate from the political advice in the Prime Minister's private office.

In a single-party government, the political weight needed to achieve policy coordination is considerable. It is likely to be even more important in a coalition government. When ministers, especially those from different parties, or departments or both, are at loggerheads, authority is required to sort the situation out. The Prime Minister could well devote all his or her time to that function and still not solve the problem. Yet ministerial time is very scarce; much is done in the Prime Minister's name that the Prime Minister knows little about. The much needed policy coordination function will not be achieved unless reduced priority is given to the other tasks of the office. This cannot be achieved by the bureaucracy; the choices are political. MMP adds, in a dynamic fashion, to the challenges of executive coordination.

MINISTERS, CABINET, AND CABINET COMMITTEES

Cabinet consists of ministers of the Crown, but not necessarily all ministers—some ministers may be designated by the Prime Minister as outside Cabinet. The offices of most Cabinet ministers are located together in the Beehive, separate from other MPs. Section 6 of the Constitution Act 1986 states 'A person may be appointed and may hold office as a member of the Executive Council or as a Minister of the Crown only if that person is a member of Parliament.' It is a key element of our system of government that only MPs should be ministers. It is often said to be the essence of responsible government because Cabinet is, in the words of Bagehot, 'a *hyphen* which joins, a *buckle* which fastens, the legislative part of the State to the executive part of the State'.[12]

Section 6(2) of the Constitution Act has two neat qualifications to the basic constitutional requirement that a Cabinet minister must be a member of Parliament. It provides that:

> (2) Notwithstanding subsection (1) of this section,
> (a) A person who is not a member of Parliament may be appointed and may hold office as a member of the Executive Council or as a Minister of the Crown if that person was a candidate for election at the general election of members of the House of Representatives held immediately preceding that person's appointment as a member of the Executive Council or as a Minister of the Crown but shall vacate office at the expiration of the period of 40 days beginning with the date of the appointment unless, within that period, that person becomes a member of Parliament; and
> (b) Where a person who holds office both as a member of Parliament and as a member of the Executive Council or as a Minister of the Crown ceases to be a member of Parliament, that person may continue to hold office as a member of the Executive Council or as a Minister of the Crown until the expiration of the 28th day after the day on which that person ceases to be a member of Parliament.

As noted in Chapter 2, the purpose of that provision was to allow rapid changes in government after a general election, even before the final official results are

[12] W. Bagehot, *The English Constitution*, London, 1945, p.12.

available. Under MMP, the time limit on the tenure of defeated ministers may affect the composition of caretaker governments while negotiations to form a new government take place.

The Constitution Act 1986 also provides for the appointment of parliamentary under-secretaries who must also be MPs. Section 9(1) states that a parliamentary under-secretary 'holding office as such in respect of any Ministerial office shall have and may exercise or perform under the direction of the Minister concerned such of the functions, duties, and powers of the Minister of the Crown for the time being holding that office as may from time to time be assigned to the Parliamentary Under-Secretary by that Minister'. This office, which is similar to that of junior minister in other parliamentary systems, allows for the workload of ministers to be spread. But under-secretaries do not attend Cabinet meetings and what they do really depends on how much the minister is prepared to delegate to them.

Ministers can be appointed who do not sit in Cabinet and in recent years this has frequently been the case. Recently, Cabinet has numbered about twenty ministers who, between them, hold more than forty portfolios. There are plenty of arguments in favour of reducing both the number of Cabinet ministers and the number of ministerial portfolios—such rationalisation is very desirable.

There has been some discussion that Cabinet government should be reformed by allowing the appointment of ministers who are not MPs. The likelihood of this being discussed further under MMP is considerable, especially if small minority governments occur. One proposal has come from political scientist Nigel Roberts. After studying what occurred in Norway and Denmark, he suggested that it should be permissible to choose ministers from among non-parliamentarians. Such ministers would have the right to speak in Parliament but not to vote. The suggestion has the advantage of increasing the availability of talent for the demanding and important post of Cabinet minister. The requirement, however, for ministers to be drawn from MPs, and to be intimately aware of the pressures of that environment, also contributes to the executive's accountability to Parliament.

Cabinet is the power-house of New Zealand government. As the *Cabinet Office Manual* observes, 'Cabinet is the central decision-making body of Executive Government.'[13] Most important decisions made by government are made by Cabinet or Cabinet committees; others are made by individual ministers. An incredible amount of decision-making power is concentrated in the New Zealand Cabinet. Many problems are pushed up through our governmental system for resolution by Cabinet. Subject to the restraints mentioned in Chapter 1, the New Zealand Cabinet:

---

13 *Cabinet Office Manual.*

- acts as final decision-maker on all important matters of policy;
- approves the content of all regulations, which are laws made under the authority of statutes;
- decides the content of government bills to be introduced to Parliament;
- makes the decisions on government spending;
- coordinates the administration and gives orders to the public service on how to carry out administration; and
- acts in ways designed to further its own political survival.

In 1970, B.E. Talboys, then an experienced minister and later Deputy Prime Minister, characterised Cabinet in the following way:[14]

> In New Zealand all the major decisions are made by Cabinet whether or not they involve more than one department. In fact, it is Cabinet which governs. It is Cabinet which determines the financial authorities granted to Ministers and unless a Minister has this authority he cannot spend, regardless of what the relevant Act may say. The sanction is not that of the law, of course; it is that of his Cabinet colleagues.

Essentially Cabinet is a committee that makes decisions. But it is a committee sitting in secret, unlike a city council, for example, so there is no need for grandstanding. Skills in committee work are of great advantage to ministers; their work as MPs gives them plenty of such experience. In many respects, we have, in New Zealand, a system of government by committee: Cabinet and its committees, caucus and its committees, the party organisation and its committees, the select committees of Parliament, the policy committees of the various parties, the electorate committees of constituency MPs in their home electorates. In fact an MP's life in politics is one long committee meeting discussing almost the same issues at every gathering; only the membership changes. In politics one learns a great deal about collapsing committees which are causing problems, by-passing them, or rendering their work redundant. People have to convince others of the worth of their ideas; that is also true of Cabinet.

The Cabinet system is flexible. Each administration is free to change it, including the structure of Cabinet committees, which are a very important part of the New Zealand Cabinet system. Most important decisions are thrashed out at Cabinet committees, sometimes over a period of weeks, where ministers can enter into discussions with officials.

Cabinet committees have great advantages:

- They allow issues to be considered in greater depth than is possible at full Cabinet.

[14] B.E. Talboys, 'The Cabinet Committee System', 33 *New Zealand Journal of Public Administration*, 1970, p.3.

- They enable ministers to question and probe public servants on proposals, and engage in dialogue with them. (Public servants do not attend full Cabinet.)
- They enable a number of ministers, not just the minister in charge of the proposal, to be fully conversant with a topic before it comes to full Cabinet.
- They improve the coordination and cohesion of Cabinet.

Cabinet committees meet regularly every week or every two weeks, on mornings when Parliament is not sitting. It is an important feature of this system that all Cabinet ministers are free to attend the meeting of any committee.

The New Zealand Cabinet committee system is extensive and systematic. As at 18 March 1996, there were ten committees and four subcommittees, as follows:

- Cabinet Strategy Committee (CSC), and Subcommittee on Defence and External Relations (SDE) and Subcommittee on Intelligence and Security (CIS) and Subcommittee on Civil Defence and Terrorist Emergencies (CIV);
- Cabinet Committee on Enterprise Industry and Environment (CIE);
- Cabinet Social Policy Committee (SPC);
- Cabinet Committee on Education, Training and Employment (ETE);
- Cabinet Committee on Treaty of Waitangi Issues (TOW);
- Ad Hoc Cabinet Committee on Implementation of Proportional Representation (IPR);
- Cabinet State Sector Committee (STA), and Subcommittee on State Wages (WAG);
- Cabinet Committee on Expenditure Control and Revenue (ECR);
- Cabinet Committee on Legislation and House Business (LEG); and
- Cabinet Appointments and Honours Committee (APH).

Although each of the main political parties in office tends to run a different structure of Cabinet committees, that structure is announced, it is publicly available, and the memberships are also public knowledge. In each administration there will be a key Cabinet committee that discusses the key decisions of the administration. This was the Cabinet Policy Committee under the Fourth Labour Government and the Cabinet Strategy Committee under the succeeding National Government.

Information about the Cabinet system is rightly prized by people who want to influence the outcome of government decisions. The 1996 *Cabinet Office Manual* is the Bible in this respect, setting out information and procedures which those involved with government must know. But information on paper is also somewhat misleading. Certain topics tend to be 'run' by certain ministers and their views on them will be decisive. There are usually four to six senior ministers in a single party Cabinet who are the crucial decision-makers. The committee minutes and the Cabinet papers simply cannot capture the dynamic of the Cabinet decision-making process, the essence of which is an interchange between ministers and officials.

The business of Cabinet and its committees is carried out under the supervision of the Secretary of the Cabinet, a high-ranking permanent public servant who heads the unit that services Cabinet. The *Cabinet Office Manual* sets out the rules by which items come to Cabinet and the form submissions should take.

Although only ministers are allowed to send papers to Cabinet, most papers for Cabinet and Cabinet committees are written for ministers by their public servants. Some matters must go to Cabinet—regulations, certain appointments, international treaties, general budgetary decisions. Issues of dispute between ministers or between departments also go to Cabinet as ultimate arbiter of such disputes. Otherwise, however, the guidance about what should go to Cabinet and what should not is delightfully vague but realistic. Paragraph 3.8 of the *Cabinet Office Manual* offers this gem: '[a]s a general rule, Ministers should put before their colleagues the sort of issues on which they themselves would wish to be consulted.' It is hard to see how a more precise test would be possible since it is a matter of politics whether a minister can get away with making a decision without going to Cabinet. Generally they cannot. Owing to the doctrine of collective responsibility discussed below, Cabinet as a collective can always overrule an individual minister's decision, even a Prime Minister's decision, unless the law states that the decision is for a minister alone.

Under MMP, Cabinet continues to consider the same key issues as in the past. Minority government Cabinets must negotiate with other parties for parliamentary support but continue to make their own decisions in the same way. Coalition Cabinets are a forum for interparty negotiations on each issue but the same criteria determine what those issues are; politically sensitive issues must be taken to Cabinet if the health of the coalition is to be preserved.

Submissions to be considered by the full Cabinet each Monday must be with the Cabinet Office by Thursday morning so that they can be processed and distributed to ministers on Friday for reading over the weekend. Each committee has its own deadline for receiving papers. The New Zealand Cabinet Office is a remarkably efficient organisation. It arranges the agenda, distributes papers, and prepares minutes of decisions for Cabinet and all its committees within extremely tight timeframes. Although these functions are under the formal control of the Prime Minister, in reality the Cabinet Office functions with a great deal of independence. To a large extent, the agenda arranges itself, depending upon what papers have been prepared for Cabinet consideration. There may be as many as thirty or forty items for a full Cabinet meeting and, with the reports of Cabinet committees, the total can be much higher than that. Cabinet committees may have only a couple of papers to consider or as many as twenty.

The Cabinet Office attempts to police strictly deadlines for receiving papers for Cabinet and its committees, requiring a ministerial explanation and the permission of the chair before accepting a late paper. Apart from protracted interdepartmental bargaining in formulating papers, there can be powerful political pressures to undermine this. One technique greatly disliked and actively discouraged by the Cabinet Office is that of tabling late papers at the Cabinet meeting itself, so that ministers and their departments have not read them in advance. This practice, known as an 'end run', can result in a Cabinet agreeing to a proposal that ministers have not had the chance to consider properly and which has not been through a Cabinet committee. Some elements of the Labour Government's restructuring of the machinery of government dealing with the environment were dealt with in this way, notably the creation of the Forestry Corporation. Where a department disagrees with a Cabinet paper, a paper to the department's minister, with alternative recommendations, can also be used by a minister in this way.

Generally speaking, most proposals to Cabinet have been looked at pretty carefully—or at least there has been an opportunity to look at them carefully, which is not quite the same thing. Individual ministers may decide to be more or less involved in formulating Cabinet papers. Some may simply sign a paper up to a Cabinet committee, leaving more detailed consideration of its contents until later. Some ministers will want a hands-on role in writing or amending important papers before signing them. Rarely, a minister will refuse to sign up a paper prepared by officials.

Some administrations have had senior officials sitting through deliberations of some Cabinet committees as a matter of course. Such 'permanent' officials provide a source of consistent advice across the range of issues considered by those committees, and help officials to understand the direction of ministers' thinking. Otherwise, at Cabinet committees, officials working on an issue wait outside the committee room when it is being discussed and can be called in and questioned by ministers. This is usually a quite helpful interchange that can clarify the nature and implications of the proposals being considered, as well as the range of ministerial and departmental views. Sometimes such interchanges illustrate weaknesses in the proposals not evident from the papers themselves. Such discussions often result in decisions different from the recommendations. The prospect of questioning by ministers helps to concentrate the minds of public servants.

There are a couple of further quality assurance checks on the papers considered by Cabinet and Cabinet committees. Each paper to a Cabinet committee must be accompanied by a form, a CAB100. This is signed by the minister submitting the paper, and by a senior official in the relevant department. The minister certifies whether consultation on the issues raised in the paper has taken place or should take place with the government caucus, other parliamentary parties and other interested groups. The senior official must certify that the views of relevant departments have been sought and are accurately reflected in the paper. If relevant departments do not appear to have been consulted, the Cabinet Office may refuse to accept a paper. Standing committees of senior officials have been used by the National Government to iron out, or at least clarify, differences between departments before issues are considered by ministers.

A Cabinet comprising ministers who have a sense of confidence and a unified sense of purpose can decide big and controversial policy issues with ease. Where there is division and an atmosphere of political adversity, it is hard to decide any big policy and several meetings of Cabinet and committees may be required.

Full Cabinet meetings start at 10.30 a.m. on a Monday, break for lunch about 1 p.m., resume at 2.15 and can continue until 5 p.m. With a big agenda, however, Cabinet cannot enter detailed discussion on every issue. Cabinet discussions are often very short and lengthy debate is not encouraged, but Cabinet meetings often last all day. This is partly because of the length of the agenda and partly because political developments are also often discussed in some detail. There are no papers about them but, on a contentious and difficult matter, lengthy debate is sometimes held in Cabinet. But the main forum for such debates tends to be a Cabinet committee.

Full Cabinet meetings conform to a general pattern under each administration. The following sorts of items are usually discussed at each meeting:

- *Engagements.* The Prime Minister reviews ministers' engagements for the coming week—sometimes there will be discussions over a particular speech a minister is proposing to give or a report which is being released. This serves to alert ministers to what their colleagues are doing and focus attention on how the political week is likely to develop. Sometimes emergencies occur which require immediate Cabinet attention and there is discussion about what to do about them at the beginning of the meeting; serious flooding is an example.
- *Regulations.* At the beginning of the formal Cabinet agenda come the statutory regulations for consideration. Since Cabinet approves more than 300 of these most years, there are always some. Usually they deal with matters of detail, but they are law and therefore require close scrutiny. Sometimes they are not approved, or are sent back for reconsideration or amendment. The regulations can vary from a simple revocation, to an increase in fees charged for some government function, to an enormous wad of complicated food and drug regulations.
- *Cabinet committee reports.* All the decisions and discussions held by Cabinet committees in the previous week are minuted and sent to full Cabinet, including decisions on government bills by the Cabinet Legislation Committee. Quite often, some of the committees' decisions are discussed again and they can be and sometimes are altered. No Cabinet committee decision is operative until the full Cabinet has noted the decision and left it unaltered.

- *Other submissions by ministers.* These papers can range from insignificant matters calling for no discussion, right through to matters of the most far-reaching policy significance, which attract considerable ministerial discussion. Where a matter appears to require further discussion or some more information, it will be referred to a Cabinet committee for consideration. A big policy item that comes straight on to the agenda of full Cabinet is unusual, unless it is urgent; there is a strong preference for big policy items to be thrashed out in Cabinet committee, where officials can attend.
- *Oral items.* A normal Cabinet agenda will have more than thirty items on it and requires a lot of reading and attention from ministers. But each minister is encouraged to raise oral items at the conclusion of the agenda. These will be matters which ministers feel their colleagues should know about or may have some views on. They are often important and sometimes time-consuming.
- *Particular topics.* Sometimes Cabinet sets aside time for a discussion on particular topics; economic policy was dealt with by the Fourth Labour Cabinet in this way on several occasions. Cabinet will also have discussions about the political situation from time to time.

At full Cabinet meetings, ministers sit around an egg-shaped table in the Beehive. There is a separate room for Cabinet committee meetings. The debate is chaired by the Prime Minister or senior minister present. Votes are hardly ever taken in Cabinet or its committees; discussion proceeds until there is a clear consensus that is summed up by the chair. If no consensus is apparent, particularly in committees, the chair may decide that an issue should be deferred for further consideration at another committee or full Cabinet meeting. Often the recommended decisions in the Cabinet paper under consideration will be changed in order to achieve more agreement. Extended debate is not common; there are usually only two or three contributions on any item.

Each decision taken by Cabinet and its committees is carefully minuted and becomes the source of authority for action in the entire government machine. Cabinet minutes are known within the governmental system as Cabinet 'greens', which is the colour of the paper on which they appear. They are the authoritative collective will of the government and are followed pretty faithfully within the governmental system. The Cabinet Office maintains a system for monitoring compliance with Cabinet greens that require further reports to Cabinet or its committees.

Because the Cabinet committee system is extensive, the number of papers considered each week is large, and the range of policy proposals is often important, there needs to be an overall perspective on the whole scene—in other words, policy coordination. Otherwise various elements of the government can start to work against each other. Overall goals must always be kept in mind; they are easily lost sight of when there is wide-ranging policy action on many fronts.

MINISTERIAL RESPONSIBILITY

The idea of ministerial responsibility is often said to be one of the great protections of our constitutional system. It is supposed to protect against the abuse of power by ministers. But just what the doctrine is and how it works are open to question. In an instructive study Professor Geoffrey Marshall in the United Kingdom has likened ministerial responsibility to the procreation of eels—which, of course, is a slippery subject.[15] Under MMP, the doctrines of ministerial responsibility in New Zealand are in a particularly volatile state.

There are two strands to the doctrine of ministerial responsibility: the collective responsibility of Cabinet and individual ministerial responsibility.[16] They do relate to each other but they are also quite distinct. We discuss them in turn.

Collective responsibility

Cabinet decisions are made by Cabinet acting collectively. The doctrine of collective responsibility of the Cabinet reinforces this. As summarised by Professor Marshall, it has three essential elements: confidence, unanimity, and confidentiality.

The Cabinet must collectively enjoy the confidence of the House of Representatives in order to continue in office. If the government loses a vote of confidence in Parliament, it must resign. A parliamentary vote on the granting of supply to the government (Imprest Supply and Appropriation Bills) is automatically a confidence vote.[17] The Prime Minister can declare any vote to be one that is regarded as a confidence vote, meaning that the government will resign if it loses. This can be a useful threat if other parties would rather not face an election but, if used too often, it could backfire on a government.

Under FPP, since a single party always had a majority, there was little chance of a government losing a vote of confidence. This situation is quite different under MMP. A minority government depends for its existence entirely on the support of other parties in confidence votes. The breakdown of a coalition agreement could also be manifested in loss of a vote of confidence. In a very real sense, MMP restores Parliament's capacity to make and unmake governments. The public will probably not take kindly to early general elections and may punish at the polls those who precipitate them. Nevertheless, collective responsibility in this sense will be more important than before.

---

15 G. Marshall, *Constitutional Conventions: The Rules and Forms of Political Accountability*, rev. ed., Oxford University Press, Oxford, 1986, p.54.

16 This section draws particularly on material in: M.S.R. Palmer, 'The Conventional Wisdom of Ministerial Responsibility in New Zealand', in *Public Law in New Zealand: Cases, Materials, Commentary and Questions*, eds. M. Chen & G. Palmer, Oxford University Press, Auckland, 1993; and M.S.R. Palmer, 'Toward an Economics of Comparative Political Organization: Examining Ministerial Responsibility', 11 *Journal of Law, Economics & Organization*, 1995, pp.164–88.

17 D. McGee, *Parliamentary Practice in New Zealand*, 2nd ed., GP Publications, Wellington, 1994.

Unanimity and confidentiality are the other elements of the doctrine of collective responsibility. Once Cabinet makes a decision, all Cabinet ministers must support it publicly, and Cabinet discussions leading up to it must remain confidential. These elements promote the idea of unity within the Cabinet and the government. They reinforce the incentives for party unity that are powerful anyway, owing to the unpopularity that accompanies disunity.

The essence of the doctrine appears in the 1996 *Cabinet Office Manual*:

> 3.4 Decisions at Cabinet and Cabinet Committee meetings are usually reached by consensus. Votes are rarely taken. Once a decision has been made, however, it is to be supported collectively by all Ministers, regardless of their personal views and whether or not they were at the meeting concerned.
>
> 3.5 The convention of collective responsibility is an essential underpinning of the system of Cabinet Government, whereby Ministers are required to advise the Sovereign (in practice, the Governor-General) on matters of public importance. Ministers whose opposition to a Cabinet decision is such that they wish to publicly disassociate themselves from it must first resign from the Cabinet.

The confidentiality aspect of collective responsibility is less powerful than it used to be and is less relevant than it is in Britain. The Official Information Act 1982 does not treat Cabinet proceedings as necessarily deserving of special protection. It does provide grounds for withholding information that are related to protecting Cabinet discussions, but these can be outweighed by the public interest. Leaks of Cabinet disagreements have become more frequent but, if too frequent, they could indicate that a government is seriously disunited. Under MMP, that is likely to lead to a government falling.

The unanimity and confidentiality elements of collective responsibility have important consequences for the way the system works. The first consequence is that every government looks more unified that it is. This has a number of advantages. First, it avoids confusion as to what the government's policy is. Second, it enables the people to know who is responsible and to hold them accountable. Every minister must be prepared to defend every policy the government has, and that advances the value of cohesion and purposefulness. The doctrine helps the Cabinet to continue to act together, in the knowledge that the public does not know about their past differences.

The idea is well summed up in the expression of Benjamin Franklin at the Declaration of Independence on 4 July 1776: 'Yes, we must, indeed, all hang together or, most assuredly, we shall all hang separately'.[18] The unanimity element

---

[18] Remark to John Hancock, at the Signing of the Declaration of Independence, 4 July 1776, in *The Oxford Dictionary of Quotations*, 3rd ed., Oxford University Press, Oxford, 1979, p.218.

is the quintessential ingredient of the adversary system of politics generated by the Westminster system. There can only be one view in the government itself and all the members of Cabinet must defend it. The principle goes further. Those who hold office as ministers or under-secretaries outside Cabinet are also bound by the doctrine, despite the fact that they have no voice in making the Cabinet decision.

The doctrine has further important consequences. It is a definite ingredient of prime ministerial power. When the Prime Minister sums up Cabinet discussions as to what the government's policy is, no minister will contest it. It is a useful management tool for keeping in line ministers who disagree with the policy. In single-party governments, it has meant that there is a solid block in the government caucus in favour of the Cabinet policy. Cabinet goes to caucus with one view and one voice. Collective responsibility is one of the factors in producing strong executive control over Parliament.

A drastic example of the application of the doctrine resulting in the dismissal of a New Zealand minister came in 1982. The Hon. Derek Quigley, a minister in the Muldoon Government, made a speech that included some observations which could have been construed as critical of the government's development policies, known as 'Think Big'. It was not so much what was actually said that seems to have caused the trouble, as much as the inferences drawn from it. The then Prime Minister, Sir Robert Muldoon, said that the minister should either apologise to his colleagues or resign; the 'speech went well beyond the limits of collective responsibility in which cabinet ministers worked'.[19] The Prime Minister drew a distinction between what a backbencher could say and what a minister could say.

In effect, it was the Prime Minister who decided what collective responsibility meant in the circumstances; he could have ignored the speech. In essence, the doctrine of Cabinet collective responsibility is a political axiom, politically enforced when it is expedient to do so. For example, the same Prime Minister took no action in 1981 when the Minister of Maori Affairs said on television that he supported a South African rugby tour of New Zealand when it was government policy to support the Gleneagles Agreement, which opposed such tours.

Ministerial responsibility is a constitutional convention and, as such, it is in a state of continuous evolution. It is bound to evolve further in an MMP environment. No doubt, as the *Cabinet Manual* suggests, the convention of collective responsibility is an essential underpinning of the system of Cabinet government. Collective responsibility in New Zealand under MMP is likely to change and develop. It will come under increasing pressure, but it will not disappear, and neither should it. The government can have only one policy and the entire Cabinet must be prepared to support it or resign. On the other hand, coalitions will place

19 *Press*, 15 June 1982, quoted in P.A. Joseph, 'The Honourable D.F. Quigley's Resignation Strictly Political Not Constitutional', 1 *Canterbury Law Review*, 1982, p.428.

increased strain on the unanimity principle, especially as an election approaches. Complex arrangements may possibly evolve to allow ministers to differ, even publicly, yet remain together in government. Free votes, without party discipline being enforced, are sometimes permitted on some subjects in Parliament; liquor legislation, abortion law, and capital punishment are standard New Zealand examples. One way to lessen the rigours of the doctrine may be to allow more such votes.

A strong case can be made to the effect that ministerial responsibility is the key to the effective working of Cabinet government. Under FPP in particular it was the doctrine of collective responsibility, combined with the threat of dissolving Parliament if Cabinet did not get its way, that allowed Cabinet to become master of the Parliament which created it. Collective responsibility is the element that fuses the executive and legislative branches of government. The rise of modern political parties, with their organisational skill and their ability to encourage people to vote, institutionalised and reinforced the control that Cabinet came to exert over a small New Zealand Parliament. This helped to make the New Zealand system of Cabinet government under FPP one of the most streamlined in the world.

Ironically, the strength of the unanimity element can be seen as undermining the enforcement of the doctrine of individual ministerial responsibility in a single-party majority government. Sheltering behind the requirement of unanimity and an impregnable Parliament any majority, an incompetent minister could be kept in office for a considerable period. Demands for dismissal of individual ministers, on grounds of individual responsibility, often led to considerable efforts by the entire parliamentary party to support the minister. Ministers may have done something wrong but if they and their colleagues collectively want them to stay, it is likely that they will stay. In this way, collective responsibility can operate to frustrate the application of individual responsibility.

Individual ministerial responsibility

The essence of the doctrine of individual ministerial responsibility is that ministers are individually responsible to Parliament for their own activities and the activities of their public servants in administering their ministerial portfolios. The employees of the department are the minister's agents; everything they do, they do in his or her name. In the eyes of the law, the permanent official is an anonymous instrument of the minister.[20]

But how can it be realistic for a minister to have to accept responsibility for every action of the public servant? Where a public servant acts contrary to policy

---

[20] *Report of the Royal Commission of Inquiry on the State Services in New Zealand,* Wellington, 1962, p.31.

and instructions without any knowledge of the minister, why should the minister be responsible? A famous Minister of Works, Bob Semple, once said he was responsible but not to blame for faults in tunnel construction, carried out by the Department of Railways and caused by laxity in the organisation of the department. Semple told Parliament: '. . . there is a great difference between responsibility and blame. How can one blame a man for the conduct of thousands of workers under his control.'[21] In New Zealand this seems to have come to mean that a minister does not resign because his or her official has blundered.

But the popular focus on ministerial resignations misses the constitutional point of ministerial responsibility. The constitutional doctrine of individual ministerial responsibility is primarily about requiring ministers to answer in Parliament and fix up mistakes. They must inform Parliament about and explain to it the activities of their departments and the exercise of their powers and duties. They should also investigate problems, fix them, and report the results to Parliament.

These apparently simple aspects of ministerial responsibility have important consequences. The government is legally responsible for acts of the servants under a minister's control and can be sued in respect of them. A minister can be asked questions in Parliament and by the media about things that may have gone wrong; a minister, and no one else, is responsible to Parliament in that way. A minister must articulate the policies being followed and defend them. He or she is supposed to see that the department functions efficiently. The chief executive of the department is answerable to the minister for this. There must be continuing consultation between the minister and his or her departmental officers on a day-to-day basis. Where mistakes and errors have occurred, the minister is responsible for putting them right and for changing policies and procedures where necessary. These implications of individual ministerial responsibility are vital to the functioning of New Zealand's system of government. Yet, when ministers are called to resign, they are usually obscured by political invocations of ministerial responsibility.

A dramatic recent debate over the implications of ministerial responsibility in New Zealand arose over the deaths of fourteen people in 1995 when a viewing platform erected by the Department of Conservation at Cave Creek on the West Coast collapsed. A commission of inquiry conducted by District Court Judge G.S. Noble inquired into the tragedy and reported to the government.[22] The commissioner found that there was one dominant or proximate cause of the collapse and a number of secondary causes. The dominant cause was that the platform was not constructed in accordance with sound building practice. The secondary

21 267 *New Zealand Parliamentary Debates*, p.43 (12 October 1944).

22 Report of the Commission of Inquiry into the Collapse of a Viewing Platform at Cave Creek Near Punakaiki on the West Coast, H.2, *Appendices to the Journal of the House of Representatives*, Wellington, 1995.

causes were that there had been a failure to provide qualified engineering input into the design, and that the people who did the design were not qualified. There had been a failure to manage the construction adequately. There had been a failure to comply with a number of laws in its construction. There was a failure to inspect. There was an absence of warning signs. There was what the judge called 'systemic failure'—the lack of a proper project management system.

How does the doctrine of ministerial responsibility apply to these facts? The minister, the Hon. Denis Marshall, did not know of the plans relating to the platform. He had not personally been involved with them. He did answer questions about the incident and took responsibility for ensuring such an event would not happen again. Attention, however, focused on whether he should resign. The minister relied publicly on a passage that appeared in the second edition of this book, to the effect that, since he did not know of these things and did not have any involvement in them, he should not resign.

The commission of inquiry found that the culture of the department was one of trying to do more with fewer resources. The judge was not suggesting that lack of money was the cause of the Cave Creek collapse, yet he felt that the Department had not been adequately resourced and that this had induced the culture which led to an enthusiastic band of dedicated employees doing things the way they did. Should the minister have been held accountable for that? If the government as a whole made budgetary decisions that affected the culture of a department, what was the responsibility of the individual minister? These questions, like most involving ministerial resignations, are political and cannot be answered by abstract constitutional or administrative doctrine. In any event, in this case the minister did not resign at the time of the tragedy and the Prime Minister did not ask him to do so.

The Minister of Conservation said, shortly after the tragedy, that he had a commitment to implement ministerial responsibility, not to shrink from it by resigning. He did, after the tragedy, implement a number of steps to improve the management systems of the Department of Conservation, with particular attention to safety. He also secured further funds for the department. He accomplished the task that he set himself to his own satisfaction. He then resigned. In his speech of resignation to the House of Representatives he concluded as follows:[23]

> On ministerial responsibility, Ministers should at the very least publicly make themselves accountable and ensure that the errors will not occur again. I believe I have done that. I said in the House last November that I am profoundly sorry. Today I am taking a further step to express my sorrow for what happened that fateful day at Cave Creek. This is a personal decision, which I feel is the correct course of action for me now. In

[23] 65 *New Zealand Parliamentary Debates, Weekly Hansard* p.12, 922 (30 May 1996).

> resigning from the ministerial responsibility for conservation I hope that the steps I have helped put in place to ensure the safety of visitor facilities will be able to proceed without any lingering distraction. I have informed the Prime Minister of my decision and he has accepted my resignation.

This resignation, many months after the events to which it related, is a puzzling addition to the annals of ministerial responsibility in New Zealand. In many ways, the truth of the matter seems to have been that the minister felt personally that he had to resign. No doubt, the political pressure had been intense for an extended period and there had been media comment for many months on the events relating to the tragedy.

There was also another complicating aspect to accountability for the Cave Creek tragedy. The public administration reforms outlined in Chapters 5 and 6 have complicated the issues of ministerial responsibility and accountability in New Zealand government. The State Sector Act 1988 and the Public Finance Act 1989 have imposed a more transparent and public accountability regime on chief executives of public service departments. Because of this, and the greater openness of official information, chief executives are more in the public eye than they used to be, relative to their political masters. As discussed also in the next chapter, this has led to something of an uneasy interface in practice between the political wing of government and its administrative element. Those tensions were highlighted in the Cave Creek matter. No doubt further consideration will be given to these issues in the future. Our instinct is that, notwithstanding the profound nature of the reforms to the state sector in recent years, the doctrine of ministerial responsibility will continue to occupy a fundamental place in defining the system of political and administrative accountability in New Zealand government. In essence, we consider that the electorate will always demand that ministers, drawn from Parliament to direct the executive, should be responsible to the electorate's representatives in Parliament for what occurs in the public sector. This may be the case even where there is no formal ministerial responsibility in the strict sense.

The question of ministerial resignations comes down to a question of what is 'wrong' in the conduct of a minister and what should the minister do when his or her conduct is 'wrong'. Opinions on what constitutes misconduct differ and must be exposed to political debate. In New Zealand we hear frequent calls for the resignation of ministers but very few actual resignations. Many of the calls for resignation, and in any year there will be several, are hollow and politically motivated. They are inevitable because the whole concept of ministerial responsibility is a political one.

The idea that resignation is the only sanction of the doctrine of ministerial responsibility requires refinement. It is not correct to say that either the minister walks the plank and resigns, or nothing happens; a minister's actions can be criticised publicly or privately by the Prime Minister, or extensive public criticism can cause a change in policy. There are many ways in which the doctrine of responsibility places pressure on ministers.

In the end, whether a minister's actions warrant his or her resignation is a question of judgement and that judgement has to be made by the Prime Minister and Cabinet. That is where the buck stops. There are some instances where resignation would be constitutionally desirable. Ministers who are guilty of personal impropriety should most certainly resign or the Prime Minister should call for their resignation and recommend their dismissal if they refuse. What constitutes impropriety was discussed in detail by a commission of inquiry held in 1980 into the Marginal Lands Board loan affair. The Minister of Lands had made representations to the board on behalf of two applicants, one of whom was the daughter of the Minister of Agriculture. (Hence the affair was dubbed New Zealand's 'Daughtergate'.) The minister described them as personal friends; the board was administered from his department. The Minister of Agriculture had also intervened in their application. The commission found there was no impropriety, although the Minister of Lands had been 'unwise'[24] and the Minister of Agriculture 'extremely unwise'.[25]

The commission decided that there is impropriety where the act complained of is done with intent to procure an improper advantage (an advantage outside the true merits of the application). It is an objective standard, the commission said. The commission found that no impropriety was present on the facts of these cases. Had it done so, resignation would have been inevitable.

Finally, a spectacular example of the operation of the doctrine of ministerial responsibility occurred in 1986 involving premature delivery of copies of the Budget to people who were not entitled to them. The Hon. Roger Douglas, Minister of Finance, discovered that some distribution arrangements for the Budget, made within his office, did not meet the overriding requirement for total Budget security.

Those arrangements concerned the couriering of Budget documents so that they could have been read by people not entitled to them before the minister delivered his speech in the House. None of those concerned were commercial people and apparently no advantage was taken of the situation by any of the recipients. The minister felt, however, that the arrangements were improper, and in his view, indefensible. So he tendered his resignation.

The Prime Minister, the Rt Hon. David Lange, refused the resignation in the course of a letter dated 12 August 1986:

---

[24] Report of the Commission of Inquiry into Allegations of Impropriety in Respect of Approval by the Marginal Lands Board of an Application by James Maurice Fitzgerald and Audrey Fitzgerald, Part I, H.5, *Appendices to the Journal of the House of Representatives*, Wellington, 1980, p.93.

[25] *Ibid.*, p.103.

> I have consulted with some of our colleagues. All the soundings which the Deputy Prime Minister and I have taken indicate strong support for your remaining in the Ministry.
>
> I have decided not to accept your resignation. That decision and the reasons for it must not be seen as questioning in any way the most honourable character of your letter and its proposed course of action.
>
> You begin, as I do, with the basic principle of our Constitution—that Ministers are responsible to Parliament for the actions of their officials. As you indicate, the action of your office in this case is a serious and indefensible breach of the principle of the inviolability of the budget. That is a principle of the highest importance in our parliamentary and governmental system. It is the more so because improper personal advantage might arise from its breach, although there is in fact no evidence of that here.
>
> In your letter you accept responsibility for the action, and you accept that responsibility without equivocation or qualification. To accept both the responsibility and the blame for actions of which you had no knowledge enhances the accountability of our system of ministerial government.
>
> The breach was not, however, your act. You did not know of it in advance. You could not reasonably have been expected to know of it. The principle is undoubted that you do not have to defend that error—indeed, as you say, it cannot be defended. And this is not a case in which you should or even could have been expected to take prior steps to prevent this breach, given the existence of the clear principle of budget confidentiality.
>
> You have moreover taken steps, immediately on learning of the bare facts, to have the relevant details assembled. The government will be taking further action to determine whether anyone took advantage of the early release of the budget information. It will as well ensure that procedures designed to prevent any such disclosure will be strengthened. It is the responsibility of the State Services Commission to consider whether disciplinary action is appropriate for the officials involved.
>
> I began this letter by referring to the honourable character of your tender of resignation. So far as I am aware, the only modern New Zealand example of a Minister resigning for wrongdoing followed upon a Commission of Inquiry finding of individual wrongdoing *by that Minister*. No such offer has, it seems, ever been made by a New Zealand Minister who was in no way at fault.

In this case, the Minister of Finance felt so affronted personally by what had happened that he felt compelled to offer his resignation. He could not be talked out of it. By doing so, he was under no obligation to defend the distribution of the Budget which had taken place. He felt quite unable to make such a defence. It was this fact that impelled him to resign. He said repeatedly to Geoffrey Palmer when he found out about it: 'There is no way I can defend this.' Had the minister himself prematurely disclosed the contents of the Budget to some unauthorised people, he would personally have been guilty of blameworthy conduct and his resignation would have been accepted. The British precedents on that were clear. Hugh Dalton's resignation as Chancellor of the Exchequer was accepted by Prime Minister Attlee when Dalton had communicated to a reporter some details of the Budget as he was going into the House of Commons to deliver it.

The tendering of his resignation by the Hon. Roger Douglas certainly cleared the air over the issue, but the Prime Minister was clearly entitled not to accept it for the reasons given in the letter.

The importance of individual ministerial responsibility may well be sharpened in an MMP environment. Under MMP, ministers' performance in their portfolios will be more open to close select committee scrutiny. Where there are coalition or minority governments, the government will be less able to close ranks and bring the parliamentary shutters down on probing actions from MPs. It is quite possible that Parliament will want to hold individual ministers more strictly to account than it has in the past. Minority governments in particular may find it more desirable to contemplate the resignation of an individual minister than the resignation of the government as a whole. Because of this, it is quite possible that MMP will have the important effect of encouraging ministers, and therefore public servants, to lift their game. Ministers may need to understand their policies better, advocate them more effectively, and be better policy analysts than they have sometimes been in the past.

5 The Public Service and Crown Entities

The public service is the machinery of government. If Cabinet and individual ministers direct something to be done, or the law so requires, it is usually the public service that does it. The public service also advises Cabinet ministers as to what they should want done. Because of this, and because they generally have more information, expertise, and time to think than ministers, public servants have power. The reality of the New Zealand public service is not, however, the all-powerful potential for manipulation portrayed by the TV series *Yes Minister.* New Zealand public servants do as they are directed and offer advice to the best of their professional ability. Reforms to the public sector over the last ten years have dramatically altered the environment in which they work. Core government departments have been restructured. Some of them, as examined later in this chapter, have been replaced by an 'alphabet soup' of Crown-owned companies (SOEs, TEIs, CRIs, CHEs), which take their place alongside Crown entities and other quangos.

DEPARTMENTS: WHAT THEY DO

The number and names of government departments have changed enormously since the last edition of this book in 1987. In the 1990s, academics have classified different departments (whether called ministries or departments) according to their primary function. An updated version of such a classification is provided in Table 5.1 below.[1]

Although government departments can be established by statute, since the late 1980s the Legislation Advisory Committee has argued that departments should be established simply by Cabinet direction under the legal authority of the royal

[1] Based on J. Boston, 'Reorganising the machinery of government, objectives and outcomes', in *Reshaping the State: New Zealand's Bureaucratic Revolution*, eds. J. Boston *et al.*, Oxford University Press, Auckland, 1991, p.252, and R. Mulgan, *Politics in New Zealand*, Auckland University Press, Auckland, 1994, p.132.

Table 5.1: List of departments

Central agencies	**Mainly delivery of goods and/or services**
Department of Prime Minister and Cabinet	Department of Conservation
State Services Commission	Department of Corrections
The Treasury	Department for Courts
	Crown Law Office
Mainly policy advice	Ministry of Foreign Affairs and Trade
Ministry of Agriculture	Government Superannuation Fund Department
Ministry of Commerce	Department of Internal Affairs
Ministry of Cultural Affairs	National Library of New Zealand
Ministry of Defence	The Police
Ministry of Education	Public Trust Office
Ministry for the Environment	Serious Fraud Office
Ministry of Fisheries	Department of Statistics
Ministry of Forestry	Department of Survey and Land Information
Ministry of Health	Ministry of Transport
Ministry of Housing	Valuation New Zealand
Ministry of Justice	
Ministry of Pacific Island Affairs	**Mainly taxes and transfers**
Ministry of Research, Science, and Technology	Customs Department
Te Puni Kokiri (Ministry of Maori Development)	Inland Revenue Department
Ministry of Women's Affairs	Department of Labour
Ministry of Youth Affairs	Department of Social Welfare
Review and audit	
Audit Office	
Education Review Office	

prerogative. Since a department is part of the Crown, ministers of the Crown have the flexibility to create departments, though abolishing departments requires legislation.[2] There is likely to be pressure against this flexibility where there is a minority government under MMP. In that case, opposition parties with a majority in Parliament may press for departments to be created, or even structured in particular ways, as a means to achieve their policy ends despite a government's wishes.

CHIEF EXECUTIVES: WHAT THEY CAN DO

The old public service was an entity in itself, with many rules and procedures laid down by the 'control' agencies—the State Services Commission and the Treasury.

2 See Legislation Advisory Committee, *Departmental Statutes: Report No. 4*, Wellington, 1989. Application of public sector accountability regimes to a new department, such as the State Sector Act 1988, can be accomplished by Cabinet through order-in-council but removal requires an act of Parliament.

The State Sector Act 1988 and the Public Finance Act 1989 have drastically reformed the New Zealand public sector.[3]

According to its long title, the State Sector Act is:

> (a) To ensure that employees in the State services are imbued with the spirit of service to the community; and
> (b) To promote efficiency in the State services; and
> (c) To ensure the responsible management of the State services; and
> (d) To maintain appropriate standards of integrity and conduct among employees in the State services; and
> (e) To ensure that every employer in the State services is a good employer; and
> (f) To promote equal employment opportunities in the State services; and
> (g) To provide for the negotiation of conditions of employment in the State services.

A key feature of the new regime is the role of each chief executive—the head of each government department.

Section 32 of the State Sector Act provides that:

> The chief executive of a Department shall be responsible to the appropriate Minister for—
> (a) The carrying out of the functions and duties of the Department (including those imposed by Act or by the policies of the Government); and
> (b) The tendering of advice to the appropriate Minister and other Ministers of the Crown; and
> (c) The general conduct of the Department; and
> (d) The efficient, effective, and economical management of the activities of the Department.

Section 33 of the act provides that:

> in matters relating to decisions on individual employees (whether matters relating to the appointment, promotion, demotion, transfer, disciplining, or the cessation of the employment of any employee, or other matters) the chief executive of a Department shall not be responsible to the appropriate Minister but shall act independently.

Section 33 of the Public Finance Act provides that:

> (2) The Chief Executive of a department shall be responsible to the Responsible Minister for the financial management and financial performance of the department and shall comply with any lawful financial actions required by the Minister of Finance or the Responsible Minister.

---

3 See, in general, J. Boston, J. Martin, J. Pallot, P. Walsh, *Public Management: The New Zealand Model*, Oxford University Press, Auckland, 1996; and State Services Commission, *Working Under Proportional Representation: A Reference for the Public Service*, Wellington, 1995.

> (3) The Chief Executive shall be responsible to the Responsible Minister for compliance with the financial reporting requirements of this or any other Act.

The effect of these and other provisions is that chief executives run the public service. Each chief executive is appointed on contract for a term of up to five years by the State Services Commissioner. (Although the Cabinet can reject a proposed appointment, it must do so publicly.) He or she has an annual performance agreement and performance is reviewed against it at the end of each year by the State Services Commissioner in consultation with the relevant minister and others. Each chief executive is the employer of the employees in a department and is subject to the same employment laws as private sector employers. The chief executive decides how to deploy available resources, within the limits set out by Parliament, Cabinet, and the relevant minister.

The idea of the reforms was to remove stultifying levels of bureaucracy and to give managers freedom to manage, while holding them accountable for doing so. Together with the employment and spending powers of chief executives are a series of related accountability documents, required by the Public Finance Act and the Cabinet. These give effect to the traditional constitutional relationships between the Parliament, ministers, and the public service, but do so more transparently than in the past. The 'estimates' of appropriations each year are known as the Budget and are the basis on which Parliament votes money to ministers. As outlined further in Chapter 6, the estimates are supported by other documents, including departmental forecast reports, annual and half-yearly financial statements, purchase agreements, and strategic business plans. Departments may also produce corporate plans, which bring together information in these documents with other aspects of organisational values, objectives, structure, and activities.

Some have criticised the new system for emphasising individual vertical relationships between ministers, chief executives, and public servants at the expense of collective relationships between all ministers and across the public service. And, especially in the first few years, the public sector reforms concentrated on reinforcing the vertical relationships through new accountability documents—especially the chief executive's performance agreement and the departmental purchase agreement. The performance agreement tells the chief executive what he or she must particularly concentrate on during the upcoming year, sets out his or her rights and obligations, and makes sure that he or she is aware of how his or her personal performance will be assessed. The purchase agreement, as outlined further in Chapter 6, is an annual agreement between the minister and the chief executive about all the things the department is expected to do during the forthcoming year, and how much it will cost. The idea of actually planning and writing down in advance what departments are supposed to do in systematic documents that are then regularly reviewed was a new concept for the New Zealand public service—and is regarded with awe and trepidation by public servants overseas.

Because Cabinet as a collective can generally override an individual minister, public servants must always have regard to the interests of the government as a whole. The concern that the new public sector accountability regime did not sufficiently emphasise the collective interests of the government as a whole has also been addressed through specific measures in the early 1990s:

- *Strategic result areas (SRAs):* The Cabinet as a collective agrees each year on a handful of key SRAs that define the emphasis a government wants to put on its activities that year. Examples include economic strategy, crime strategy, and Treaty of Waitangi settlements.
- *Key result areas (KRAs):* These are formulated in each chief executive's annual performance agreement to define the key results he or she is expected to achieve in that year. They are supposed to be accompanied by milestones specified in advance to provide more concrete guidance to allow easier assessment. KRAs reflect SRAs and are, in turn, reflected in the purchase agreement between a chief executive and his or her minister. KRAs are usually known throughout a department and, ideally, are further reflected in the performance agreements of individual managers and staff. Chief executives' performance agreements also now contain a standard clause requiring them to have regard to the collective interests of government.
- *Officials committees*: Committees have always been a feature of public service life. Between 1990 and 1996 the National Government has relied more on officials committees as a way of coordinating views and resolving arguments between public servants from different departments before they are considered by ministers. In particular, standing committees of senior officials that mirror Cabinet committees have become important features of the bureauucratic landscape—including the Officials Strategy Committee, the Officials Committee on Expenditure Control, the Officials Social Policy Committee, the Officials Committee on the Implementation of Proportional Representation, and the Officials Treaty Strategy Committee.

The State Services Commission has this to say:[4]

> Since the passage of the State Sector Act 1988 relationships between Ministers and chief executives have developed in two ways. Some chief executives have become more visible, publicly asserting responsibility for the management of resources and defending actions which, in the past, would have been dealt with by Ministers. Equally, some

[4] State Services Commission, 'The Public Service and Government', in *Public Service: Principles, Conventions and Practice—Guidance Material*, Wellington, 1995, pp.4–5.

> Ministers have exercised a more direct control over departments, particularly (but not always) where issues have become 'political' in character.
>
> Though the reforms embodied in the State Sector Act 1988 can be said to have established (or even confirmed) an agency relationship between Ministers and their departments or chief executives for the specification of social or political outcomes and the delivery of contributory outputs, in practice the relationship is not clear cut. Martin notes[5] that 'while it is constitutionally proper for the Minister to be in charge; it is managerially unsound for Ministers to run their departments . . . The ideal relationship is one of trust between two people linked inextricably at least for a time . . .'
>
> Thus, 'Ministers should not have operational responsibility for the routine performance of departments. They must have, however, some form of 'early warning system' so that they are alerted to potentially controversial matters very quickly.'[6]
>
> The State Sector Act 1988 envisages that Ministers will not normally involve themselves in the day-to-day management of their departments. The general relationship between Minister and chief executive should be characterised as:
>
> - departments being extensions of the Minister acting in the Minister's name and in accordance with the Minister's wishes and direction
> - chief executives under the Public Finance Act 1989 having a delegated authority to enable the production of contracted outputs in the most efficient and effective manner and being accountable for the exercise of this authority.

On the face of it, the system of accountability mechanisms instituted by the State Sector Act and the Public Finance Act should allow the constitutional relationships between Parliament, ministers and the public service to be focused more clearly and transparently than in the previous system, which was partly based on implicit understandings and knowledge of past practice. But it is not clear that this is the general understanding of commentators to date. The way in which the state sector reforms have been implemented should not be allowed to obscure the constitutional truths that lie behind them and are unaltered by them. Among these, the doctrine of ministerial responsibility is the key fundamental, as canvassed in Chapter 4. The move to managerial accountability of public servants for operational decisions cannot mask the political accountability of ministers.

It remains to be seen how the new system will respond to MMP. It is likely that MMP will create increased stress on the public service, but the instruments of vertical accountability between ministers and chief executives are probably robust

---

5 J. Martin, 'Remaking the State Services', in *The Fourth Labour Government: Politics and Policy in New Zealand*, eds M. Holland & J. Boston, 2nd ed., Oxford University Press, Auckland, 1990, p.130.

6 *Cabinet Office Manual*, Wellington, 1996, para 2.57.

enough to cope. The coordination and horizontal relationships between different departments may need further strengthening, especially in a coalition government where public servants are responding to demands from ministers of different political parties. It may be that the central agencies, the Department of Prime Minister and Cabinet, the State Services Commission, and the Treasury, will have a greater role to play in ensuring that the collective interests of a coalition government as a whole are adhered to by individual departments.

PUBLIC SERVANTS: WHAT THEY SHOULD DO

In the words of a 1962 Royal Commission on the State Services, New Zealand 'has been so well served for so long by loyal, incorruptible, and politically neutral State servants that it may be inclined to assume that this is part of the natural order of things'.[7] That situation undoubtedly still holds, although the public service has altered its shape dramatically since 1962.

The *Public Service Code of Conduct*,[8] issued by the State Services Commission in prescribing minimum standards of integrity and conduct for the public service under section 57 of the State Sector Act 1988, establishes three general principles of conduct that all public servants are expected to observe:

(i) Employees should fulfil their lawful obligations to Government with professionalism and integrity.

- Employees are obliged to serve the aims and objectives of the Minister. Employees should ensure that their personal interests or activities do not interfere with, or appear to interfere with, this obligation.

(ii) Employees should perform their official duties honestly, faithfully, efficiently, respecting the rights of the public and their colleagues.

- Employees should carry out their duties in an efficient and competent manner, and avoid behaviour which might impair their effectiveness.
- In performing their duties, employees should respect the rights of their colleagues and the public.
- Employees should perform their duties honestly and impartially, and avoid situations which might compromise their integrity or otherwise lead to conflicts of interest.

---

7 *The State Services in New Zealand*, Report of the Royal Commission of Inquiry, Wellington, 1962, para 20.

8 State Services Commission, *Public Service Code of Conduct*, Wellington, 1995, p.9. See also *Public Service: Principles, Conventions and Practice—Guidance Material*, Wellington, 1995, composed of ten papers on different aspects of the public service.

(iii) Employees should not bring their employer into disrepute through their private activities.

— Employees should avoid any activities, whether in connection with their official duties or otherwise, which might bring their department into disrepute, or jeopardise its relationships with Ministers, clients, or the general public.

The key element running through these obligations is that the New Zealand public service is politically neutral—loyal to whatever government is in power at any time. This is a corollary of the doctrine of ministerial responsibility. There can be tension between the need for officials to be politically neutral and offer their best advice, and the need to do what ministers direct. As para 2.64 of the *Cabinet Office Manual* states:

> Public servants must act in such a way that their department maintains the confidence of its current Minister and also of future Ministers. Advice given to Ministers must be honest, impartial and comprehensive. Although regard must be had to the policies and priorities of the government of the day, the advice given by officials should be 'free and frank', so that Minister can take decisions based on all the facts and an appreciation of all the options.

This tension is heightened by MMP, since public servants have more to do with the political negotiations between parties, whether regarding particular policies, legislation, or the formation of a government itself. In general, public servants must act in accordance within their minister's instructions, but they must also pay close attention to the need to be, and to be seen to be, politically neutral. The tension of political neutrality of public servants is likely to be most keenly felt during the formation of a new government and in advising on the formulation of legislation.

As indicated in previous chapters, the formation of a government under MMP is a fraught time of political manoeuvering among constitutional niceties in an unstructured environment. An important part of negotiations between political parties is likely to concern certain policies held dear by them. It would be desirable for full information and advice concerning those policies to be available—for example, advice regarding the cost of a policy might be useful for all parties. Yet the public service, which is expert in providing such information and advice, must maintain its political neutrality while, at the same time, being loyal and accountable to incumbent ministers who belong to one (or more) of the negotiating parties.

The controversy that attended the costing of opposition parties' policies by the Treasury at the request of ministers before the 1993 election illustrates the dangers in this situation. Specific rules of procedure for dealing with requests for costings were confirmed following this, in order to preserve the non-partisan, apolitical nature of the public service.[9] But a more general constitutional understanding of the circumstances in which a minister should ask for public servants' interaction with political parties during the formation of a government remains unclear.

Of less constitutional moment, but more frequent occurrence, is the negotiation of policy or the passage of legislation under a coalition or minority government. In a coalition government, every Cabinet decision is the subject of interparty political negotiation but it generally takes place within the relatively structured confines of the Cabinet decision-making machinery. In a minority government, every piece of legislation is potentially the subject of political negotiation with, at least initially, few procedural rules. The practices governing how such consultation takes place and the role of public servants evolve under each government. The *Cabinet Office Manual* states:

> 2.66 Consultation and negotiation between the government and other political parties is the responsibility of Ministers. Public servants may however be called upon to support Ministers in this process. Officials should obtain clear instructions from their Minister on the nature of the contact, and whether they will be supporting a briefing or supporting a process of consultation and negotiation between Ministers. Any contact between public servants and representatives of political parties within or outside the government should take place only with prior Ministerial approval.
>
> 2.67 Public servants may on occasion be asked by their Minister to meet representatives of political parties without the Minister present. On such occasions all those involved should clearly understand that officials are only to provide a briefing on the issues. As a matter of practice, officials should keep a record of the discussion and consider providing a copy of that record to all those who attended the meeting as well as to the Minister.

A particularly difficult aspect of the legislative process for a public servant under a minority government is advising a select committee dominated by opposition parties. Constitutionally, a public servant advises a select committee privately (rather than appearing as a public witness) at the committee's invitation, but with the consent and on behalf of the minister. Public servants in this position must attempt to provide information and advice to a committee to the best of their professional ability, without undermining the minister's position on any particular matter. This relationship did not need to be so explicitly understood in the past when the government always dominated Parliament and had a majority on select committees. Under MMP, however, a general understanding of this role should be reached

---

9 State Services Commission, 'The Public Service and Government', in *Public Service: Principles, Conventions and Practice—Guidance Material*, Wellington, 1995, p.13.

between the executive and Parliament. In June 1996 the State Services Commission issued guidelines on the relationship between officials and select committees that represents the conventional constitutional relationship.[10] Three paragraphs of the summary of these guidelines in the *Cabinet Office Manual* captures their flavour:

> 5.87 To assist its members with consideration of a Bill, a select committee will usually ask the responsible Minister to provide officials to act as advisers to the committee. These officials attend at the committee's request, not as of right. Their role is to assist the committee with information on the legislation and on its implementation and administration.
>
> 5.88 As a general practice, the officials advising a select committee should represent the government's view to a select committee. However, officials are not responsible for justifying policy, or disclosing details of how a policy evolved; that is the Minister's responsibility. It is essential that departmental advisers are sufficiently experienced to provide frank and correct information and to exercise good judgment.
>
> 5.89 Officials should keep their Minister fully informed of any contact with a select committee, should err on the side of caution before committing themselves or their Minister to a position, and should seek leave to withhold comment and consult the Minister when that seems prudent.

If the nature of this key set of relationships in New Zealand's constitution is not understood and accepted by ministers, public servants, and parliamentarians, they could end up being altered unwittingly in response to a particular crisis rather than by a considered approach.

SOEs AND OTHER GOVERNMENT COMPANIES

Although the public service, contained in government departments, is the core of the public sector, many other significant organisations are also considered to be part of the public sector although they are not government departments, in particular, state-owned enterprises (SOEs), Crown health enterprises (CHEs), Crown research institutes (CRIs), and tertiary education institutes (TEIs).

In fact, the reforms of the core public service started with the development of the SOE reforms. In 1985 the Labour Government decided there were serious inadequacies in the operation of massive New Zealand trading enterprises that were run as ordinary government departments, including the electricity system, the telephone system, the Post Office, commercial forests, property-owning organisations, and several banks.

---

10 State Services Commission, *Public Servants and Select Committees—Guidelines*, Wellington, 1996.

The classic departmental structure combined with rigid public service administration methods, and the constant potential for political influence on management decisions through ministerial responsibility, promoted an environment that meant these operations were not run in a business-like manner. The economic performance of state trading activities left great room for improvement. The Tongariro electricity scheme was estimated to take ten years to build; in reality it took twenty years. Administrative expenditure by the Post Office Savings Bank (primarily on staff) grew 75 per cent in real terms in ten years, while total real assets fell 37 per cent. Its market share in 1986 was just over half what it was in 1985. State Coal posted losses in twenty out of twenty-one years. This poor record meant that the economy as a whole experienced lower growth than it should have and those organisations soaked up resources which could have been used more profitably elsewhere. Over twenty years, the taxpayer poured the equivalent of 10 per cent of New Zealand's 1986 income into five major state trading organisations: the Post Office, the Ministry of Energy, the Forest Service, the airways system, and the trading activities of Lands and Survey. In 1986 the net post-tax return to the government, and therefore the taxpayer, on that investment was exactly zero.

In December 1985, the government announced, in an *Economic Statement*, five principles to underlie the management of state-owned enterprises:[11]

(a) Responsibility for non commercial functions will be separated from major trading state owned enterprises;
(b) Managers of state owned enterprises will be given a principal objective of running them as successful business enterprises;
(c) Managers will be given responsibility for decisions on the use of inputs and on pricing and marketing of their output within the performance objectives agreed with Ministers so that the managers can be held accountable to Ministers and Parliament for their results;
(d) The advantages and disadvantages which state owned enterprises have, including unnecessary barriers to competition, will be removed so that commercial criteria will provide a fair assessment of managerial performance;
(e) Individual state owned enterprises will be reconstituted on a case by case basis in a form appropriate for their commercial purposes under the guidance of Boards comprising, generally, members appointed from the private sector.

These principles were reflected in the State-Owned Enterprises Act 1986, which applied to five existing state-owned corporations[12] and created nine

11 Minister of Finance, *Economic Statement to the House of Representatives,* Wellington, 1985.

12 Air New Zealand Limited, New Zealand Railways Corporation, Petroleum Corporation of New Zealand Limited, Tourist Hotel Corporation of New Zealand, and the Shipping Corporation of New Zealand Limited.

new state-owned enterprises[13] to take over trading operations of government departments.

The influences on SOEs are intended to be a mix of private sector efficiency incentives (reflecting their primarily commercial nature) and public sector accountability measures (reflecting the fact that they are owned by the government). The principal objective of every state enterprise is to be a successful business. The act provides that they are to be good employers, exhibit a sense of social responsibility, and operate profitably and efficiently. The directors of these enterprises are mostly people who have had extensive experience in successful businesses. SOEs are registered companies under the Companies Act. In addition, the SOE Act sets out a number of public sector accountability mechanisms. All the shares in each SOE are held by the Minister of Finance and the Minister for SOEs and cannot be sold unless there is specific legislative authority. The powers of ministers in respect of the enterprises are carefully defined by the act. They can direct the board to include or omit statements from the statement of corporate intent, which means, in effect, that the overall strategy of the enterprise is controlled by ministers. They determine the dividends to be paid. The Official Information Act 1982 and the Ombudsmen Act 1975 apply to SOEs and they are audited by the Audit Office.

The statement of corporate intent (SCI) is a key instrument of accountability. Section 14 of the act provides that each statement of corporate intent deal with the current financial year and the two following years and contain the following information:

- objectives;
- nature and scope of activities;
- ratio of consolidated shareholders' funds to total assets, and definitions of those terms;
- accounting policies;
- performance targets;
- estimate of intended distribution of profits and reserves to the Crown;
- what information is to be provided to the shareholding ministers;
- procedures for acquiring shares in any company or other organisation;
- activities for which the board seeks compensation from the Crown; and
- the board's estimate of the commercial value of the Crown's investment and the manner of reassessment.

---

13 Airways Corporation of New Zealand Limited, Coal Corporation of New Zealand Limited, Electricity Corporation of New Zealand Limited, Government Property Services Limited, Land Corporation Limited, New Zealand Forestry Corporation Limited, New Zealand Post Limited, Post Office Bank Limited, and Telecom Corporation of New Zealand Limited.

The annual report and audited consolidated financial statements must be provided and the dividend payable. SOEs are required to provide a report on their operations for the first six months of the financial year as well as an annual report at the end of the year. All the information described above must be laid before Parliament.

The act provides for a clear separation of commercial and non-commercial objectives. SOEs can be held to account for performance and the return on taxpayers' investment against clear commercial objectives. On the other hand, non-commercial functions can be undertaken by an SOE if ministers negotiate an explicit agreement (and payment) for that to be done.

Since a policy of privatisation was announced in 1988, many SOEs have been sold. In fact, all five of the original existing SOEs and effectively four of the ninc original new SOEs have been privatised. Yet the SOE framework as an organisational form has endured. More SOEs have been created periodically since 1987, as other spheres of state activity have been reformed. In general, the SOE form has tended to be used for trading activities which the government wants to continue owning for some political or economic reason but which it wants to be subject to as many private sector efficiency incentives as possible. The SOE form is not a guarantee of efficiency. Ministers can still use various levers in the SOE framework to interfere with SOE management decisions. After all, ministers are the legal owners of the business. In 1991–92 the chair of Electricorp resigned because of the ministerial role taken in setting electricity prices. But the SOE form probably removes commercial management from political interference as far as is possible in a government-owned enterprise, given the need to meet public sector accountability standards.

The drive for introducing managerial efficiency into the state sector continued with the State Sector Act 1988 reforms to the core government departments as outlined in the first portion of this chapter. And further, specialist, frameworks that combined efficiency incentives of a corporate form with public sector accountability mechanisms have been developed, based on the SOE model:

- Tertiary education institutes (TEIs): established under the Education Act 1989 to compete for government money to provide tertiary education services to students (e.g. universities and polytechnics);
- Crown research institutes (CRIs): Established under the Crown Research Institutes Act 1992 to compete with private sector institutions for government money to conduct scientific research;
- Crown health enterprises (CHEs): Established under the Health and Disability Services Act 1992 to compete with private sector hospitals for government money to provide health services to the public;

These forms owe much to the SOE model but have various tweaks in their regime here and there that reflect the nature of the sectors in which they operate. (And, interestingly, the latter two forms did not create the Treaty of Waitangi legal obligations on government in the way that section 9 of the SOE Act did.)

CROWN ENTITIES AND QUANGOS

In addition to government departments and SOEs and their cousins, there is an amorphous multitude of other public sector agencies that are often known as 'quangos'. A quango is a quasi-autonomous national (or non-) governmental organisation. It is an acronym that describes a variety of corporations, companies, committees, tribunals, and other miscellaneous organisations loosely connected to government. In the United Kingdom, quangos are sometimes called non-departmental public bodies. The acronym is not short for 'quite unacceptable and nasty government offshoot'.

Quangos defy easy categorisation but it is useful to identify three different 'sorts':

- *Crown entities* such as corporations, commissions, or other corporate bodies set up by statute and subject to the accountability requirements in the Public Finance Act 1989;
- *Other statutory bodies* such as tribunals, professional organisations, and producer boards; and
- *Other bodies established by government*, such as informal advisory committees.

By royal prerogative, the Crown can set up an organisation with no formal legal status. A variety of bodies are set up by statute but do not meet the test that defines Crown entities, which are the best defined of these bodies and have a status and set of financial accountability provisions under the Public Finance Act 1989. In 1991 the government agreed to a recommendation by the Finance and Expenditure Select Committee that a body is a Crown entity for these purposes (and hence listed in the fourth schedule to the Public Finance Act) if it is a body corporate (other than an SOE):[14]

— in which the Crown owns a majority of the voting shares; or
— for which the Crown has the power to dismiss a majority of the members of the governing body or, where no such body exists, has the power to dismiss the chief executive, and replace the governing body or the chief executive which is primarily responsible to the Crown; or
— for which the Crown has the right to more than fifty percent of their net assets on their disestablishment; or

14 Report of the Finance and Expenditure Committee on *The Inquiry into Reporting by the Crown and its Sub-entities to the House of Representatives*, 1.4A *Appendices to the Journal of the House of Representatives*, Wellington, 1991.

- — in respect of which the Crown would be expected to assume any residual liabilities other than pursuant to a guarantee; or
- — which Parliament considers to be owned by the Crown and deems to be Crown entities.

At the time of writing there were over seventy individual Crown entities, including the Accident Rehabilitation and Compensation Insurance Corporation, Creative New Zealand, the Commerce Commission, the Lotteries Commission, the Special Education Service, and the Testing Laboratory Registration Council. The schedule also lists groups of Crown entities such as business development boards, fish and game councils, and regional health authorities.

The reasons why Crown entities and other quangos are established vary even more than their form of legal organisation. They are set up:

- to avoid political control and having a minister responsible for the organisation;
- to provide a measure of independence;
- to relieve ministers of responsibility for detailed or specialised tasks;
- to carry out, fairly, certain regulatory functions involving adjudication;
- to fulfil the desire to bring outside people into the management of the activity; and
- to allow for representation of special interests in the administration of some activity.

Given the fact that we are a small country, the number, variety, and complexity of quangos is astonishing. One feature of a quango is that ministers usually get to appoint the members. And the people appointed are not usually public servants. Ministers make thousands of appointments to some 400 bodies: statutory corporations, boards, companies, committees, tribunals, and other quangos. These appointments go through the Cabinet Appointments and Honours Committee, in accordance with guidelines in a 1995 Cabinet Office Circular (CO (95) 6) and Cabinet Office forms. Most appointees to quangos are paid or receive expenses. Most of the jobs are never advertised. Political affiliation is usually important in the process of appointment to quangos. This may become more contentious under MMP, raising the issue of whether the process of appointment should be transparent, or perhaps subject to parliamentary scrutiny.

Crown entities and quangos have some positive features. They can help to diffuse concentrations of power and they can allow citizens to participate in the activities of government. But there are some important weaknesses in quangos as they have developed in New Zealand. The first is a familiar one. A body may have been established long ago. Its performance has never thereafter been re-examined. Has it done a good job? Has it done what it was supposed to do? Has it, in fact, done anything? Has the nature of the job changed over time? Does it duplicate work done elsewhere? These questions are seldom asked. They should be. There is much to be said for quangocide—an occasional but systematic massacre of quangos. We must stop the habit of continually establishing new bodies without ever reviewing old ones to see if we still need them.

In 1986 the Labour Government embarked on a great quango hunt. The aim was to:

- eliminate unnecessary quangos;
- save money;
- reorganise quangos to better achieve their objectives;
- improve the accountability of quangos; and
- discourage the creation of new quangos.

That material was analysed by the government and decisions taken—fifty-six quangos were axed, until the exercise faltered because of the emergence of other priorities. Those destroyed included the Building Performance Guarantee Corporation, the Communications Advisory Council, the Transport Advisory Committee, and the Seed Potato Certification Advisory Committee. There is a good case for a review of quangos being made in the life of every Parliament. They multiply so quickly in response to particular issues that they should be periodically and consistently purged.

It is important that there are adequate checks on how coercive powers are used by quangos. This is especially so in an MMP environment if a government wants to avoid increased scutiny or criticism of its own actions by transferring powers to independent bodies. It is of concern, then, that serious doubts exist about the public accountability of quangos in New Zealand. The standing orders of the House of Representatives ensure that all quangos can be effectively scrutinised by select committees, if desired, but select committees may not have the time or interest to be able to devote as much time as necessary to quangoland.

Otherwise, quangos without a statutory basis are accountable to whichever minister sets them up, according to the terms on which they are set up—which could vary enormously. Bodies established by statute that are not Crown entities may have some accountability requirements in their establishing legislation but these are often of varying importance and quality. Under the Public Finance Act 1989, Crown entities have the most developed set of financial accountability requirements, depending on what sort of Crown entities they are.

Under the Public Finance Act, every Crown entity must provide to Parliament:

- audited annual financial statements in accordance with generally accepted accounting practice, including: statement of financial position, an operating statement, a cash flow statement, a statement of financial performance;
- a statement of commitments;

- a statement of contingent liabilities; and
- such other statements as are necessary fairly to reflect the financial operations of the Crown entity for the financial year and its financial position at the end of the year.

Crown entities that exist primarily to provide goods or services, as listed in the fifth schedule to the Public Finance Act (and may also be listed in the sixth schedule), must also deliver to the responsible minister, to lay before Parliament:

- a statement of objectives, specifying the classes of outputs to be produced during the next financial year; and
- a statement of service performance, reporting the classes of outputs produced by the Crown entity over the past financial year, compared with the previous statement of objectives.

Crown entities that exist primarily to manage assets, which are listed in the sixth schedule to the Public Finance Act (and may also be listed in the fifth schedule), must deliver to the responsible minister, to lay before Parliament:

- a draft statement of intent relating to the next three financial years that specifies similar information as is required of SOEs (as noted earlier in the chapter); and
- an annual report containing the Crown entity's profit or dividend and such information, including a comparison against the statement of intent, as is necessary to enable an informed assessment of its financial performance to be made.

Financial reporting is the primary instrument of accountability for Crown entities. It provides Parliament, and any interested members of the public, with information to scrutinise performance. In addition, as noted in Chapter 6, the executive practice of requiring a purchase agreement between a minister and a department has been extended to Crown entities. Those that receive public money are asked to agree with the responsible minister on what goods or services it produces with that money, in a purchase agreement or similar document, suitably modified to recognise any statutory independence of the entity. Crown entities that request more public money are subject to similar scrutiny and Cabinet procedures as government departments, as covered in more detail in the next chapter.

Crown entities and quangos can be important, but the most important aspects of their performance are not always captured by financial accountability. Those set up by statute, such as producer boards, tribunals, and occupational licensing bodies, can have significant coercive powers. In a 1991 report, the Finance and

Expenditure Committee identified the lack of reporting on exercise of these powers as important:[15]

> the committee considers it important that there be reporting on the use of coercive powers. Occupational licensing bodies could be required to report, for example, on the impact of restricting entry to the occupation. Tribunals could be required to report on their workload and the timeliness of their decisions. Producer boards, which currently provide financial statements to the House even though the Crown no longer has a financial interest in them, could be required to change the content of their reporting to the House and report on their use of the powers conferred on them by Parliament.

In reporting to the committee the following year, the Law Commission took ten pages just to list the bodies to which Parliament had granted coercive powers, broken down into the eight categories of: administrative tribunals, local organisations, funding bodies, advisory bodies, services, producer boards, trading corporations, and control and supervisory bodies.

Crown entities and quangos need to be accountable for the exercise of their coercive powers, as well as their financial performance, to at least the same extent as the core public service.

---

15 *Ibid.*, p.19.

6 Public Finance

Money has always been a core concern of the Westminster constitution. A large part of the historical development of constitutional relations between the English Crown and Parliament can be seen as a struggle over who has the power to tax and to spend. The Magna Carta and the 1688 Bill of Rights, both of which are part of New Zealand law, were vitally concerned with this. One of the most interesting and significant constitutional developments of the modern New Zealand constitution has also concerned expenditure. The Public Finance Act 1989, its 1992 and 1994 amendments, and the Fiscal Responsibility Act 1994, lead the world in setting standards of modern financial accountability for a government.

SUPPLY AND PARLIAMENT

Lack of financial resources is perhaps the most major constraint on the policies of any government. The power of Parliament over finance is a key element in our system of government. This is reflected in sections 21 and 22 of the Constitution Act 1986:

> 21. Bills appropriating public money—The House of Representatives shall not pass any Bill providing for the appropriation of public money or for the imposition of any charge upon the public revenue unless the making of that appropriation or the imposition of that charge has been recommended to the House of Representatives by the Crown.
>
> 22. Parliamentary control of public finance—It shall not be lawful for the Crown, except by or under an Act of Parliament,—
>
> (a) To levy a tax; or
>
> (b) To raise a loan or to receive any money as a loan from any person; or
>
> (c) To spend any public money.

These sections reflect the balance worked out in the battles between the Crown and Parliament in Britain over 300 years ago. The Crown retains the right to propose and Parliament retains the right to approve. This is also reflected in the legislative requirements on the executive and in the standing orders of the House of Representatives relating to public finance. Section 4 of the Public Finance Act 1989 states:

> (1) No expenditure of public money shall be made other than in accordance with an appropriation by an Act of Parliament.
>
> (2) No expense or liability shall be incurred by the Crown in relation to any transaction for which expenses or liabilities are required to be appropriated . . other than in accordance with an appropriation by Act of Parliament.
>
> (3) A separate appropriation shall be made for—
> (a) Each class of outputs contained in the Estimates . . ; and
> (b) Each category of benefits or other unrequited expenses contained in the Estimates; and
> (c) Each category of borrowing expenses contained in the Estimates . . ; and
> (d) Each category of other expenses contained in the Estimates . . ; and
> (e) Each capital contribution contained in the Estimates; and
> (f) Each purchase or development of capital assets contained in the Estimates; and
> (g) Each repayment of debt contained in the Estimates . .
>
> (4) Any money or expenses or liabilities appropriated under subsection (3) of this section may be incurred only in relation to that appropriation and for no other purpose.
>
> (5) The authority to expend cash or incur expenses or liabilities under an Appropriation Act shall lapse at the end of the financial year to which that Act relates.

Around these provisions the government financial systems function. The main appropriation in each year is included in the Appropriation Bill that accompanies the Budget—the government's principal annual statement of economic and fiscal policy. It must be introduced before the end of July each year, unless the House makes a resolution to the contrary. (The government's financial year runs from 1 July until 30 June.) There are a limited number of exceptions to the requirement of annual parliamentary appropriation:

- when the government requires money in anticipation of the Budget being passed by Parliament, it can introduce an Imprest Supply Bill to be passed by Parliament to tide the government over;
- Parliament can make a multi-year appropriation of up to five years, e.g., for expenditure relating to Treaty of Waitangi settlements (section 4(6));
- in the last three months of a financial year or the first three months of the next financial year, the Minister of Finance can approve unappropriated expenditure

of money that occurred in the last three months of the financial year, up to a limit of 1 per cent of the amount appropriated for a vote for the year. This requires the Minister of Finance to table in the House a report by the relevant minister on each instance of unappropriated expenditure (section 12);
- under certain situations of a declared state of emergency the Minister of Finance can approve expenditure to meet the emergency, which must be included in an Appropriation Bill for confirmation by Parliament (section 13).

Parliamentary appropriations are known as the granting of 'supply' and the key votes in Parliament on Imprest Supply and Appropriation Bills are automatically matters of confidence. Without supply, the government cannot continue. That fact is potentially the biggest check of all on executive action. In an MMP environment, especially under a minority government, the granting of supply will no longer be assured, as it was under single-party majority governments. Governments may fall over a refusal of Parliament to grant supply and it is conceivable that Parliament could be dissolved without ensuring that sufficient supply is available for the day-to-day running of government. This, however, seems unlikely. Few political parties would want to be seen as responsible for the political problems that would result from the government running out of money. And, as the Clerk of the House, David McGee points out: 'The question of whether sufficient financial authorisation exists to carry on the government is always a matter which the Governor-General is entitled to seek assurances about from a Prime Minister before acceding to a request from the Prime Minister to dissolve Parliament for a general election.'[1]

FISCAL RESPONSIBILITY AND THE BUDGET PROCESS

The Fiscal Responsibility Act 1994 introduced a comprehensive regime of reporting requirements on the government's fiscal and economic policies. The genesis of the act was in the desire of the former Minister of Finance, Hon. Ruth Richardson, to entrench principles of fiscal responsibility for future governments to follow. It is difficult, however, to stop future governments from doing what they want if they have a majority in Parliament. So the Fiscal Responsibility Act 1994 has few substantive requirements on government; rather, it relies on publicity and reporting requirements on governments to tell Parliament and the public what fiscal and economic policies they propose to pursue, what effects they are likely to have, and to justify any departures from specified principles of 'responsible' fiscal management.

1 David McGee, *Parliamentary Practice in New Zealand*, 2nd ed., Wellington, GP Publications, 1994, p.332.

In its long title, the Fiscal Responsibility Act 1994 is stated to be:

> An Act to improve the conduct of fiscal policy by specifying principles of responsible fiscal management and by strengthening the reporting requirements of the Crown and, in particular, —
>
> (a) By requiring the Minister of Finance to report regularly to the House of Representatives on the extent to which the Government's fiscal policy is consistent with the specified principles of responsible fiscal management and to justify in his or her report any departures made by the Government from those principles; and
>
> (b) By requiring all the Crown's financial reporting to be in accordance with generally accepted accounting practice; and
>
> (c) By requiring the Minister of Finance —
>
> (i) To publish, at least 3 months before the start of each financial year, a budget policy statement containing the Government's long-term objectives for fiscal policy, its broad strategic priorities for the Budget for that financial year, and its fiscal intentions for that and the next 2 financial years; and
>
> (ii) To lay before the House of Representatives, on the day on which the first Appropriation Bill relating to a financial year is introduced, a fiscal strategy report assessing the consistency of the Budget with the budget policy statement and providing progress outlooks for the next 10 years, and an economic and fiscal update prepared by the Treasury for the next 3 years; and
>
> (iii) To publish, in December of each financial year, an economic and fiscal update prepared by the Treasury for the next 3 years; and
>
> (iv) To publish, before each general election, an economic and fiscal update prepared by the Treasury for the next 3 years; and
>
> (v) To lay before the House of Representatives, towards the end of each financial year, a fiscal update prepared by the Treasury for that year, including forecast estimated actual financial statements for the Crown.

As with most topics in this book, a full account of the New Zealand Budget process could do with a whole volume to itself.[2] It is a complex and continually evolving set of processes and structures in both the executive and Parliament. The executive Budget-making processes are dominated by a Cabinet committee (currently the Committee on Expenditure Control and Revenue, ECR), the Minister of Finance, and Cabinet Office circulars and Budget circulars. The usual Budget process involves bids by each minister (prepared by the department) for his or her votes, bilateral meetings between each minister and the Minister of Finance, a process of scutiny of all bids by the Treasury, by an Officials Committee on Expenditure Control (OCEC), and by the ECR. The timetables are tight, the

---

2 See, in general, State Services Commission, *Working Under Proportional Representation: A Reference for the Public Service*, Wellington, 1995, Ch. 5.

Table 6.1: Timetable for Parliament's annual financial cycle

By 31 March	(1.1)	**Budget Policy Statement** published and referred to Finance and Expenditure Committee (FEC)
Within six weeks of (1.1)	(1.2)	FEC reports to House on the Budget policy statement
	(1.3)	Budget policy statement debate
May/early June	(2.1)	**Appropriation (Supplementary Estimates) Bill** introduced (no debate)
May/June	(2.2)	Select committees consider supplementary estimates and report to the House
By 30 June	(2.3)	Appropriation (Supplementary Estimates) Bill debated (five hours for whole bill)
By 30 June [end of financial year]	(3.1)	First **Imprest Supply Bill** for following financial year introduced and debated (four hours for whole bill)—debate may be combined with debate on Appropriation (Supplementary Estimates) Bill (five hours for both bills)
By 31 July	(4.1)	**Appropriation (Estimates) Bill** introduced (no debate) and **Budget** delivered [and **Fiscal Strategy Report** and **Economic and Fiscal Update** tabled] followed by Budget debate (fifteen hours)
Within two months after Budget delivered (4.1)	(4.2)	Select committees examine estimates and report to the House
Within two months after Budget delivered (4.1)	(4.3)	FEC considers the Fiscal Strategy Report and the Economic and Fiscal Update tabled with the Budget and reports to the House
Within three months after Budget delivered (4.1)	(4.4)	Estimates debate (ten hours) with select committee chairpersons leading off debate on each vote
	(4.5)	Debate on third reading of the Appropriation (Estimates) Bill (four hours) completed—debate may include reference to Fiscal Strategy Report and Economic and Fiscal Update and the FEC's report
Within three months after Budget delivered (4.1)	(5.1)	Second **Imprest Supply Bill** for financial year introduced and debated (four hours for the whole debate)—debate may be combined with debate on third reading of Appropriation (Estimates) Bill (four hours for both bills)
September/October	(6.1)	**Crown financial statements** for previous financial year tabled
September/October	(6.2)	**Annual reports** and **financial statements** for previous financial year of **departments** and **Offices of Parliament** tabled
October–December	(6.3)	FEC reviews Crown financial statements for previous financial year and reports to the House by first sitting day in new calendar year
October–December	(6.4)	Select committees review performance in previous financial year and current operations of individual departments and offices of Parliament and report to the House by first sitting day in new calendar year
November	(6.5)	**Annual reports** and **financial statements** for previous financial year of many **Crown entities**, **public organisations** and **state enterprises** tabled
	(6.6)	Select committees review performance in previous financial year and current operations of individual Crown entities (sixth schedule), public organisations and state enterprises and

		report to the House within six months of annual report being tabled
By February	(6.7)	**Appropriation (Financial Review) Bill** introduced (no debate)
February	(6.8)	Debate (three hours) on Crown's financial position as reflected in the FEC's report on Crown financial statements for previous financial year (second reading of Appropriation (Financial Review) Bill)
By 31 March	(6.9)	Financial review debate (five hours) on performance in previous financial year and current operations of individual departments and offices of Parliament (committee stage of Appropriation (Financial Review) Bill)
	(6.10)	Third reading of Appropriation (Financial Review) Bill (no debate)
April/May	(6.11)	Debate (five hours) on performance in previous financial year and current operations of individual Crown entities (sixth schedule) and public organisations
	(6.12)	Debate (five hours) on performance in previous financial year and current operations of individual state enterprises

cases must be well argued, and the processes are strict (especially in the last few years). Under MMP governments are likely to continue to adhere to these requirements. Coalition governments, however, may find it difficult to preserve the confidentiality that has traditionally accompanied the executive processes of Budget decision-making. And minority governments may well want to consult other parties in order to gauge the likely parliamentary reception of their Budgets.

Once budgetary decisions are confirmed by Cabinet and the estimates tabled in the House with an Appropriation Bill, the Budget speech, a fiscal strategy report, and an economic and fiscal update, there is a further series of parliamentary procedures. These procedures were revisited in 1995 by the Standing Orders Committee, which recommended a number of changes to streamline proceedings and improve the timeliness of some events. The Budget Policy Statement required by the Fiscal Responsibility Act provides an early indication of the government's fiscal objectives and strategic priorities. This is likely to be a document of increasing importance under MMP and could prove to be a focus for a coalition or minority government flagging its intentions and testing the support of other parties.

The debate on the Budget itself is an opportunity for general debate in the House. Standing Order 321 provides that, following the delivery of the Budget, the estimates stand referred to the Finance and Expenditure Committee which may examine a vote itself or, as it commonly does, may refer it to a subject select committee for examination. Committees must report back to the House on the estimates within two months of the Budget, as must the Finance and Expenditure Committee on the fiscal strategy report and the economic and fiscal update accompanying the Budget. The third (final) reading of the main Appropriation Bill must be completed within three months of the Budget, according to Standing Order 326.

The Standing Orders Committee provided a useful guide to the likely timetable for the parliamentary Budget process, which is set out in Table 6.1.[3]

One of the most interesting and innovative changes to standing orders in 1996 was the establishment of a financial veto procedure. This was introduced in recognition of the long-standing constitutional conventions surrounding the Crown's financial initiative—that it is for the Crown, not ordinary MPs, to propose expenditure increases. The parliamentary rules surrounding this were inconsistent (e.g., ordinary MPs could propose reductions in tax). The Standing Orders Committee developed a procedure designed to 'enable the Government to retain control over the fiscal aggregates while allowing members an opportunity to propose initiatives involving minor amounts of expenditure which do not affect the overall integrity of the government's budget or the government's forecast financial position.'[4] The result is that ordinary MPs can initiate proposals involving expenditure or taxation, but if the government certifies that a bill, amendment or motion 'would have more than a minor impact on the Government's fiscal aggregates' or a change to a vote would have 'more than a minor impact on the composition of the Vote', then Standing Order 311 provides that it will not be passed. The government's certification must state 'with some particularity' the nature of the impact and the reason why the government does not concur. The government's certificate must be tabled and can be debated. There are serious political implications in this. A government may prefer the money not to be spent, but may feel, from a political point of view, that it does not want to exercise the veto. Furthermore, the whole process has not yet been made consistent with section 21 of the Constitution Act, which needs to be altered to allow the procedure devised by the Standing Orders Committee to be followed.

How the budgetary and financial process will evolve in an MMP environment is an intriguing question. Because of the importance of public money, it is likely that the budgetary process in the executive or the House will set the scene for some of the toughest political battles of the new environment. Governments may fall over budgetary disputes. The Budget policy statement may evolve into a proxy for a coalition agreement, or a statement of what policies a minority government has support for pursuing. The information provided in the budgetary process is likely to be a focus for political and public debate.

ACCOUNTING AND ACCOUNTABILITY

It is no accident that the words 'accounting' and 'accountability' have a common root. A lot of what the people's representatives in Parliament would want to know about the administration of government concerns who spent how much and for

[3] Standing Orders Report, Wellington, 1995, pp.70–1 (format modified from original).
[4] Standing Orders Report, Wellington, 1995, p.61.

what. For this reason, the Public Finance Act 1989, reinforced by the Financial Reporting Act 1993, represents a revolution in accountability in New Zealand government.

Modern accounting practices are now a world away from the stereotypical image of grey people adding up numbers. Numerical accuracy is still important, but an audit by an accountant now involves not just adding up figures but also examining the systems by which figures and other information are collected, recorded, and presented to managers, and the systems which control the authorisation of expenditure, compliance with legislative requirements, and identifying significant issues that should be known by those concerned with the entity being audited.

For years it was accepted in New Zealand, as it is still accepted everywhere else in the world, that it is a sad and unfortunate fact of life that it is too difficult for a government to comply with the modern accounting practices with which private sector businesses must comply. That has now changed in New Zealand since the Public Finance Act requires the Crown, departments and Crown entities, and offices of Parliament, to adhere to 'generally accepted accounting practices' or GAAPs.

According to section 2 of the Public Finance Act, GAAPs are either financial reporting standards approved by the Accounting Standards Review Board or accounting standards which 'are appropriate in relation to' the entity and 'have authoritative support within the accounting profession in New Zealand'. The Accounting Standards Review Board is composed of between four and seven members with knowledge in business, accounting, economics or law, appointed on the recommendation of the relevant minister. It is established by the Financial Reporting Act 1993 to review and approve financial reporting standards for both the private and public sectors in New Zealand, after consultation with those who would be affected by them. As at 30 June 1995, ten financial reporting standards had been approved by the board, all proposed by the New Zealand Society of Accountants.

The result is that the financial accounts of every government department, SOE, Crown entity, and of the Crown itself in aggregate, must be examined and audited to the same standards as the private sector. In particular, and uniquely in the world for governments, the New Zealand Government now accounts on an accruals rather than a cash basis, i.e., it takes notice of expenditure when it incurs the obligation to pay rather than when it actually pays out the cash. The move to accrual accounting is a profound change; it ensures, among other things, that government takes account of the full value of the assets that it employs in the pursuit of its policies. There are some wrinkles in these standards to take account of things that occur in the government and not in the private sector. And there are some general requirements imposed by the Treasury, in 'Treasury Instructions' issued under section 80 of the Public Finance Act 1989, in order to ensure consistency of accounting policies in the public sector. Otherwise, the requirements to adhere to GAAPs and to be audited represent the primary checks on the accuracy of government reporting information.

THE CONTROLLER AND AUDITOR-GENERAL AND THE AUDIT OFFICE

Parliament's watchdog over financial expenditure is the Auditor-General, who audits the accounts of the government and reports to Parliament on maladministration in financial matters. The Auditor-General is also the Controller, who checks the legality of issues of money to the Crown. The main power of the Auditor-General is the power of reporting to Parliament.

'The Audit Office conducts audits of government departments to provide assurance to Parliament that the departments are performing and accounting for their performance in a manner consistent with Parliament's intentions.'[5] The Auditor-General is the auditor of the government's accounts, of all public money and public stores, not only of central but also of local government. In essence, he or she is responsible for the audit of the whole public sector, more than 3600 entities in all. This includes schools, government departments, SOEs, Crown entities, and local government entities. In order to carry out audits, the Auditor-General directs the Audit Office as its chief executive, but he or she may and does contract out a number of these audits to private sector accounting firms; about a quarter are currently dealt with in this way.

The office's report on the 1995 audit of government departments notes that it provides a summary of the assurance provided as a result of:[6]

- auditing the financial statements for the year ended 30 June 1995;
- assessing financial and service performance management;
- assessing the control environment;
- auditing compliance with legislative requirements;
- identifying significant issues arising from the audit.

The overall conclusion of this report was:[7]

> The results of the audit of departments' 1994–95 financial statements show that, on the whole, assurance can be given that they have achieved a good standard of performance and accounting for that performance. In particular, reported information is generally reliable and financial management is generally sound.

---

5 *Report of the Controller and Auditor-General: First Report for 1996*, B.29[96a] *Appendices to the Journal of the House of Representatives*, Wellington, 1996, p.11.

6 *Ibid.*, p.12.

7 *Ibid.*, p.24.

> Nevertheless, scope for improvement exists, especially in some departments' cost allocation systems and in many departments' service performance measurement and reporting. In this last respect, our future attention will focus on the appropriateness of the performance measures used, and in the other respects we will continue to monitor the position and make any recommendations necessary for further improvement.

The Auditor-General can have full access to all relevant material in order to carry out that function. Under section 27 of the Public Finance Act 1977 he or she can have access to all bank accounts and may require evidence to be given on oath. There is also power to surcharge those responsible for a deficiency or loss or for failing to account fully and properly for money or stores for a number of reasons stated in the Public Finance Act 1977.

In carrying out these great powers the Auditor-General is protected in much the same way as a High Court judge, and can only be removed from office upon an address from the House of Representatives. The Offices of Parliament Committee in Parliament, chaired by the Speaker, and not the executive government, conducts the annual estimates and financial review of the Audit Office. The Auditor-General has close relations with the Finance and Expenditure Committee of Parliament and often provides expert audit staff to assist select committee inquiries into financial administration.

The Auditor-General, who also carries out value for money audits that often cast light on particular government policies, is an important check against financial corruption and inefficiency in government. Mercifully, documented cases of financial corruption have been exceedingly rare. Corruption is an everyday part of government administration in many countries and we can be grateful that we are essentially free from it in New Zealand. As the Chief Ombudsman Sir Brian Elwood told Parliament in 1995,'We are indeed fortunate in New Zealand in that the process of government appears to be remarkably free from the taint of graft and corruption.'[8] Perhaps that confidence was dented in 1994, when the then Auditor-General himself, Mr J.T. Chapman, resigned on the basis that his personal financial situation was incompatible with his maintaining the independence of the Auditor-General. He was subsequently indicted for offences involving dishonesty in relation to his expenses. In a report presented to the House, the auditor of the administration of the Audit Office in the wake of Mr Chapman's resignation stated: 'The public of New Zealand has the right to believe that the Auditor-General is beyond reproach. The person holding this office should be leading by example and setting standards for others.'[9]

---

8 *Report of the Ombudsmen for the Year Ended 30 June 1995*, Wellington, 1995, A.3 *Appendices to the Journal of the House of Representatives*, Wellington, 1995, p.8.

9 *Report on the Audit of the Administration of the Audit Office consequent on the resignation of Mr J. T. Chapman as Controller and Auditor-General on 10 October 1994*, Wellington, 1994.

The Auditor-General is restricted to commenting on the administration of policy, not on the desirability of the policy itself. But obviously where she or he finds money is being wasted, that is likely to bring the policy itself into question in many cases. Sometimes the activities of the Auditor-General attract a high degree of media and political interest, as in the instances of the expenditures of public money on the commanding officer's house at the Ohakea Air Force base or the police purchases of flak jackets. More usually, the Auditor-General's activities involve detailed and painstaking studies of accounts and cataloguing instances of waste. For example, the second report of the Controller and Auditor-General for 1996 set out a study that had been carried out of how local authorities were meeting their obligations under the Local Government Act to look at the advantages and disadvantages of different options for service delivery and whether significant contracts should be put out to tender. The conclusion was that they were handling the issues adequately, although there was room for improvement. In particular, procedures and standards of documentation often fell short of those required to ensure full and proper accountability.

The Auditor-General also looked closely at the operation of cemeteries by local authorities. In 1991 the officer had reported there were approximately 150 cemetery trusts operating in terms of the Burial and Cremation Act 1964 and it was recommended then that local authorities should be made responsible. The Auditor-General found that important accountability issues had not been addressed and that structural problems needed to be reviewed. He also looked at the operation of reserve boards and Provincial Patriotic Councils. Putting the spotlight on these obscure organisations and highlighting weaknesses in administration, accountability, and legislation is a valuable function. But the same report also addressed matters of more moment, particularly the administration of the Resource Management Act 1991 by regional councils.

The Auditor-General is also the Controller, whose function is to check the legality of issues of money to the Crown. Money can only be paid out of the Crown Bank Account following the issue of a warrant by the Governor-General. Under section 22 of the Public Finance Act 1989 the Audit Office, in performing the Controller function, is required to certify that the amount in a warrant can be lawfully paid before the warrant can be submitted to the Governor-General. This requires that there is legal authority for the payments and that the purpose to which the money is to be put is lawful.

The Controller function is a fundamental and important check upon government but it is little known. Money cannot be spent unless there is legal authority for the expenditure. In his 1984 report, the Auditor-General stated that no discretion exists in exercising the Controller function by accepting assurances that subsequent validating legislation could be passed where there was no legal authority. This went back to an earlier incident where a previous Auditor-General accepted the assurance of the then Prime Minister, Sir Robert Muldoon, that he would secure passage of legislation authorising the building of the Clyde dam after millions had already been spent, but there was no legal authority. Under MMP it would be most unwise to give such assurances in any event, since it will be more difficult to predict the future vote of Parliament, especially under a minority government. The Controller should form his or her own view of the legal authorisation for expenditure.

There are some problems with the role and structure of the Audit Office. It can be argued that the dual role of the Auditor-General, in commissioning independent audits of the executive and in directing the conduct of most of them, is inconsistent. It is also constitutionally odd that the Audit Office, which conducts independent audits of executive government entities, is itself an executive department with its own minister. The Chapman affair further suggests that the effectiveness of accountability through the Offices of Parliament Committee needs attention. Finally, how the Controller function operates in an accrual accounting environment and in an MMP era of minority and coalition governments needs to be debated. In general, it seems that a fundamental review of the role of the Controller and Auditor-General and the Audit Office is constitutionally overdue.

It is likely that, under MMP, the role of the Controller and Auditor-General will take on greater constitutional and political importance. There are likely to be greater demands on the office and the reports he or she makes may more often have political consequences, especially where maladministration is exposed. The office's role in helping select committee inquiries will also become more important. The office of the Auditor-General is a key constitutional office that is likely to flourish and develop further in the new environment, but, to do so, requires a robust constitutional basis and a new accountability regime.

ACCOUNTABILITY DOCUMENTS

The primary documents relevant to the financial accountability of the government are:

- *Estimates of appropriations*: These are the requests by ministers to Parliament for money to fund government activities. They have to be accompanied by details about objectives, expenditure trends over the past five years, what 'outputs' the money will be spent on and what revenue will be received;
- *Departmental forecast reports*: These give details for each department of its expenses in producing outputs that are bought by ministers and the revenue each department receives. Unusually, in international terms, they must comply with generally accepted accounting practices. These reports include a statement

of each department's financial position and cash flow statement and the main indicators of each department's performance;

- *Annual and half-yearly financial statements*: These are reports by each department, and by the Crown as a whole, on its finances. They are audited and must accord with generally accepted accounting practices.
- *Purchase agreements*: These describe what each minister purchases from his or her department, including the quantity, quality, and cost of the department's outputs. A purchase agreement is not legally binding. It goes into a greater level of detail than the information in the estimates of expenditure that are considered by Parliament. It provides a mechanism for a minister to be very clear about what he or she wants a department to do, within the limits set down by Parliament. A minister may employ a purchase adviser to advise him or her when negotiating a purchase agreement with a department;
- *Strategic business plans:* These are supposed to outline the key strategies a department uses to achieve its vision and purpose, including strategies dealing with marketing, human resources, capital expenditure and asset utilisation, information technology, organisation, production, and financial performance.

Note again the terminology. A 'vote' is the amount of money that Parliament authorises, or 'appropriates', for a minister to spend on activities in his or her portfolio, e.g., Vote:Justice contains the appropriations able to spent by the Minister of Justice. This chapter will focus particularly on the estimates as the basis on which Parliament votes money to ministers.

It is important to appreciate the nature and amount of the information that can be obtained from the Budget. The Budget (estimates of appropriations) provides a lot of information to MPs, and the public in general, as illustrated in Figure 6.1 from the 1996/97 Estimates.[10]

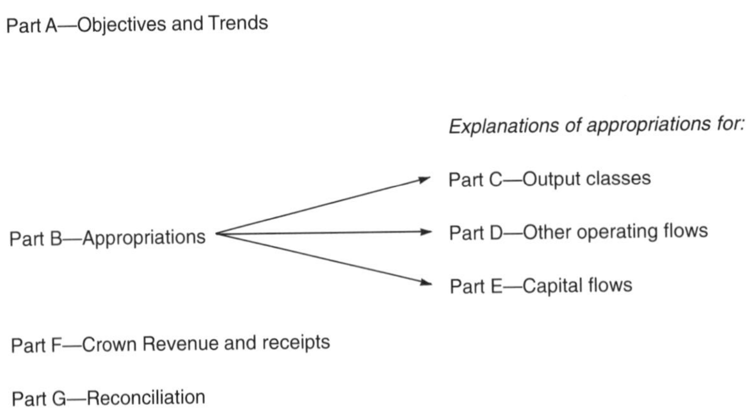

Figure 6.1: Layout of each vote

Parts A, B, C, E, and F of the estimates provide particularly important information for a general reader. Points about some of these are noted below, together with illustrative extracts from relevant parts of the 1996/97 Estimates.

Objectives and trends

Part A of each set of vote estimates provides a commentary on the minister's objectives for each vote, and an analysis of the trends within the vote over the previous five years. These are associated with the 'outcomes' the government is seeking in each area. In 1996/97, for example, the statement of objectives (part A2) for Vote:Justice included the following text:[11]

> **Part A1—Objectives for Vote Justice**
>
> The appropriations sought in Vote Justice will make an important contribution to Government's strategic goals of social cohesion, community security and economic growth by providing: justice policy advice, strategic assessment, and advice on the allocation of resources across the justice sector; electoral services to enable Parliamentary elections and polls to be conducted with integrity, impartiality, efficiency and professionalism; equity promotion and protection services; advice on law reform; and services relating to the provision of legal assistance.
>
> Justice policy advice includes advice on fundamental constitutional matters such as rights, the body of law and democratic processes, and the relationship between Treaty partners, access to workable and accepted dispute resolution mechanisms; fair and efficient markets; preventing and minimising the impact of crime; and the effective operation of agencies responsible for delivering these services.

Appropriations

Part B of each set of vote estimates details appropriations to ministers, whether they are to be used by a department or someone else, and a comparison with the previous year's appropriations (and estimated outturns or results of that previous year). The 'outputs' are used to achieve the government's desired 'outcomes'. In 1996/97, Part B for Vote:Justice included the following information in relation to departmental and non-departmental output classes:[12]

> **Part B1—Details of 1996/97 Appropriations**
>
> **Departmental Output Classes**
>
> D1 Ministerial Servicing $1,705,000
>
> Services relating to replies to Ministerial correspondence and Parliamentary

---

10 *Estimates of Appropriations for the Government of New Zealand for the Year Ending 30 June 1997*, B.5, Vol.I, p.x.

11 *Ibid.*, Vol. II, p.863–4.

12 *Ibid.*, Vol. II, pp.870–1.

questions on issues which relate to or impact on the justice portfolio, and advice on Ministerial appointments.

D2 Policy Advice $11,737,000

Strategic and policy advice on public law policy, responses to crime policy, family policy, commercial and property law policy, legal advice and law reform, strategic assessment and purchase advice across the justice sector, and the development and implementation of a justice information strategy.

D3 Contract Management $169,000

Management of contracts (or memoranda of understanding) with Crown Entities and other bodies funded through Vote Justice.

D4 Management of the Parliamentary Electoral System $13,388,000

Conduct of Parliamentary elections, by-elections, referenda and polls.

Total Appropriations for Departmental Output Classes $26,998,000

Non-Departmental Output Classes

O1 Policy Advice $3,347,000

The purchase of policy advice from the Law Commission on the review, reform and development of all aspects of the law in New Zealand.

O2 Equity Promotion and Protection Services $8,571,000

The purchase of impartial and independent conciliation processes and services from the Human Rights Commissioner and the Race Relations Concilator to investigate and resolve complaints relating to discrimination and to promote human rights issues and racial harmony, the purchase of a service from the Police Complaints Authority, independent of the Police, to investigate incidents and investigate and resolve complaints against the Police; and the purchase of services from the Privacy Commissioner on privacy issues relating to the collection and disclosure of personal information and the privacy of individuals.

O3 Administration of Legal Services $4,072,000

The purchase of services from the Legal Services Board, including the administration services of the Legal Services Board and District Legal Services Committees, funding for community law centres, management of pilot schemes and research.

O4 Provision of and Access to Legal Services $69,751,000

The purchase of services from the Legal Services Board to make payments of legal aid, and to make legal assistance available.

O5 Provision of Electoral Services $18,372,000

The purchase from the Electoral Commission of services relating to the registration of political parties, the conduct of education and information programmes and other activities to promote public awareness on electoral matters, and advisory services on electoral matters; and the purchase from the Electoral Enrolment Centre (New Zealand Post Ltd.) of services relating to the maintenance of electoral rolls, including all activities required to register electors and produce electoral rolls as is required by law.

Total Appropriations for Non-Departmental Output Classes $104,113,000

Output classes

Part C of each set of vote estimates provides further explanation of the details of the classes of 'outputs' which the minister purchases with the money in the vote, i.e., what goods and services the minister gets for his or her public money. The quality, quantity, timeliness, and cost of the classes of outputs are described in the estimates, i.e., how many things the minister buys of a particular sort, how good they are, whether they are delivered on time, and how much they cost. In 1996/97, Part C for Vote:Justice included the following information: [13]

Output Class D4—Management of the Parliamentary Electoral System

Description

Under this output class the Minister of Justice will purchase services relating to the conduct of Parliamentary elections, by-elections, referenda and polls; the appointment and training of returning officers; the printing of voting papers; publicity programmes concerned with voting procedures and voting places, nominations and other matters; and the provision of polling places in accordance with legislative requirements. It also includes administrative support needed in the reforms of the electoral system.

Quantity

The expected number of elections, by-elections and polls:	1
The expected number of information requests (public enquiries)	100
The expected number of plans for the conduct of elections and polls	4

Quality

The criterion for elections and polls conducted is that legislative and administrative requirements are met as set out in the Electoral Act, Returning Officers Instruction Manual and Circulars and Instructions.

All elections, polls and referenda will be conducted according to this criterion.
Information on electoral matters will be provided to the public according to this criterion.

The criteria for information provided are:

- response is accurate and relevant
- meets professional standards of presentation

[13] *Ibid.*, Vol. II, pp. 877–8.

- all options are explored
- is appropriate for target audience.

Critical factors will be met in planning for the conduct of elections/polls.

These factors are:

- Electoral project management plans exist for the conduct of by-elections, elections and polls. These identify: all key actions and tasks to be undertaken, task responsibilities, task duration, necessary completion dates and resource needs.
- Relevant legislation and regulations required to conduct elections and polls are available.
- Recommendations and proposed changes approved by Officials Committee and Government have been actioned.
- Draft submissions to secure necessary appropriation of resource have been prepared.

Timeliness

All elections, polls and referenda will be conducted by due date.
Response to requests for information on electoral matters will be completed within 15 working days of receipt.
Target dates for electoral project management plans are met.

Cost

Outputs in this class will be provided within the appropriated sum of $13,388,000 including GST. The GST exclusive sum of $11,960,000 will be funded from revenue Crown of $11,421,000.

Although this sort of information can be difficult to specify in relation to some services received by ministers (e.g., policy advice from officials), the requirement to do so and to report on performance concentrates the minds of public servants and enables ministers to impose binding performance requirements on the public service and others receiving public money. Ministers can buy goods and services from their departments (departmental outputs), or from other people (non-departmental outputs). And they can employ independent 'purchase advisers' to advise them on what they should buy, what performance they should expect, and who they should buy it from.

Since 1993, the government has imposed (though not by legislation) a further set of more detailed accountability requirements on departments and others receiving public money (subject to the statutory independence of some of those bodies), such as purchase agreements.

A purchase agreement sets out the quality, quantity, timeliness, and cost of outputs at a greater level of detail than do the estimates. The estimates provide information about goods and services that ministers buy at 'output class' level—groups of similar sorts of goods and services. A purchase agreement between a minister and a department, or other entity, provides the information underlying this—at 'output' level. Purchase agreements between a minister and a department are not legally binding as both are elements of one entity, the Crown. They can also be revised at any time to take into account new developments or circumstances. The purpose and scope of the 1995/96 purchase agreement between the Minister of Justice and Secretary for Justice were stated as follows:

Purpose and Scope

General Principle

2 The objective of the purchase agreement is to provide the Minister of Justice with information to assess the strategic importance and value of Ministry outputs and to make comparisons with similar outputs across both the public and private sectors. By allowing meaningful comparisons of value and cost, the output descriptions in this agreement should assist the Minister of Justice to select those outputs that conform to the Government's strategy and which, in the Minister's opinion, represent value for money. This purchase agreement sets out the outputs the Minister of Justice has agreed to purchase, their performance attributes and costs and the terms and conditions of the agreement. The purchase agreement should allow the Minister to

- determine which outputs to purchase;
- agree to appropriate cost, quantity and quality standards for desired outputs;
- determine the provider where there are alternative providers to choose from;
- assess the risks and obligations associated with delivery;
- record and change decisions;
- subsequently verify that the output has been delivered; and
- hold the provider accountable for the delivery of the specified output.

Other organisations that receive public money, such as Crown entities, are separate legal entities from the Crown. A purchase agreement or memorandum of understanding between a minister and those entities cannot override legislative requirements on those entities (or, indeed, legislative requirements on departments) as to how to go about their activities. It is, however, constitutionally desirable for such entities to provide information to the relevant minister, on behalf of Parliament, about the way in which they have spent the public money they receive through the minister and to provide information about their objectives in advance through a mechanism such as a purchase agreement or a memorandum of understanding. This derives from the constitutional position of the responsible minister in relation to the appropriations made by Parliament to the minister. Such a document should, of course, pay due regard to the independent statutory functions, duties, and powers imposed on an entity. A good example is the memorandum of understanding that the Law Commission concluded with the Minister of Justice for 1995/96.

As an example of the content of an ordinary departmental purchase agreement, the 1995/96 purchase agreement between the Minister of Justice and the Secretary for Justice provided the following information:

- summary of outputs purchased;
- terms of agreement, including: purpose and scope, accountabilities (powers and obligations), definition of terms, term of agreement, procedures for amending and updating, monitoring and reporting, monitoring against cost, assessment of results, rewards and sanctions for output delivery, coverage, dispute resolution, payment, signed statements;
- government outcomes and Ministry of Justice output classes;
- output schedules for each output class;
- definitions of quality criteria for policy and legal advice;
- contracts quality criteria; and
- the initial version of the year's work programme.

Capital flows and aggregate information

There is a basic accounting distinction between 'operating' flows (spending or receiving money) and 'capital' flows (adding to or subtracting from the value of an asset). Until the financial management reforms, the government did not keep track of the value of its assets through rigorous accounting systems (and other governments still do not). It was not surprising, then, that the government made decisions about its assets that often looked wasteful or odd. If the rate at which a hospital runs down through wear and tear over the years (let alone more major changes in value) is not reflected in its value to government, then it is not surprising that the hospital is not well maintained.

Since the revolution in public sector financial management and the application of GAAPs, departments and other public sector entities face the costs of depreciation and maintenance and account for the value of their assets. Part G of the estimates provides Parliament and the public with information about capital payments made to departments and other entities and a statement of estimated and forecast net worth for each department, Crown entity and SOE a minister is reponsible for.

The information in the estimates is useful in relation to what goes on within a particular vote but also in making appropriations between votes and in getting an idea of the financial performance of government overall. Owing to the application of GAAPs, international financial markets are assured that the financial accounts of the New Zealand Government provide an accurate picture of its financial position, which is not the case with many governments. And Parliament, political parties, the media, and voters can also examine in general terms where the government gets its money, where its money goes, and how much the government is worth.

part three

parliament

7 MPs and Other Parliamentary Inhabitants

INTRODUCTION

There are few legal requirements as to what members of Parliament (MPs) have to do. There is no job description for the position either. Section 55 of the Electoral Act 1993 provides that an MP vacates his or her seat if he or she:

- misses a whole session of the House unless he or she has permission of the House;
- takes an oath of allegiance to, or becomes a citizen of, any foreign power;
- is convicted of a crime punishable by two or more years in prison, or is convicted of a corrupt practice;
- becomes a public servant;
- becomes mentally disordered;
- resigns, dies;
- has his or her election declared void by a court; or
- is proved to the satisfaction of a select committee to have acted for reward to secure the purchase of someone's land by the Crown.

Yet, in practice, MPs find that they have many different roles. Within his or her community, an MP is seen as a sort of community leader, with obligations to represent the interests of the local area. Within a political party, an MP is a leader and a representative—of the beliefs of the party. Within Parliament, an MP is a lawmaker. Within the executive, an MP may be a Cabinet minister or, otherwise, is a key opinion leader with the potential to create trouble.

And in each of these arenas MPs interact with a variety of other people, groups, and institutions. In particular, Parliament is populated by a wonderful array of inhabitants who generally go unnoticed by the public. Aside from MPs, these include the researchers and staff of political parties, officers of Parliament, and the parliamentary bureaucracy including the Parliamentary Service Commission, the Office of the Clerk of the House of Representatives, and the Parliamentary Library.

In 1946 Sir Arnold Nordmeyer wrote: 'Parliament is essentially a representative body, a cross-section of national life. Fortunately it does not consist of experts: it is composed of ordinary people—men and women who, as they are wise, will give heed to what experts have to say, remembering always that the experts are at least sometimes wrong.'[1]

THE MP IN THE COMMUNITY

Before MMP, all MPs represented electorates. In an MMP Parliament there are now two types of MP, as detailed in Chapter 2: those who represent constituency electorates and those who are elected on the party list. Sixty MPs are elected from general electorates, sixteen of which must be located in the South Island. More seats (currently five) represent Maori who opt to be on the Maori electoral roll. There has been a long tradition in New Zealand of MPs carrying out extensive electorate work—conducting clinics with their constituents and helping with governmental problems they may have. The extent to which party list MPs engage in these activities will be worth watching, but it is expected that political parties will want to ensure that list MPs stay in touch with the public and provide services to voters, perhaps in those areas where the party has no electorate MPs.

An MP is invited to many official functions within the electorate and asked to officiate at many different ceremonies such as the opening of buildings and bridges, conventions and celebrations of various sorts, and sports gatherings; the opening day of bowling clubs throughout New Zealand sees MPs and local body politicians in attendance. Indeed, an MP will usually have so many invitations that, if he or she accepted them all, any ordinary family life would be impossible. An MP also functions as a political organiser in the community, often engaged (with his or her family) in organising political meetings, fund-raïsing, and attending and speaking at political meetings.

In New Zealand an MP has close contact with the public. This makes for a sensitive political environment in which many members of the public can transmit their concerns directly and personally to their MP. Most constituency MPs conduct a weekly clinic in their electorates so that members of the public can meet their MP. Many people telephone MPs to point out some weakness in government administration and complain about a policy.

MPs act as a sort of clearing house for complaints, many of them genuine, a proportion from cranks. The advent of the Ombudsmen does not appear to have caused any change in the number of complaints against the bureaucracy and

[1] A. Nordmeyer, 'A Critical Examination of the Functioning of Parliament', 8 *New Zealand Journal of Public Administration,* 1946, p.3.

requests for help received by MPs, but the presence of Ombudsmen does give MPs a useful avenue of referral for their constituents' grievances.

This community work is an important feature of representative democracy. Because MPs are generally required to be in Parliament Buildings, when Parliament is meeting, most work has to be done at weekends or Fridays (or Monday, except for Cabinet ministers).

In order to assist MPs in helping the public, in the mid-1980s the government introduced a system of paid electorate secretaries for MPs—a long overdue reform. In preparing for MMP in 1996, the Parliamentary Service Commission reviewed support arrangements for MPs and, among other things, decided that:

- all MPs will continue to be provided with an office in Parliament and an executive secretary;
- constituency MPs will have two full-time equivalent electorate support staff and receive a budget of $55,000 for electorate office running costs, technology, postage, and printing;
- list MPs will have one full-time equivalent out-of-Wellington support staffer and a budget of $34,200 for out-of-Wellington office running costs, technology, postage, and printing.

Giving help to the public is an important part of an MP's job. Requests from constituents cover a wide range—social welfare benefits, housing, immigration, and legal problems are the staples but enquiries can range over the full ambit of government activity. Sometimes the MP is like a traffic officer directing people to the right place to have their problem solved. On other occasions, the MP can actually help by getting in touch with the relevant government department or by making representations to a minister. Indeed, correspondence to ministers is probably the most frequent, though not the only, way in which MPs help members of the public.

These functions require the MP to be a good listener, to have an extensive knowledge of various institutions in society, and a range of personal contacts in a variety of fields. An MP needs some of the professional competence of, among others, an accountant, social worker, psychologist, medical practitioner, lawyer, financial expert, environmentalist, and trade union secretary.

Information is one of the things that constituents most need. If you do not know much about the system, it seems designed to clobber you. Everything seems against you. Help appears remote. The provision of basic information about many matters would help to lessen the burden that many in our society are forced to carry. Things have become much more complex than they were even a few years ago and this makes the task of communicating the basic information more difficult.

In appropriate cases, publicity can be used to further constituents' causes. MPs are in a position of influence and authority and their intervention on behalf of constituents who have been hard done by can produce redress. The MP is an important check against excesses that can develop in the bureaucracy. And, from the point of view of an MP's work in Parliament, constituency work is an excellent indicator of what is wrong with particular laws and policies.

THE MP IN PARLIAMENT

In Wellington the MP inhabits a different world, a strange sort of parliamentary subculture. Most MPs from out of Wellington live in boarding houses or flats near Parliament while the session is on. They usually eat and drink at Bellamy's, a well-provisioned catering service at Parliament now run under private contract. At the beautifully refurbished Parliament Buildings, back in use in 1996 after some years of restoration, other facilities are available to MPs, who generally work long hours. Parliament is a self-contained community; the MPs are part of it, but they are not all of it. There are the messengers, the officials of Parliament, the people who run Bellamy's, the members of the party research units, the members of the Parliamentary Press Gallery, the Hansard reporters, the secretaries, the librarians, and the staff of the select committees. Most of them are allowed to eat and drink in Bellamy's.

A full travel service is available. MPs travel a lot and not just between their electorates and Wellington. They are entitled to free unlimited air travel on all scheduled air services within New Zealand, and to free rail travel. They enjoy certain concessions on overseas travel after they have served more than one term in Parliament. Free overseas trips available to MPs are considerable; most of these relate to conferences and other meetings to which members are sent as official delegates. Considerable discussion takes place in the caucuses, and sometimes votes are cast, as to which MPs should go on a trip. MPs also enjoy unlimited free telephone calls all over New Zealand and free use of postal facilities.

Many MPs are often together at official receptions and cocktail parties. The world of Parliament in Wellington is a strained and artificial one. Tensions arise from political and personal conflict. This, combined with the ceaseless travelling for many, makes it hard for MPs to function as normal human beings and to sustain personal relationships. The toll upon their health and family life is also substantial. Members must attend each sitting of the House unless they are granted leave of absence by the Speaker or, more frequently in practice, by the party whips, who are MPs with the job of maintaining discipline among MPs in each party.

The House is run under an extensive system of rules called the standing orders. In 1995 these were comprehensively overhauled in preparation for MMP. One of the changes was to the times Parliament meets, which are now: Tuesdays from 2 p.m. to 6 p.m.; Wednesdays from 2 p.m. to 6 p.m. and 7.30 p.m. to 10 p.m.; and Thursdays from 10 a.m. to 1 p.m. and 2 p.m. to 6 p.m.

During the hours the House is not sitting, MPs have plenty to occupy them. Party caucus meetings are held on Tuesday mornings. On Tuesday evenings caucus committees are likely to meet. Wednesday mornings are set aside for select committee meetings. Select committees are now entitled to have one meeting a week of up to three hours a week while the House is sitting.

Since 1984, Parliament has been sitting regularly. It sits for between twenty-five and twenty-eight weeks, amounting to between seventy-five and eighty-five sitting days a year. Because the New Zealand Parliament is small, attendance has been much more rigorously enforced than in other Parliaments and special leave is required for periods of absence.

In between the constant round of meetings and sittings in the chamber, MPs need to read the hundreds of bills introduced in Parliament each year and the hundreds of papers tabled, as well as prepare speeches for delivery, both inside and outside the House of Representatives. MPs are forced to cut corners. They cannot do everything. The workload for MPs is very heavy indeed; for ministers who are also expected to carry out the duties of MPs as well as their ministerial duties, it can be cruel.

One interesting question under MMP will be the extent to which distinctions are drawn in practice between constituency MPs and party list MPs. Will both sets of MPs have the same status in Parliament? Will constituency MPs be more independent of their parties than list MPs? Will list MPs concentrate more on national policies and constituency MPs more on matters of local concern? In the House itself, there has at least been a change in terminology. The standing orders now allow members to refer to one another by name using honorifics rather than by constituency or ministerial portfolio (but MPs are still not permitted to address one another as 'you').

This raises the issue of the true function of an MP. Should he or she be regarded as a representative of the people, speaking for them in Parliament and thereby moderating the action of the government? Should he or she be regarded as someone who has a serious part to play in the legislative process, scrutinising legislation to show up anomalies and to contribute policy ideas? Should he or she be thought of as the local trouble-shooter who helps people when they are in difficulty? Or should the MP simply be content to secure sufficient political skills to become an apprenticed member of the executive? Most MPs aspire to be in Cabinet, although it is possible that under MMP, with a larger Parliament and a different dynamic, this expectation may change. Should the MP be regarded as a servant of the political party to which he or she is affiliated so that he or she can contribute to it ideas for policy, keep the party faithful happy, and work to see that the party is elected to government? Or is the MP the watchdog for the people on the actions of the executive?

The MP in New Zealand tries to perform all these functions, but usually excels at none of them. Because MPs' energies are dissipated among many activities, we are in danger of losing any adequate definition of the function. It should be observed, however, that the balance of time and effort spent by individual members on the various aspects of their work varies greatly according to their own interests and talents. With MMP there will be further evolution in the nature and functions of the duties of MPs.

POLITICAL PARTY CAUCUSES

A caucus is the name given to the weekly meeting of MPs of a political party. You will find no reference to it in any law; from a formal constitutional point of view it hardly exists. But in truth it is an important component of our governmental and political system. Caucuses are important committees in a system of government by committee. Under FPP, since a single party was in government, its caucus functioned as something of a rival to Cabinet, or at least a countervailing force. Previous editions of this book suggested that a government caucus could be best understood as an instrument by which a party that controls the executive can ensure and perpetuate its domination of Parliament.

Under MMP, since several parties are likely to share in governmental power (whether as coalition or minority governments), no single caucus has the ability to cement the fusion of executive and legislature. But the caucus of each party remains important as the means of ensuring party discipline in parliamentary negotiating and decision-making. Cabinet ministers must continue to pay close attention to the attitudes of their caucus (or caucuses) in order to be sure of parliamentary support for the government's initiatives. It could be argued that the greater number of parties existing under MMP has made it easier for MPs to change parties and therefore has made party discipline harder to enforce so that Cabinet cannot so easily dominate its caucus(es). On the other hand, it may be that the power of party organisations over the rankings in the party lists, and hence the continuation of list MPs' parliamentary careers, may increase party discipline over list MPs.

In the late 1980s the Labour Party caucus in government proceeded as follows:

1. Reading of the minutes
2. Correspondence
3. Matters arising
4. Leader's report
5. Procedures Committee report
6. Whips' report
7. Members' requests (items that members have asked to be put on the agenda)
8. Ministers' requests (matters which ministers wish to be raised)
9. Reports from select committees
10. General business.

The 1996 *Cabinet Office Manual* recognises the role of caucus in providing (para 5.37) that all draft bills are referred to government caucus(es), with the responsible minister in attendance, after approval by Cabinet and before being introduced into the House. It also recognises (para 4.80) that many appointments to statutory bodies involve reference to the government caucus(es).

Caucus is still a primary instrument by which tight party discipline is observed in the New Zealand Parliament. Labour MPs are pledged to vote in the House in accordance with caucus decisions. And although National has no such formal requirement, the difference in practice has been more apparent than real. In New Zealand all divisions in the House (except on conscience issues, usually in members' bills) are subject to the whip. The result is that it is very rare indeed for MPs to cross the floor of the House; this happened no more than fifteen times from 1950 to 1990. In the United Kingdom, however, it is quite a common occurrence.

Votes are frequently held in a caucus, although a united Cabinet is not often defeated in a government caucus. That does not mean caucus is without influence. Caucus follows a handful of important issues closely—employment and labour relations were two prominent examples in the 1980s Labour Government caucus.

From the New Zealand literature that does exist, a number of conclusions can be reached about caucus:

- caucus acts as a sounding board of public and party opinion;
- the role of caucus is becoming increasingly important;
- caucus functions as an institutional check on the actions of ministers;
- caucus offers an opportunity for full and frank discussion in secret;
- caucus is a source of ideas and suggestions on policy;
- caucus provides an opportunity to settle differences and promote unity;
- caucus scrutinises legislation;
- caucus conducts enquiries into policy;
- caucus discusses appointments;
- parliamentary strategy and tactics can be discussed and planned at caucus;
- caucus forms an important communication link; and
- caucus elects the parliamentary leader and deputy leader and, in the case of the Labour Party, Cabinet ministers.

For the governing party perhaps the most important role of caucus is as a sounding board for the state of public opinion on questions of the day. It is probably true that the more controversial an issue, the more caucus will be concerned with it. And on some issues caucus may decide that the policies of the ministry are unacceptable and must be changed. The best short description of caucus we have seen comes from former National Party speaker, Alfred Allen. He wrote in 1971:

> . . . at caucus meetings, where all are regarded as equal, and some prove themselves a little more equal than others, Members are extremely outspoken and the utterances and actions of individual Members come under very close scrutiny. A word picture of a Member is often so vividly painted that it enables him to see himself clearly as others see him.
>
> While Cabinet Ministers form the executive Government, they are always ready and willing to bring all matters of major importance before caucus before becoming irrevocably committed to any course of action. While it is unusual, I have on occasions seen the strongly presented recommendation of a Minister turned down in no uncertain manner and on other occasions a Cabinet decision reversed or abandoned.[2]

Caucus committees can do valuable work. The number of caucus committees in parties varies from time to time. There is a pronounced tendency to set up ad hoc committees as issues arise. The National Government in 1982 had twenty-three caucus committees; the Labour opposition sixteen. In 1996 the National Party in government had seven core committees. The Labour opposition had eleven committees. The performance of caucus committees tends to be uneven. It depends to a large extent on the interests of the members and the importance of the issues with which the committee deals.

In addition to their caucuses, political parties have substantial research units housed in Parliament Buildings. The members of the units are appointed by the party leaders and paid for from public funds. The 1996 decisions on support services to parties by the Parliamentary Service Commission include:

- each party in Parliament other than the party providing the Prime Minister receives a pool of funding of $57,176 per MP for the leader's private office, policy and communication budgets;
- each party receives a budget of $20,000 per MP on a pooled basis for research support, and communications including whips' offices.

Research units dig up information requested by members, prepare background papers on particular topics and speech notes, help with the drafting of questions and notices of motion, monitor the debates in Parliament, and prepare material for rebuttal. They also provide information for inclusion in press statements and keep in touch with people outside Parliament sympathetic to the political party they serve, to secure comment and information on topics that come up in Parliament. They draft papers and act as a secretariat to caucus committees. The central concern of the research units, however, is the quick production of information, in a simple form, for use in parliamentary debate.

---

2 E.A. Allen, 'The Role of Whips and the Caucus in the New Zealand Parliament' (1971) 52 *Parliamentarian* 37.

MMP, especially coalition governments, is likely to change greatly the role of party caucuses. They may decline in importance as the role of select committees grows. In a coalition government it is likely that the government caucuses will meet separately, but special arrangements for briefings by ministers of each caucus are likely to be made.

THE SPEAKER

The Speaker has the key role in controlling the proceedings of the House. The way in which the Speaker discharges the responsibilities of the office is an important influence in setting the standard of debate in regard to both its propriety and its relevance to the matter being discussed. The Speaker is responsible for keeping order. When the Speaker stands up, any member speaking must be silent and resume his or her seat. The Speaker is responsible for ensuring that the standing orders governing debate are observed. The Speaker can:

- direct a member to discontinue his or her speech if that member 'persists in irrelevance or tedious repetition' (Standing Order 110);
- order members whose conduct is 'highly disorderly to withdraw immediately from the House during such period (up to the remainder of that day's sitting) as the Speaker or Chairman may appoint' (Standing Order 87);
- name and, with the approval of the House, suspend a member whose conduct is grossly disorderly for increasingly lengthy periods depending on the number of offences (Standing Orders 88, 89, and 91); and
- adjourn the House, in the event of grave disorder, if the Speaker thinks it necessary to do so (Standing Order 50).

The Speaker occupies a position of great historical importance in New Zealand. The Speaker has usually been the nominee of the party in government, a fact which may be thought to have eroded his or her independence. There is no constitutional reason why the Speaker needs to be a member of the governing party. After the election of 1993, in which the National Party found itself returned to office with a very slender majority, a member of the Labour opposition, the Hon. Dr Peter Tapsell, was elected Speaker.

The Speaker chairs the Parliamentary Service Commission, a function introduced in 1985 which has added substantially to the duties of the Speaker and the importance of the office. The office of Speaker has taken on further and enhanced importance as a result of the changes made to the standing orders of the House in 1995. The Speaker chairs the important Business Committee which, as discussed in the next chapter, has a great deal to do with determining the conduct of business in the House. The Speaker is also involved in discussions leading to the appointment of officers of Parliament.

The 1995 Standing Orders also change the procedures for the election of Speaker. There is no debate on the issue; members who want to be considered nominate themselves. Where there are two nominations there is a personal vote. Where there are three or more nominations, members are asked to stand in their place and state which member they vote for. There is no proxy voting on this matter. This method of election may further strengthen the independence of the Speaker's position in the New Zealand Parliament.

The Standing Orders Committee that reported in 1995 discussed whether, on appointment, the Speaker should become an independent member and withdraw from his or her political party. In the end it was decided that the Speaker should remain a member of his or her party, although that may change after further experience with MMP. [3]

Considering the circumstances of their appointment, New Zealand Speakers have done well in the past in protecting the rights of the minority. Both the independence and the powers of the New Zealand Speaker have increased in recent years, and this trend is likely to develop under MMP as Parliament becomes more distinct from, and independent of, the executive government.

THE PARLIAMENTARY SERVICE AND OFFICE OF THE CLERK

Parliament used to be run through a government department called the Legislative Department, responsible to a minister. There were grave objections to such a structure. The minister, a member of the executive, was in a position to make decisions about the running of the legislature which favoured the party in government at the expense of the opposition. Over the years, Parliament was so starved of resources that it was difficult for MPs to carry out their duties in a satisfactory manner. This was changed with the passage of the Parliamentary Service Act 1985. Section 4 of the act established a Parliamentary Service Commission to provide 'to members of the House of Representatives such administrative and support services as may be necessary or desirable'.

The Speaker chairs the commission and has important practical responsibilities for the running of Parliament and expenditure of the funds. Other members include the Leader of the House and the Leader of the Opposition or their nominees, and four other members—two from the government and two from the opposition. In effect this group has all the responsibilities that a minister would have over a government department. This arrangement makes it impossible for the administration of Parliament to be dictated by the government of the day or to be based on partisan party considerations.

[3] *Report of the Standing Orders Committee on the Review of Standing Orders*, I.18A *Appendices to the Journal of the House of Representatives*, Wellington, 1995.

Section 29 of the Parliamentary Service Act provides for the commission to appoint a general manager who is responsible to the Parliamentary Service Commission for 'the efficient and economical administration of the Parliamentary Service'. The types of activities funded by Vote:Parliamentary Service, according to the 1995/96 estimates are:

- support services to individual MPs' offices in Wellington and their electorates, and travel services for MPs;
- research and library services, including computing facilities;
- catering services through Bellamy's;
- buildings maintenance, security services, messenger services;
- policy advice to the Parliamentary Service Commission and the Speaker; and
- personnel and accounting services to MPs and other parliamentary agencies.

Thousands of people visit Parliament every year. Security is provided twenty-four hours a day, seven days a week for the whole of the parliamentary complex. The standing orders provide that the responsibility for the proper use of facilities and grounds rests with the Speaker. With Parliament often the focus for demonstrations, and with the occasional bomb threat, there is a need for adequate security in and around Parliament. Public tours of Parliament have become increasingly popular and tour guides are provided.

The House of Representatives is broadcast by radio all the time it sits. It has been broadcast since 1936. It is also available to television. Reporters from the news media are accredited by the Speaker as members of the Press Gallery where they are given some accommodation in offices and can report the proceedings of the House and its select committees. For its knowledge of what goes on in Parliament, the public is dependent to a large extent upon the media.

The great information resource available to members of Parliament is the Parliamentary Library. As at 1995, that library had a collection of more than 700,000 volumes and 333,000 microfiche documents, including every book published in New Zealand, and it contains a number of unique features. It has an up-to-date newspaper index dating from 1924 and using 600 index headings. An index of articles, appearing in a multitude of periodicals, is kept under subject headings. The library operates a reference service so that a trained librarian will help any member secure information on any topic. The library expects to respond to around 14 200 enquiries in the 1995–96 year. Where members indicate a special interest, the library makes arrangements for them to receive material on the subject on a continuing basis. The Parliamentary Library provides computer terminals that can give instant access to a wide range of statistical material.

Parliamentary support services are, however, more extensive than the Parliamentary Service. The Office of the Clerk of the House of Representatives carries out vital constitutional functions. This is headed by the Clerk of the House, Mr

David McGee. The clerk, appointed by the Governor-General on the recommendation of the Speaker of the House, is responsible to the Speaker.

According to the Report of the Office of the Clerk for the year ended 30 June 1995,[4] the office's functions include:

- administrative and support services for the House and select committees;
- advice to the Speaker and MPs on parliamentary law and procedures;
- scrutiny of material prepared for the House and its committees;
- recording of all proceedings by the Hansard reporters;
- administration of the parliamentary printing contract of bills and reports and the agreement for broadcasting the proceedings of the House; and
- determination of the question to put to voters in a citizens' initiated referendum and determination of whether such a petition has been signed by the required 10 per cent of eligible electors.

Advice on parliamentary procedure is required by all MPs from time to time. There are 398 standing orders governing conduct in the House, plus a set of rulings from Speakers relating to procedural matters. And there are other complicated features of parliamentary law, such as privilege, upon which expert advice is required. The Clerks-at-the-Table, headed by the Clerk of the House of Representatives himself, provide the Speaker and MPs with the advice that actually allows Parliament to function.

The select committees of Parliament are serviced by support staff. There are, at the time of writing, twenty-three committee clerks who act as secretaries to the committees, assisted by twelve assistant clerks who provide technical advice and draft background papers and reports for the committees. In addition, specialist staff with particular expertise are engaged from time to time. If select committees are going to fulfil their proper role they must have available to them quality advice independent of the government. Within the clerk's office there is also the Serjeant-at-Arms, who is responsible for discipline within the chamber of the House and who handles parliamentary relations with overseas Parliaments.

4 *Report of the Office of the Clerk of the House of Representatives for the year ended 30 June 1995*, A.8 *Appendices to the Journal of the House of Representatives*, Wellington, 1995.

8 What Happens in Parliament

INTRODUCTION

One of the primary constitutional doctrines of the Westminster system of Parliament is parliamentary sovereignty. In essence this means that Parliament can do whatever it wants to do, in particular that it can pass any law it wants to. There are now generally acknowledged to be some limits on this, including laws that previous Parliaments have said require a special parliamentary majority to amend. As mentioned in Chapter 14, it is also possible that, in very extreme circumstances, a court would refuse to enforce some laws that a Parliament might pass, although this has never happened. Most important, Parliament is restrained from abusing its power by the effect of public opinion, particularly as felt by politicians through elections, as well as by international obligations and constitutional conventions.

Despite some limits, the power of Parliament is constitutionally impressive and has been revitalised by MMP. Under FPP, since one party controlled a majority in Parliament and formed the Cabinet, parliamentary sovereignty was effectively wielded by the Cabinet—the executive. Under MMP this may continue to be so under coalition governments with a majority in Parliament, but the power of coalition partners to bring down the government would be exercised through Parliament. And a minority government owes not only its existence, but the passage of every piece of legislation, to its ability to persuade a majority of MPs to vote with it.

As Michael Rush of the University of Exeter has pointed out, parliamentary control is often taken to be an alternative way of stating ministerial responsibility, a distinguishing feature of parliamentary government which is itself:

> . . . that form of government in which the executive is drawn from the legislature and is constitutionally responsible to it. This fusion of personnel and power is a constitutional arrangement which seeks to limit the exercise of political power by two devices: first, by arguing that the executive or government derives its authority to govern initially by securing and subsequently retaining the confidence of sufficient members—usually a

> majority—of the legislature; and second, by rendering members of the government individually and collectively accountable to the legislature for the exercise of their powers. It therefore follows that constitutionally the legislature can prevail upon the government to change its policies or, more drastically, bring about a change of government.[1]

The Constitution Act 1986 brought together a number of important provisions of the law relating to the New Zealand Parliament:

- 'There shall be a Parliament of New Zealand, which shall consist of the Sovereign in right of New Zealand and the House of Representatives' (section 14).
- The House of Representatives has as its members persons elected under the provisions of the Electoral Act who shall be known as members of Parliament (section 10).
- The House of Representatives 'shall be regarded as always in existence, notwithstanding that Parliament has been dissolved or has expired' (section 10).
- The 'Parliament of New Zealand continues to have full power to make laws' (section 15).
- The term of Parliament is '3 years from the day fixed for the return of the writs issued for the last preceding general election of members of the House of Representatives, and no longer' (section 17). This provision cannot be repealed except by a 75 per cent majority voting for it in the House, or by a poll of electors.
- The Governor-General may summon, prorogue or dissolve Parliament (section 18). This power, of course, is exercised on the advice of ministers.
- One provision, which appeared in the Constitution Act 1986 for the first time, requires Parliament to meet 'not later than 6 weeks after the day fixed for the return of the writs' after any general election (section 19).

Regarding the last provision, it had been common in the past for Parliament not to meet for months after an election, a situation that was regarded as unfortunate. With the arrival of MMP, the provision will take on new practical importance because of the negotiations that may be necessary to form coalition or minority governments. Ultimately the government must have the confidence of the House of Representatives and the fact that Parliament must meet within a certain period may assist and test the formation process.

THE FUNCTIONS OF PARLIAMENT

The functions of Parliament are:

- to raise the money by which the business of government may be conducted and to approve the expenditure of money;

---

1 M. Rush, *Parliamentary Government in Britain*, Pitman, London, 1981, p.1.

- to consider and pass bills into law;
- to provide a place for the airing of grievances;
- to act as a check on the manner in which government is actually carried out;
- to serve as a forum for party political contest.

The passage of laws through Parliament gives those laws legitimacy because there they are approved by the elected representatives of the people. Under FPP, legislation had become more a function of the executive branch of government. It will be interesting to see the degree to which, under MMP, Parliament can exert an influence over the content of legislation compared with the executive. Parliament now has the capacity to curb the executive; the degree to which it does so will depend on the nature of the particular government and whether it enjoys a majority in the House.

For more than sixty years the New Zealand Parliament has revolved around party political contest. Much time was spent in party political attack and defence: the opposition attacked the party in government and the government members defended it. We have had a combative, adversary style of politics in which neither side gives any quarter, and much effort is wasted in perpetual party conflict and constant electioneering.

Given the importance of political parties in our system, it would be idle to suggest that political confrontation can be removed from Parliament. But some have expected that the introduction of MMP will usher in a new approach in which, to some extent, bargaining and cooperation replaces confrontation. Where there are more than two parties represented in the House and the government does not have a majority, there may be greater incentives to reach a consensus on policy matters. It may be damaging to your own political interests to mount a vicious attack on a political adversary if, next month or next week, you need their support. In 1995 the Bolger Government did not have a majority in the House but it was able to consult other parties on matters of importance to them and often to adopt policies that reflected the views of others, particularly in securing agreement to policies against French nuclear testing. Such approaches may occur more often under MMP.

WHAT PARLIAMENT DOES

The daily programme for Parliament is determined by the printed order paper that comes out every day Parliament is in session. Orders of the day must be disposed of in the order they appear on the paper. Usually the opposition determines how long the debate will last on each measure. It may debate some bills down to the closure at every stage and vote against every provision in them, or it may decide to allow a measure to be passed with little or no debate. The power of the opposition, in a Parliament where there is a majority government, is primarily a power to delay by debating.

The opposition is free to debate matters down to the closure, which is a motion 'that the question be now put'. The Speaker has the discretion whether to accept such a motion if he or she believes it is reasonable to do so under Standing Order 141. Such motions are accepted only after considerable debate. But where the debate has become tedious and repetitious and no new arguments are being advanced, it is accepted. These provisions still exist in the new standing orders adopted in 1995 but they are qualified by a new development, the establishment of a powerful Business Committee. For example, the Speaker may not accept a closure motion if the time for the debate is prescribed by standing orders or by a determination of the Business Committee. This adjustment has been made to allow for the different pressures of MMP that will occur in managing the business of the House.

The Business Committee is chaired by the Speaker. Every party with six or more members is entitled to be represented at each meeting of the committee by a member nominated by the party leader. One member can also represent all parties with fewer than six members in a government coalition, and another represents all parties with fewer than six members who are not in a government coalition. Standing Order 77 provides that the committee reaches its decisions 'on the basis of unanimity or, if this is not possible, near-unanimity having regard to the numbers in the House represented by each of the members of the committee'. The Speaker is the judge of that.

The Business Committee has the power to determine:

- the order of business to be transacted in the House;
- the time to be spent on an item of business;
- how the time is to be allocated on an item among the parties;
- the speaking time of individual members of an item.

In effect the Business Committee has the power to override standing orders and produce managed debates in terms of time and also the agenda to be pursued by the House. Obviously, where unanimity or near unanimity cannot be obtained the provisions in the standing orders will continue to apply, but the Business Committee will be a powerful influence on what occurs in the House. And most of what happens is likely to be the result of cooperative solutions produced by the committee. The government will go to the committee with its desires; opposition parties will have their own agendas. Compromises will be reached. That is a far cry from the days when the government bent the Parliament to its will, regardless of the views of the opposition. It is ironic that, although the new legislative process makes it easier for the public to know what is going on, it is possible that the Business Committee may obscure that transparency by arriving at arrangements and deals to put measures through quickly and to abridge the ordinary legislative processes.

Under the 1995 revisions to Standing Orders, at 2 p.m. each day the House sits there is general business, which consists of:

1. First reading of bills (there is no debate).
2. Announcement of the presentation of petitions, papers and reports of select committees.
3. Questions for oral answer (including urgent questions).
4. Debate on a matter of urgent public importance (if allowed by the Speaker).
5. A general debate (on Wednesdays only).
6. Consideration of reports of the Privileges Committee.

Among the other business that the House deals with, in an order likely to be determined primarily by the Business Committee, is:

- *Government orders of the day*, including: government bills, the Address in Reply debate, debate on the Prime Minister's statement, consideration of the performance and operations of Crown entities;
- *Members' orders of the day:* primarily members' bills, and consideration of reports of inquiries carried out by select committees; and
- *Private and local orders of the day:* private and local legislation.

Legislation is examined further in Chapter 9. The new standing orders provide for a new, important, non-legislative debate. Standing Order 341 requires the Prime Minister, at 2 p.m. on the first sitting day of each year, to make a statement 'reviewing public affairs and outlining the Government's legislative and other policy intentions for the next 12 months'. The statement must be made available no later than 10 a.m. on the day it is given to each party leader. After the Prime Minister makes the statement there is a debate on it.

VOTING IN PARLIAMENT

The standing orders adopted in 1995 changed the system of voting in Parliament, borrowing from a system the Standing Orders Committee had seen in the Netherlands. The new system of voting in the House is a three-tiered one:

1. *Voice vote.* Questions are initially determined on a voice vote: 'aye' or 'no'. If there is doubt about the result, or a party wishes to record its dissent, the second step would be taken.
2. *Party vote.* When a party vote is called, a member from each party in the House will state the number of votes the party is casting. Members not voting with

their party or independent members would also declare their votes at that time. Parties can record an abstention.

3. *Personal vote.* After a party vote, a member may request a personal vote. This is similar to a division in the old system. The bells are rung, tellers are appointed, the doors are locked, and each member's vote is recorded, but again abstentions are permitted. The Speaker no longer has a casting vote, although he or she has a deliberative vote. In the event of a tie the question is lost.

These are novel provisions designed with MMP specifically in mind. It will be interesting to see how well they work or whether adjustments are needed. As Parliament came to an end in 1996, the Standing Orders Committee reported that the new system appeared to be working well.

Another new element that was added in the 1995 revision of standing orders is to permit proxy voting—an MP can authorise another MP to vote in his or her absence. This is designed to replace the old system of 'pairs', which could be effectively administered only when there were two parties. Members who give proxies must sign them, date them, and indicate who is to exercise the proxy. In the case of personal and party votes, proxies may be exercised for a number equal to no more than 25 per cent of a party's membership in the House. There are so many demands on MPs' time that it is often necessary for them, and particularly for ministers, to be absent from Parliament. It is in the public interest that they can be.

PARLIAMENTARY QUESTIONS

Parliamentary questions offer MPs an important opportunity to question and probe the Ministers of the Crown about the administration of their departments and their policies. Each year, much information is elicited by parliamentary questions, and a good deal of it is information that would not otherwise become available to the public. In 1984–85 there were 1902 oral and 3609 written questions. A decade later, in 1995, there were 1178 oral questions and 9884 written questions. Parliamentary questions are an important instrument of ministerial responsibility for the conduct of public affairs.

A minister may be asked questions relating to public affairs with which he or she is officially connected. Notice in writing must be given of questions; they are printed on the order paper. Replies must be concise and confined to the subject matter of the question. Although replies are usually drafted by public servants, ministers take a close interest because they will be answering the question and may immediately face supplementary questions on the same topic. Each day the House sits there is a question time, which lasts as long as it takes to deal with the questions.

Questions for oral answer must be lodged with the Clerk between 10 and 10.30 a.m. on the day they are to be answered. Twelve questions may be accepted for oral answer each day. Questions are allocated to parties in proportion to their membership in the House. The Business Committee decides the weekly allocation and rotation of questions. Questions can also be dealt with in writing without being asked and answered orally in the House. But they are recorded in Hansard. In practice, a vastly greater number of questions are dealt with in this way than are dealt with orally. When an MP has lodged a question for written answer it is printed on a notice paper circulated by the clerk and the reply to the clerk for delivery to the member must be given not later than the fifth working day after the appearance of the notice of the question.

There is also a procedure for the asking of urgent questions about events that arise after the lodging of oral questions. Questions may also be put to a member, who is neither a minister nor the speaker, relating to any bill, motion, or public matter of which the member has charge. This is most frequently used to question the chairs of select committees concerning activities for which they are responsible.

Difficulties have often arisen in the House when members have not been happy with the answer given by a minister and supplementary questioning, which is permitted for oral questions, did not elicit what the members considered to be an appropriate answer. The 1995 standing orders make an important innovation to deal with this problem. Standing Order 375 provides that 'An answer that seeks to address the question asked must be given if it can be given consistently with the public interest.' The intention is that the Speaker will apply a 'reasonableness' test to this standing order. Another change has allowed hypothetical questions and questions seeking an opinion, which were previously excluded. It remains to be seen how far these innovations will put ministers under greater pressure to account for government policies and actions. Answering questions in Parliament in a manner that gives little away is an art in which many ministers take pride. The conduct of the House is frequently rowdy and disorderly at question time because of answers that are too long or do not address the question. The Standing Orders Committee wanted a better standard of behaviour, but such aspirations are not easily achieved in the New Zealand Parliament.

Questions are asked in Parliament on many different topics for many different purposes. Some examples of the most common techniques follow. First come the 'patsy', or 'Dorothy Dix', questions—asked of a minister by a political ally—to allow the minister to show him or herself and the government in a good light. The member knows the answer before asking the question, but some of Parliament's listening audience may not.

The 1995 Standing Orders Committee report deplored the use of these questions and said that somewhat more rigorous questions from government backbenchers could improve the behaviour of the House at question time and that Speakers should be supported in their attempts to discourage this type of questioning.

The reverse of the patsy question occurs when a member who has a shrewd idea of the answer to his question seeks to embarrass the government with it. Sometimes members will ask a series of questions designed to build up a body of information on a particular topic or policy that can be used later in other debates or in some other way. Constituents or pressure groups may be interested in having information on a topic.

Parliamentary questions can be used to assemble information on particular topics or pursue in depth the actions of ministers. Sometimes oral questions can be concentrated on a particular minister or a particular topic. They are important instruments in holding the government to account and probing the executive. In the 1980 Marginal Lands Board loan affair, the opposition directed eighty-two oral questions and thirty-five written questions at ministers, probing for information. Eventually the government decided to establish a Royal Commission of Inquiry to investigate the whole matter. Here are a couple of examples of the questions that were asked:

> Mr PREBBLE (Auckland Central) to the Minister of Lands: Did Mr and Mrs Fitzgerald give him a complete account of their financial history and holdings before he wrote to the Marginal Lands Board in January on their behalf?
> Hon. V.S. YOUNG (Minister of Lands): No, it was not necessary. Their representation to me was to seek the board to review an earlier decision. On my request, Mr and Mrs Fitzgerald furnished my office with evidence in support of the review.
> Mr Prebble: How could the Minister assure the board that the Fitzgeralds were not buying the property for speculative purposes if he did not know their financial history?
> Hon. V. S. YOUNG: All those matters will be considered at the inquiry.
> Mr Lange: If the Minister did not solicit their financial background from Mr and Mrs Fitzgerald, how was it that in his letter of 25 January he gave details of their residential properties, the collateral security on them, and the wish of the mortgagee not to have that security discharged?
> Hon. V. S. YOUNG: All those matters will be considered at the forthcoming inquiry.
> Hon. M. B. R. Couch: Did the Minister adopt the same procedure when I appealed to the Marginal Lands Board on behalf of Mr Harrington, one of my constituents?
> Hon. V. S. YOUNG: Yes, exactly the same.
> Mr SPEAKER: Order! I did not call the Minister. The Postmaster-General's question was not related to the original question, which was about the affairs of Mr and Mrs Fitzgerald.
> Mr Moore: What evidence did the Minister provide to the Marginal Lands Board if it did not contain information about the finances of the couple involved?

Hon. V. S. YOUNG: I take it the member is referring to the Fitzgerald case. All those matters will be considered at the forthcoming inquiry.[2]

Rt. Hon. W. E. ROWLING (Leader of the Opposition), on behalf of Mr PREBBLE (Auckland Central), to the Minister of Lands: When did he first become aware of the possibility that a false declaration had been made in connection with the application of J. M. and A. Fitzgerald for a Marginal Lands Board loan?
Hon. DAVID THOMSON (Acting Minister of Lands): On 30 June 1980.
Mr Lange: If the Minister of Lands was aware on 30 June 1980 that there had possibly been a false declaration to the Marginal Lands Board, why was there a delay until the third week of August 1980 before the matter was referred to the Police?
Hon. DAVID THOMSON: I have no doubt that the honourable member can get that question answered in the report of the commission of inquiry.
Mr D. M. J. Jones: Am I correct in recalling that only yesterday in the House the Opposition was informed that, within 24 hours of the Marginal Lands Board getting a Crown Law Office opinion on the matter, the matter was referred to the Police? It could hardly have been done more promptly than that.
Hon. DAVID THOMSON: The proceedings of the House yesterday are a matter of record.
Rt. Hon. W. E. Rowling: Can the Minister indicate whether the delay referred to was based on negligence or unwillingness to act?
Hon. DAVID THOMSON: The right honourable gentleman can have his prurience satisfied in the report of the commission of inquiry.
Mr Lange: It's a cover-up!
Mr SPEAKER: Order! I do not need that type of interjection from the honourable member. I find it entirely disorderly. I do not need to have the honourable member chipping away at me now. That is disorderly, too. I require the Minister to withdraw his comment, because it infringes Standing Order 80, which states that answers shall not contain argument or controversial matter. All that is required of the Minister is to give the answer to the question. He will withdraw his last comment.
Hon. DAVID THOMSON: I withdraw.
Mr D. M. J. Jones: Will the Minister assure the House that Government departments and Government boards will continue to seek Crown Law advice, and not commence prosecutions on rumour created by people who are not interested in the real truth?
Hon. DAVID THOMSON: I would certainly hope so.
Mr Lange: If the matter was referred to the Police within 24 hours of receipt of Crown Law opinion, why did it take 7 weeks to resolve that matter by Crown Law opinion?
Mr SPEAKER: I do not know that that is a question the Minister of Lands can properly

2 430 *New Zealand Parliamentary Debates*, p.1329.

answer, because the Minister of Lands is not in charge of the Crown Law Office. I can allow the member to rephrase his question.
Mr Lange: When was the Crown Law opinion sought by the Minister of Lands?
Hon. DAVID THOMSON: Again I repeat my advice to the member. He can have his curiosity satisfied by reading the report of the commission of inquiry.[3]

PETITIONS TO PARLIAMENT

The right to petition Parliament for redress of grievances is acknowledged as a fundamental principle of our constitution. It is a right that goes as far back as Parliament itself. Petitions on a wide variety of topics are presented to Parliament. Some call for an alteration in the general law; others ask for some reconsideration of an administrative decision. Everyone has the right to present a petition and it is Parliament's function to consider the petition and make recommendations to the government about what should be done. Petitions are dealt with in more detail in Chapter 13.

SELECT COMMITTEES

Parliamentary select committees have long been a strong and positive feature of the New Zealand Parliament. The 1985 changes to standing orders completely reorganised the system of select committees and vastly extended their jurisdiction and powers. The purpose of the change was to strengthen the accountability of government to Parliament by more systematic, comprehensive scrutiny of Government activity. The potential for parliamentary control of the executive was greatly enhanced. Select committees have become, in the words of the 1995 Report of the Standing Orders Committee, the 'workhorses' of Parliament.[4] In 1994–95, the subject committees met for a total of 1359 hours and twelve minutes; each committee met for an average of 113 hours.[5] MMP should make the select committee system of the New Zealand Parliament even more significant in the system of government.

The functions of select committees in the New Zealand Parliament are:

- *To examine bills:* all bills stand referred to a select committee for consideration after the second reading, except those to which urgency is accorded by the House, and Appropriation and Imprest Supply Bills;

---

3 433 *New Zealand Parliamentary Debates*, p.3042.
4 *Report of the Standing Orders Committee on the Review of Standing Orders*, I.18A *Appendices to the Journal of the House of Representatives*, Wellington, 1995, p.31.
5 *Ibid.*, p.36.

As is explained further in Chapter 9, this involves scrutinising bills that have been introduced, reading or hearing submissions from the public on them, considering departmental reports, making amendments to the bills, and reporting them back to the House for further consideration. New Zealand goes further than other Commonwealth Parliaments in providing such extensive consideration of legislation with systematic public input. As was pointed out in 1995, 'Governments are coming to rely on the Select Committee system to provide for the public discussion and refinement of the legislation.'[6]

- *Inquiries:* to monitor and conduct special investigations into the policy, administration, and expenditure of government agencies (including Crown entities).

Select committees are empowered to initiate their own inquiries. They are not dependent on receiving a direction from the House of Representatives itself. Terms of reference are formulated and advertised and submissions may be requested. Particular state agencies will be asked to appear before the committee to provide information and to be questioned. A good example of such an inquiry is the one that the Justice and Law Reform Committee completed in 1995 into the Race Relations Conciliator.[7] The report canvassed various administrative and policy issues that had arisen in relation to the office. It produced a lengthy report that was highly critical of several aspects of the management of the office and the administrative decisions taken. This caused the government to review aspects of the organisation of the office and its relationship with the Human Rights Commission.

Select committees can inquire into virtually any subject of government policy, expenditure, and administration, and the decision whether to conduct such an inquiry will depend upon how important and politically significant the committee members consider the topic to be. Whether the recommendations made are taken up will be a question for the government, although it is obliged by standing orders to make a formal response to such select committee reports and the recommendations not more than ninety days after the report has been presented to the House.

- *Financial scrutiny.* As outlined in Chapter 6, the estimates of expenditure accompany the annual Budget statement by the Minister of Finance. The Budget and the estimates stand referred to the Finance and Expenditure Select Committee, which may examine each particular vote itself or refer it to any of the subject select committees for examination. There is a debate in the House on the estimates where issues relating to particular votes or expenditures can be

---

6 *Ibid.*, p.31.

7 *Report of the Justice and Law Reform Committee Inquiry into the Race Relations Conciliator*, 1.7A *Appendices to the Journal of the House of Representatives*, Wellington, 1995.

raised. The standing orders now provide for the Finance and Expenditure Committee to conduct or allocate to the other committees the task of conducting a financial review of the performance and current operations of each individual department, office of Parliament, Crown entity, public organisation, or state-owned enterprise. There is also an opportunity to debate these in the House.

- *Consideration of petitions* presented to the House. As noted earlier in this chapter, select committees also consider petitions.

The balance of work of a particular select committee will vary from year to year depending largely on how many bills are to be considered. Some committees, such as Justice and Law Reform are likely to have a heavy legislative load. Others, such as Foreign Affairs, Defence, and Trade, will usually have a lighter legislative load, leaving more time for inquiries. But all subject committees will have a mix of legislative, inquiry, and appropriation work. In 1994–95 committees spent 50 per cent of their time on legislative scrutiny.

There are currently twelve standing select committees organised around areas of government activity determined by ministerial portfolio. They are:

- *The Commerce Committee:* commerce, communications, energy, regional development, and tourism;
- *The Education and Science Committee:* education, science, and technology, including all Crown research institutes;
- *The Finance and Expenditure Committee* (FEC): government finance, insurance, superannuation, taxation, and the auditing of the Crown's financial statements and departmental financial statements. This committee has a number of unique functions. In addition to the functions related to the estimates and to entities' financial performance noted above, the FEC examines and reports on the Crown's annual financial statements and the report of the Auditor-General on those statements, the annual Budget policy statement and fiscal strategy report, and Reserve Bank monetary policy statements;
- *The Foreign Affairs, Defence and Trade Committee:* customs, defence, foreign affairs, and trade;
- *The Government Administration Committee:* central government advisory services, official information, security intelligence, statistics, and services to Parliament;
- *The Health Committee:* health.
- *The Internal Affairs and Local Government Committee:* internal affairs and local government, including consideration of all local bills;
- *The Justice and Law Reform Committee:* corrections, courts, Crown legal services, justice, police, privacy, and serious fraud;
- *The Maori Affairs Committee:* Maori affairs;

- *The Primary Production Committee:* agriculture, fishing, and forestry;
- *The Social Services Committee:* employment, housing, immigration, labour, and social welfare;
- *The Transport and Environment Committee:* conservation, construction and development, environment, land information, surveying, transport, and transport safety.

There are some other standing specialised committees:

- *The Business Committee.* As discussed in the previous chapter, the Business Committee has a vital role in determining the business of the House, the manner of its organisation, and the membership of the select committees.
- *The Regulations Review Committee.* As discussed further in Chapter 10, the Regulations Review Committee examines and reports to the House on regulations—subordinate legislation made by the executive under the authority of an Act of Parliament. The committee is an important curb on executive power.
- *The Privileges Committee.* This committee sits as required to determine questions of privilege, as discussed later in this chapter.
- *The Officers of Parliament Committee.* This committee supervises the work of the officers of Parliament, dealing with their appropriations and related functions.

The House retains the power to set up other select committees and it often does so for special purposes. The proceedings of all committees are open to the public and the media during the hearing of evidence, including submissions from government departments. There is special provision for evidence to be taken in private by unanimous agreement of the committee. The same requirement is necessary for evidence to remain secret. All committees have identical powers to travel round New Zealand to hear submissions. They have the power to call for persons, papers, and records to be placed before them. They may carry out their functions through subcommittees. They must observe those rules of natural justice that are now prescribed in the standing orders.

The enlarged Parliament has enabled the membership of select committees to be increased from five MPs to eight, which is of considerable benefit to the operations of the committees themselves. Membership of these committees reflects the balance of the parties in the House but it is ultimately determined by the House on the recommendation of the Business Committee. A select committee may, in its report, indicate the differing views of members—in effect, set out minority views.

Ministers are no longer members of the subject select committees, although they figure prominently on the Privileges Committee, which includes the most senior members of the House. This was done in an attempt to separate the executive from the parliamentary function. In an MMP Parliament, this is likely to be a significant factor in holding ministers accountable to Parliament. They are likely to be expected to appear personally in front of select committees and explain their policies and their decisions. Already, the Minister of Finance appears in front of the Finance and Expenditure Committee to explain his or her thinking about the forthcoming Budget, as set out in the Budget policy statement required to be tabled before the end of March each year. There is also a growing practice of committees requesting ministers to appear before them with regard to their estimates of expenditure.

As the inquiry function of committees develops further in an MMP environment, the actions of public servants are likely to come under increased scrutiny. Public servants have traditionally provided information and advice to select committees—'serviced' them—in relation to legislation with which their department is particularly concerned. But the constitutional convention of ministerial responsibility is clear that, in performing both these functions, public servants are acting on behalf of their minister. Sometimes, when select committees are concerned with policy or politics, it will be more appropriate for public servants to refer questions to their ministers. It is also possible that ministers may instruct their public servants not to help select committees in certain ways or regarding certain matters. This then becomes an issue between the committee and the minister.

Under a minority government, or when a coalition does not have an agreed policy on an issue, a government may not automatically be able to command the numbers in the House to secure agreement to its policies. This is one of the essential differences that MMP causes in our constitution. Government policies may have to be the subject of amendment and alteration in order to secure the necessary support if they are to gain parliamentary approval. Often the most convenient forum for hammering out such arrangements will be the select committee, where the issues are being considered. The membership of the committees reflects the distribution of party support in the House. This may lead the relationship between committees, ministers, and public servants to become strained. If this happens too frequently, select committees will probably push for more independent resources and advisers to assist them in holding the executive to account. Select committees may, however, emerge as very significant places for policies to be brokered; they will have looked at the public submissions and heard the views of all the parties represented on the committee. Among the fascinating issues raised by MMP, none will be more important than to try to chart how the select committee system evolves in the new parliamentary environment.

PARLIAMENTARY PRIVILEGE

Parliamentary privilege is an ancient and extensive branch of the law and custom of Parliament. Under section 242 of the Legislature Act 1908, the New Zealand

House of Representatives enjoys the same privileges as the British House of Commons enjoyed on 1 January 1865. Although it seldom exercises them, privilege gives Parliament great powers and their unlimited character gives rise to constitutional difficulties, which have been debated in New Zealand in recent years. Parliamentary privilege is in the words of one English authority, 'exceptional, peculiar and discretionary'.[8]

The essence of parliamentary privilege is the freedom of the House of Representatives to conduct its proceedings without interference by the Crown, the courts, or bodies outside Parliament. The struggles of Parliament in the United Kingdom against the Crown were embodied in the Bill of Rights 1688, which is part of New Zealand law and which provides, in Article 9: 'That the freedom of speech and debates or proceedings in Parliament, ought not to be impeached or questioned in any court or place out of Parliament.'[9]

This was designed to protect freedom of speech—obviously an important value in the functioning of the country's central democratic institution. The New Zealand Bill of Rights Act 1990, which protects certain fundamental rights and freedoms, also declares that the legislature is bound by the provisions of the act. It can be strongly argued that the law relating to parliamentary privilege in New Zealand is in breach of some of the requirements of the New Zealand Bill of Rights Act. These are complicated issues that cannot be considered here, but we expect further changes to the law of parliamentary privilege in New Zealand.

The manner in which these matters have developed in New Zealand, however, has left the law relating to parliamentary privilege with some oppressive features which, in 1995, the Parliament moved to improve. Among the problems were:

- the uncertain scope and range of parliamentary privilege;
- the existence of power in Parliament to fine or imprison and otherwise punish for contempt;
- lack of protection for the rights of strangers to Parliament who become enmeshed in its proceedings;
- the fact that select committees did not appear to be obliged to follow the rules of natural justice when dealing with matters that could damage individuals;
- the fact that individuals were increasingly being named in the House and attacked by MPs and there was no right of reply in respect of such attacks.

Allegations that have been made in recent years include the following:

- that a businessman attempted to buy political support by offering donations;

---

8 O. Hood Phillips, *Constitutional and Administrative Law*, 4th ed., Sweet & Maxwell, London, p.168.

9 The Privy Council examined the range of parliamentary privilege in *Prebble* v. *TVNZ* [1993] 3 *NZLR* 513 in a decision that dealt with article 9 of the Bill of Rights 1688.

- that a named solicitor systematically fleeced a friendly society;
- that well-known business figures have been guilty of tax evasion and conspiracy to defraud;
- that named legal firms have approved and participated in criminal fraud;
- that senior named government officials have failed in their duties and should be charged with conspiracy to pervert the course of justice.

One important principle is that people who are accused of criminal behaviour should be tried in the courts. Specific charges should be laid. If the charge is serious, there is a right under the law to a jury trial. Being tried before a parliamentary select committee brings elements of politics into the equation; it is not the appropriate forum for dealing with such matters.

In 1996 some important developments occurred in New Zealand on issues of privilege. Mr S.J. Cushing brought a case against the Hon. Winston Peters. He sued Mr Peters in the District Court for defamation and succeeded in obtaining damages. Mr Peters' defence was based on the fact that he had not named Mr Cushing in any statements he made outside the House, but had named him only in the House; he argued that he could not be sued for what was said in the House. The District Court judge took the view that the statement made by Mr Peters in the House could be used for the purposes of the law of defamation as identifying the person about whom Mr Peters was speaking outside the House. Mr Peters had raised with the Privileges Committee of Parliament the fact that he was being sued for what was apparently said in the House, but the committee recommended to the House that it should not intervene in the proceedings and it did not do so. The Privileges Committee took the view that the matter should be argued out in the courts which would be well aware of the arguments based on Article 9 of the Bill of Rights 1688.[10]

A look at some of the cases of privilege dealt with by the New Zealand Parliament may show more clearly the nature of the problems.

- In 1896 the New Zealand House of Representatives fined a banker £500 for refusing to supply information asked for by a select committee. Journalists have also been fined on two occasions. It is doubtful that legal authority actually exists for the House to fine, although certainly there is power to imprison.
- In 1968 a newspaper headline 'Statistical Claim is Made that Four MPs in NZ are Probably Homosexual' was branded a breach of privilege, although, in view of the editor's expression of regret, no further action was taken.[11]

---

10 *Report of the Privileges Committee on the Question of Privilege* referred on 11 June 1996 concerning the action *Cushing* v. *Peters* in the District Court at Wellington, New Zealand, I.15A *Appendices to the Journal of the House of Representatives*, Wellington, 1996.

11 358 *New Zealand Parliamentary Debates*, p.2725.

- Several cases where publication in the news media of what occurred in select committee hearings not open to the public have been held a breach of privilege.
- An editorial saying that the Speaker of the House was willing to permit derogatory interjections based on racial prejudice and that he would not intervene to stop them was declared to be a serious breach of privilege and the editor was censured, although no further action was taken when the editor expressed his regret.
- Statements in a television interview with the transvestite, Carmen, in which it was alleged that one MP was a homosexual and a number were bisexual, were held to be breach of privilege. The House expressed its strong disapproval and reprimanded Carmen, but took no further action.

The Privileges Committee of Parliament deals with cases where the Speaker finds, upon a complaint made by a member, that there is a prima facie breach of privilege that ought to be examined. The committee attempts to conduct the inquiry as fairly as possible, and in accordance with normal judicial principles. When a matter has been referred by the Speaker, the committee meets to formulate a charge so that the person involved may know with some precision what he or she is being accused of. The committee allows people to be represented by counsel. During hearings witnesses are examined on oath by committee members.

Where an MP wishes to raise a question of privilege, it must be referred, in writing, as soon as possible, to the Speaker, who then rules whether a question of privilege is involved. Where the issue involves another member of the House, the member raising the matter must fully inform the other member of the matter.

Standing Order 387 provides that the Speaker, in considering whether a matter constitutes a question of privilege, 'takes account of the degree of importance of the matter'. A question of privilege is not involved if 'the matter is technical or trivial and does not warrant the further attention of the House'.

In 1995 the standing orders were changed to ensure that a member who makes an allegation of breach of privilege may not serve on an inquiry into that allegation. Attempts were also made to clarify what amounts to a contempt of the House. Standing Order 392 says that the House may treat as a contempt any act or omission which:

(a) obstructs or impedes the House in the performance of its functions, or
(b) obstructs or impedes any member or officer of the House in the discharge of the member's or the officer's duty, or
(c) has a tendency, directly or indirectly, to produce such a result.

Because these tests are vague, an effort has been made to spell out some examples of contempts in order to illuminate the concept. For example, deliberately attempting to mislead the House or a committee is a contempt. So is offering bribes to members (which is also a breach of ordinary criminal law). Refusing to answer a question or provide information required by the House or a committee is another example. So is disobeying an order of the House.

The 1995 Standing Orders made two other important reforms that impinge upon privilege. Where a stranger to the House has been referred to in the House by name or in such a way as to be readily identifiable, the person may make a submission to the Speaker in writing:

(a) claiming to have been adversely affected by the reference or to have suffered damage to their reputation as a result of the reference;
(b) submitting a response to the reference; and
(c) requesting that the response be incorporated in the parliamentary record.

Such a submission must be made within three months of the reference having been made, it must be succinct, and it must not contain anything offensive. The Speaker then considers the matter and may decide to have it incorporated in the parliamentary record. In doing this he or she makes no judgment as to the truth of the reference made in the House, or the response.

Requirements are also imposed on select committees to ensure that they respect the rights of people. A committee may not inquire into or make findings in respect of allegations of crime by persons who are named or otherwise identifiable, without the express authority of the House. MPs who have made allegations of crime or expressed a concluded view on any conduct or activity of a criminal nature may not participate in any select committee inquiry into that person's responsibility. Both MPs and those appearing before the committee may make complaints about the apparent bias of any MP.

The standing orders also now provide that at any stage during a select committee's proceedings it may consider hearing, in private, evidence that may contain allegations against or seriously damage the reputation of a person. The committee may also invite that person to be present during the hearing of such evidence. Any person who claims that his or her reputation may be seriously damaged by the proceedings of a select committee may make written submissions and the committee may invite such a person to give evidence orally. Such people will be informed of or given copies of any evidence that may seriously damage their reputation and will be given a reasonable opportunity to respond. Such a person may ask that further witnesses be called in his or her interest. Where evidence is given or a statement is made that contains allegations against or that may seriously damage the reputation of a person, the committee is now obliged to inform that person of the evidence or statement and to give him or her a reasonable opportunity to respond by written submission or appearance. A person whose reputation may be seriously damaged by the proceedings of a select committee may request from the clerk of the committee a copy of all the material concerning him or her. The committee may furnish such material if it considers this necessary to prevent serious damage to the person's reputation.

These changes have done much to reduce the risk of abuse of Parliament's power against citizens. But standing orders are not the law of the land. They are rules governing Parliament's conduct that can be changed at any time. Parliament's powers of privilege remain legally unlimited and potentially draconian, in line with the doctrine of parliamentary sovereignty. Parliament retains the power to imprison. It can be argued that further reform is needed, that Parliament should lose its exceptional and anomalous powers and should lose its ability to punish strangers for contempt. There is a good argument for transferring these matters to the ordinary courts. It may no longer be generally acceptable for the House of Representatives to be the sole judge of the extent of its own privileges. If the power of parliamentary privilege were dealt with by statute, it would give the courts power to interpret that statute and declare what the law is.

9 Legislation

INTRODUCTION

To legislate means to make laws. Legislation is the enactments of a legislator or legislature—Parliament. The power to legislate is one of the most fundamental constitutional powers of a civil society and issues relating to its location and processes are of the greatest importance. As the New Zealand Law Commission said in 1990: 'Legislation is central to our legal system. It is the principal source of new law. It has an essential and pervasive role in our national life.'[1]

Under section 15 of the Constitution Act 1986, Parliament in New Zealand has as one of its prime constitutional functions 'full power to make laws'. The laws it makes are called statutes, or acts of Parliament. Before they are passed by Parliament, draft acts are called bills. Acts are the most important laws, but they are not the only laws.

Most acts of Parliament contain authority for the Governor-General in council to make laws called regulations to deal with matters of detail that may be necessary for an act to operate. Often, quite important matters are contained in regulations. They are made by the executive branch of government, not by Parliament; though Parliament maintains oversight of them and can, if it considers it necessary, disallow them under the Regulations (Disallowance) Act 1989. So important are regulations that we have reserved a separate chapter for them—Chapter 10. There are also laws made by local authorities, called by-laws, and some other entities have power to make laws of this character.

Another important source of our law is the common law, which consists of judge-made rules built up over the years by judges in New Zealand, as influenced by such rules developed in other common law jurisdictions such as Australia, Britain, Canada, and the United States. Common law is based on a system of precedent and it governs many important matters in the law relating to government.

---

1 Law Commission, *Report No. 17: A New Interpretation Act To Avoid 'Prolixity and Tautology'*, Wellington, 1990, p.1.

For example, the law relating to the royal prerogative is common law. So are the bulk of the administrative law rules concerning judicial review of administrative action.

In this chapter we focus on legislation and its intricacies. As President Woodrow Wilson wrote, when he was still a professor at Princeton, '[o]nce begin the dance of legislation, and you must struggle through its mazes as best you can to its breathless end—if any end there be.'[2] The dance of legislation is intricate. Each bill is a different dance, each dance has many different steps and, under MMP, even different partners. The dance requires perseverance, stamina, and a large degree of esoteric knowledge. The purpose of the process is not to provide an obstacle course for good ideas but to provide checks and balances and quality controls and democratic scrutiny of the content of new legislation.

MMP adds to the complexity of the legislative processes and provides new mazes though which a bill must travel on its journey to becoming an act of Parliament. The biggest change to the legislative process resulting from MMP is likely to be a lessening in executive control over the content of legislation passed by Parliament, especially under a minority government. The character of legislation may change—it may be harder to pass controversial legislation but easier to pass technical, uncontroversial bills. It is also likely that less legislation will pass in MMP Parliaments than has been the case in modern times. Many would welcome such a result, given that New Zealand has tended to pass too many laws and pass them too quickly.

TOO MUCH LAW?

Many countries have a Parliament with two chambers and any bill must pass through them both in order to become law. Many countries also have formal constitutional limits on what matters may be legislated. Others allow legislation to be determined by the legislature itself, whereas in New Zealand the traditional pattern has been that, to a large extent, the executive determines the content of legislation. These factors have combined to produce the charge by many that New Zealand suffers from hyperlexis—an overactive law-making gland. Certainly the sheer quantity of legislation in New Zealand is impressive.

One school of thought says that our fast law-making procedures allow our laws to be kept up to date easily and encourage a flexible approach. The other view is that the speed and simplicity of our legislative procedures have traditionally made it too easy for the executive branch of government to do what it likes, to take power that it does not really need, and to smother us all in red tape. Both views contain important elements of truth. It is all a question of balance. Statistics

---

2 W. Wilson, *Congressional Government: A Study in American Politics*, 15th ed., (originally published 1885), Johns Hopkins University Press, Baltimore, Maryland, p.397.

alone do not say everything about the bulk of New Zealand legislation. Not all acts of Parliament are long and complex, although many of them are. And many of the acts passed by the New Zealand Parliament each year are amending acts, patching up anomalies that have been discovered or making provision for new policies and developments. But to give some impression of the volume of New Zealand legislation, Tables 9.1 and 9.2 show the pattern:

Table 9.1 Numbers of acts and regulations

Year	*Total number of acts passed*	*Days Parliament sat*	*Total number of regulations passed*
1956	123	67	224
1957	124	80	281
1966	140	78	222
1967	182	99	289
1976	182	96	332
1977	206	118	340
1985	219	104	343
1986	154	81	383
1994	179	77	287
1995	108	79	328

Table 9.2 Printed pages of acts and regulations

Year	*Acts*	*Regulations*
1956	1355	1202
1957	1173	1134
1966	1969	1339
1967	1563	1942
1976	2361	1960
1977	2872	1526
1985	1587	1649
1986	1584	2108
1994	4295	1650
1995	1332	2823

As well as the new law that is added each year, there is the law that remains from previous years. There are more than 600 general acts in force in New Zealand, including a number originally passed in London. There are 2000 local acts (that relate to a particular locality) and private acts (that relate to a particular person, group, or corporation). And there are something like 4000 regulations. It is a lot of law to understand and follow. The conscientious citizen wishing to read his or her legal obligations would read for a long time. In 1990, the Law Commission estimated that around 4000 new pages are added to the volumes of legislation each year, subordinate as well as primary.

In 1978 Sir Kenneth Keith gave a graphic description of the bulk of the New Zealand statute book:

> The New Zealand Statute book is enormous. It now runs to well over 60 volumes of an average of 800 pages each. In 1931, 29 volumes were consolidated into eight volumes (which were annotated and had an index volume), in 1957 those eight volumes plus a further 33 were reprinted in 16 volumes and in the last 19 years we have had a further 54 volumes. There is some relevant legislation not included in those volumes—including applicable British statutes. Not every page of those 70 volumes—which must contain something like 15,000,000 words—is still part of the law; indeed a few volumes are completely superseded. The basic 1957 reprint does however still contain much extant material—about one third of the more than 600 principal public Acts which are in force.[3]

Since that time the quantity has increased. We can read today with a wry smile the complaints which were made about inadequate consideration of legislation in New Zealand nearly fifty years ago. In 1932 the editor of the *New Zealand Law Journal* wrote:[4]

> We have recently witnessed our Parliament spending 11 weeks in session. At the end of 10 weeks, five new legislative enactments were added to the Statute book. Then, after setting out to break previously deplorable records with a last minute endurance test of continuous sitting—with only intervals for meals, for even legislators must feed—four days' sitting resulted in the passing of seven Acts, containing nearly 200 clauses, all of a highly technical nature and most of them of far-reaching importance.
>
> The system is entirely wrong and fraught with all kinds of danger and possibility of injustice. The time has long since passed when proposed legislation should be available for a reasonable period before its final consideration by Parliament.

New Zealanders tend to exhibit an innocent and misplaced faith in the efficacy of legislation. We also undervalue the importance to the community of good law flowing from good law-making procedures. We seem to be addicted to passing legislation for the sake of it, and to believe that legislation can cure our innermost ills. This superfluity of legislation is in part a response to political demands. The government must be seen to be reacting; if it passes a law it can be said to be doing something. In response to other pressures, legislation is passed for which there is no legal need. As a respected New Zealand judge, Sir Alexander Turner, wrote in 1980: 'The belief is widely held, that there is no human situation so bad but that legislation properly designed will effectively be able to cure it.'[5]

Some legislation results from pressure groups that wish to enhance their status

---

3 K.J. Keith, 'A Lawyer Looks at Parliament', in *The Reform of Parliament*, New Zealand Institute of Public Administration, ed. J. Marshall, Wellington, 1978, p.26.

4 'Hasty Legislation: A Wrong System', 8 *New Zealand Law Journal*, 1932, p.117.

5 A. Turner, 'Steering the ship of state—functions of Parliament', 10 *Victoria University of Wellington Law Review*, 1980, p.209.

by legislation, for example, the Music Teachers Act 1981. For many occupational groups it is not the public interest that requires legislation, but their own private interest. Music teachers had had an act since 1928. Because only about 1500 music teachers were registered and thousands of others were not, they wanted compulsory registration, but the government was not prepared to allow that policy. There was no rational analysis about the need for this law, which was unnecessary. The music teachers could have formed an incorporated society under the Incorporated Societies Act and done all the things that were being done under the act. There was no need to change the law of New Zealand to accomplish the teachers' aims. They wanted the legislation, however, because they had some already, they wanted it to confer status, and they wanted it because it might have been a step towards compulsory registration. The economic purpose of such legislation would be to restrict competition and the public interest would clearly not be served by such statutory interventions. But many of the pressures to pass law are like these and they have to be carefully examined. The lesson is quite simple. The basic question in respect of every proposed bill should be, *why is this law necessary?*

There are a good many things about which it is better not to legislate. Legislation gives the state its legitimate authority to exercise its coercive powers over citizens and it should not be entered into lightly. The wholesale creation of new criminal offences in an effort to regulate behaviour often creates great problems in law enforcement and leads to community disrespect for the law. New Zealanders have failed to appreciate the limits on legal sanctions as a means of ordering society; moral purity cannot be brought about by legislation. Not only should we pass fewer laws, we should go through the statute book and see what can be cut out.

The dangers that flow from the rapid passing of legislation are obvious enough:

- legislation is not sufficiently scrutinised to detect flaws, omissions, and anomalies;
- there is not enough time for the public to participate in the parliamentary process by making their views known;
- inadequate scrutiny produces more amending legislation later on;
- Parliament, as the people's watchdog, is brought into public disrepute and people lose faith in it;
- changes in the law come less to the attention of the public;
- the passage of law comes to depend less on reasoned argument;
- the law itself is brought into disrepute.

By 1996, however, it can be said that the legislative process has been reformed quite drastically and there is now a much better opportunity to scrutinise legislation effectively before it is enacted. MMP is likely to make the passage of legislation more difficult because it will require a greater degree of consensus. This will ensure that MPs think twice before embarking on legislation. It may cause more rigorous examination of whether a statute is really needed and what other non-legislative options may be available.

THE LEGISLATIVE PROCESS WITHIN THE EXECUTIVE

Issues relating to legislation in New Zealand have been examined closely by the Legislation Advisory Committee (LAC), a standing committee established in 1986 comprising experts drawn from the legal profession, the academic world, and government. The LAC has a close association with both the Law Commission and the Ministry of Justice, but acts independently of government.

In 1996, the LAC's terms of reference are:

- to scrutinise and make submissions to the appropriate body or person (usually a select committee) upon aspects of bills introduced to Parliament affecting public law or raising public law issues;
- to report to the Minister of Justice or the Cabinet Committee on Legislation and House Business (LEG) on aspects of legislative proposals referred to it by the minister or the committee; and
- to advise the Minister of Justice on such other topics and matters in the field of public law as the minister from time to time refers to it.

In particular, the LAC concentrates on ensuring that adequate protection is given to an individual dealing with a government agency or personally affected by the operation of an act. Some examples are: licensing procedures, adequate rights of appeal, avoiding the creation of wide, subjective powers exercisable by officials, and checking that powers of entry are justified and appropriately cast.

The LAC is sometimes involved in legislation before it is introduced but in recent years most of its work has centered on making submissions to parliamentary select committees. The LAC has shown it can do much to provide a systematic monitoring of the quality of our legislation, though limited resources mean that its scrutiny is limited only to those bills it considers most in need of examination. In 1995 it made submissions to select committees regarding thirty-seven bills.

One of the LAC's most important functions has been to formulate a document entitled *Legislative Change—Guidelines on Process and Content.*[6] This has been endorsed by the Cabinet as the Bible, in conjunction with Chapter 5 of the *Cabinet Office Manual*, on legislative process within government. Unfortunately, the LAC guidelines frequently are not followed and it is a continuing struggle to try to maintain the quality of legislation.

The LAC guidelines point out, sensibly, that the rules for the functioning of our society are increasingly found in legislation—the criminal law and electoral

6 *Report No. 6*, rev. ed., Wellington, 1991.

law, for example, and the rules for regulating relations between individuals, such as family law and the law of contract; regulating of activities in modern industrial society, such as safety rules and industrial relations; rules relating to health education and welfare; and laws relating to business and taxes. The report goes on to point out that new legislation needs to be effective and must be as understandable and accessible as possible.

The LAC formulated nine general questions that must be asked about all legislative proposals. These have been updated and integrated into a required format for submissions to LEG to be given a priority on the government's legislative programme. The resulting 'Format for Submissions to LEG on Draft Bills Ready for Introduction' in Appendix 6 of the 1996 *Cabinet Office Manual* is a useful checklist for anyone in scrutinising a bill or act and is reproduced in full here:

OFFICE OF THE MINISTER OF [XX]

TITLE [Give the full title of the draft Bill]

1 **Proposal**

Briefly state what is proposed in the paper.

2 **Policy**

a Briefly summarise the policy to be implemented in the Bill. (Give references and dates of key Cabinet and Cabinet committee decisions.)

b Indicate any aspects of the Bill which are likely to be contentious.

c Explain why a Bill is required.

d Indicate any outstanding policy issues and explain why these have not yet been resolved.

3 **Compliance**

Indicate whether the Bill complies with each of the following, with reasons if the Bill does not comply (list each sub-heading):

a The principles of the Treaty of Waitangi

b New Zealand Bill of Rights Act 1990

c The principles and guidelines set out in the Privacy Act 1991. (If the Bill raises privacy issues, indicate whether the Privacy Commissioner agrees that it complies with all relevant principles.)

d Relevant international standards and obligations.

e Guidelines in the Legislation Advisory Committee report, *Legislative Change: Guidelines on Process and Content* (revised edition, 1991).

4 **Consultation**

Summarise the consultation that has taken place under the following categories, as well as the results of that consultation:

a Relevant government departments or other public bodies
b Relevant private sector organisations and public consultation processes
c Government caucus(es) and other parties represented in Parliament.

5 Creating New Agencies or Amending Law Relating to Existing Agencies

a If the legislation will create a new agency, will the Ombudsmen Act 1975 and the Official Information Act 1982 apply? If not, why not? (The Office of the Ombudsman should be consulted on this issue and its views summarised.)

b If the legislation will create a new agency that is legally separate from the Crown, will it be included as a Crown entity in the Fourth Schedule to the Public Finance Act 1989 and, as appropriate, in the Fifth, Sixth and Seventh Schedules? If not, why not? (The Treasury should be consulted on this issue and its views summarised.)

c If the legislation will amend the existing coverage of the Ombudsmen Act 1975, the Official Information Act 1982 or the Local Government Official Information and Meetings Act 1987, explain why. (The Office of the Ombudsman should be consulted on this issue and its views summarised.)

6 Allocation of Decision-Making Powers

a Does the draft legislation involve the allocation of decision-making powers between the executive, the courts and tribunals?

b Have the criteria relating to the qualifications and responsibilities of decision-makers and the procedures they follow (set out in paragraphs 65–84 of Legislation Advisory Committee, *Legislative Change: Guidelines on Process and Content* (revised edition, 1991) been applied?

c If not, state departures from the criteria and reasons for these.

7 Associated Regulations

Will regulations be needed to bring the Bill into operation? If so, briefly summarise the regulations which will be needed, their likely timing (taking into account the 28-day rule), and the likely size of the drafting task involved in developing them.

8 Definition of Minister/Department

Does the Bill contain a definition of Minister, department (or equivalent government agency), or chief executive of a department (or equivalent position)? (The Cabinet Office should be consulted on this issue and its views summarised.)

9 Parliamentary Stages

a Indicate the date by which the Bill should be introduced and the date by which it should be passed.

b Indicate the Select Committee to which it is proposed that the Bill be referred.

10 Recommendations

The basic format for recommendations in submissions for approval of a Bill for introduction is as follows:

'I recommend that the Committee:

a note that the [XX] Bill holds priority XX on the legislation programme;

b note that the Bill . . . [briefly summarise the main purpose of the Bill];

c approve for introduction the [xx] Bill;

d agree that the Bill be:

(i) introduced on [date];

(ii) referred to the [xx] Committee for consideration;

(iii) enacted by [date].

[signature of Minister]
[name and title of Minister]

At present, most legislative proposals are prepared within the executive government by officials in the department within which the topic falls. Although, under MMP, it is likely that members' bills will be more seriously dealt with and passed more often than in the past, especially under minority governments, it is still likely that most legislation will be initiated by the government.

The government's involvement with legislation is managed at ministerial level by the Cabinet Committee on Legislation and House Business (LEG) and confirmed by the full Cabinet. LEG's functions are:

- to make recommendations to Cabinet on the government's legislation programme;
- to determine the drafting priority to be accorded to individual proposals;
- to examine draft bills to ensure that their policy content has been approved by the appropriate Cabinet committee and that relevant requirements of the *Cabinet Office Manual* have been satisfied; and
- to authorise for reference to Cabinet draft bills and amendments to bills and to coordinate the passage of government legislation through the House.

LEG meets each week to approve bills for introduction and to discuss questions relating to legislation with parliamentary counsel and officials. The legislative programme is the government's legislative plans and priorities. Each parliamentary term, usually early in the year (and at the end of each calendar year), the Cabinet Office invites ministers to submit bids for the programme. The ministers do this in consultation with their officials and all bids are then forwarded to LEG, which discusses the bids from each minister and arrives at a set of priorities that is then approved by Cabinet. The resulting document is known as the legislative programme and current practice is to keep it confidential to the government.

The priorities established determine the order in which government bills are drafted. Drafting of bills, except for tax bills, is carried out by professional lawyers appointed for that purpose in the Parliamentary Counsel Office and known as parliamentary counsel. But no drafting can take place until the department has prepared drafting instructions and the necessary Cabinet approvals have been given. Departmental solicitors prepare instructions for parliamentary counsel, which should be written in ordinary narrative prose and not in the form of a draft bill. Whatever form they are initially formulated in, parliamentary counsel must go through an elaborate process to ensure that a bill is free from defects.

A great deal of pressure is generated within government for the rapid production of bills. Each minister and department always think their own bill is the most important. But sometimes circumstances change so that a bill that seemed urgent when the programme was settled later turns out to be quite unnecessary and does not proceed. In contrast, items that were never even included in the programme can later assume great importance and must be given top priority. Politics is about priorities and bills are the legislative vehicles for political programmes. The management of the legislative programme of the government, therefore, requires continuous and careful attention. Hitches and anomalies in the law are often found that are thought to require urgent repair. Because there is so much law to draft, priorities often mean that some measures are not reached for years.

So that as many anomalies as possible can be ironed out of the legislation before its introduction, printed copies of draft bills are circulated within the executive. This has two advantages. First, it enables the sponsoring department to secure the agreement of other affected departments or parties. Second, it reduces the number of potential embarrassments by removing the mistakes or oversights. By the time the bill is actually introduced to the House, it has already been widely discussed, negotiated and thought about within the government. As a result, many public servants outside Parliament are far better informed about the detailed provisions in a bill than are the parliamentarians formally in charge of passing it. Usually, the executive branch of government has taken a stance on the legislation before the public has a chance to consider it. In the course of this process, the minister often becomes committed to important details. The Cabinet itself will have considered the legislation before its introduction, as will the government caucus.

In the past, this consideration used to take place in secret, but MMP has introduced much more emphasis on consultation into policy-making processes—not only with all relevant government agencies, but also with relevant interest groups and with other political parties. The acceptability of legislation can be influenced significantly by those in the community most directly affected by the proposed measures.

THE LEGISLATIVE PROCESS IN PARLIAMENT

Government bills are introduced into the House by ministers, but other members of Parliament can introduce bills too. A bill may be introduced as:

- *a government bill:* dealing with a matter of public policy introduced by a Minister;
- *a member's bill:* dealing with a matter of public policy introduced by a member who is not a minister;
- *a local bill:* a bill promoted by a local authority that affects a particular area only;
- *a private bill:* a bill promoted by a person or body of people for the particular interest or benefit of that person or group.

A bill must relate to one subject area only, although the standing orders sometimes permit omnibus bills, which make amendments to many different areas of the law. This restriction is designed to ensure that bills are not treated like a train to which separate and unrelated carriages are added for the legislative journey in a way that will impede public scrutiny and debate on the proposed law. The 1995 provisions in standing orders concerning omnibus bills will certainly cut down the opportunity for fast-tracking legislation through the House without allowing adequate scrutiny.

From the beginning of 1996, the legislative process in the New Zealand Parliament has been changed by drastic and enlightened revisions to Parliament's standing orders. The basic rule is that each bill must be read by the House three times in order to be passed. The processes are as follows:

Introduction and first reading

The Leader of the House informs the clerk by 1 p.m. on a sitting day of the government's intention to introduce a bill. Printed copies must be delivered to the clerk, who will circulate the bill to members. The first reading of bills takes place as the first order of general business each day but there is no debate and no vote at this stage.

In 1995, the Standing Orders Committee of Parliament called for the expansion and improvement of the explanatory notes that appear at the front of the bill when it is introduced. The committee recommended that these notes 'should include discussion on the policy the Minister or member in charge is intending to implement through legislation and matters it is intended be remedied. They should cover issues that would be included in the present introductory speech.'[7] Following that practice should allow for a much more informed parliamentary and public debate on a bill.

---

[7] *Report of the Standing Orders Committee on the Review of Standing Orders*, I.18A *Appendices to the Journal of the House of Representatives*, Wellington, 1995, p.54.

Whenever a bill contains any provision that the Attorney-General feels is inconsistent with any of the rights and freedoms contained in the New Zealand Bill of Rights Act 1990 he or she must indicate to the House what the provision is and how it appears to be inconsistent. This must be done before the second reading and consideration of the bill by a select committee. This means that the committee can consider carefully whether the proposal merits Parliament overturning one of the fundamental rights and freedoms contained in the Bill of Rights.

Second reading

This is a debate in the full Parliament about the principles and objects of the bill. It takes place after MPs and the public have had the opportunity to get to grips with what is actually in the bill and think about it, but before select committee consideration. The second reading cannot ordinarily take place before the third sitting day following its introduction. The debate is limited to two hours, consisting of twelve speeches lasting ten minutes, unless the Business Committee decides otherwise.

Select committee consideration

A bill stands referred to a select committee unless the House has accorded urgency to its passing. The member in charge of the bill moves a motion nominating which committee will consider the bill after its second reading. Where a special committee is to be established for the purpose, notice must be given. Committees must examine bills to determine whether they should be passed in the form in which they have been introduced. The committee is empowered by the standing orders to recommend amendments to the bill, although these must be consistent with its principles and objects. A select committee may divide a bill into separate parts and report on them separately at different times.

The vital importance of select committee scrutiny in the New Zealand Parliament lies in the ample opportunity given to members of the public to make submissions on a bill. They can do so in writing, but they can also ask to be heard and almost invariably will be heard if they ask. Usually a minimum of four weeks is allowed for the preparation of submissions, although it is up to the committee and practice is flexible. Committees will often travel to different parts of New Zealand to hear submissions.

Since 1996, select committees have been obliged to report on a bill within six months, unless the time is extended by the House. This is designed to stop the previous practice of burying bills at select committee stage and taking no action on them. If a committee fails to report on time, then the bill is automatically set down for its next stage in the House. When the committee has completed its consideration, it will report the bill back to the House with its recommended amendments; it must distinguish between those amendments adopted unanimously and those adopted by a majority.

Consideration of select committee report

The select committee report is presented to the House in writing and is debated after MPs have had time to read and consider it. At the conclusion of the consideration of the final report on a bill, the Speaker asks that the amendments recommended by the committee by majority be agreed to. Then the question is put whether the bill should proceed. A debate on a select committee report can last up to two hours—twelve ten-minute speeches, unless the Business Committee decides otherwise.

An important innovation in the 1995 revision of standing orders was that, with any amendments a select committee makes to a bill, it should include an extensive commentary of what it did in considering the bill, how it conducted its proceedings, what it found, and other matters of concern. Committees must also show which amendments have been unanimously agreed and which amendments have been adopted by a majority. Unanimously agreed amendments are automatically adopted by the House when it decides that the bill should proceed. Those agreed by a majority have to be voted on by the House. These changes should make the legislative process more transparent and may induce more cooperative behaviour within committees.

Committee of the Whole House

The Business Committee may decide that a bill does not require consideration by the House sitting as the Committee of the Whole House (known as the committee stage). Otherwise the Committee of the Whole proceeds to examine the nuts and bolts of the bill to determine whether it properly incorporates the principles of the bill as read a second time by the House. Amendments may be made to each clause at the committee stage. For a government bill, a minister will often move a supplementary order paper (SOP) containing amendments designed to improve the bill from a technical and legal point of view. At this stage, too, a bill may also be divided up into separate bills if it lends itself to this treatment.

Once the Committee of the Whole has completed its consideration it will report the bill to the Speaker presiding in the House. In the Committee of the Whole, MPs may make multiple three-minute speeches, with ordinary members allowed three speeches on the short title of the bill and four speeches on other clauses or provision. Ministers are allowed more. But, again, the Business Committee may impose limited time debates at this stage or decide that the entire Committee of the Whole stage should be waived.

Third reading and passage

A bill can be recommitted to a Committee of the Whole House, although this does not often happen. It usually occurs where some oversight has been discovered that needs to be rectified. The whole debate on the third reading is limited to twelve speeches of ten minutes, a total of two hours unless otherwise determined by the Business Committee. Once the third reading debate is over and the motion agreed to, the bill has been read a third time and it is passed by the House. To become law, it needs only to be printed fair by direction of the clerk and presented to the Governor-General for the royal assent. In the course of this process the clerk can correct minor clerical and typographical errors. Once the bill has been signed into law, one copy is deposited with the Registrar of the High Court at Wellington and one is retained by the clerk. The new law will be printed and sold by the Government Printer.

There are small differences in parliamentary procedure for members' bills, local bills, and private bills. For private bills, which are relatively rare, usually no more than one or two a year, special procedures providing for the giving of notice, advertising, deposit, and inspection must be followed. There are also special procedures for local bills and local legislation bills, again dealing with notice, deposit, and inspection. Both these categories of bill can be introduced even though the House is adjourned and is not due to meet again within fourteen days and the bill appears to the clerk to comply with standing orders. With the agreement of the Business Committee, a government bill or a member's bill can be introduced the same way.

For members' bills and local bills there is a system of rationing. No more than three notices for the introduction of members' bills may be lodged on the same day. The clerk conducts a ballot to determine the order separately for local bills and members' bills. For members' bills the clerk rejects any notices above three. This rule, which is a great deal more liberal than it used to be, shows clearly that members' bills are a much more important part of the legislative process than the old private members' bills. Under MMP, particularly under a minority government, there is a much higher chance that such bills will be enacted. There is also provision for them to be taken over by the government and to advance as a government bill.

SELECT COMMITTEE SCRUTINY

One of the most important features of the legislative process in recent years has been the stronger role being played by the select committees of Parliament in the content of legislation. In 1978 twenty-six bills were referred to select committees; in eighteen cases, hearings were open to the news media. In 1986, eighty-three bills were referred to select committees, and referral is now mandatory, except for bills introduced and passed under urgency as well as Appropriation and Imprest Supply Bills. And all committees are now automatically open to the public and the media. This mandatory referral was one of the principal recommendations of the first edition of this book in 1979 and it is a step that should do much to improve the quality of legislation passed by Parliament.

In his annual report tabled in Parliament in 1978, the Secretary for Justice observed:

> Our own experience is that Parliament through its Select Committee system is playing a larger role than formerly in the shaping of at least what may be called law reform legislation. In last year's report I adverted to the increasing tendency for interested groups or individuals to make submissions on a particular Bill. This is by no means confined to those whose interest is purely a matter of the pocket. I believe too that parliamentary committees are more ready than they were even a few years ago to alter Bills in details and in principles alike. This trend must be a source of gratification for those who wish to see our parliamentary system strengthened but I do not know that the public at large is fully aware of it.[8]

MPs feel that their most constructive legislative role occurs in select committees, as is indicated by the remarks Dr Martyn Finlay made when he retired from Parliament in 1978:

> In a committee, however, Opposition members should reconcile themselves to the inevitable and accept the fact that the Government's majority must ultimately prevail and its proposals carry the day. Opposition there ceases to be fruitful, and destructive criticism should give way to constructive suggestions, making the best of a bad job. Similarly, there is a responsibility on Government members in committee to regard the rights of minorities and consider reasonable concessions . . . It pleases me greatly that in committee one can to a very considerable extent put aside party affiliation and all members can work cooperatively.[9]

Since then there have been marked developments. Now all bills go to select committees for public submissions and are usually changed in light of these. The changes made will include drafting changes but also frequently changes of substance and policy. It is not unknown for bills to emerge from select committees almost totally rewritten, although Standing Order 282 requires that amendments must be relevant to the subject matter of the bill and consistent with its principles and objects. Close attention to legislation can be expected under a minority government since the majority of committee members will not be from the government. The development of the select committee role and public participation in the content of legislation has become a major and positive feature of the New Zealand legislative process.

---

8 *Report of the Department of Justice for the Year Ended 31 March 1978*, Wellington, 1978, E.5 *Appendices to the Journal of the House of Representatives*, Wellington, 1978.

9 421 *New Zealand Parliamentary Debates*, pp.4299–300.

LEGISLATIVE DRAFTING AND ACCESS TO THE LAW

The Parliamentary Counsel Office drafts all government bills and all regulations. There were twelve parliamentary counsel as at the beginning of 1996. In recent years there has been dissatisfaction within government circles about delays and bottlenecks caused by the drafting of bills within the Parliamentary Counsel Office. As a result, the Statutes Drafting and Compilation Amendment Act 1995 and an associated order in council has allowed the Inland Revenue Department to draft its own legislation.

Parliamentary counsel always attend when a bill they have drafted is being deliberated upon by a select committee and draft amendments at the direction of the committee. With MMP this may become a source of tension since drafting can reveal issues of policy and the question of whether parliamentary counsel work for the executive or Parliament is likely to be highlighted. In the light of MMP, the role and accountability regime of the Parliamentary Counsel Office could do with further examination. Parliamentary counsel, appointed by the Governor-General on the advice of the Prime Minister, would appear to have some duties independent of the government of the day. Yet, despite its name, the Parliamentary Counsel Office is not a true office of Parliament. The Statutes Drafting and Compilation Act 1920, which established the Parliamentary Counsel Office, provides that their drafting of government bills is at the direction of ministers and that the Prime Minister or Attorney-General can also direct them to report on the drafting of private members' bills.

The 1995 Report of the Standing Orders Committee highlighted the increased significance and frequency of members' bills and was concerned to ensure a consistent standard of excellence in drafting all legislation. The committee believed that 'the ideal situation would be that all legislation, including Members' Bills, should be drafted by the Parliamentary Counsel Office'.[10] Yet, because of the allegiance of the PCO to the government, the committee called for an expansion of the independent drafting facility in the Office of the Clerk to cover those situations where parliamentary counsel are not available. This sets up two sources of legislative drafting with potentially conflicting and inconsistent standards. Different styles of legislative drafting can have direct and important legal effects when courts are interpreting legislative language. Procedures and institutions must be developed quickly to resolve this difficulty.

Much of the law passed is incomprehensible to ordinary people. In his book *Access to the Law*, the Canadian minister M. L. Friedland has asserted: 'The state has an obligation to ensure that its laws are available in an understandable fashion

---

10 *Report of the Standing Orders Committee on the Review of Standing Orders*, I.18A *Appendices to the Journal of the House of Representatives*, Wellington, 1995, p.59.

to laymen.'[11] That should be our goal. It is a fundamental premise of the rule of law in a democratic society.

The New Zealand approach to drafting acts is similar to that of the United Kingdom. Both have tended to use what is known as the detailed approach. Statutes in New Zealand do not confine themselves to general principle, but are inclined to spell out everything, often in detail of tedious and incomprehensible prolixity, inflating the statute book considerably in the process.

Many complaints have been made about the drafting techniques employed in modern times. In England in 1966, two leading authors, Megarry and Wade, wrote: 'Statutory draftmanship has now attained a level of professional technique which too often endangers clarity and logic'.[12] Lord Scarman, in a celebrated lecture delivered in England, remarked that 'statutes are complex and detailed often to the point of unintelligibility and seldom contain any broad declaration of principle'.[13]

Sir William Dale, in a comparative study of legislation in England and certain continental countries, concluded that United Kingdom acts came out badly by comparison. He concluded:

> Features making for obscurity or length, usually both, in United Kingdom Acts are—
>
> (a) long, involved sentences, and sections;
> (b) much detail, little principle;
> (c) an indirect approach to the subject-matter;
> (d) subtraction—as in 'Subject to . . .', Provided that . . .';
> (e) centrifugence—a flight from the centre to definition and interpretation clauses ('the famous freak of modern law givers');
> (f) poor arrangement;
> (g) schedules—too many and too long;
> (h) cross-references to other Acts—saving space, but increasing the vexation.[14]

Sir William suggests that a new technique of drafting be introduced.

> We need at least to reduce the verbal impediments; to be less fussy over detail, to be more general and concise; and to situate each rule where it belongs, in an orderly and logical development. On this level, the question is largely a matter of style and arrangement. A more profound change is also desirable: a determination to seek the principle, to express it, and to follow up with such detail, illuminating and not obscuring the principle, as the circumstances require.[15]

---

11 M.L. Friedland, *Access to the Law*, Methuen, Toronto, 1975, p.1.
12 R.E. Megarry, and H.W.R. Wade, *The Law of Real Property*, 3rd ed., Stevens, London, 1966, p.v.
13 Scarman, Lord, *English Law—The New Dimension*, Stevens, London, 1974, p.4.
14 W. Dale, *Legislative Drafting: A New Approach*, Butterworths, London, 1977, pp.331–2.
15 *Ibid.*, p.335.

The counter-arguments that parliamentary counsel would advance for their present approach are:

- The general approach often does not fit the specificity of the purpose wanted by the government;
- Lack of detail would lead to substantial doubt continuing until resolved by the courts;
- Litigation is expensive and should be avoided where possible;
- Leaving the matter to the courts detracts from the power of the House of Representatives whose job legislation is, and the general approach gives too much power to the courts to 'legislate';
- The courts have become accustomed to the detailed approach and change now would be difficult for them.

The purpose of the Law Commission, under section 3 of the Law Commission Act 1985, is 'to promote the systematic review, reform and development of the law for New Zealand'. The commissioners are drawn from the highest level of the legal profession. Past presidents have been Sir Owen Woodhouse and Sir Kenneth Keith. Section 5 of the act instructs the commission 'to advise the Minister of Justice on ways in which the law of New Zealand can be made as understandable and accessible as is practicable'.

Some years ago, the Law Commission was given a specific brief to examine and review the language of legislation in New Zealand. The terms of reference were:

- To propose ways of making legislation as understandable and accessible as practicable and of ensuring that it is kept under review in a systematic way; and
- To ascertain what changes, if any, are necessary or desirable in the law relating to the interpretation of legislation.

In 1990 the Law Commission produced a major report,[16] which pointed out there has been a growing emphasis on plain drafting, and it produced a new Interpretation Act that it recommended be enacted. Interpretation acts contain the rules that are binding on courts when interpreting the acts passed by Parliament. The development of a new approach to interpretation was a necessary ingredient in making the law more understandable. In 1993 the commission produced a further report on the format of legislation, recommending changes to the design and typography of legislation.[17] This was endorsed by the Justice and Law Reform

16 Law Commission, *Report No. 17: A New Interpretation Act To avoid 'Prolixity and Tautology'*, Wellington, 1990.

17 Law Commission, *Report 27: The Format of Legislation*, Wellington, 1993.

Select Committee and, at the time of writing, was being examined for adoption. In 1996, the Law Commission produced two parts of a substantial *Legislation Manual* to guide all those involved in the law-making process on the structure of legislation (function and arrangement of component parts of legislation) and the style of legislation (such matters as plain language, gender-neutral expression, the use of the Maori language, and punctuation).[18]

The move towards plain English drafting has come some distance in recent years in New Zealand. As one famous advocate of the new method of drafting has said: 'It is strange that free societies should thus arrive at a situation where their members are governed from cradle to grave by texts they cannot understand'.[19] In a democracy people ought to be able to understand the laws they are supposed to obey, but this is much easier said than done. Many more New Zealand acts now contain statements of objects and principles, but too much law is still unnecessarily wordy and obscure. Such laws can impose heavy costs on both the government and the community, they can reduce the efficiency of government administration, they can cause dispute and doubt, and they can waste time and money. Often they end up having to be interpreted through litigation in the courts, which is also expensive and wasteful. Laws can and should be written in a way that is both intelligible and legally certain.

New Zealand has not given enough attention to providing aids to finding the law. In 1978, for the first time, the tables setting out the names of the public acts of the New Zealand Parliament and the statutory regulations in force were published as a separate volume. That list now covers 320 pages, which itself gives some indication of the volume of law we have. For the most part, the tables list the acts and regulations in alphabetical order by name; there is some cross-referencing, but unless you know the name of the act or regulation you are looking for, there is a good chance you will not find it.

By constrast, the State of Iowa in the United States reprints its entire statute law every year, together with a comprehensive index. The compiler divides up the codes into topic headings, and ensures that the index contains every conceivable cross-reference to the headings. The headings include such topics as education, social welfare, environment, commerce, and so on. Within each chapter there is room for subdivision. Each section of the law within such a code has a unique number, so that it is easy to identify a particular provision.

For those trying to keep track of parliamentary papers, the *Parliamentary Bulletin* is invaluable. Compiled by the Office of the Clerk of the House of Representatives, it allows people to chart the progress of bills through the Parliament. It is, however,

---

18 Law Commission, *Report 35: Legislation Manual Structure and Style*, Wellington, 1996.

19 Francis Bennion quoted in Susan Krongold, 'Writing Laws: Making them Easier to Understand', 24 *Ottawa Law Review*, 1992, p.495.

not enough. The day is long past when a lay person could attempt to keep abreast of changes in our legislation. For one thing, it would cost too much. In 1996, a full set of annotated New Zealand statutes cost $3131. Unfortunately, however, much of this would be printed in the form of loose acts; the official bound volumes of statutes are years behind. At the beginning of 1996 the volumes for 1993, 1994, and 1995 had not been published. The Chief Parliamentary Counsel, under the direction of the Attorney-General, is obliged by the Acts and Regulations Publications Act 1989 to arrange for the printing and publication of copies of acts and regulations. Yet it is impossible to buy a complete set of New Zealand's regulations from the Government Bookshops. Some of them are simply out of print. The problem of accessibility is even more marked in relation to court judgments—an important source of law. It is difficult and expensive to get copies of unreported judgments.

Using the Iowa approach to presenting the law would be simpler than the system now used. But in today's age of computer databases and the Internet, much more could be done to make the law accessible to the public. It should be possible to store on computer an authoritative version of all New Zealand statute law, which is kept constantly updated with amendments, legislative history, and references to cases that interpret provisions, and which is accessible to everyone online and/or on computer disk.

Commercial suppliers do now provide versions of the New Zealand statutes on CD-Rom, online, and in printed form at considerable cost to those who can afford it. At the time of writing there is at least one full-text information site on the Internet, operated by a private supplier, that includes full transcripts of Hansard, parliamentary bills, and statutory regulations as well as the text of current legislation. Private suppliers have filled the gap because up-to-date versions of the law are essential, particularly for the legal profession. Compared with these private enterprise efforts, the official programme seems to have lagged behind. Yet the government has a responsibility to ensure that a single, accurate, authoritative version of the statute law is printed and available to those who need it, without undue cost. If citizens in society are expected to observe the obligations imposed on them by law, they should be able to find out what that law is. It is hard to see that this need is currently being properly met. Much more attention needs to be given to presenting the law in an intelligible and accessible format.

In conclusion it may be added that, under MMP, there is likely to be less coherence in the legislation as a result of political compromises. This may increase concerns about the quality of legislation that flows out of an MMP Parliament.

10 Regulations and Red Tape

WHAT ARE REGULATIONS?

As was pointed out in the last chapter, there are three major species of New Zealand legislation: acts, regulations, and by-laws. The last two are sometimes called 'subordinate' legislation.[1] That may suggest that they are always concerned with minor matters, and they often are, but the New Zealand Parliament has passed acts allowing for regulations to be made on all manner of things. This chapter explores the use of the regulation-making power in New Zealand and assesses the strength of the protections that are available against it.

By-laws can be made only where an act of Parliament confers power upon an organisation to make them. The most common source of by-laws in New Zealand are local authorities, which are examined further in Chapter 11. Most by-laws deal with matters that come under the control of local authorities and are made under authority conferred by Parliament in the Local Government Act 1974 and other statutes.

Regulations are made under the authority of statutes; a statute will state that regulations can be made on various topics. One statute containing some extensive powers to make regulations is the Conservation Act 1987. Section 48 of that act, as amended, contains a list of fifteen subjects upon which regulations can be made. These include:

- prescribing forms for licences and leases made under the act;
- providing for the care, management, and protection of natural or historic resources or conservation areas;
- prohibiting, controlling, and restricting the entry of the public into any conservation area;
- prescribing conditions and charges for the use of huts, camping sites, picnic places, and other facilities in conservation areas;

1 D.C. Pearce, *Delegated Legislation in Australia and New Zealand*, Butterworths, Sydney, 1977.

- power to prescribe criminal offences by regulation that impose fines up to $5000 for non-compliance with the regulations or any 'lawful direction or requirement made under this Act or any such regulations . . .'; and
- providing for 'such matters as may be contemplated by or necessary for giving full effect to this Act and for its due administration'.

It is important, when examining the power given in an act of Parliament to make regulations, to study closely the wording of the provision to see what comes within its range. When regulations are made, parliamentary counsel must certify, before approval by Cabinet, that the regulations in question fall within the scope of the empowering act. Here is what section 48A of the Conservation Act 1987 says about the power to make regulations relating to freshwater fisheries:

> (1) Without limiting section 48 of this Act, the Governor-General may from time to time, by Order in Council, make regulations for all or any of the following purposes:
>
> (a) Providing for the establishment of an advisory user group for the Taupo Fishery, and prescribing its functions, powers, proceedings, and other necessary matters:
>
> (b) Prescribing a total allowable catch in respect of any freshwater fish, freshwater fishery, or method of fishing for freshwater fish:
>
> (c) Prescribing the forms and classes of licence to fish for freshwater fish or sports fish, and providing for the issue of such licences and for the disposal of fees for such licences and of fines recovered under this Act:
>
> (d) Providing for the Minister to appoint agents and authorise such agents and Fish and Game Councils to issue, on such conditions as may be prescribed in the regulations, licences authorising the holder to fish for sports fish, and providing for licence fees to be paid to such agents and such Councils:
>
> (e) Prescribing the scope and effect of licences to fish for freshwater fish or sports fish or any specified class of licences, and providing for licences issued in respect of any region to be available in any other region or regions or in all regions:
>
> (f) Regulating or prohibiting the taking or possession or sale of any specified freshwater fish:
>
> (g) Providing for the issue, refusal, renewal, suspension, revocation, modification, and imposition by the regulations or the Director-General of conditions on licences for persons who wish to acquire or be in possession in prescribed circumstances of fish taken for the purposes of sale:
>
> (h) Providing for the recognition of licences granted under any other Act as licences for the purposes of this Act:
>
> (i) Providing for the variation, renewal, and evocation of licences to fish for freshwater fish or sports fish and for the refusal of the issue of licences in certain cases:
>
> (j) Providing for the payment to a Fish and Game Council of any fines or licence fees for the purposes of the distribution, rearing, cultivation, or protection of

sports fish in the area under the jurisdiction of that Council, or, with the approval of the Minister given upon or subject to such conditions as the Minister thinks fit, for the purpose of applying the same or any part thereof either alone or jointly with any other Council, or for any related purpose approved by the Minister:

(k) Providing for the payment to the Director-General of any fines or licence fees for the purposes of the distribution, rearing, cultivating, or protection of freshwater fish in any area, or with the approval of the Minister given upon or subject to such conditions as the Minister thinks fit, for any related purpose:

(l) Prohibiting, restricting, or regulating the use of electric fishing devices for the taking of freshwater fish or sports fish, including . . . :

(m) Regulating, restricting, or imposing conditions on the canning, smoking, freezing, or other preserving of trout or other specified freshwater fish and the possession thereof when canned, smoked, frozen, or otherwise preserved; and providing for the inspection of canneries, smokehouses, freezing chambers, refrigerating works, and any premises (not being a dwellinghouse) where freshwater fish are canned, smoked, frozen, preserved, treated, dressed, or stored:

(n) Requiring and authorising the provision of devices and facilities to permit or control the passage of freshwater fish or sports fish through or around any dam or other structure impeding the natural movement of fish upstream or downstream:

(o) Authorising the establishment of fish hatcheries by Fish and Game Council, or the Department, and regulating the management and operation of such establishments:

(p) To prohibit or impose conditions and restrictions on the possession, or the retention in captivity, or the transfer to or release into any waters, of any live aquatic life:

(q) Prescribing the conditions of, and rentals payable in respect of, fishing competitions.

(2) Any such regulations—

(a) May apply generally throughout New Zealand or New Zealand freshwaters or be made to apply only within such area or areas as may be defined in that behalf:

(b) May apply special conditions or confer special rights in relation to fishing by specified communities.

The range of matters that may be dealt with by regulations made under this section is extensive, but it is not unlimited. The language is very specific. On the other hand, not all the topics for which regulations can be made could be classed as administrative detail.

WHY DO WE HAVE REGULATIONS?

Regulations are inevitable in a modern and complex state where high technology, often dangerous, is in use. The grant of some legislative power to the executive branch of government is an inevitable feature of all modern democracies. A number of reasons are advanced to justify the use of regulations. Parliament does not have the time to consider everything so it should leave detail to the executive branch. Then there is the technicality of much subject-matter, which is not fit for statute law. Regulations also provide flexibility and the opportunity to experiment. And, it is suggested, emergency conditions requiring instant action can best be handled by regulations.

A large number of regulations are made in New Zealand every year, in most years more than 300. The figure has not fallen below 200 since 1961, when 178 regulations were made. The largest number made in a single year was 393 in 1986. It is important to add, however, that a large number of regulations are revoked each year. In 1986, for example, the total number of revocations was 421. In 1979 a total of 209 were revoked.

Conceding that regulations are necessary does not mean that the way in which they are made is satisfactory, or that the protections available to the citizen against them are adequate. Regulation-making forms one of the most important sources of executive power in modern governments, the power to make law instantly. Of course we are being a little unfair when we stress the instant quality of regulations. The speed of law depends on your point of view. To the unwary citizen, a regulation may come like a bolt out of the blue. To the public servant who has been plodding away in his or her specialised area for years, trying to get the department, parliamentary counsel and Cabinet to make the regulation he or she believes to be essential, the process may seem much slower. There are plenty of cases of draft regulations languishing in departments for years because they do not have enough priority to rate action.

The power to make regulations probably assumes greater importance under MMP. Where there are governments with minority support in Parliament or a coalition with some uncertainties within it, a Cabinet may not always want to run the gauntlet of Parliament to get its policies adopted. It may instead use its power to the full to make regulations from statutes already passed. So the use of regulations to advance government policy could well increase, and the protections against the abuse may be tested more than in the recent past. Fortunately, the level of these protections has been well developed since a special select committee was established in 1986 to review them. The Regulations (Disallowance) Act 1989 was passed allowing motions of disallowance to be passed in Parliament to strike down regulations.

A well-known British report on ministers' powers, the Donoughmore Report published in 1932, stated in some detail the orthodox constitutional theory concerning regulations. That theory was echoed in the 1962 New Zealand parliamentary report on delegated legislation. The main principle of the orthodox theory is that making law by regulation is legitimate, even desirable 'within certain limits and under certain safeguards'.[2]

The reasons for the view are:

- regulations are convenient for dealing with detail—pressure on parliamentary time is great;
- technical matters cannot be effectively scrutinised by Parliament;
- administrative machinery provisions make for a cumbersome statute, the drafting of which requires a degree of forseeability, which is impossible;
- regulations allow for flexibility and experimentation more readily than statute; and
- in the modern state quick action is often needed.

It is also important to recall why regulations as a form of law are fundamentally different from statutes. Those reasons are:

- regulations are not enacted by Parliament;
- regulations can be made without warning, creating important changes in the law with no political or public debate before the event;
- the normal processes of political representation do not work nearly as directly for regulations as they do for acts of Parliament; and
- the control exercised by non-elected public servants over the content of regulations appears to be greater than their control over the content of statutes.

A serious danger with regulations lies in their capacity to erode the position of Parliament by dealing with important principles and policies that ought to be decided by Parliament.

LEST WE FORGET . . .

New Zealand has, at some points in its history, demonstrated a stunning indifference to the dangers of rule 'by decree' through regulations and some of the statutes that permitted it are recalled here so that the sad history is not forgotten.[3] It is often said that statutes contain the most important laws and that regulations contain only administrative detail, but this distinction has often not been observed in New Zealand. For many years, important facets of our national life could be controlled by regulation. The powers given to the executive by the Economic Stabilisation Act 1948 allowed the government to control prices, wages, and take almost every economic measure conceivable (short of raising taxes) by regulation. Fortunately, that legislation has now been repealed, but more than 200 regulations

---

2 Report of the Delegated Legislation Committee 1962 (Algie Report), *Appendices to the Journals of the House of Representatives*, Wellington, 1962.

3 M.A. Sieghart, *Government by Decree*, Stevens, London, 1950.

were made under the act. One worrying feature was that the act contained no statement of the principles in accordance with which the regulation-making power was to be exercised. Too often in the past, Parliament signed a blank cheque to the executive to pass whatever regulations it liked. As Prime Minister Sir Robert Muldoon remarked in 1976: '. . . you can do anything provided you can hang your hat on economic stabilisation'.[4]

The Economic Stabilisation Act 1948 provided in section 11:

> (1) The Governor-General may from time to time, by Order in Council, make such regulations (in this Act referred to as stabilisation regulations) as appear to him to be necessary or expedient for the general purpose of this Act and for giving full effect to the provisions of this Act and for the due administration of this Act.

Section 3 stated that the general purpose of the act was to promote the economic stability of New Zealand. The act then went on to authorise regulations for all or any of the following purposes:

- regulating the marketing of any goods or classes of goods for the general purpose of the act;
- equalising as far as possible the net returns received or payable in respect of any goods or classes of goods, and for that purpose imposing levies in respect of any goods or classes of goods;
- the recovery of subsidies paid out of public monies in respect of any goods or classes of goods; and
- providing for the appointment of officers and committees and other bodies and defining their sanctions and powers.

In 1980, Ms Deborah Shelton wrote a lengthy thesis entitled 'Government, the Economy and the Constitution'. After nearly 400 pages of close analysis, especially of regulations made under the Economic Stabilisation Act, her conclusion is arresting: 'Constitutional theory and practice have diverged alarmingly.'[5] Ms Shelton pointed out the dilemma:

> The conclusion that cannot be avoided is that the coherence of the constitution is breaking down. There are two possible responses to this collapse of coherence; either to allow the gap between theory and practice to widen even further, paying lip service to the theory when it is convenient, or, as has become more frequent, repudiating the theory because of the divergence of theory and practice.
>
> The other alternative is to formulate a constitutional theory and practice that reflects

4 R. Lewis, 'How Mr Muldoon Waved a Big Stick Over the Unions', *The Times,* 14 April 1976, p.18.

5 D. Shelton, 'Government, the Economy and the Constitution', unpublished LLM thesis, Faculty of Law, Victoria University of Wellington, 1980.

> the expectations and understandings of New Zealand society and government and that attempts to control these new powers of the executive through the democratic process.[6]

For more than thirty years New Zealand tolerated a statute that allowed things to be regulated not by Parliament but by the executive, things which most Western governments would never have dreamed of regulating in peacetime—prices, remuneration, and interest rates. It was these powers more than any others that led to comparisons of New Zealand to Albania and raised fundamental questions about the rule of law here. Since that time we have moved towards a new realism about the need to control the powers of the executive through the democratic process.

The Public Safety Conservation Act 1932, which was repealed in 1987, was potentially the most dangerous and repressive piece of legislation on the New Zealand statute books. The act was used only twice in forty-four years. The first time was at the outbreak of war in 1939, when regulations were promulgated under the act; these were later brought under the authority of the Emergency Regulations Act 1939. The second occasion was the 1951 waterfront dispute, an episode that can hardly be classed as one of the finer moments for the rule of law in New Zealand.

Section 2(1) of the Public Safety Conservation Act 1932 provided:

> If at any time it appears to the Governor-General that any action has been taken or is immediately threatened by any persons or body of persons of such a nature and on so extensive a scale as to be calculated, by interfering with the supply and distribution of food, water, fuel, or light or with the means of locomotion, to deprive the community or any substantial portion of the community of the essentials of life, or if at any time it appears to the Governor-General that any circumstances exist, or are likely to come into existence, whereby the public safety or public order is or is likely to be imperilled, and a state of national emergency or of civil defence emergency has not been declared under the provisions of the Civil Defence Act 1962 in respect of those circumstances, the Governor-General may, by Proclamation approved in Executive Council . . . declare that a state of emergency exists throughout New Zealand . . .

When a proclamation of emergency had been made, section 3 of the act gave power to the Governor-General:

> . . . to make all such regulations as he thinks necessary for the prohibition of any acts which in his opinion would be injurious to the public safety, and also to make all such other regulations as in his opinion are required for the conservation of public safety and order and for securing the essentials of life to the community.

The 1951 regulations made pursuant to the Public Safety Conservation Act 1932 contained unduly onerous provisions. The definition of strike included failing to

---

6 *Ibid.*

work overtime. The minister was empowered to end strikes by notice in the *New Zealand Gazette*. Freedom of expression in relation to declared strikes was prohibited. Processions, public meetings, and the display of posters could be prohibited. The publication of statements made at public meetings that were likely to aid or abet the continuance of a declared strike became a criminal offence. The regulations placed in the hands of a receiver all the funds of unions that were parties to a declared strike. The minister was empowered to suspend awards and industrial agreements. The regulations authorised the temporary employment of members of the armed forces for any kind of work specified in writing by order of the minister. Picketing was made an offence. Special powers of entry without a warrant were given to the police.

In 1951 an unsuccessful attempt was made to challenge in court the use of the act and the validity of the regulations made under it.[7] The climate for judicial review of subordinate legislation has changed considerably since then and now a court might embark upon judicial review in an appropriate case. A 1960 amendment to the Public Safety Conservation Act offered some check on the arbitrary use of the act. If Parliament was not sitting when the proclamation declaring the emergency was made, then Parliament must be called together and sit not later than seven days after the proclamation was made. And the regulations expired after fourteen days from being tabled in the House unless they were confirmed by resolution.

An apt legal description for civil society undergoing a proclamation of emergency under legislation of this character comes from the Duke of Wellington's description of martial law: 'Martial law is neither more nor less than the will of the general who commands the army. In fact martial law means no law at all.'[8] Such arbitrariness is contrary to the fundamental constitutional principle of the rule of law. The best protection against government by regulation is to stop Parliament passing acts which empower it.

In general, the most potent variety of regulation relates to emergencies and, significantly, some of these regulations are more difficult to challenge before a court. For example, section 79(1) of the Civil Defence Act 1983 empowers the Governor-General to make regulations 'for such matters as are necessary or expedient for the purpose of securing the public safety and generally safeguarding the interests of the public during any state of national or civil defence emergency'. There are occasions when the public good requires the use of repressive powers. Who could argue that an outbreak of foot and mouth disease in New Zealand would not warrant taking drastic steps? But that does not mean that the taking and using of drastic powers should be beyond all control or review either in

7 *Hewett* v. *Fielder* [1951], *NZLR* 755.

8 *Hansard*, 1851, Vol. CXV, col. 880.

Parliament or in the courts. Such review must be available to ensure that great powers are used only when appropriate. The people who have created the powers should not be the judge of that.

CABINET AND REGULATIONS

Regulations are often made by 'order in council'. To make an order in council means that the Governor-General and Cabinet ministers meet and the Governor-General signs the regulations proposed by ministers at the Executive Council meeting. These are meetings of the Executive Council, as distinct from Cabinet (which the Governor-General does not attend). Actually, regulations are approved by Cabinet before being sent to the Executive Council, where they are discussed. Meetings of the Executive Council do not need to be attended by all ministers; two ministers plus the Governor-General constitute a quorum. However, para 5.72 of the 1996 *Cabinet Office Manual* requires that 'the Minister responsible for an item on the Executive Council agenda must be present at Executive Council to answer any queries from the Governor-General or must have briefed another Minister who will be present'.

Chapter 5 of the *Cabinet Office Manual* has an extensive set of rules governing the making of orders in council. It stresses:

- the need to check that regulations are in fact needed;
- the desirability of consultation with affected groups;
- the need for consultation within the government;
- the need for Cabinet approval of the underlying policy;
- the requirement for parliamentary counsel to consider whether the regulations are within the powers granted in the act;
- the need for the regulations to be accompanied by a submission in a set format (similar to the one quoted in Chapter 9 regarding submissions on legislation);
- a Cabinet requirement that regulations shall not come into force until at least twenty-eight days after they have been notified in the *New Zealand Gazette* (published each Thursday);
- encouragement to departments to prepare a schedule of regulations likely to be required each year, taking into account the time needed for policy development and consultation, policy approval by Cabinet, drafting, approval of the Regulations by Cabinet, and the twenty-eight day rule (with an absolute minimum of six weeks between completion of drafting and the date on which they come into force).

In December 1994 the Minister of Finance and the Deputy Minister of Finance published a policy and discussion paper on business compliance cost reduction.[9]

[9] Rt Hon. W. F. Birch, Hon. Wyatt Creech, *Business Compliance Cost Reduction: A Government Policy and Discusssion Paper*, December 1994.

Compliance costs are the costs to private sector bodies of interacting with the government in meeting an obligation. The purpose was to reduce excessive compliance costs of existing regulations and legislation. One result of the programme is that from 1 January 1996 all Cabinet papers on policy issues that involve compliance costs must contain a compliance cost statement briefly summarising the compliance cost implications of the proposal.[10] Detailed reports must be prepared where there is a risk of substantial compliance costs. These reports are available under the Official Information Act 1982.

PARLIAMENT AND REGULATIONS

For many years regulations were simply published in the *Gazette* and were inaccessible. But in 1936 the Attorney-General Hon. H.G.R. Mason ordered that they be published in volumes each year and that they were to be drafted by parliamentary counsel. He was also responsible for the passage of the Regulations Act 1936. It took longer for Parliament to take any interest in regulations, despite periodic criticisms that were made about their use.

In 1962 Sir Ronald Algie, an MP and Speaker of the House of Representatives who had been a minister of the Crown, chaired a parliamentary select committee that considered the situation in New Zealand and made some recommendations for change, which were adopted. The committee praised the new form of regulation-making power that the government had approved in 1961. The new form was designed to ensure that the courts could review whether a regulation fell within the scope of the power given in the Act to make regulations. The courts, not the executive that made the regulation, would be the ultimate judge. And it was designed to ensure that 'the precise limits of the law-making power conferred by Parliament are set down as clearly as possible . . .'[11] The Algie committee also considered that all regulations made should be laid upon the table of the House of Representatives so that they could be discussed there if members wished. The Regulations Act 1936 was amended to provide that all regulations 'shall be laid before the House of Representatives not later than the 16th sitting day of the House of Representatives after the day on which they are made'.[12]

A major recommendation of the Algie committee was that the Statutes Revision Committee of Parliament be empowered to consider regulations referred to it to determine whether the House's attention should be drawn to the regulation on a number of grounds, such as that it trespasses unduly on personal rights and liberties or that it made some unusual or unexpected use of the powers conferred. The

[10] Cabinet Office Circular CO(95) 14, 'Compliance Cost Assessment Framework', 29 November 1995; *Cabinet Office Manual*, Wellington, 1996, para 4.24.

[11] Report of the Delegated Legislation Committee 1962, p.12.

[12] Regulations Act 1936, s.8, as amended by the Constitution Act 1986, s.27.

standing orders of Parliament were amended accordingly, with a procedure for allowing the regulation to be referred to the committee if five members of the House request it during a parliamentary recess.

The procedure existed from 1962 until 1985 but it was used on only eleven occasions. In most of those cases, the Statutes Revision Committee took a modest and cautious view of its power. Nevertheless, it was made clear that the power to report adversely to the House on a regulation would be used on appropriate occasions. In a 1976 case involving an amendment to the rock lobster regulations, which placed an absolute prohibition on the hand-picking of rock lobsters, the committee took the view that the regulation went further than was necessary and was an undue trespass on personal liberty. It recommended that the regulation be amended, revoked, or replaced, a recommendation which was implemented by replacing the total ban with the introduction of a closed season.

In 1980 the Statutes Revision Committee examined the Remuneration (New Zealand Forest Products) Regulations 1980, which were revoked before the committee concluded its deliberations. Nonetheless, the committee continued its work and pointed out to the House its view of the undesirability of 'the practice whereby the provisions of an Act of Parliament may be waived or amended by the Executive through its Regulation-making powers'.[13]

In 1985, as a result of policy pledges in Labour's open government policy, big changes were made. The Statutes Revision Committee recommended changes to standing orders to 'enable a more effective and comprehensive Parliamentary scrutiny and control' of delegated legislation.[14] Submissions were heard and the evidence showed that the existing system was not ensuring the effective scrutiny of delegated legislation. Part of the problem was that the Statutes Revision Committee had not really concentrated on regulations because it had too much other work to do.

To remedy the situation, a special Regulations Review Committee was established. Since 1986, it has produced a large number of reports and has provided a check on the wrongful use of regulations. Unlike other select committees, it does not consider policy, but is concerned only with the tests relating to delegated legislation set out in the standing orders.

All regulations are automatically referred to the Regulations Review Committee, which is, by tradition, chaired by an opposition MP. The committee can consider any regulation-making power contained in all bills under consideration by other select committees. And it can deal with any other matter relating to regulations. It can also consider draft regulations. Where a complaint about a regulation is made

---

13 *Report of the Statutes Revision Committee* 1980, Wellington, 1981, p.12.

14 Statutes Revision Committee 1985, *First Report on Delegated Legislation*, Wellington, 1985, p.3.

to the chairman of the Regulations Review Committee or to the committee itself, the complaint must be placed before the committee. And Standing Order 197 requires that the complainant must be given an opportunity to be heard unless all the members of the committee agree to proceed no further with the complaint. This novel provision prevents a majority of committee members from avoiding a proper inquiry into a matter that could be politically embarrassing.

In examining a regulation, Standing Order 196 says that the committee must consider 'whether it ought to be drawn to the special attention of the House' on one or more of the following grounds, that the regulation:

(a) is not in accordance with the general objects and intentions of the statute under which it is made:
(b) trespasses unduly on personal rights and liberties:
(c) appears to make some unusual or unexpected use of the powers conferred by the statute under which it was made:
(d) unduly makes the rights and liberties of persons dependent upon administrative decisions which are not themselves subject to review on their merits by a judicial or other independent tribunal:
(e) excludes the jurisdiction of the Courts without explicit authorisation in the enabling statute:
(f) contains matter more appropriate for parliamentary enactment:
(g) is retrospective where this is not expressly authorized by the empowering statute:
(h) was not made in compliance with particular notice and consultation procedures prescribed by statute:
(i) for any other reason concerning its form or purport calls for elucidation.

These grounds are potent. Under these tests, great practical help has been given to aggrieved people. But there is more: the Regulations (Disallowance) Act 1989 provides that the House of Representatives may, by resolution, disallow any regulations or provisions of regulations. Furthermore, a regulation can be automatically disallowed if a motion put forward by a member of the Regulations Review Committee is not disposed of within twenty-one sitting days. Although this procedure has yet to be used, it puts heavy artillery in the hands of the committee.

It is likely that the Regulations (Disallowance) Act 1989 will be used in MMP Parliaments. Because the government may not enjoy a majority, it may be tempted to use regulations rather than an act of Parliament to advance its policies. Regulations may, therefore, be used in doubtful situations. Interestingly, Parliament can disallow a regulation for any reason or no reason; it is not limited to the grounds in the standing orders quoted above. And the experience of the Regulations Review Committee itself in the last few years provides ample evidence that other effective remedies are available.

Consider the case of Mr Edward, who owned and operated a chemist shop in Rotorua. It is a story about the imposition of the policy that the user should pay for the cost of government services and the silly effects this policy can have in individual cases, if it is not applied with discernment. For approximately $500, Mr Edward obtained from the United Kingdom a second-hand weighing machine,[15] which he installed outside his shop for public use. The rather sophisticated machine, which provided a computer printout, had a British certification as an approved weighing instrument. Mr Edward was advised by the Labour Department that, under the Weights and Measures Regulations 1987, he was required to apply for New Zealand certification of the machine, which would cost him $2000. Mr Edward went to his MP, who complained to the Regulations Review Committee. The committee's inquiry was extensive and its report trenchant.

The committee found it 'astonishing' that the machine would have to undergo such expensive accuracy tests. It found that the regulation trespassed unduly on personal rights and liberties and meant that people's rights depended on administrative decisions that are not subject to review on their merits. It recommended that such weighing machines should either be excluded from the regulations or that certificates of accuracy issued by other countries belonging to the International Organisation of Legal Metrology should be recognised.[16] The regulations were changed to recognise such certificates and everyone lived happily ever afterwards.[17] Note that this result was secured under the standing orders; the Regulations (Disallowance) Act 1989 was not involved.

A more difficult case arose in 1994 concerning a complaint relating to the Whitebait Fishing (West Coast) Regulations 1994,[18] which changed the whitebait season on the West Coast and shortened it. They were made under the statutory power contained in the Conservation Act 1987 set out earlier in this chapter. A complaint about the regulations was made to the Regulations Review Committee. The complainants said that the level of consultation undertaken was inadequate, the process of consultation was seriously flawed, there was no scientific evidence to justify the measure, and the Department of Conservation had failed to follow its own act, in particular section 17A:

> Subject to this Act, the Department shall administer and manage all conservation areas and natural and historic resources in accordance with—

---

15 Regulations Review Committee, *Report on the Inquiry into Fees Charged under the Weights and Measures Regulation 1987*, I.16 *Appendices to the Journal of the House of Representatives*, Wellington, 1987–90, p.9.

16 *Ibid.*, p.12.

17 Weights and Measures Regulations 1987, Amendment No. 1, SR 1987/123.

18 Regulations Review Committee, *On a Complaint Relating to the Whitebait Fishing (West Coast) Regulations 1994* I.16A *Appendices to the Journal of the House of Representatives*, Wellington, 1994.

(a) Statements of general policy approved under section 17B or section 17C of this Act; and
(b) Conservation management strategies, conservation management plans, and freshwater fisheries management plans.

The department said it had power to make regulations under section 48A and this was not qualified by the part of the act quoted above. Any plans conflicting with regulations would be unenforceable. The minister was free to consult in a manner satisfactory to him.

In its report, the committee told the House that the regulations were not made in compliance with particular notice and consultation procedures prescribed by the statute and that other matters should be brought to the House's attention. It recommended that the whitebait fishing season be extended to close on its former date (and this was done by the government). It also found that consultation with Maori had been inadequate and said that further consultations should be carried out. The committee stated that the procedure for making regulations should be compatible with matters of management planning under the provision quoted above. It also recommended that more research be undertaken on the whitebait fishery to generate data on catch records that would assist in determining the status of the fishery in the long term.

Over the years the Regulations Review Committee has made some important recommendations. It has noted some instances of acts 'containing Regulation-making powers that are so wide that they authorise the delegation of legislation that more properly falls within the province of Parliament itself'.[19] It has reported on regulations that are made under statutory provisions allowing provisions in acts of Parliament to be changed by regulation.[20] It is important to note, before we deal with the capacity of the courts to declare regulations invalid, that the parliamentary remedies are much wider than those the courts can provide.

REGULATIONS IN THE COURTS

Regulations are law, but they must be made under the authority of an act of Parliament. In the event of a dispute concerning an act, it is the job of the courts to interpret what the statute means. With regulations, the courts have wider powers. Not only can they interpret regulations, but they can also declare a regulation to

---

19 Report of the Regulations Review Committee 1986, *Regulation Making Powers in Legislation* I.16A *Appendices to the Journal of the House of Representatives*, Wellington, 1986, p.4.

20 Report of the Regulations Review Committee, *Inquiry into the Resource Management (Transitional) Regulations 1994 and the principles that should apply to the Use of Empowering Provisions Allowing Regulations to override primary legislation during a Transitiional Period*, I.16C *Appendices to the Journal of the House of Representatives*, Wellington, 1995.

be invalid and of no effect if it is outside the ambit of the power laid down in the enabling act. For example, a regulation made under the Conservation Act 1987 that attempted to control the price of television sets would be struck down. This is called by lawyers the doctrine of *ultra vires*. That act gives no power to make regulations for that purpose.

The courts examine regulations to ensure that they are made within the scope of power granted by Parliament. Two examples demonstrate the process and the restraint it imposes upon the executive.

The Toheroa Regulations 1955 provided that: 'No person shall open toheroa in any place below high-water mark.' The purpose was, apparently, to prevent pollution of the toheroa beds, but the wording of the regulation went a very long way indeed: it would prevent the opening of toheroa on board ship. The regulations were made under the authority of the Fisheries Act 1908 (where 'fish' includes 'shellfish'), which gave the Governor-General power to make regulations for the following purposes, among others:

- generally to regulate sea fishing in New Zealand;
- to prohibit or regulate the possession of any fish;
- to prohibit the deposit on any oyster bed of any substance;
- to set apart waters or adjacent areas for the propagation of fish; and
- any other purpose for which regulations are contemplated or required by the act.

The court decided that the regulations were outside the power conferred by the act and were void. Nowhere did the act give express power to make regulations governing the opening of shellfish. None of the provisions could be interpreted as granting such a power.[21]

In the second example, the Education (School Age) Regulation 1943 made under the Education Act 1914 gave an education board power to transfer pupils or to refuse to enrol pupils 'for the purpose of ensuring that the best use is made of all accommodation and educational facilities available in school . . .'. In 1954, twelve-year-old Vernon Smith was enrolled in Auckland School A. In February 1955, because of zoning decisions, the board transferred him to School B. In February 1956 he was transferred to School C. In August 1958 he was transferred to School D. Vernon's father would not send him to the last school, but the boy was refused tuition at his old school and his father was charged under the provisions of the Education Act governing truancy. The prosecution failed because the court held that the regulations were invalid. The act provided that the Governor-General was authorised to make regulations 'for any purpose for which Regulations are by this Act authorized or required to be made, and generally for any purposes which

[21] *Strawbridge* v. *Simeon and others* [1959] *NZLR* 405.

he thinks necessary in order to secure the due administration of this Act'. The court refused to be put off by that language. It would always inquire into any question of law that the Governor-General might be required to decide, and would also decide whether the Governor-General would reasonably have formed any opinion, whether law or fact. Justice Turner, therefore, examined the purposes that the Governor-General could have considered as necessary for the due administration of the act and found nothing to justify the regulation. All that was needed was to set a maximum number beyond which new enrolments might not be accepted. Another provision in the Education Act gave the Governor-General power to 'make such Regulations as he thinks necessary or expedient for avoiding doubt or difficulty which may appear to him to arise in the administration of the principal Act by reason of any omission or inconsistency therein, and all Regulations shall have the force of law, anything to the contrary in the principal Act notwithstanding'. That provision appeared to do great evil: to allow the executive to make regulations contrary to provisions in a statute. But still Justice Turner was unmoved. He construed it strictly, and there was, he said, no doubt or difficulty.[22]

The case is a classic example of how far a court will go, in a case where justice requires it, to strike down a regulation that is unfair and oppressive, even though the power given to make regulations is very wide. The power is drafted widely to try to prevent the courts from reviewing regulations. Sometimes the courts will give in without a struggle. For example, they tend not to interfere easily with regulations dealing with emergency situations. And there are few occasions where a regulation is outside the power given to make it. Where a specific power is granted to make a regulation on a specific topic, and the regulation is within the power, the court is powerless to strike it down.

There are, however, some interesting arguments yet to be had in the courts as to whether a regulation can be struck down by the court because it is in breach of the New Zealand Bill of Rights Act 1990. Should such arguments succeed, a new avenue of constitutional protection against delegated legislation will be opened.

REGULATIONS UNDER MMP

In a famous, some would say infamous, book called *The New Despotism*, published in 1929, Lord Hewart, when he was Lord Chief Justice of England, declared that delegated legislation had become 'a persistent and well-contrived system, intended to produce, and in practice producing, a despotic power which at one and the same time places Government departments above the Sovereignty of Parliament and beyond the jurisdiction of the Courts'.[23]

22 *Reade* v. *Smith* [1959] *NZLR* 996.
23 Lord Hewart of Bury, *The New Despotism*, Benn, London, 1929, p.14.

In New Zealand in the late 1990s it is not possible to make such a charge. Between 1986 and 1996 protection against government by regulation has substantially increased. Parliament, the executive, and the courts all share responsibilities for different aspects of delegated legislation. Parliament has two tasks. The first is to scrutinise the scope of enabling provisions in each bill to see that they are not too broad. The second is to determine whether the executive's use of its powers to make regulations falls outside the established tests. It is the court's role to apply and interpret the law and hold, where appropriate, that regulations are *ultra vires*. Under MMP, all branches of government are likely to be more concerned with the use of regulations. The executive is likely to be tempted to use them to get around the parliamentary process and Parliament and the courts will need to scrutinise them even more closely.

part four

restraints on government

11 Public Opinion and Information

INTRODUCTION

In a democracy, public opinion can provide a substantial check upon the use of power. The most important barometer of public opinion is the election of Parliament at least every three years. Although the elections are for MPs and the expression of party preferences, the government can be said to be on trial. Political parties compete for more votes in Parliament and therefore more influence over the conduct of government. Because, under MMP, a number of parties are likely to be represented in Parliament and none may have a majority, bargaining between the parties will often be needed in order to form a government and to pass legislation. In that bargaining, information is power; the availability of information is the key to the democratic character of MMP. And much of that bargaining may occur in public, or at least with an eye to how it will look if made public. Under MMP, public opinion is likely to be a greater driver of policy and legislative decision-making. This, in our view, will encourage more participation in decision-making and will result in a greater demand for information.

Public opinion can be expressed in a number of ways on a continuing basis. Public opinion polling, which is frequent and sophisticated, can and does measure the preferences of the public not only for commerce, which is interested in people's buying preferences, but also for political parties, who are interested in people's political and policy preferences. Systematic survey research has made a big difference to modern politics. Politicians pay close attention to public opinion polls and often try to frame their activities to secure favourable ratings.

Politicians also try to ascertain voters' views about issues on which they may have to vote in Parliament. Under MMP, electorate MPs will see constituents in clinics. List MPs, too, will no doubt see members of the public to listen to their concerns and help them with their problems. Hard-working MPs can learn a lot about the state of public opinion: people write them many letters, they listen to people in the community, they are exposed to the views expressed in the media.

The media are an important influence on public opinion, for it is through them that the majority of citizens receive most of their information about public affairs. The media have a responsibility not only to make information available but also to act as a forum for public debate. Letters to the editor, talkback radio, television current affairs programmes, and news reports all feed into the intricate web of complexities that form public opinion in a modern democracy.

The political process is, in many ways, a continuous interchange between the decision-makers and the public about the directions in which policy should travel. Criticism of policies and performance is a necessary ingredient of the democratic process and the spotlight of public scrutiny on politicians, particularly ministers, can be very harsh. In order to participate effectively in the formation of policy and its evaluation, it is necessary to have information. Under modern laws, people are entitled to a great deal of information about government and this has made government less remote and has meant that its policies are more sceptically examined by both the media and the interested public.

In this chapter, we consider the Official Information Act, the media, lobbying, and referenda.

OFFICIAL INFORMATION

The Official Information Act 1982 has enhanced the public's ability to find out what is going on within government and to exert some influence on policy formation. Greater opportunity for continuing public participation will improve all important decisions and will be more democratic.

Information bestows power. Governments collect copious amounts of information for all sorts of reasons. In New Zealand, the government had a near monopoly on official information until the passage of the Official Information Act 1982. Because more official information is available, Parliament and the public should find it easier to scrutinise, check, and hold to account the executive branch of government. As a famous American judge, Justice Brandeis, once said: 'Publicity is justly commended as a remedy for social and industrial diseases. Sunlight is said to be the best of disinfectants; electric light the most efficient policeman.'[1]

The principal rule in New Zealand is that official information must be made available to those who request it unless there is good reason to withhold it. The presumption is in favour of disclosure.[2]

The Danks Committee report, from which the 1982 legislation sprang, was a document of high quality and considerable liberality. Titled *Towards Open*

1 Louis D. Brandeis, *Other People's Money and How the Bankers Use It*, R. Adams, ed., A.M. Kelley, New York, 1971.

2 See generally, I. Eagles, M. Taggart & G. Liddell, *Freedom of Information in New Zealand*, Oxford University Press, Auckland, 1992.

Government, the report came in two parts. The reasons the committee articulated for more open access to official information could be summarised as follows:

- a better informed public can better participate in the democratic process;
- secrecy is an important impediment to accountability when Parliament, press, and public cannot properly follow and scrutinise the actions of government;
- public servants make many important decisions that affect people and the permanent administration should also be accountable through greater flows of information about what they are doing;
- better information flows will produce more effective government and help towards the more flexible development of policy. With more information available, it is easier to prepare for change;
- if more information is available, public cooperation with government will be enhanced.

The Danks Committee concluded:

> The case for more openness in government is compelling. It rests on the democratic principles of encouraging participation in public affairs and ensuring the accountability of those in office; it also derives from concern for the interests of individuals. A no less important consideration is that the Government requires public understanding and support to get its policies carried out. This can come only from an informed public.[3]

The Official Information Act applies to all government departments, ministers, and most government entities. It does not apply to MPs, the courts, tribunals, Royal Commissions, and other inquiries, or to the Parliamentary Service Commission. (Ministers must therefore be clear about when they are holding information as ministers and when they are holding it as MPs.)

The purposes of the act, as stated in section 4, are:

> (a) To increase progressively the availability of official information to the people of New Zealand in order—
> (i) To enable their more effective participation in the making and administration of laws and policies; and
> (ii) To promote the accountability of Ministers of the Crown and officials,—
> and thereby to enhance respect for the law and to promote the good government of New Zealand:
> (b) To provide for proper access by each person to official information relating to that person:
> (c) To protect official information to the extent consistent with the public interest and the preservation of personal privacy.

3 Committee on Official Information, *Towards Open Government,* Vol. 1 *General Report,* December 1980, p.14.

The prime principle is stated in section 5—'the information shall be made available unless there is good reason for withholding it'.

Section 6 of the act provides a number of reasons that are regarded as being conclusive for the withholding of information. Those reasons, as amended by the Official Information Amendment Act 1987, are that the information would be likely:

(a) To prejudice the security or defence of New Zealand or the international relations of the Government of New Zealand; or
(b) To prejudice the entrusting of information to the Government of New Zealand on a basis of confidence by—
  (i) The government of any other country or any agency of such a government; or
  (ii) Any international organisation; or
(c) To prejudice the maintenance of the law, including the prevention, investigation, and detection of offences, and the right to a fair trial; or
(d) To endanger the safety of any person; or
(e) To damage seriously the economy of New Zealand by disclosing prematurely decisions to change or continue Government economic or financial policies relating to—
  (i) Exchange rates or the control of overseas exchange transactions:
  (ii) The regulation of banking or credit:
  (iii) Taxation:
  (iv) The stability, control, and adjustment of prices of goods and services, rents, and other costs, and rates of wages, salaries, and other incomes:
  (v) The borrowing of money by the Government of New Zealand:
  (vi) The entering into of overseas trade agreements.

Where those reasons are applicable the information will not be given unless the government wants to release it.

There is a further list of more common reasons where a balancing test comes in. Under section 9 of the act these are justifications for withholding information *unless* 'in the circumstances of the particular case, the withholding of that information is outweighed by other considerations which render it desirable, in the public interest to make the information available' to:

(a) Protect the privacy of natural persons including that of deceased natural persons;
(b) Protect information where the making available of the information
  (i) Would disclose a trade secret; or
  (ii) Would be likely unreasonably to prejudice the commercial position of the person who supplied or who is the subject of the information: or
(ba) Protect information which is subject to an obligation of confidence or which any

person has been or could be compelled to provide under the authority of any enactment, where the making available of the information—

(i) Would be likely to prejudice the supply of similar information, or information from the same source, and it is in the public interest that such information should continue to be supplied; or

(ii) Would be likely otherwise to damage the public interest;

(c) Avoid prejudice to measures protecting the health or safety of members of the public; or

(d) Avoid prejudice to the substantial economic interests of New Zealand; or

(e) Avoid prejudice to measures that might prevent or mitigate material loss to members of the public; or

(f) Maintain the constitutional conventions for the time being which protect—

(i) The confidentiality of communications by or with the Sovereign or her representative:

(ii) Collective and individual ministerial responsibility:

(iii) The political neutrality of officials:

(iv) The confidentiality of advice tendered by Ministers of the Crown and officials; or

(g) Maintain the effective conduct of public affairs through—

(i) The free and frank expression of opinions by or between or to Ministers of the Crown or members of an organization or officers and employees of any department or organization in the course of their duty; or

(ii) The protection of such Ministers, members of organisations, officers, and employees from improper pressure or harassment; or

(h) Maintain legal professional privilege; or

(i) Enable a Minister of the Crown or any Department or organisation holding the information to carry out, without prejudice or disadvantage, commercial activities; or

(j) Enable a Minister of the Crown or any Department or organization holding the information to carry on, without prejudice or disadvantage, negotiations (including commercial and industrial negotiations); or

(k) Prevent the disclosure or use of official information for improper gain or improper advantage.

Clearly, there is not a great deal of precision in most of those tests and the categories are broad. This makes the decision-making process a critical element of the legislation. In marginal cases, it is not easy to predict whether the information sought will be released. The guidance given and decisions made by the Ombudsmen are critical here.

Where a request for information is made—and it can be made by any New Zealand citizen or permanent resident—it needs to be specified, in the words of the act, 'with due particularity'. It is best, clearly, to apply in writing, but there are no formal requirements of any kind, although it will be difficult if you do not know what you are looking for. So that people know what is available under the act, the Ministry of Justice publishes a most useful and comprehensive directory of information[4] which includes details of all departments and organisations covered by the act, what they do, what sort of documents they hold, a list of all manuals and similar documents containing policies, principles, rules, or guidelines that the department applies, and a statement of how to obtain access to information, including details of which officers to get in touch with. The publication is revised every two years. It is important to note that all information held is subject to the act, not just that acquired after the act came into force.

Requests can be made to ministers, departments, or organisations—in fact to anyone holding the information wanted. Usually it is best to make the request about information held by the department rather than by the minister because the minister's office does not keep and file nearly as much information as departments do. Most paper comes up to the minister's office and goes back to the department. In the act as it first operated, decisions on requests had to be made 'as soon as reasonably practicable'. But it became evident that this led to delays, and the 1987 amendments require decisions to be made within twenty working days of the request. There is provision to extend the time limits in some circumstances—there may be a large quantity of information that requires a lot of time to search through, consultations may be needed. Where there is an extension, notice must be given to the person who has requested the information, specifying the reasons for it and its length.

Where information is supplied, section 15 of the act provides that charges 'shall be reasonable and regard may be had to the cost of the labour and materials involved in making the information available'. Charges can be required to be paid in advance.

Section 16 of the act specifies a number of ways in which the information contained in a document may be made available:

- by providing a reasonable opportunity to inspect the document
- by providing a copy of the document
- as a written transcript, where it is a recording or similar matter
- by giving a summary of its contents
- by furnishing oral information about its contents.

Documents can have material deleted from them if there is reason to withhold some of the information. The information must be made available in the way

[4] Ministry of Justice, *Directory of Official Information: Te Rairangi Whakatu Whakahaere Kawantanga,* Wellington, 1995.

preferred by the person requesting it, unless that would impair efficient administration or there is a good reason under the act.

Requests for information can be refused on the grounds specified in section 18. These are:

- That good reason exists for withholding the information in terms of the tests discussed earlier.
- That, for some sensitive categories, the existence of the information can be neither confirmed nor denied—this ground can be used only to protect from disclosure information that falls into one of the conclusive grounds or special grounds stated in the act. Terrorism information is an obvious example.
- Where making the information available would be contrary to a specific act.
- Where making the information available would amount to a contempt of court or of the House of Parliament.
- Where the information is or will soon be publicly available.
- Where the information or document does not exist or cannot be found.
- Where the information cannot be made available without substantial collation or research.
- Where the information is not held by the department, minister, or organisation dealing with the request.
- Where the request is frivolous or vexatious or the information requested is trivial.

Where a request is refused, the department, minister, or organisation must, if the applicant asks, give the reasons for refusal. (There are some exceptions to this—if giving this information would prejudice the interest protected by the refusal.)

The applicant must also be informed that he or she has the right to ask the Ombudsmen to review the decision. Where such a request is made, the Ombudsman investigates the matter in much the same way as is done for complaints against administration. The Ombudsman has no power of decision, but can recommend as he or she thinks fit. The Ombudsman can make recommendations where he or she feels that the request should not have been refused or that the decision complained of is unreasonable or wrong. The Ombudsman's opinion and reasons are reported to the appropriate department, minister, or organisation, as well as to the complainant. Where such a recommendation is made, the information must be made available within twenty-one days, unless the Governor-General, by order-in-council, directs otherwise. This collective veto by Cabinet was inserted in 1987 to replace the veto by individual ministers, which had been the most controversial feature of the act.

In the early days of the act's operation, ministerial vetoes were quite common—ten were issued before the 1984 election, and only one partial one since. In the view of the Danks Committee, the courts should not be the final arbiters. They said:

> We believe that in the New Zealand context there are convincing reasons not to give the courts ultimate authority in such a matter. The system we favour involves the weighing of broad considerations and the balancing of competing public interests against one another, and against individual interests. If the general power to determine finally whether there should be access to official information were given to the courts, they would have to rule on matters with strong political and policy implications.[5]

The committee defended the veto on the grounds of ministerial responsibility and accountability to Parliament. The collective veto is a much more solemn and deliberate process than one minister, in the privacy of his or her office, deciding whether a veto ought to be applied. The veto has not been used since the amendments were made.

Moreover, the order-in-council may be made only for the reasons given in the decision reviewed by the Ombudsman. Those reasons will have resulted from a process of argument, reason, persuasion, and possible compromise. It would not be appropriate for the government to rely on a reason that had not been subjected to such a refinement process.

In addition, the person whose request for information has been declined can seek a judicial review of the making of the order-in-council. The court can consider whether the order has been properly made. This change, made in 1987, went against the view of the Danks Committee. Further, unless the court is satisfied that the application has not been reasonably or properly brought, the Crown will pay the applicant's costs. This ensures that the ordinary person's remedy is a real one. There have, however, been no decisions by the courts under these provisions and only a handful under the act. Perhaps the Ombudsmen's investigatory powers resolve disputes to the satisfaction of all parties.

The number of complaints to the Ombudsmen under the Official Information Act has been steadily increasing. In the year ended 30 June 1995, 1093 complaints were received or actioned, up significantly from the 343 complaints in the year ended 31 March 1986. Delay complaints have consistently made up a significant part of that caseload, but refusals of requests are now the main cause. When Chief Ombudsman Sir George Laking left the office in 1984 his report noted that there 'have been instances of an over-protective attitude towards the release of information by some agencies'[6] and to some extent this attitude continues. In the end, under the sort of legislation we have, the attitudes of those working in government are critical to how the act works. Some departments have at times been obstructive to the extent of delaying replies to queries by the Ombudsman when investigating a complaint.

---

[5] Committee on Official Information, *Towards Open Government*, Vol. 2: *Supplementary Report*, Wellington, 1981, p.8.

[6] *Report of the Chief Ombudsman, G. R. Laking on Leaving Office*, A.3A *Appendices to the Journal of the House of Representatives*, Wellington, 1984, p.9.

THE MEDIA

The news media are a key vehicle for public opinion acting as a check upon government.[7] The ways in which news is reported, editorial opinion is expressed, television and radio current affairs programmes are handled, all affect the public's capacity to probe and question government decision. The knowledge that such scrutiny will occur acts as a constraint upon the making of the decisions themselves. How potent a force the media can be in alerting public opinion to the actions of government depends on many factors. It is fair to say that although the media in New Zealand function as a reporter of events, their capacity to probe and question is less highly developed. And the amount of probing the media can do is shaped by how interested the public is in the fruits of that sort of journalism. If people do not buy newspapers or watch the television programmes that undertake such a task, then there will be less investigation.

If the public must rely on the media to find out what is going on in government, how reliable is that message? Not all the reforms needed in our system of government concern our public institutions. A great deal of change is also required in private organisations such as the media.

We consider that serious criticisms can be made of the New Zealand media's treatment of government and politics.[8] One of the problems with the constitutional and political system is the media's performance; if the media were of a better standard, the political system would function better. In the world of media excellence 'analysis and intelligence are valued above all else'.[9]

The media are a centre of power in the political system; they represent, literally, the ways by which the people are connected to power. The nature of the media's own power, the way it is exercised, and the accountability for it are all constitutionally important issues. The media are subject to the market and subject to the law. Both pose substantial restraints on media activities, but not in a way that aids the performance of the *constitutional* function. So how does the media exercise power and what are their obligations?

> The media have an obligation to provide information to the public about the functioning of the executive government, the decisions it takes, the inputs to those decisions, the public debate surrounding them, and the consequences. The media have a similar function in relation to Parliament—reporting what is done and said in Parliament, the work of its select committees, scrutinising government legislation, policy and expenditure. There is also an obligation to provide information to the public on the

---

7 See, generally, J. McGregor, ed., *Dangerous Democracy?—News Media Politics in New Zealand*, Dunmore Press, Palmerston North, 1996.

8 Much of this section draws on G. Palmer, *New Zealand's Constitution in Crisis: Reforming our Political System*, John McIndoe, Dunedin, 1992, Ch.9.

9 D. Halberstam, *The Powers That Be*, Chatto & Windus, London, 1979, p.132.

> activities of political parties, including caucuses as well as the party organisations in policy-making and the selection of parliamentary candidates . . .
>
> Sufficient accurate information must be imparted to provide the consumer of the media with the essence of what the government's policy is. Journalists are free to say 'The Government stinks' if they wish, but that ought to be separate from a factual account of the government's actions. The United Kingdom Royal Commission formulated the relevant standard for this problem. It said '. . . if a newspaper purports to record and discuss public affairs, it should at least record them truthfully. It may express what opinions it pleases . . . but opinions should be advocated without suppressing or distorting the relevant facts.[10]
>
> In both television news and political journalism in New Zealand these distinctions are frequently not observed. Fact and comment are jumbled up, the material is highly selected and slanted. Thus the stream of ideas in the political marketplace is polluted at the source. Television is the major influence on the political process. The way in which the distinction between fact and comment should be applied in television is by no means an easy issue. The amount of hard information imparted by television news in New Zealand is small. The images are selected and edited down so far as to often be distorted and misleading. The public is left not with substance but with image. And so politics is becoming more about images and less about policy.
>
> The implications of increasing television dominance for the political system in New Zealand have not been analysed systematically so far as I know. The question has to be asked whether television is inherently incapable of offering the audience any reliable analysis. There is also a question as to how much depth we can reasonably expect in the news. No-one can manage to publish all the news that is fit to print, although that should be easier in New Zealand than most places given its size and the fact that not a great deal happens here . . .
>
> The New Zealand media have bright spots—they are free from government control and reasonably robust. Their constitutional faults, in a symbiotic way, mirror the faults in the functioning of the political system itself. The quality of journalism in New Zealand needs to be improved if we are to improve the quality of government and the public's ability to participate in it.[11]

The complexity of the policy-making system under MMP poses grave challenges to the media in New Zealand. It is likely that MMP will make Parliament, the public service, and government decision-making more generally sensitive to public

---

[10] Report of *Royal Commission on the Press 1947–49*, reprinted in *Reader in Public Opinion and Communication*, eds B. Berelson & M. Janowitz, 2nd ed., Free Press, New York, 1966, pp.541–2.

[11] G. Palmer, *New Zealand's Constitution in Crisis*, pp.203, 204.

opinion. If that is the case, the activities of the media may be even more important than they have been in the past. Any emphasis or slant in the communication of information can affect the voting preferences of the public. Selection of issues can play a role in setting the political agenda and the parliamentary agenda. Practising politicians are acute observers of media output and they often interact with journalists in order to get their own views across to the public.

Furthermore, under MMP the policy-making process is likely to contain a greater variety of views on policy and many more opportunities for lobbyists to influence the course of the policy and legislative processes. Journalists will have to be diligent in investigating nuances of compromises and deals. They will have to interpret and dig behind positions taken by different political parties, interest groups, and select committees, and compare them with ministers' statements and public servants' advice.

MMP will pose particular challenges to the journalists who work in the parliamentary Press Gallery.[12]

> The parliamentary press gallery is the centre of political reporting in New Zealand and has the most important role in carrying out the constitutional function of the media. It is the only segment of the media which devotes its activities entirely to politics and government. Its performance, therefore, is central to the public understanding of policy issues and the political process. Obviously the press gallery does not operate in isolation from the rest of the media. Gallery journalists are much affected by trends in journalism generally and the pressures which drive them. But they also have particular problems of their own due to the way they are organized and the place where they work. Their central difficulty is lack of some coherent conception of what they are supposed to be doing.
>
> The press gallery comes within the purview of the standing orders of Parliament which provide that any organisation whose representative infringes the standing orders of the house may be excluded from representation in the press gallery. The rules of the parliamentary press gallery are approved by the Speaker and cover such matters as accreditation. Membership is restricted to those whose primary duties are 'to cover politics and to report to the public what is happening in Parliament'. Full accreditation goes to those who work in the gallery on a full time basis. There are about 50 [now 45] such reporters. Associate members can be appointed if they can demonstrate a need for frequent access to Parliament. Currently there are about 40 [now 30] associate members . . .
>
> observations on the gallery's range of reportorial functions . . :

12 *Ibid.*, pp.214–15 and 219. Also, see Alister Browne, 'Reporting the Politicians: Feasting in the Gallery', in *Dangerous Democracy?—News Media Politics in New Zealand*, ed. J. McGregor, Dunmore Press, Palmerston North, 1996.

- reporting Parliament
- reporting Select Committees
- reporting ministerial announcements and press conferences
- reporting on the activities of the Opposition
- reporting statements made by MPs
- trying to find out what went on in Caucus meetings
- preparing reports of official government documents, reviews, commissions, reports and studies
- finding out what is going on in government departments and reporting on it
- reporting on Cabinet to the extent this is possible
- interviewing and profiling ministers and MPs
- preparing background reports on issues, preparing analysis of political issues and prospects
- covering regional and national conferences of political parties
- covering party candidate selections and backgrounding them
- analysing annual reports tabled in Parliament
- preparing summaries of legislation introduced into Parliament
- reporting on the conduct of New Zealand's foreign relations
- providing reports on economic policy and the state of the economy.

These functions are impossibly broad, yet specialisation appears to be very limited. Most members of the gallery have to turn their hand to most of the above tasks at some time or other.

The gallery journalists attend press conferences, and concentrate on reporting them, ministerial press statements, press conferences, and documents released by the Government or tabled in the House. They also write weekly round-ups containing their opinions on various issues and the government's performance. They will also spend a lot of time on political stories—splits and divisions, if any can be discerned in either the opposition or the government . . .

Some observers make the point that it is necessary to develop other means of conveying the information. Dr Les Cleveland and Mr Brian Conroy have written:[13]

> For example, a great deal has been said in recent years about the need for a more extensive presentation of the work of Parliament, but it is unrealistic to expect newspapers and radio and television services as they are at present constituted to cope with this task. The chief deficiencies of their present coverage are the episodic nature of their reportage, its lack of explanatory depth and its superficiality on all but the major topics of current political debate. A great deal of information currently

[13] L. Cleveland & B. Conroy, 'Government Agencies and the News Media: A Better Working Relationship', 2 *Public Sector*, 1979, pp.2, 10, 12.

> available in departmental reports and other published documents, or located in the deliberations of select committees goes largely unreported. Furthermore, during each session a considerable output of legislation in the form of bills and regulations is available for detailed analysis.

Perhaps the technological revolution will come to the rescue of democracy. The development of cable and satellite TV, multimedia computing, and the Internet brings enormous reservoirs of information within easy reach of those who can afford the equipment. The New Zealand Government, many departments, and political parties have already established home pages on the World Wide Web, which is part of the Internet. As the ease of access increases, and the cost decreases, people will be able to get precise and accurate information about what they are interested in directly from the relevant sources anywhere in New Zealand or the world. The media must, therefore, concentrate even harder on investigation and interpretation to make 'news'.

LOBBYING

Politics is not merely the 'clash and adjustment of interests and groups'.[14] Pressure group activity is not all politics, but it is a big chunk of it. The issue here is to what extent lobbying will increase under MMP and how it will be carried out. Several things are clear. First, select committees, already important in the system, become more so under MMP and appearances at select committees will be vital to groups who want to influence their deliberation. Second, every MP will be of greater importance than before. In an MMP Parliament there may be issues that will be determined not by the will of the government but by the will of the Parliament, which is not always the same thing.

The trouble with the term 'lobbying' is that it has good and bad connotations. Lobbying can be educative, informative, and improve the quality of decisions in a thoroughly democratic manner. Or it can be malign and corrupting. Lobbying involves an attempt to exert influence, but this can either be 'proper' or 'improper', according to the point of view of the person examining the conduct. In New Zealand, as in other countries, there would be substantial disagreement about what is and is not appropriate.[15]

As Will Rogers put it, 'A lobbyist is a person that is supposed to help a Politician to make up his mind, not only help him but pay him.'[16] Or, if it is not money,

---

[14] B. Crick, *The American Science of Politics*, University of California Press, Berkeley, California, 1959, p.127. Compare this approach with that adopted in the classic work, V.O. Key Jr, *Politics, Parties and Pressure Groups*, 5th ed., Crowell, New York, 1964.

[15] Lester W. Milbrath, *The Washington Lobbyists*, Rand McNally, Chicago, 1963, p.7. Congressional Quarterly Inc., *The Washington Lobby*, 4th ed., 1982, 1, 3.

[16] W. Rogers, *The Autobiography of Will Rogers*, Avon, New York, 1949, p.14.

then blandishments of some other description may be used, even 'the lever of lust'.[17] Many lobbyists, like diplomats, assist their craft by providing good dinners. Indeed, the law in the state of Wisconsin used to forbid any lobbyist to buy or give any legislator anything, a meal, a drink, or even a cigar.[18] At best, lobbying looks like political work, at its worst, it looks like bribery.

New Zealand abounds with organisations that are formed to promote various kinds of activity. There are trade organisations such as the Employers Federation, the Manufacturers Federation, the Retailers Federation, and Federated Farmers. There are professional organisations such as the New Zealand Law Society, the New Zealand Nurses Association, the Post-Primary Teachers Association, and the New Zealand Educational Institute. There are organisations such as the Council of Trade Unions, which represent thousands of workers. Recreation organisations such as the New Zealand Rugby Football Union and the New Zealand Deerstalkers Association represent particular points of view. The network of these pressure groups influences government at every turn by making representations to ministers, to MPs, to public servants, to parliamentary select committees, to caucus committees, and even, on occasion, to Cabinet committees.

It has been said that a politician is a person kept upright by pressure on all sides, which suggests that there is something sinister about the influence of pressure groups. But in a democracy it is inevitable that people with similar interests will organise themselves to protect those interests. Often new interests will not be well represented among the chorus of entreaties sung to government, but if the interest to be promoted strikes a chord in the community, the organisation will follow.

The tactics of pressure groups vary from issue to issue and from organisation to organisation. Some will offer campaign contributions to political parties. Those with big memberships will threaten to conduct a campaign through the media against certain government decisions. Perhaps the most effective weapon of the pressure group in an MMP environment is to provide all the relevant decision-makers with *information* about how a decision will affect people and to make *rational arguments*, based on that information, as to why any policy should or should not be adopted.

Despite the confidential nature of the decision-making process, most arguments in favour of a policy need, finally, to withstand the scrutiny of the public gaze. Governing by giving in to the demands of pressure will not produce good policy or sound government, but only incoherent zigzags in policy.

---

17 N.J. Orstein & J. Elder, *Interest Groups, Lobbying and Policymaking*, Congressional Quarterly Inc, Washington, 1978, p.97. Gambling halls and hotels filled with women lobbyists were apparently common in Washington in the mid-nineteenth century.

18 W.H. Young, *Ogg and Ray's Introduction to American Government*, 12th ed., Appleton-Century-Crofts, New York, 1962, p.742.

Lobbyists may make clear and logical policy arguments based on solid information. Or they may engage in political threats or inducements. In the latter case, they may resemble politicians rather than advocates. Express or implied threats are a sort of political bargaining. The support or opposition of a large organisation that may translate into gain or loss of electoral support is leverage. These threats can be given credibility in a number of ways well known to New Zealand MPs—telegrams, letters to MPs and ministers, a campaign of letters to the editor, phone calls, visits to the electorate office, the mounting of a petition to be presented to Parliament, and so on. Decision-makers in New Zealand tend to take seriously the carefully expressed views of an individual citizen; they tend to be a bit more cynical when they receive fifty identically worded letters.

Influencing policy involves making some judgements about public opinion. Public policy not only involves public opinion, but may involve the black arts of influencing that opinion by means of media pronouncements and public relations techniques.

Because of the clear abuses that can be associated with lobbying, attempts have been made to regulate it. In the United States it has been regulated by law since 1946.[19] Given the nature of democracy and the constitutional guarantees of freedom of expression, such regulation would never be easy and the legislation has proved to be ineffective.

In the House of Commons at Westminster, it has long been the case that MPs take on positions as 'consultants' or agents for particular interests and are remunerated. This ought not to be misunderstood. Bribery of an MP is a breach of privilege and a number of rules require interests to be declared. Strict control over members' conduct and over lobbying can be exerted through the rules of parliamentary privilege. But it is clear that MPs at Westminster provide advice on parliamentary relations and are paid to do so. This can be found from the Register of Members' Interests.[20] In other words, the MPs themselves are lobbyists. Lobbying in the House of Commons appears to be unregulated except by the rather ill-defined protections offered by parliamentary privilege. The same is true of New Zealand, but the British practice of having MPs as lobbyists has never been adopted in the New Zealand Parliament. Obviously MPs have preferences for and loyalties to some groups more than others, but to turn that into some formal relationship for a fee, as occurs among British backbenchers, would be undesirable.

The Australians have ventured into voluntary regulation of lobbying, under a scheme administered by the Department of Administrative Services. There is no legal compulsion backing the scheme, but failure to register means that access to

---

19 Federal Regulation of Lobbying Act 2 *United States Code* Annotated sections 261–70.

20 A.G. Jordon & J.J. Richardson, *Government and Pressure Groups in Britain*, Clarendon Press, Oxford, 1987, pp.265–73.

the person to be lobbied will be denied. In other words, there will not be any appointments. When the scheme was established in 1984, ministers were advised not to deal with lobbyists not fulfilling the registration requirements.[21] The Guidelines for Registration of Lobbyists are quite explicit: '*lobbyist* means a person (or company) who, for financial or other advantage, represents a client in dealing with Commonwealth Government Ministers and officials'.[22]

Looking at the nature of the law in other jurisdictions, it may seem to be desirable for possible excesses to be curbed in New Zealand by some light regulation. There is a very small amount now. Strangers are not permitted in the lobbies generally and certainly not while a division is in progress.[23] It should be remembered, however, that the criminal law does have some application to lobbying and will curb the grosser abuses.[24] The real problem is that it is hard to make such regulation effective and there are many practical problems associated with it.

A register of members' interests is a reform that should be seriously considered for the New Zealand Parliament.[25] It would simply require MPs to disclose their pecuniary interests. The *Cabinet Office Manual* applies such disclosure to ministers and the same rules could easily be applied to all MPs. Furthermore, a register of lobbyists could be adopted dealing with those who would influence both ministers and MPs, as well as members of the public service. Both these measures could be adopted by resolution of the House. The contents of both registers should be publicly available. There is quite enough authority, within the standing orders and powers of parliamentary privilege, to give such a regime the necessary teeth. Measures like these would add transparency to some of what goes on at present, but they would not provide great protection against undesirable practices. It should be noted, however, that the 1995 Standing Orders contain stricter rules about pecuniary interests.

Moderate as these suggestions are, it will be difficult to get them adopted until there is some public incident that stirs public dissatisfaction and creates a demand for action. But, as has happened overseas, such rules are not likely to achieve much. New Zealand has been remarkably free of the sort of abuse that has given lobbying a bad name in other countries. But it might be prudent to act in advance of demand and such a move might help to restore the reputation of the political process.

---

21 Peter Sekuless, *Lobbying in Canberra in the Nineties—the Government Relations Game*, Allen & Unwin, North Sydney, 1991, p.81.

22 *Ibid.*, p.85. The full guidelines are set out.

23 New Zealand House of Representatives, *Speakers' Rulings 1867–1980*, Wellington, 1982, 136; D. McGee, *Parliamentary Practice in New Zealand*, Government Printer, Wellington, 1985, p.32.

24 See the Crimes Act 1961, ss. 102, 103 and the Secret Commissions Act 1910.

25 G. Palmer, *Unbridled Power*, 2nd ed., Oxford University Press, Auckland, 1987, p.129.

We expect that MMP will make the task of lobbyists much more time-consuming but that they will find it easier to stop the government from acting. Lobbying is likely to be more continuous and to have less of an all-or-nothing outcome for the term of a particular government than has been the case in the past.

CITIZENS' INITIATED REFERENDA

From time to time important public issues in New Zealand are decided by referendum, that is to say they are voted on at a poll of electors. Questions for which the procedure has been used over the years in New Zealand include:

- the introduction of MMP (1992 and 1993);
- control of alcoholic liquor—the issue of prohibition, continuance, or state control was voted on every three years for many years until the passage of the Sale of Liquor Act 1989;
- licensing hours, i.e., end of six o'clock closing (1967);
- whether the term of Parliament should be extended to four years (in 1990);
- conscription during peace (1949); and
- the control of off-course betting on horse races (1949).

Referenda can be in two forms. A referendum can be advisory, not producing any change in the law but providing a guide for politicians who make the final decision by voting in Parliament. The 1992 referendum on whether to vote further on changing the electoral system was advisory. Or a referendum can have a legally binding effect, as did the 1993 referendum on whether to introduce MMP.

A related method of decision-making is the free vote in Parliament. Under that system, which has been used in recent years for liquor legislation, the capital punishment issue, and abortion and homosexual law reform legislation, MPs do not vote in accordance with a party line but according to their own consciences. The tangles into which Parliament often gets itself over these issues, particularly abortion, is partly a result of parliamentarians being in the unaccustomed role of having a free vote and not having a means of working out new groupings, and partly because of the passionate views of the community.

Deciding whether to put issues to a referendum poses problems. The formulation of a particular issue can cause great confusion. Questions must be put so that people understand them; refinements cannot be incorporated if the issue is to remain comprehensible. Most important issues of public policy are very difficult to represent in neutral language in a simple question. Also, referenda are expensive to conduct if, as in New Zealand to date, they are conducted on the same basis as general elections. If an indication of public opinion on an issue is wanted, public opinion polls may be just as good. Nonetheless, referenda do give everyone a chance to be heard. And they must reduce the level of public dissatisfaction with some types of decision.

Referenda are commonly used in the United States. The most dramatic provisions are contained in the Constitution of the State of California, article 4, section 1 of which states that 'the people reserve to themselves the power to propose laws and amendments to the Constitution, and to adopt or reject the same, at the polls independent of the Legislature, and also reserve the power, at their own option, to so adopt or reject any act, or section or part of any act, passed by the Legislature'.

The Royal Commission on the Electoral System in New Zealand, which reported in 1986, examined the use of referenda. Many submissions to the commission supported the increased use of referenda and the range of views was wide. The commission's general conclusion was opposed to the introduction of widespread referenda as a means of deciding public issues. It said:

> In general, initiatives and referenda are blunt and crude devices which need to be used with care and circumspection. Their frequent use would amount to a substantial change in our constitutional and political system. They would blur the lines of accountability and responsibility of Governments and political parties, and blunt their effectiveness. In our view, those elected to govern should be able to do so without formal reference to the people as a whole, provided they can be formally held to account at regular and frequent intervals, provided they are responsive to an informed public opinion, and provided there is continued development of restraints on the power of Government such as through parliamentary select committees, the Ombudsmen, the Official Information Act, and administrative review through the courts. There are other ways through which popular opinion can be expressed and have an effect on the legislative and decision-making processes. Initiatives and referenda can adversely affect minorities. There are very real practical difficulties. It is our view that under our present political and constitutional system, the regular use of initiatives and referenda would detract from rather than enhance the ways our democracy generally works.[26]

The commission saw merit in conducting referenda on constitutional issues—it even recommended them for some of its own recommendations, including the introduction of the new voting system, MMP, which was brought in as a result of two referenda. In the commission's view, all referenda should be regarded as binding on Parliament. Where a referendum is to be held, there should be special legislation concerning its questions and procedures in each case.

The commission's views did not settle the question of the future use of referenda in New Zealand.[27] The National Government passed the Citizens Initiated

---

26 Report of the Royal Commission on the Electoral System, *Towards a Better Democracy*, Wellington, December 1986, pp.175–6.

Referenda Act 1993, which enables issues to be subjected to an indicative referendum that is not binding on the government or the Parliament. At the time of writing one such referendum has been held in 1995 on the question: 'Should the number of professional fire-fighters employed full-time in the New Zealand Fire Service be reduced below the number employed on 1 January 1995?' The use of the referendum was heavily criticised, because it appeared to be promoted by a trade union in order to win an industrial relations argument. The firefighters received a heavy majority against the proposition put, but it did not appear to affect government policy. There was also criticism that it cost $9 million to hold the referendum.[28]

In order to promote a referendum under the act, it is necessary to present a petition to Parliament with supporting signatures of 10 per cent of eligible electors. On current figures, that would amount to something like 240,000 voters. This is a high threshold to meet and it is not surprising that, by the middle of 1996, only one proposal had met it. A formidable amount of time and effort is required to collect that number of signatures. Many will not find the task worthwhile, given that, even if the referendum attracts a majority, it is not binding on the government.

The range of matters that may be subjected to an indicative referendum is almost limitless. There is no specific guidance as to the scope or nature of the permitted subject matter of the referendum, a situation which the Chief Justice said 'may seem extraordinary' in a case that came before him concerning the wording of a proposed referendum on battery hens.[29] ('Should the production of eggs from battery hens be prohibited within five years of this referendum?') In theory, questions could be put to a referendum that Parliament would have no power to do anything about, for example, to change the All Black captain.

It costs $500 to file a petition asking for a referendum and the Clerk of the House of Representatives has a role in determining the question that can be put as well as checking the signatures. The act also restricts the amount of money that can be spent on publicity promoting or opposing a referendum. Every person who either alone or in combination with others, knowingly spends more than $50,000 on advertisements published or broadcast either in relation to a petition or in the promotion of one of the answers to the precise question to be put to

---

27 See A. Simpson (ed.), *Referendums: Constitutional and Political Perspectives*, Department of Politics, Victoria University of Wellington, Wellington, 1992; and M. Gobbi, 'The Quest for Legitimacy: A Comparative Constitutional Study of the Origin and Role of Direct Democracy in Switzerland, California and New Zealand', LLM thesis, Faculty of Law, Victoria University of Wellington, 1994.

28 B. Edlin, 'A grand exercise in ballot box absurdity', *The Independent*, 8 December 1995, p.10.

29 *Egg Producers Federation of New Zealand* v *Clerk of the House of Representatives*, Eichelbaum CJ, 20 June 1994, High Court, Wellington CP 128/94.

voters, commits an offence. Returns of expenditure have to be kept. The procedures for conducting the poll are largely the same as those stipulated for the taking of an electoral poll under the Electoral Act 1993. There is no requirement for the production of any official objective material explaining the issues.

Just what role citizens initiated referenda may play in the future is not easy to predict, but the portents are not favourable.

12 Local Government

LOCAL GOVERNMENT IN THE PAST

Following the end of Crown colony government in New Zealand, the Imperial Parliament at Westminster gave New Zealand a constitutional structure that contained an elaborate set of arrangements for what, today, may be considered local government.

The New Zealand Constitution Act 1852 contained eighty-two sections. It provided for a General Assembly, which consisted of a House of Representatives elected for a period of five years, an upper House of legislative councillors nominated by the Crown, but holding office for life, and the Governor. As well as the General Assembly, there were provincial legislatures in six provinces, later ten.

The provincial councils were designed to carry out in each province the work of subordinate legislation and administration, and to ease the burden of work of the General Assembly. As two early analysts observed: 'Though the machinery devised was faulty, the principle was a sound one, and well-suited to the circumstances of the young Colony. The centres of population were distinct and isolated, and the difficulties of transit and communication great.'[1] The chief executive of each province was a superintendent directly elected by the people for a term of four years.

The provinces endured from 1856 to 1876 when the Vogel Government abolished them. The destruction of the provinces is an interesting historical issue in itself. Centralism versus provincialism was a key political issue between 1856 and 1876 and the battles were hard fought.

A recent biography of E.W. Stafford, an important nineteenth-century political figure, indicates how parochial politics were in early New Zealand.[2] Stafford, who was leading the government in 1868, was moved to say in Parliament:

1 J. Hight & H.D. Bamford, *The Constitutional History and Law of New Zealand*, Whitcombe & Tombs, Christchurch, 1914, p.264.

2 Edmund Bohan, *Edward Stafford, New Zealand's First Statesman*, Hazard Press, Christchurch, 1994.

> I shall now urge our friends to take every opportunity of pointing out how miserably insufficient the present political system is to meet the wants of the people, and of demonstrating how, whatever little efficiency it once possessed, has as a rule died out. The honourable member always forgets that there is a large portion of the Colony which does not belong to the large centres of population. He has never got beyond the time when New Zealand consisted of six small fishing villages, as was the case when the Constitution Act was passed in 1852. He speaks as if these six little villages still represented the people of New Zealand. He ignores the fact that provincial government in New Zealand is, for the most part, reduced to a petty central power, and that the most despotic government ever seen in the country is what might be styled the rump of a provincial government. The provincial system has been tried and found wanting, and cannot long survive.[3]

The provincial system lasted only another eight years. Stafford had a consistent policy of attempting to weld a nation out of New Zealand's disparate and far-flung settlements. As he remarked to the Parliament on a later occasion: 'If we heard less of the provinces, and more of the people of New Zealand, our legislation would be more beneficial'.[4] The critical argument which ultimately sealed the fate of the provinces in New Zealand was the principle that the power which raises the taxes should be the spending power directly responsible to the people on whom those taxes are levied. So on 1 November 1876 the provinces perished.

New Zealand had a Municipal Corporations Ordinance as early as 1842. This established that each settlement of 2000 souls was a borough comprising a body corporate of 'the Mayor, Alderman and Burgesses'. But the constitutional foundations of this ordinance were insecure and it was eventually disallowed, to be followed, in 1845, by a Public Roads and Works Ordinance. Local government as we understand it today proceeded in fits and starts until the passage of the Municipal Corporations Act 1867, which provided for a uniform urban territorial authority structure, although its application was not mandatory.

Although the centralist tradition triumphed in 1876, New Zealand's citizens initially resisted the central power, which they saw as a vehicle that was going to impose taxes on them but do nothing else. The settlers were strongly independent and, in many instances, wanted to resist government as much as they could.

The historical record shows that, because of the way in which the debate on the abolition of the provinces proceeded, very little conceptual thinking was done about what pattern of local government should be adopted in New Zealand. Local government really started life as a practical and operational contrivance lacking any fundamental constitutional conception. It is a defect from which we still suffer.

---

3 Hight & Bamford, *The Constitutional History and Law of New Zealand*, p.291.
4 *Ibid*, p.294.

Local government was strengthened when the provinces were abolished and the Municipal Corporations Act 1876 brought all existing entities under the same act, and provided for the creation of new ones. One of the principal consequences of the abolition of the provinces was the passage through the Parliament of the Counties Act 1876, which created sixty-three counties in rural areas with elected councils. A new and complementary Municipal Corporations Act was passed the same year. From 1876 onwards local bodies multiplied, with many ad hoc authorities being added such as harbour boards, rabbit boards, and water boards.

LOCAL GOVERNMENT IN THE PRESENT

Local government remains a necessity. But because, early on, New Zealand had a more elaborate and overblown system of provincial government than it needed, the destruction of that arrangement appears to have acted as a disincentive to create any adequate local government structure since.

Far from having a federal system where power is shared, New Zealand has an incredibly strong, centralised, unitary system of government. The powers of local government depend not upon any constitutional document, but on the will of the Parliament as expressed, from time to time, in the Local Government Act 1974.

Although this may seem to be an unsatisfactory situation, which needs to be altered, it is difficult to arrive at some conceptual understanding of the appropriate role of local government. There is a notable absence of constitutional analysis in New Zealand on the role of local government. As Dr Kenneth A. Palmer points out: 'The theory and place of local government in the political system does not derive from any formal constitutional entitlement.'[5] He goes on to point out that the history of local government depends primarily on the policies and expectations of central government. And although local government has evolved considerably, particularly in recent years, its evolution has been essentially pragmatic. If New Zealand adopts a written constitution, that would be an ideal opportunity to insert the constitutional principles that should govern local government in New Zealand. But we must know what it is we want. There has been a dearth of debate and thinking about local government; it is time there was some.

The closest we have in New Zealand to a developed theory about the purposes of local government is contained in section 37K of the Local Government Act 1974, which was inserted at the time of the 1989 amendments. It provides as follows:

---

5 K.A. Palmer, *Local Government Law in New Zealand*, 2nd ed., Law Book, Sydney, 1993, p.23. This is an important book on the law relating to local government. See also G. Bush, *Local Government and Politics in New Zealand*, Auckland University Press, Auckland, 1995.

The purposes of local government in New Zealand are to provide, at the appropriate levels of local government,—

(a) Recognition of the existence of different communities in New Zealand:

(b) Recognition of the identities and values of those communities:

(c) Definition and enforcement of appropriate rights within those communities:

(d) Scope for communities to make choices between different kinds of local public facilities and services:

(e) For the operation of trading undertakings of local authorities on a competitively neutral basis:

(f) For the delivery of appropriate facilities and services on behalf of central government:

(g) Recognition of communities of interest:

(h) For the efficient and effective exercise of the functions, duties, and powers of the components of local government:

(i) For the effective participation of local persons in local government.

The amendments made to the act in 1989 were highly significant; they amounted to some of the most radical reforms ever made to the structure of New Zealand local government. The aim of the changes was to make local government more effective, more democratic, more accountable, and more economical.

One of the features of these reforms was to reduce the number of local authorities and *ad hoc* local bodies that had grown up over the years. The schemes of reorganisation were prepared by the Local Government Commission and electors' ability to frustrate these amalgamation and reorganisation plans was removed by changing the law allowing polls on the issue. The result of all this activity was to prune the number of authorities drastically and simplify the structures. Before the reforms there were territorial authorities made up of cities, boroughs, districts, counties, and towns. Afterwards there were cities and districts, both with mayors.

To appreciate the magnitude of the changes, consider what happened to the previous Auckland territorial authorities. There were eleven cities, sixteen boroughs, four counties, a drainage board, a scenic board, and a number of reserve boards. These were replaced by four new cities and three district councils.[6] The rationalisation and consolidation throughout the country was extensive.

6 J.B. Ringer, *An Introduction to New Zealand Government: a guide to finding out about government in New Zealand, its institutions, structures and activities*, Hazard Press, Christchurch, 1991, p.242.

Elected regional councils were set up across the country with specific rating powers in 1989. They were based on water catchments. They received important powers following the passage of the Resource Management Act 1991.

So in 1996 the essential structure of local government in New Zealand comprises:

- Regional councils, which absorbed many functions of many of the previous special purpose authorities.
- Territorial authorities, which are district councils and city councils.
- Special purpose authorities, which have been greatly reduced following abolition of power boards, harbour boards, and area health boards. But licensing trusts, which sell liquor in some areas, are surviving examples.
- Community boards established under the Local Government Act have to be approved by the council within whose area the community is, although there can be an appeal to the Local Government Commission if a petition to set one up is refused. The council may delegate functions to the board as well. Broadly, boards perform advisory and community liaison functions.
- Community trusts can be established by local authorities. Usually these are for the purpose of receiving surplus funds for the profit or sale of trading enterprises such as a port company. The Auckland Community Trust is perhaps the best known of these.

THE FUNCTIONS AND POWERS OF LOCAL GOVERNMENT

While local government in New Zealand is subordinate to central government and ultimately is controlled by legislation passed by Parliament, it is nonetheless invested with substantial law-making and regulatory powers. Most people probably think of local authorities as being responsible for roading, water, sewerage, parks and reserves, and collecting the rubbish. But they have a much wider range of responsibilities, particularly of a regulatory character. A good example is the power to grant consents required under the Resource Management Act 1991. But there are many others: administering the standards for buildings and ensuring compliance with the codes, noise control, dog registration, and running libraries and other civic amenities such as town halls.

Local governments carry out a variety of health and environmental functions, such as registration and inspection of premises that sell food for public consumption. They often hold substantial amounts of land and carry out public works. They are sometimes engaged in housing activities and encouraging industrial development. They must provide cemeteries. They have functions concerning noxious plants, litter, clean air, animals, offensive trades, wildlife, and civil defence. They regulate billiard rooms, shooting galleries, amusement galleries, massage parlours, and aspects of the liquor laws.

The most important power of local authorities is that to levy rates. Rating, a form of tax on freehold or leasehold property, is by far the most important source of revenue available to local government. The law about rating, which is found primarily in the Rating Powers Act 1988, is highly complex and gives rise to many disputes. Councils have a choice of methods for striking a rate. The rate can be on the capital value of property, or the unimproved value of the land, or a council can choose the annual value system. There is also power to levy rates on a differential basis, which means that local authorities can vary the effects of any of the three base systems by imposing uniform annual charges and can determine the appropriate spread of the rating burden. There are a number of exemptions from rates: some Crown land comes into this category, as does much land used for educational, religious, and charitable purposes.

The legal powers enjoyed by local government come entirely from statutes passed by the New Zealand Parliament. Local government also has power to pass its own laws—called by-laws. These have to be agreed by the elected representatives of the council but they can relate only to topics about which Parliament has given local authorities the power to make laws. A local authority has no inherent law-making power and by-laws cannot contradict the general law of the land. Section 14 of the By-laws Act 1910 provides that a by-law will be invalid if it is 'repugnant' to the laws of New Zealand.

The act controls the validity of these laws and it also provides that the Minister of Local Government may confirm by-laws if the authority decides to seek that confirmation. If this is done, the confirmation prevents any issues being raised about the regularity of the processes used to pass the by-law. The Local Government Act lays down the procedure for making by-laws. Notification (twenty-one days' notice) must be given so that people can think about the law and make representations before the council adopts it.

Often the by-laws adopted are standard ones that have been worked up and published by the Standards Council of New Zealand under the Standards Act 1988. The council produces model by-laws on a number of subjects; there is advantage in the uniform approach this practice allows.

As canvassed in Chapter 10, the doctrine of *ultra vires* is the most potent check against the making of regulations and by-laws that are too wide. The law limits the powers of a local authority to those given by statute. A local authority cannot legislate widely, and its officials can do only those things and carry out those functions authorised by statute. This doctrine has given rise to a wider range of case law in the courts about how far local authorities can go in exercising their powers. In one case, for example, a court held that a power to make by-laws 'concerning the construction and repair of buildings' did not authorise the prohibition by by-law of erecting some buildings unless they were designed by a registered architect or engineer.[7] Where by-laws are breached, it is officers of the council who bring prosecutions in the courts.

Apart from the doctrine of *ultra vires* under which all subordinate legislation including regulations can be challenged, by-laws can also be challenged in court because they are 'unreasonable'. A famous English case, which took the same approach as is taken in New Zealand courts, held that a by-law that prohibited the playing of any instrument or singing in any public place within 50 yards of a dwelling house, after being required by a constable or inmate of such house to desist, was not a reasonable exercise of power to make by-laws for the good rule and government of the borough and the suppression of nuisances.[8]

One of the problems with local government has been that, in recent times, courts exercising their power of judicial review have become an important element in refining local authority decisions. On matters such as rates, judicial review has tended to take the place of the decisions of elected people. This is partly because the statute law is unsatisfactory and various efforts have been made recently to rectify that. But the real issue is: once the framework is properly established, what powers ought elected representatives have?

In recent years, judicial review has been sought over a number of local authority funding decisions. The courts have tended to expand the range of matters into which they will allow judicial review. Most of the cases involve review of funding decisions made under the Rating Powers Act 1988 and the Local Government Act 1974.[9] But a 1996 decision of the Court of Appeal has clarified matters.

In *Wellington City Council* v. *Woolworths and others*,[10] the Court of Appeal concluded that the scheme of the rating legislation implies that a rating system, in whatever form, remains primarily a taxation system and not a system inherently based on user pays. The legislation imposes significant obligations with respect to process, all of which were met by the council, but the substantive decision-making power is not expressly circumscribed. The legislation proceeds on the premise that the wider substantive judgements are made by the popularly elected representatives exercising a broad economic, social, and political assessment. The President of the Court of Appeal, Sir Ivor Richardson, says at pages 12–13 of the court's judgment:

> To confine the acceptable justification for the differentiation to those differences as correspond or are reasonably related to enjoyment of the benefit of services provided by the territorial authority is to ignore the scheme of the legislation and to disregard the breadth of the statutory powers. The legislation permits a territorial authority in

---

7 *Hanna* v. *Auckland City Corporation* [1945] *NZLR* 622.
8 *Kruse* v. *Johnson* [1898] 2 QB 91.
9 For example, *McKenzie District Council* v. *Electricity Corporation of New Zealand* [1992] *NZLR* 41.
10 CA 17/96, CA 46/94, judgment of the court delivered by Richardson P., 24 May 1996.

> making those choices which impact on the incidence of rates to make its own judgment as to what is appropriate and equitable. The decision-making is the prerogative of the local authority subject to the statutory limitations and process constraints already referred to—and to amenability to judicial review.

Because the powers of local government are currently defined by statute, the role of the courts is to determine whether councils have neglected to consider relevant matters, have considered irrelevant matters, have failed to consult or follow statutory procedures, or have reached a decision so unreasonable that no reasonable council could ever have made it. The court does not substitute its own judgment for that of the council. Again, Sir Ivor Richardson, at page 15 of the court's judgment, said:

> . . . there are constitutional and democratic constraints on judicial involvement in wide public policy issues. There comes a point where public policies are so significant and appropriate for weighing by those elected by the community for that purpose that the courts should defer to their decision except in clear and extreme cases. The larger the policy content and the more the decision making is within the customary sphere of those entrusted with the decision, the less well equipped the courts are to reweigh considerations involved and less inclined they must be to intervene.

THE ACCOUNTABILITY OF LOCAL GOVERNMENT

As has already been outlined, the law is one of the key elements in the accountability of local government. More frequently than in central government, the capacity of local government to carry something out is questioned. But the democratic procedures of elections, not the law, are the most important element of local government accountability.

A lengthy statute sets out how the local electoral system works.[11] Elections are held every three years, usually on the second Saturday in October. The most recent local body elections were in 1995. Every parliamentary elector automatically qualifies as a 'residential elector' for local body elections if his or her registered address is within the region, district, or community. But, unlike parliamentary elections, non-resident ratepayers who occupy premises within the district or who are nominees of a corporate property occupier, may vote in local body elections. This is a controversial provision. The Labour Government abolished it; it was restored by National.

All New Zealand citizens and permanent residents may vote in local body elections, although there are restrictions if they have been out of New Zealand for

[11] Local Elections and Polls Act 1976, but this needs to be read in conjunction with the Local Government Act 1974.

lengthy periods—three years in the case of a citizen and twelve months in the case of a permanent resident. Citizens and permanent residents can stand as candidates, but a person who is a candidate for a territorial authority or community board cannot be a candidate for a regional council election. Unlike elections for Parliament, postal voting can be used for local authority elections. This is usually done because it achieves higher returns than conventional voting through a polling booth.

Polls can also be conducted on local government issues. A common example concerns polls on special loans raised by territorial authorities for public works. Where 15 per cent of the ratepayers for a district who represent at least 15 per cent of the rateable properties in the district petition for a poll, it must be held.[12] Polls are also required for approval of reorganisation schemes to establish new local authority districts or regions. If the local authority wishes, it can conduct referenda on any matter relating to services or policy, although the results of these are not binding.

OTHER PUBLIC LAW CHECKS ON LOCAL GOVERNMENT

Other instruments are available to secure democratic accountability. If a person wishes to complain about the decision of a local authority, he or she can write to the Ombudsmen, as is further outlined in Chapter 13.[13] This power does not extend to reviewing decisions made by a full council, but it does allow the investigation of matters of administration, advice recommended by council officers, or recommendations of council committees. The result, in practical terms, is that almost all local authority decisions can be examined by the Ombudsmen because they are usually the result of advice, recommendations, and actions by committees. The Ombudsmen conduct their investigations in private but they will have access to all the files of the local authority. Although the Ombudsmen have no direct power to alter decisions, in practice their recommendations are usually followed.

The Ombudsmen also have an important role in another instrument of local government accountability: the Local Government Official Information and Meetings Act 1987. This is similar to their role with respect to official information held by central government and has been dealt with in more detail in Chapter 11. They deal with complaints where information has not been given to someone requesting it from the local authority. There are exceptions; under section 5 of the act, as with central government, the presumption is that official information held by the local authority shall be made available 'unless there is good reason for withholding it'.

12 Local Authorities Loans Act 1956 s. 34A(6).
13 Ombudsmen Act 1975, s. 13.

The local authority is obliged to provide reasonable assistance to the person making the request. The local authority must also publish a handbook or guide to the structure of the authority, the committees and membership, working manuals, and other public information that will enable people to participate more effectively in council affairs.

Conclusive 'good reasons' for withholding official information are if making that information available would be likely to prejudice the maintenance of the law, including the prevention, investigation, and detection of offences and the right to a fair trial, or to endanger the safety of any person. As with the application of the Official Information Act to central government, there may also be other reasons for withholding information unless, in the particular case, those reasons are outweighed by other public interest considerations. These reasons, in section 7, are generally the same as many of the corresponding reasons in the Official Information Act as quoted in Chapter 11, with one additional reason:

> 7 (2) (ba) In the case only of an application for a resource consent, or water conservation order, or a requirement for a designation or heritage order, under the Resource Management Act 1991, to avoid serious offence to tikanga Maori, or to avoid the disclosure of the location of Waahi tapu; . . .

Public attendance at meetings is also dealt with by the 1987 act, which governs virtually all meetings of local authorities, including committee meetings. A provision says that, for the purposes of the act, any meeting at which no resolutions are put or decisions made is not a meeting. So social occasions, informal meetings, and briefing sessions are not covered. The general rule is that every meeting of a local authority shall be open to the public. The grounds upon which the public can be excluded are stated in the statute and they are both elaborate and discretionary. The grounds are, broadly, where allowing the meeting to remain open would be likely to result in the disclosure of information that would be protected from disclosure under the provisions relating to official information set out above. Resolutions excluding the public must follow a prescribed form and must state the subject considered, the reason for the passing of the resolution, and the grounds. Exclusion resolutions must be put when the meeting is open to the public. Improper exclusions could be tested through a complaint to the Ombudsman or by judicial review through the courts. Local body members also have to observe legal rules about conflicts of interest.

Local authorities are also accountable through civil liability in damages for wrongs they do. A recent case from Invercargill that went to the Privy Council neatly illustrates the point. The city issued a building permit to a builder to build a house. The building inspector was negligent in inspecting compliance with the permit and the foundations were not properly laid, resulting in serious damage to the house many years later. By that time the builder concerned had gone out of business, so the owner sued the city council, alleging negligence in carrying out the duty to inspect. It was held that the law of negligence, which was interpreted in New Zealand as allowing the city to be sued, was a valid application of common law principles.[14]

The New Zealand Bill of Rights Act 1990, covered further in Chapter 15, will be relevant to the way in which local government exercises a number of its powers—for example, the right to freedom of expression and public assembly, freedom of movement and residence, the rights of minorities, and freedom of association.

A further set of checks on the activities of local government stems from the power of parliamentary select committees (as outlined in Chapter 8) to investigate their activities, and this occurs quite frequently, particularly in the scrutiny of local bills promoted by local authorities. These bills are sometimes designed to bail local authorities out of situations they should never have got into and their conduct will come under review before any bill is passed to alter the law.

The Treaty of Waitangi (examined in Chapter 16), is also of importance to local government. Where local government breaches the principles of the treaty, Maori may make a claim to the Waitangi Tribunal. The tribunal has interpreted its powers to extend to local authorities on the ground that the Crown is responsible for acts or omissions of the authorities.[15] And, in exercising its powers under the Resource Management Act, local government is under a series of obligations to take into account treaty principles and a number of other factors relating to Maori.

As outlined in Chapter 6, the Auditor-General is the watchdog over local authority financial matters. Extensive legal requirements are imposed on local authorities concerning management structures, annual policy and activity reports, financial performance reports, and accounting matters. The Auditor-General conducts the audits of the accounts (these can be contracted out) and can make reports to Parliament and conduct special investigations where he or she thinks money has been wasted or procedures are inappropriate.

Under the Public Finance Act 1977, the Auditor-General can consider and assess the personal liability of local authority members for losses incurred where the expenditure has been unlawful, or an unlawful liability has been incurred, or the authority has wilfully or negligently failed to enforce the collection of money it was lawfully entitled to receive. In certain circumstances, officers can be surcharged.

REGIONAL GOVERNMENT AND THE FUTURE

One important feature of the Resource Management Act 1991 was to encourage a tier of regional government; the act actually gives regional govern-

14 *Invercargill City Council* v. *Hamlin* [1996] 1 *NZLR* 513.
15 *Waitangi Tribunal Report on Manukau Harbour*, Wellington, 1985, p.99 (Wai 8).

ment something substantive to do. The new tier of local government, called regional government, was formed around water catchments for the express purpose of dealing with resource management. It was remarkable how well water catchments fitted new regional boundaries, although there were, as there always will be in New Zealand, enormous disputes about where the lines should be drawn. Catchment boards and regional water boards were replaced by directly elected regional councils.

The logic of the resource management legislation would have been seriously affected if the tier of regional government established expressly for it had been abolished. Although the Nelson–Marlborough region was later abolished, for reasons that lacked clear principle, the main structures were left in place. It is beyond doubt that some regional organisation is necessary for the resource management legislation to function effectively. The real question, however, is whether regional government will flourish and develop in New Zealand or whether it will fail to become a critical part of the governmental structure.

Another question that needs to be considered is an issue that came up from time to time in a number of reforms sponsored by the Fourth Labour Government—devolution. From a practical and political point of view, could other services be devolved to the regions and dealt with by regional government at that level? Serious consideration has been given to this in a number of social policy areas, such as education and health. There may be other candidates for devolution, although there has not been any active recent discussion of this. Such developments would fit in with the current trend toward greater regional self-determination.

In some ways, suggesting enhanced regional government structures contains echoes of the provincial government system that was dumped unceremoniously in 1876. But times change. And if we are to breathe any life into local government in New Zealand, this is one direction that could be explored further.

A view becoming rather prominent is that local government should stick to its knitting, that it ought not to get involved in the expenditure of money in wide-ranging projects beyond its core functions. It ought to be modest, it ought to be constrained by statute from using resources. We should admit, says this strand of thought, that the instruments of political accountability do not work well in relation to local government and that the democratic processes cannot be trusted to produce fiscally appropriate results. Therefore central government ought to constrain local government closely and not allow it to develop in too generous a fashion.

Great care should be taken to avoid making judgements that local government cannot be trusted with anything important. Instead, the instruments of democratic accountability at the local level must be sufficiently robust and responsive to ensure that what occurs is democratically defensible. The great advantage of local government is that it is closer to local communities. Often, the people in a local community have greater interest than central government in administering services to their own community, and, in doing so, can take local circumstances into account.

There is an increased interest in local government, as evidenced by the high number of candidates in the 1995 local body elections. This is a very good sign, from which everyone involved in local government can take considerable encouragement. But if local government in New Zealand is ever to avoid being the poor relation of central government, a focused theory must be developed about its proper scope and function.

There are many unanswered questions concerning local government in this country; it needs to be the subject of a proper debate. Should New Zealand be developing a constitutional place for local government around a framework of permissive powers constrained by principles of local political accountability? Or should local government be severely restricted in its activities and subject to the most limited powers?

We think that it would be a wise constitutional counsel to give local government greater authority, along with a more robust accountability regime. In the event that central government makes a mess of things, and that will happen from time to time, it is useful to have another government structure with elected decision-makers who can provide some counterweight to developments at the central level.

But nothing is likely to be achieved without a new Local Government Act. The present statute is one of the longest, most intricate, and unwieldy of statutes on the New Zealand statute book. It needs to be shortened, sharpened, and restructured. The trend towards a framework of permissive powers would accelerate if this task were undertaken. Local government needs a constitutional place in the sun. After 156 years of New Zealand local government history, it has yet to find it.

13 Avenues for Complaint

INTRODUCTION

There are, in modern New Zealand, many avenues through which people can complain if they think the institutions of government have done them wrong. Many independent agencies have been established to monitor and examine the conduct of various institutions of the state that have coercive powers over people. Sometimes these powers extend beyond the agencies of the state to private conduct as well, as in the case of discrimination or breaches of the Human Rights Act 1993 and the Privacy Act 1993. Often these new institutions give people a right to complain and an investigation can be conducted and the wrong put right. These remedies do not require expensive court cases and often involve no cost at all on the part of the complainant.

These institutions have grown up alongside those of representative government, of which petitioning Parliament and making representations to MPs were the time-honoured methods of trying to have a grievance put right. With the rise of the welfare state and the extensive administrative mechanisms needed to deliver health, education, and income maintenance, a substantial degree of official discretion and power was required. Such powers could be used unfairly and in 1962 New Zealand, borrowing liberally from a Scandinavian institution, established the Ombudsmen, who were empowered to look into administrative decisions and make recommendations about defects.

So successful were the Ombudsmen and their methods of investigation, that their jurisdiction was rapidly extended from central government, first to local government and then to review decisions about refusal to disclose information under the Official Information Act. Similar, although not identical, independent agencies were established over the years to deal with complaints against the police, to protect privacy, and to advance human rights and race relations. The private sector also found value in the concept of the Ombudsmen and set up officers to deal with consumer complaints in the fields of banking and insurance.

Sometimes the powers granted to these new agencies, such as the Human Rights Commission and the Privacy Commissioner, are wide and controversial. The growing number of agencies sometimes gives the impression of an increasing number of shrubs in the bureaucratic thicket. There has also been a tendency not to legislate with precision but to legislate principles and allow them to be worked out over time by the agency, for example, the Privacy Commissioner. The overall policy question in this area is whether we have overdone it in New Zealand and created too many agencies that are likely to trip over one another.

On balance, it is probably the case that the growth of these institutions since 1962 has given people greater access to justice in the sense that they have impartial agencies to whom they can complain about a wide number of matters. It is a question of maintaining a balance between bureaucracy and democracy. The independent agencies set out in this chapter increase the accountability of the officials (and sometimes the private citizens) whom they scrutinise. None of these agencies is controlled directly by the executive government (although they are funded through it), nor are they directly subject to the doctrine of ministerial responsibility. The conduct they put under the spotlight must be explained and justified, with adequate reasons, unless it is to be found wanting.

The conduct of the police, public servants, local government, and many other public authorities, as well as private organisations, are all subject to scrutiny by these agencies. They must be seen as part of the framework of democratic control and accountability of government and, in some areas, the private sector as well. Correspondingly, though, their recent proliferation suggests that it would be useful to develop a systematic, coherent model of how such independent agencies for investigating complaints should operate, backed by sound general principles, rather than creating a whole new structure with each new agency. The tendency to create such agencies may well increase under MMP. As in the United States, political parties in power under MMP may seek to cement in their policy objectives by creating independent bureaucracies to administer legislation. This reinforces the need to examine the role and structure of complaints agencies from first principles.

This chapter does not attempt to do that, but, rather, briefly introduces these agencies and explains a little of what they do and how they do it. We start with the most traditional—Parliament.

PARLIAMENT

Those who feel that something needs putting right should never neglect the oldest and, often most effective, avenue of redress of all—Parliament. Visiting an MP and pointing out a problem can result in his or her writing to the relevant minister on your behalf. Then the whole machinery of the public service swings into action to examine the gripe, respond to it, and provide an answer for the minister's consideration. The minister will write back to the MP saying what the position is and whether, in the government's view, anything is wrong. Although ministerial correspondence is usually drafted by public servants, it enjoys a high priority in the system and matters can quite often be corrected in this way.

MPs can also put down questions in Parliament that can elicit official answers from ministers, upon which they can be further questioned. Furthermore, select committees can now investigate any matters of policy, administration, and expenditure that they choose. Some grievances can be so serious that they warrant attention of this sort. And select committees in an MMP Parliament are likely to be much more active in pursuing matters, even where it is inconvenient to the government.

The time-honoured method to force parliamentary consideration of a grievance is the petition to Parliament. The right to petition Parliament for redress of grievances is acknowledged as a fundamental principle of our constitution, going as far back as Parliament itself. Petitions on a wide variety of topics are presented to Parliament; 294 were presented in 1995. Some petitions call for an alteration in the general law; others ask for some reconsideration of an administrative decision. Everyone has the right to present a petition and it is Parliament's function to consider the petition and make recommendations to government about what should be done.

Petitions must comply with the standing orders of the House. They must require the House to take some action in respect of the subject matter of the petition. They may be in English or in Maori. They must be presented to Parliament by an MP, who must deliver the petition to the Clerk of the House, who announces them to the House. They are then referred by the clerk to a select committee. Select committees can make recommendations that action be taken and Standing Order 249 requires that, if they do, the government must provide a response to the recommendation within ninety days. Petitions are not usually debated.

Standing Order 359 places a number of limitations upon petitions. If other legal remedies have not been exhausted, the House will not receive the petition. If the matter is one that could be the subject of complaint to the Ombudsmen and a complaint has not been made, it will not be considered. Neither will one on the same subject as an earlier petition that has been finally dealt with, unless substantial and material new evidence is available.

Notwithstanding these limitations, petitions have not infrequently borne fruit in New Zealand. They are an important safety valve in the political process, a last resort where there is no other hope of action. The petition against raising the level of Lake Manapouri is perhaps the most dramatic example in recent years.

The Standing Orders Committee that reported in 1995 felt that the procedures for dealing with reports on petitions were too inflexible. Under the new standing orders, reports by the government of its response to petitions are not required unless a select committee report includes recommendations to the government, in which case a response is required as outlined above.

The last report under the previous standing orders, presented to the House of Representatives in March 1994,[1] shows the wide variety of topics dealt with by petitions:

- the interpretation by local councils of the Fencing of Swimming Pools Act 1987;
- the application of fringe benefit tax on benefits provided by friendly societies;
- the Department of Conservation's approach to the citing of the Hahei Marine Reserve;
- the need to make funds available to guarantee all New Zealanders who wish to, the right to work, to meet their housing, health, and education needs;
- special needs classes and the government proposal to close them in public schools;
- burning of toxic chemicals not universally accepted as safe;
- the live sheep export trade;
- legislation on resident withholding tax and the way it affects interest earned on children's bank accounts;
- funding directed to early childhood services; and
- the desirability of dismissing Dr Don Brash from his position of Governor of the Reserve Bank.

On a number of recent petitions the government has acted in a way that went some distance towards meeting the goal of the petitioners. Some examples are listed below.

Petition No. *Name*
1996/601 *David Walsh*
Subject of petition: Requesting that the House of Representatives recommend to the government that a mechanism be provided to allow United Kingdom pensions to be paid through New Zealand support services as previously.

In 1996 the government introduced the Social Welfare (Miscellaneous) Provisions Bill. This included discretionary powers to enable the Director-General of Social Welfare to receive from an overseas pensioner an amount equivalent to his or her overseas pension, and to pay that person the rate of New Zealand benefit that would be payable if that person were not receiving an overseas pension.

1 *Report of the Parliamentary Petitions Referred to the Government by the House*, A.5 *Appendices to the Journal of the House of Representatives*, Wellington, 1994.

Petition No. *Name*
1993/185 *Marilyn Waring*
Subject of petition: Praying that the House of Representatives amend the Electoral Act to ensure equality of, and parity in, gender representation in New Zealand's elected representatives.

Decision of the government: The government agreed that greater representation of women in the House of Representatives was highly desirable. It said that one of the advantages of MMP, as described by the Royal Commission on the Electoral System, was that political parties would have an incentive to select party lists that fairly represented the electorate. It noted that section 264 of the Electoral Act 1993 provides for the appointment of a select committee in the year 2000 to review various aspects of the electoral system, including the provisions of the act dealing with Maori representation. It said that the House of Representatives might consider inviting the select committee also to examine the extent to which party lists have resulted in the better representation of women in the House and what changes, if any, to the electoral system might be made to further enhance the representation of women. It also suggested that the House of Representatives might consider inviting the select committee charged with reviewing the conduct of the 1996 general election to examine the extent to which party lists have resulted in the better representation of women in the House.

Petition No. *Name*
1991/2109 *G.O. Fenton*
Subject of petition: Praying that the House of Representatives direct the Planning and Development Select Committee to investigate the circumstances of houses sold by Coalcorp and other vendors in the Huntly East area and their depreciation in value due to land subsidence.

Referral to the government: The report of the Planning and Development Select Committee on the petition was presented to the House on 24 September 1992 and referred to the government for most favourable consideration subject to certain considerations.

Decision of the government: The government supported the select committee's conclusion that the 1987 policy was deficient. On 24 May 1993 Cabinet agreed to extend the Huntly East land subsidence policy to provide for the purchase of properties that are not necessarily materially damaged, but that are located in the area of active subsidence caused by the mining of the south section of the Huntly East mine. The policy extension provides for the Crown to purchase properties that the owners cannot sell at a reasonable price because their land is subsiding.

OMBUDSMEN

Connected to Parliament, and acting as a check on the power of the government, are the Ombudsmen. Under section 1 of the Ombudsmen Act 1975 they are appointed as officers of Parliament, which means that they are Parliament's people and owe no allegiance to the executive government, whose activities they are primarily involved in investigating. Even their funding decisions are made by the Officers of Parliament Committee rather than by Cabinet. They are appointed for five-year terms. The names have to be approved, by convention, by both opposition and government caucuses before being submitted to Parliament for approval.

There was a controversy about the reappointment of the first female Ombudsman, Nadja Tollemache, who was not reappointed after serving a five-year term. It led to a trenchant and critical statement by the Chief Ombudsman in his annual report to Parliament in 1992:[2]

> If the present system of appointment is maintained, this [evaluation of whether to reappoint an Ombudsman] must test the constitutional integrity of the government holding office for the time being. Should it take no action to nominate for reappointment it is inevitable that speculation will occur about the government's motives. It is likely to be accused of abusing its power to remove an Ombudsman who has displeased it in the resolution of complaints against it. Failure to explain its reasons for non reappointment will certainly give fuel to such speculation.
>
> The government of the day will thus always face a difficult communication problem so long as it follows the present practice as recently explained by the Minister. Such a problem inevitably leads to questions about the integrity of the institution of Ombudsmen despite the fact that a current Government may accord the institution the highest possible credibility.
>
> In my view it is time for a change to be made to the procedures used for the appointment of an Ombudsman.

Nadja Tollemache, in her report on leaving office, made similar comments:[3]

> I hope that when future appointments are made the transition can be managed in a less disruptive way. It must also be said that if the continued impartiality and fearless application of the law, particularly the Official Information Act, to all organisations of government including Ministers of the Crown and State-Owned Enterprises is to be ensured, no suggestion that reappointment might depend on government approval of

2 *Report of the Ombudsmen for the Year Ended 30 June 1992*, A.3 *Appendices to the Journal of the House of Representatives*, Wellington, 1992, p.8.

3 *Ibid.* p.46.

decisions and recommendations should be possible. There are, after all, ample safeguards in the legislation for examination of decisions considered by the authorities to be inappropriate.

In an MMP Parliament, which will usually have more than two parties, it may prove more difficult to secure agreement on the appointment of Ombudsmen and other officers of Parliament. As noted in other chapters, there is a need to reconsider the general model of the accountability structure of officers of Parliament and other organisations closely connected to Parliament: the Parliamentary Counsel Office, the Parliamentary Service, the Office of the Clerk of the House, the Office of the Controller and Auditor-General, the Parliamentary Commissioner for the Environment, and the Ombudsmen. Even compared with the other independent complaints agencies, the importance of these parliamentary offices and the sensitivity of their positions will be increased under MMP. It is imperative that their accountability structures are clear, robust, and consistent with the constitutional principles underlying the relationship between the executive and legislative branches of government.

New Zealand borrowed the idea of an Ombudsman from Scandinavia in 1962; there has been an institution of this type in Sweden since 1809. It was a bold move to pick up the idea, adapt it, and implement it, and the institution has proved a considerable success in New Zealand.[4] The Ombudsmen can investigate complaints made to them by members of the public, or can, on their own initiative, investigate any administrative decision, recommendation, act or omission of government departments, related organisations, and local authorities affecting a person individually. A large number—nearly 100—other organisations connected to government (including state-owned enterprises) are affected and are listed in the schedule to the act. As outlined in Chapter 11, Ombudsmen also have important duties under the Official Information Act 1982.

The Ombudsmen may reach the conclusion that a decision was unfair on a number of grounds. It could be:

- contrary to law;
- unreasonable, unjust, oppressive, or improperly discriminatory;
- made under an act, regulation or by-law that was unreasonable, unjust, oppressive or discriminatory;
- based on mistake of fact or law;
- made in the exercise of a discretionary power used for improper or irrelevant purpose;
- simply 'wrong'.

4 L.B. Hill, *The Model Ombudsman: institutionalizing New Zealand's democratic experiment*, Princeton University Press, New Jersey, 1976.

Where the Ombudsmen reach an unfavourable view of a decision they can say that:

- the matter should be further considered by the appropriate authority;
- the omission should be rectified;
- the decision should be cancelled or varied;
- the practice on which the decision was based should be altered;
- the act, regulation or by-law on which the decision was based should be reconsidered;
- reasons should have been given for the decision; and
- other steps should be taken.

The Ombudsmen have no power to alter decisions; they simply investigate and report on them. Nonetheless, the process of investigation itself, the power of the office, the capacity to report to Parliament, and the publicity given to the reports exert a considerable influence in righting administrative injustices and changing the way in which officials approach some tasks. More recently the Ombudsmen, as well as dealing with individual complaints, have broadened their focus, 'looking beyond the resolution of the individual complaint towards identifying underlying causes. This approach has resulted in [Ombudsmen] making suggestions of a proactive kind'.[5]

For example, where the Ombudsmen had received complaints about decisions to expel or suspend students from school, the Chief Ombudsman prepared draft guidelines setting out standards that the legislation requires the school authorities to follow. The draft has become incorporated in the Ministry of Education's guidelines for use by principals and boards of trustees. The Ombudsmen also drafted some amendments to legislation to improve some of the procedures for consideration by the ministry. The Ombudsmen have also taken a proactive role in the area of complaints by prisoners. A special pamphlet has been prepared setting out the role of the Ombudsmen in the prison system and urging inmates to use the internal complaints procedure before complaining to the Ombudsmen. They also said, in their 1995 report, that 'We believe there is a need for a comprehensive reconsideration of the conditions under which remand inmates are detained and managed.'[6]

The Ombudsmen can look at government files and recommend that decisions be altered. If no appropriate action is taken, the Ombudsmen can report to the Prime Minister and to Parliament. Every year a report is made to Parliament and a compendium of case notes is published from time to time, giving instances of decisions investigated.

---

5 *Report of the Ombudsmen for the Year Ended 30 June 1995*, A.3 *Appendices to the Journal of the House of Representatives*, Wellington, 1995, p.14.

6 *Ibid.*, p.21.

In the year ended 30 June 1995 the Ombudsmen (there are currently two of them—Chief Ombudsman Sir Brian Elwood and Ombudsman Judge Satyanand) had a total of 4707 cases under investigation, of which 4015 were disposed of during the year. In that year there were 2910 complaints under the Ombudsmen Act, of which 207 were resolved by the department or organisation, thirty-two were sustained, 264 were not sustained, 430 others were discontinued with further inquiry not warranted, 135 were declined because of lack of jurisdiction, and 498 were declined for other reasons. In 888 cases, formal investigation was not undertaken. The large majority resulted in provision of explanation, advice, or assistance; three were transferred to the Privacy Commissioner. The remaining 453 cases were still under investigation at 30 June. In 1995 the Ombudsmen disposed of sixteen complaints every working day.

The introduction of the Ombudsmen has had a healthy effect on decision-making in the New Zealand Government. They provide the check of independent scrutiny with full access to the relevant information and the possibility of publicity about erroneous government decisions that affect individuals.

The Chief Ombudsman, Sir Brian Elwood, put it well in his annual report in 1995:[7]

> 'The system' must avoid the impression that it is automatic, impersonal, pervasive and non-communicative. It can do this, in part, by listening to the concerns of individual citizens, responding appropriately against publicised objectives and by adequate communication. As simple as a statement of the potential problem may be, to avoid it the requirement is ongoing vigilance and the right to request an impartial scrutiny. The classical Ombudsman concept in an open democratic society provides the opportunity for that impartial scrutiny and hence will remain the cornerstone of the developing role of the Ombudsmen in New Zealand.

A recent development has been the establishment of private sector agencies to deal with consumer complaints. These include the Banking Ombudsman and the Insurance and Savings Ombudsman. The Banking Ombudsman scheme, which came into operation on 1 July 1992, was a world first in requiring participating banks to establish internal complaints procedures linked to an independent complaints review process. The use of the name 'Ombudsman' for private organisations requires the consent of the Chief Ombudsman.

POLICE COMPLAINTS AUTHORITY

For many years the Ombudsmen had jurisdiction to examine complaints against the police, but an internal investigation had to be done by the police first. There

---

[7] *Report of the Ombudsmen for the Year Ended 30 June 1995*, A.3 *Appendices to the Journal of the House of Representatives*, Wellington, 1995, p.8.

were some difficulties and tensions over this concerning complaints made against the police after the 1981 Springbok rugby tour of New Zealand. These and other events, particularly police shootings, led to a call for increased police accountability, which was eventually accomplished by the passing of the Police Complaints Authority Act 1988.

The act establishes an independent Police Complaints Authority who has been, since the inception of the office, a retired High Court judge, Sir John Jeffries. The authority is appointed by the Governor-General on the recommendation of the House of Representatives, which means that it is not an appointment within the power of the executive government but, in practice, requires discussion between the parties represented in Parliament.

Under section 12 of the Police Complaints Authority Act 1988, the functions of the authority are:

- to receive complaints:
  —alleging any misconduct or neglect of duty by any member of the police; or
  —concerning any practice, policy or procedure of the police affecting the person or body of persons making the complaint in a personal capacity;
- to investigate of its own motion, where it is satisfied there are reasonable grounds to carry out an investigation in the public interest, any incident involving the death or serious bodily harm notified to the authority by the Commissioner of Police, as that officer is obliged to do when such an event occurs under section 13 of the act;
- to take such action in respect of complaints, incidents, and other matters as is contemplated by the act.

The Police Complaints Authority Act provides that complaints can be made orally or in writing, but where they are made orally they must be reduced to writing as soon as practicable (section 14). The authority can decide to take no action on a complaint, on a range of grounds set out in the statute (sections 17–18). It has power to secure assistance from the police. Where the authority undertakes an investigation itself, 'it shall form an opinion on whether or not any decision, recommendation, act, omission, conduct, policy, practice, or procedure which was the subject-matter of the investigation was contrary to law, unreasonable, unjustified, unfair, or undesirable' (section 27). The authority is then required to convey its opinion to the Commissioner of Police and make such recommendations as the authority thinks fit, including recommendations that disciplinary or criminal proceedings be considered or instituted against any member of the police. The commissioner must notify the authority of the actions to be taken to give effect to the recommendations, and give reasons for any proposal to depart from, or not to implement, any recommendation. Where the commissioner takes no action or does not follow the recommendations, the authority, after considering the reasons given, may send its opinion to the Attorney-General and the Minister of Police. The Police Complaints Authority is also authorised to make public reports 'from time to time, in the public interest . . .' (section 34). The authority must make an annual report to the Minister of Justice, which must be laid before the House of Representatives.

The annual report of the authority for the year ended 30 June 1995 was nearly 100 pages long, and it contained an assessment of the authority's work. The bread and butter work of the authority lies in complaints about the police by members of the public relating to attitude, the use of force, harassment, language, and property claims. The investigations involving deaths caused by the police create most public attention. The report calls for a change in name to convey the essential nature of the office—an independent civilian oversight of the police service. It also suggests a number of possible modifications to the authority, where it thinks the act may need attention. The report also goes into detailed discussions of particular difficulties found relating to:

- suicides in police stations;
- police behaviour at a student demonstration at Otago University;
- a police shooting at Kaitaia;
- decisions on prosecutions;
- the pursuit of members of the pubic by police in vehicles—the Authority repeated the view that Police General Instructions on the subject 'are in need of radical review';[8] and
- the deployment of police dogs.

Details are also given of a large number of individual complaints. In the course of the year, 2620 complaints were received and the number has been rising since the authority was established. The statute setting up the authority is in need of some repair but there is little doubt that the institution is here to stay and has improved the public accountability of the police for the important powers they exercise.

THE HUMAN RIGHTS COMMISSION AND THE RACE RELATIONS CONCILIATOR

The Human Rights Act 1993 provides a framework to protect and promote human rights in New Zealand. New Zealand has had a Human Rights Commission since 1977 but the 1993 legislation extended the range of protections and methods of dealing with complaints where the standards have been breached. The commission comprises a Chief Commissioner (Pamela Jefferies in 1996), and the Privacy

8 Police Complaints Authority, *Annual Report for the Year Ended 30 June 1995*, G.51 *Appendices to the Journal of the House of Representatives*, Wellington, 1995, p.21.

Commissioner, the Race Relations Conciliator, the Proceedings Commissioner, and not more than three other commissioners. Like all the other agencies discussed in the chapter, it is independent of the executive government.

The Office of the Race Relations Conciliator functions alongside the Human Rights Commission and derives its legal powers from the same statute, the Human Rights Act 1993. In matters of race relations, the Race Relations Conciliator exercises the same functions as the Human Rights Commission. That office deals with complaints of racial discrimination and provides educational initiatives to promote good race relations.

The Human Rights Act is related to the New Zealand Bill of Rights Act 1990, which is designed to protect many of the same values. Essentially, the Human Rights Act deals with equality or freedom from stated grounds of discrimination, while the Bill of Rights Act also covers fundamental freedoms such as freedom of speech and religion and rights in criminal procedure. The Human Rights Act also provides practical methods of dealing with complaints when unlawful discrimination prohibited by the act occurs.

Under section 5 of the Human Rights Act 1993, the most important statutory functions of the Human Rights Commission are to:

- promote, by education and publicity, respect for and observance of human rights;
- encourage and coordinate programmes and activities in the field of human rights;
- make public statements in relation to any matter affecting human rights;
- prepare and publish guidelines for the avoidance of acts or practices that may be inconsistent with, or contrary to, the provisions of the act;
- receive and invite representations from members of the public on any matter affecting human rights;
- consult and cooperate with other persons and bodies concerned with human rights;
- inquire generally into any matter, including any enactment or law, or any practice, or any procedure, whether governmental or non-governmental, if it appears human rights may be infringed thereby;
- to report to the Prime Minister from time to time on:
    - (i) any matter affecting human rights to give better protection to human rights and to ensure compliance with the international instruments on human rights;
    - (ii) the desirability of New Zealand becoming bound by any international instrument on human rights;
    - (iii) the implications of any proposed legislation or government policy that may affect human rights.

The commission also has important responsibilities to examine all New Zealand law, policy, and practice to see whether features of it infringe the range of prohibited discrimination set up by the act or infringe the spirit and intention of the act. This task must be complete by 31 December 1998. Part of the reason for this is that section 151 of the Human Rights Act itself states the act is not to affect any other act or regulation. In other words, the Human Rights Act enjoys no primacy and other statutes can and do make discrimination lawful in particular circumstances. But section 152 of the act, which provides that other enactments and actions are not affected, itself expires on 31 December 1999. It is likely that the human rights prohibitions will then be given primacy over other statutes. The government will therefore want to be able to consider any legislation and practices that come into this category well before this expiry date. The message is that, when the year 2000 arrives, human rights in New Zealand will be even more heavily protected than they are now.

The act sets out, in Part II, a number of prohibited grounds of discrimination. These are: sex, marital status, religious belief, ethical belief, colour, race, ethnic or national origins (which includes nationality or citizenship), disability (which is defined), age (but subject to important qualifications), political opinion, employment status, family status, and sexual orientation.

The act then goes on to spell out the application of these grounds in particular contexts. They are:

- discrimination in employment matters, including a number of exceptions;
- discrimination in partnerships;
- discrimination by industrial and professional associations, qualifying bodies, and vocational training bodies;
- discrimination in access to places, vehicles, and facilities;
- discrimination in provision of goods and services;
- discrimination in provision of land, housing, and other accommodation;
- discrimination in access to educational establishments;
- other forms of discrimination, including inciting racial disharmony, sexual harassment, racial harassment, indirect discrimination, advertisements, and victimisation; and
- creation of special provisions for superannuation schemes.

The act provides an elaborate set of procedures for dealing with complaints about unlawful discrimination. The steps are:

1. Complaint to the Complaints Division of the Human Rights Commission.
2. The division may decide to investigate or not—there are stated grounds upon which it can decide not to investigate.
3. Where it decides to investigate, parties have to be informed both of the

investigation and the result. A compulsory conciliation conference can be called. It may be possible to reach a settlement. This means agreement of the parties on actions that settle the matter, which may include compensation and an apology, as well as an assurance against repetition of the conduct.

4. The Proceedings Commissioner may decide to bring civil proceedings on the complaint before the Complaints Review Tribunal. Individuals can bring proceedings directly before the tribunal in certain circumstances as well, where, for example, the Proceedings Commissioner declines to take proceedings.
5. Remedies available to the tribunal include:
   - a declaration that the defendant has committed a breach of the act;
   - an order restraining the defendant from continuing to breach the act;
   - damages for pecuniary loss, loss of benefit and humiliation, and loss of dignity as specified in the act;
   - an order that the defendant perform any acts specified in the order to redress any loss or damage.
6. Appeal to the High Court is available for any party dissatisfied with the decision.

In the year ended 30 June 1995 the Human Rights Commission received 8084 inquiries. The commission's complaints team opened 257 formal complaints, many of which involved more than one ground in the act. Fifty-six per cent of the complaints arose in the employment area; 23 per cent involved goods and services. Among the grounds, disability accounted for 20 per cent of complaints, gender for 18 per cent, age for 14 per cent, and sexual harassment for 12 per cent. Some of the settlements involved significant monetary compensation 'of at least $10,000'.[9]

One of the case studies included in the annual report of the Human Rights Commission illustrates how people can benefit from a complaint. A woman who uses a wheelchair took a return overseas flight with three other people. The travel agent sent her a medical form to be completed by herself and her doctor. She was asked some questions by the form that she considered offensive—'Is the patient's condition likely to be a source of discomfort to other passengers? (odour, appearance, conduct)'. She had to sign a declaration that she would, at her own risk, bear any consequences that air travel might have for her state of health. She complained that this was discrimination on grounds of disability, and that, during the flight, she was not seated with her companions, she was refused a window seat, and, after requesting an aisle chair so she could go to the toilet, she waited fifteen minutes and was then told by a steward that the chair was locked away and passengers would not like to see a wheelchair brought out. She also complained

---

9 *Report of the Human Rights Commission and Office of Race Relations Conciliator for year ended 30 June 1995*, E.6 *Appendices to the Journal of the House of Representatives*, Wellington, 1995, p.15.

that ground staff ignored her request to board last so that she could empty her catheter just before boarding. Following the complaint, the airline implemented a disability awareness course for ground staff. After a conciliation meeting the woman was given a written apology, several thousand dollars in compensation for humiliation and injury to feelings, and the airline agreed to review the medical form.[10]

The Race Relations Conciliator reported to Parliament separately for the year ended 30 June 1995.[11] The report records that 587 complaints were received, up significantly on 142 in 1992–93 and 273 in 1993–94. This increase is partly the result of the new legislation.

The report shows that the Race Relations Conciliator was heavily involved in educational activities as well as complaints and inquiries. Again, case studies show the benefit of a complaint. The report includes the case of a Samoan woman who contacted the office to complain that she had been dismissed by her employer for speaking Samoan in the workplace. She stated that she had been warned at a meeting with her employer that if she persisted in using Samoan when speaking with her fellow workmates she would be dismissed. She had chosen to ignore the warning.

The employer, when contacted by the office, stated that although he permitted staff to speak in their native language during their breaks he preferred that they all spoke English while working. He further stated that since she had returned to the workforce, after a year's absence, she had been a disruptive influence in the workplace and had adversely affected relationships among the staff.

As a result of discussions with the office, the manager agreed to meet with the complainant to discuss the matter. The meeting was also attended by the complainant's two immediate supervisors and several other staff. The complainant confirmed with the office that she was satisfied that the matter had been successfully concluded. The manager informed the office that the matter was resolved amicably as a result of the meeting and that the complainant had started back at work that same afternoon.[12]

In another case a Niuean parent contacted the office after her son had been suspended from the school he was attending because the family had refused to have his hair cut. The parent alleged that the boy was being indirectly discriminated against by the school's rule on hair length on the grounds of his race and his cultural expectations. The school claimed that if they allowed the boy to attend the school with his hair as it was, they would be compromising the application of the uniform and tidiness policy. Investigations made it clear that many Niueans still practised the traditional hair-cutting rites. A mediation meeting was arranged

10 *Ibid.*, p.17.
11 *Ibid.*, p.64.
12 *Ibid.*, p.106.

between the two parties and possible solutions were discussed. The outcome of the meeting was that the boy should be allowed to return to school on the condition that he wore his hair in a tidy bun. The school also agreed to alter their policy to encompass different cultural dress codes. As a result of this agreement, the matter was satisfactorily resolved.[13]

THE PRIVACY COMMISSIONER

The Privacy Commissioner is a recent addition to the band of watchdogs for the public. The Privacy Act 1993 is an important and ambitious piece of legislation designed, in the words of its long title, to:

> Promote and protect individual privacy in general accordance with the Recommendation of the Council for the Organization of Economic Co-operation and Development Concerning Guidelines Governing the Protection of Privacy and Transborder Flows of Personal Data, and, in particular,—
>
> (a) To establish certain principles with respect to—
> (i) The collection, use, and disclosure, by public and private sector agencies, of information relating to individuals;
> (ii) Access by each individual to information relating to that individual and held by public and private sector agencies; and;
>
> (b) to provide for the appointment of a Privacy Commissioner to investigate complaints about interferences with individual privacy; and
>
> (c) To provide for matters incidental thereto.

Privacy is a complex and specialised field that is rapidly evolving. We cannot hope here to more than glance at what the act does and how individuals can use it. At the heart of the statute are twelve information privacy principles which dominate everything that occurs under the statute. These are spelt out at length in section 6, and deal with:

- the purpose of collection of personal information;
- the source of personal information;
- the collection of personal information from subject;
- the manner of collection of personal information;
- storage and security of personal information;
- access to personal information;
- correction of personal information;
- accuracy etc. of personal information to be checked before use;

[13] *Ibid.*, p.109.

- an agency not keeping personal information longer than necessary;
- limits on use of personal information;
- limits on disclosure of personal information;
- the assignment of unique identifiers.

The application of these principles is no easy matter and sometimes they are not necessarily consistent with one another. It is difficult to advise, on a particular set of facts, what the answer will be. This has led to quite a deal of public confusion about what the statute does and how it applies. The Privacy Commissioner has called it a 'uniquely flexible law',[14] but its very flexibility produces vagueness and a lack of certainty.

The principal interpreter of the act is the Privacy Commissioner, who has a large number of tasks under the act. The commissioner is appointed for a term not exceeding five years by the Governor-General on the recommendation of the Minister of Justice. The present commissioner is Mr B.H. Slane, a former President of the New Zealand Law Society. Under section 13, his functions include:

- by education and publicity promoting an understanding and acceptance of the privacy principles;
- when requested to do so, conducting audits of personal information maintained by the requester;
- monitoring the use of unique identifiers and reporting to the Prime Minister on the results;
- maintaining directories of personal information;
- examining proposed legislation with privacy implications (the commissioner made thirteen reports on twelve bills in the 1995 year).

The provisions in the act concerning access to and correction of personal information are similar to those contained in the Official Information Act 1982. Part VI of the Privacy Act also deals with the commissioner's power to issue codes of practice that modify the privacy principles and there is a procedure to be followed before codes of practice are issued. (The commissioner has issued several codes, including, in 1994, a Health Information Privacy Code, and another involving the Wanganui Computer Centre, which held law enforcement information when it was privatised.) Codes are deemed by section 50 of the Privacy Act to be regulations for the purpose of the Regulations (Disallowance) Act 1989 and can therefore be disallowed by a motion passed by Parliament. The act also contains a list of privacy principles to be followed by agencies compiling public registers.

Section 67 of the Privacy Act gives the commissioner power to hear complaints made by any person that 'any action is or appears to be an interference with the

---

[14] *Report of the Privacy Commissioner for Year Ended 30 June 1995*, A.11 *Appendices to the Journal of the House of Representatives*, Wellington, 1995, p.4.

privacy of an individual'. In the year ended 30 June 1995 the commissioner received 877 complaints. Of the 128 that proceeded to a final opinion of the commissioner, twenty-six were found to have substance. A complaint may be made either orally or in writing. An action is an interference with the privacy of an individual if:

- the action breaches an information privacy principle;
- the action breaches a code of practice about public registers;
- it does not comply with Part X of the act concerning information matching;

and in the opinion of the commissioner the action:

(i) has caused or may cause, loss, detriment, damage or injury to the individual; or
(ii) has adversely affected or may adversely affect the rights, benefits, privileges, obligations or interests of that individual; or
(iii) has resulted in or may result in significant humiliation, significant loss of dignity or significant injury to the feelings of that individual.

The commissioner investigates complaints, and may investigate on his own initiative without waiting for a complaint. He can also act as a conciliator concerning the complaint. He can decide to take no action on a complaint. The commissioner must advise the complainant, and the person to whom the complaint relates, of the procedure to be adopted. He may try to secure a settlement; he has said that 'It is my practice whenever possible to endeavour to bring about a settlement.'[15] He may call a compulsory conference of the parties. Where no settlement can be reached, the commissioner may refer the matter to the Proceedings Commissioner of the Human Rights Commission, who may decide to bring civil proceedings before the Complaints Review Tribunal established under the Human Rights Act. An aggrieved individual may bring proceedings before the tribunal if he or she wishes to do so, if the Privacy Commissioner or the Proceedings Commissioner declines to do so or if the Proceedings Commissioner agrees to the individual bringing the proceedings.

Section 85 of the Privacy Act provides that the powers of the Complaints Review Tribunal to do with privacy cases include the power to grant:

- a declaration that the action of the defendant is an interference with the privacy of an individual;
- an order restraining the defendant from continuing or repeating the interference with privacy;
- damages in terms specified in the act;
- an order that the defendant perform specific acts to remedy the interference.

The tribunal may award costs against a defendant. Lack of intention is no defence to proceedings for interference with privacy.

---

15 *Ibid.*, p.11.

Certainly the Privacy Commissioner in New Zealand is armed with powers necessary to defeat the Orwellian scenario of a 'Big Brother' watching over you, an important value in a democracy. But, as the commissioner has said, 'The Office of the Privacy Commissioner is still very much in a developmental phase.'[16] How it beds in remains to be seen. To be effective in the long term, it will probably need to become more specifically focused.

THE PARLIAMENTARY COMMISSIONER FOR THE ENVIRONMENT

The Parliamentary Commissioner for the Environment is an officer of Parliament appointed under section 4 of the Environment Act 1986. The mission of the commissioner is to provide 'an independent check on the capability of the New Zealand system of environmental management and the performance of public authorities in maintaining and improving the quality of the environment'.[17]

The office is concerned with policy implementation and the policy itself, as well as individual cases of environmental mismanagement. The commissioner gives advice to Parliament, central and local government, and receives and handles complaints.

A recent example occurred when a complaint was made that Transit New Zealand proposed to build a combined bridge/embankment over the Ahuriri Estuary in Napier. The complaint was that, in its benefit–cost calculations and subsequent planning and funding allocation, Transit New Zealand did not take full account of the environmental values or the potential effects of roading. The commissioner recommended that Transit New Zealand did need to recognise all costs and benefits in its analysis, to avoid distortions and possible incorrect funding allocations. In evaluating and funding of road transport projects, it needed to develop a procedure to consider the relative importance of significant intangible values on a nationwide basis. As a result of the investigation and recommendations, Transit revised its procedures.[18]

Where people feel an environmental issue is not being handled properly, the commissioner can bring considerable weight to bear if she decides to become involved. The commissioner has, in recent times, dealt with the following issues:

- failures in implementation of the Resource Management Act 1991;
- environmental information and the adequacy of treaty settlement procedures;

---

[16] *Ibid.*, p.6.

[17] Parliamentary Commissioner for the Environment, *Annual Report 1994–95*, C.12 *Appendices to the Journal of the House of Representatives*, Wellington, 1995, p.4. The functions of the Parliamentary Commissioner are set out in section 16 of the Environment Act 1986.

[18] *Ibid.*, p.9.

- sustainable land management and the East Coats Forestry Project;
- advice to Parliament on bills with environmental implications;
- dredgings disposal in the Hauraki Gulf; and
- advice to local government on particular issues.

The commissioner follows up issues on a continuing basis to see what has been done concerning the recommendations.

THE HEALTH AND DISABILITY COMMISSIONER

The most recent addition to the arsenal of public watchdogs is the Health and Disability Commissioner, whose office was established by the Health and Disability Commissioner Act 1994. The first incumbent of the office is Robyn K. Stent. The purpose of the act is to promote and protect the rights of consumers of health and disability services and to facilitate the fair, simple, speedy, and efficient resolution of complaints relating to the infringement of those rights. The act applies to all health care providers and disability service providers.

Section 14 of the act sets out the commissioner's functions, which include:

- drawing up a Code of Health and Disability Services Consumers' Rights. (This task was completed in 1996 after extensive consultation as required by the statute);
- promoting, by education and publicity, respect for and observance of health and disability services consumers' rights;
- making public statements and publishing reports in relation to matters affecting health and disability services consumers' rights;
- investigating either on complaint or on the commissioner's own initiative, any action that appears to be in breach of the code;
- making recommendations to the Minister of Health and any other body regarding the rights of consumers;
- mediating resolution of complaints where appropriate.

The act also creates a Director of Advocacy in relation to health and disability services and a Director of Proceedings, who takes proceedings on behalf of complainants. The commissioner acts independently from these officers. The Director of Advocacy's role is to administer, promote, and monitor advocates, who are to act as advocates for health and disability services consumers, including receiving complaints from those consumers. The Director of Proceedings' function is to decide whether to institute or participate in complaint proceedings.

Where the commissioner investigates a complaint she may:

- take no action for reasons that include the lapse of time, triviality, or that the complaint was not made in good faith;

- notify other bodies such as the Ombudsmen, Privacy Commissioner or Human Rights Commission;
- notify the relevant health professional body and consult with it on the appropriate means of dealing with the complaint;
- arrange for mediation;
- make such reports or recommendations as she thinks fit;
- refer the complaint to the Director of Proceedings who can decide whether to commence proceedings before a disciplinary board of a statutory body or the Complaints Review Tribunal.

Although it is too early to assess this new office, it is clear that there are likely to be problems of overlap with some of the other agencies discussed in this chapter. And this office is not as independent as some of the others. It will be interesting to see how the advocates appointed under the act can be independent of the commissioner and how the whole system will interrelate with other health complaints statutes and professional bodies that have responsibilities in the area.

THE COMMISSIONER FOR CHILDREN

Created as a statutory officer in the Children, Young Persons, and Their Families Act 1989, the Commissioner for Children does not enjoy many resources or much independence. But he can and does investigate and report on the matters relating to the care and welfare of children. Section 411 of the act provides:

> **411. Functions of the Commissioner**—(1) The functions of the Commissioner shall be —
>
> (a) To investigate any decision or recommendation made, or any act done or omitted, under this Act in respect of any child or young person in that child's or young person's personal capacity:
>
> (b) To monitor and assess the policies and practices of the Department, and of any other person, body, or organisation exercising or performing any function, duty, or power conferred or imposed by or under this Act, in relation to the exercise or performance of any function, duty, or power conferred or imposed by or under this Act:
>
> (c) To encourage the development, within the Department, of policies and services designed to promote the welfare of children and young persons:
>
> (d) To undertake and promote research into any matter relating to the welfare of children and young persons:
>
> (e) To inquire generally into, and report on, any matter, including any enactment or

law, or any practice or procedure, relating to the welfare of children and young persons:

(f) To receive and invite representations from members of the public on any matter relating to the welfare of children and young persons:

(g) To increase public awareness of matters relating to the welfare of children and young persons:

(h) On the Commissioner's own initiative or at the request of the Minister, to advise the Minister on any matter relating to the administration of this Act:

(i) To keep under review, and make recommendations on, the working of this Act:

(2) The Commissioner shall also have such other functions as are conferred on the Commissioner by this Act or by any other enactment.

(3) Nothing in subsection (1) (a) of this section authorises the Commissioner to investigate any decision or recommendation made by, or any act or omission of, any Court.

The present commissioner, Laurie O'Reilly, bases his work on the principles set out in the United Nations Convention on the Rights of the Child 1989, which was ratified by New Zealand in March 1993.[19] The commissioner sees the primary purpose of the office as being to advance the welfare of children in New Zealand.

A 1992 ministerial review of the Children, Young Persons, and Their Families Act 1989 recommended that the Office of the Commissioner for Children be established under a separate statute to ensure independence from the Department of Social Welfare and that the commissioner be made an officer of Parliament. These recommendations have not yet been implemented.

In the annual report for the year ended 30 June 1995, the commissioner reports that he has set the following objectives for his term of office:

- To promote effective advocacy for children at every level and in every sector to ensure the welfare of children and young persons.
- To ensure that the child's voice is heard in all matters affecting the child.
- To promote knowledge and understanding of the needs and rights of children, and particularly the rights in the United Nations Convention on the Rights of the Child.
- To provide a forum for monitoring the implementation of obligations under the convention to ensure that mechanisms are developed to allow children to access their rights.

[19] Office of the Commissioner for Children, *Annual Report for the Year Ended 30 June 1995*, Wellington, 1995, p.4.

- To implement effective monitoring procedures in respect of the Children, Young Persons, and Their Families Act 1989 concerning care and protection and youth justice.
- To promote a comprehensive perspective on the overall victimisation of children and initiate research that cuts across and integrates the various forms of child victimisation.
- To be part of the community response to prevent and reduce all forms of violence.
- To promote positive parenting and develop resources for such programmes.
- To establish a comprehensive mortality review system for children.
- To initiate the formation of links between school, home, and the wider community, supporting schools in their pastoral care role.
- To establish child impact studies and assessment mechanisms in respect of legislation, policies, and practices affecting the welfare of children.

Although the act does not outline specific procedures for dealing with complaints, the commissioner does receive and consider a large number of formal complaints. The number of complaints received has been increasing rapidly, from 103 in the 1991–92 year to 147 the following year, 183 in the 1993–94 year and 350 in the 1994–95 year. In the 1994–95 year 49 per cent of complaints related to the New Zealand Children and Young Persons Service, 24 per cent were education related, and 7 per cent were custody and access related. Forty per cent of complaints were responded to by the commissioner with an opinion, 35 per cent with advice, 18 per cent were withdrawn, leaving only a small number for which there was no jurisdiction or other responses were required.

The office also responds to a large number of requests for information. These are also increasing rapidly, from 682 in the 1993–94 year to 1264 in the 1994–95 year.

The commissioner concentrates on particular problems and conducts investigations. A major concern in the 1994–95 year was bullying and the office hosted a series of seminars in conjunction with others. After an investigation involving bullying was carried out at a Christchurch college, the school acknowledged and implemented fifteen specific recommendations. These were published and, as a result, many other schools reviewed their anti-violence policies.

14 The Courts

WHAT COURTS DO

New Zealand has long enjoyed a judicial system based on British justice. There are complaints about the rather formal way in which courts conduct their business, about delays, about their cultural or gender bias, and going to law can be expensive, but, whatever charges are levelled against our system of justice, the courts enjoy a high reputation for fairness and impartiality.

What many people do not realise, is that the courts are one of the arms of government, and exert an important checking function on the executive and on Parliament. Alexander Hamilton, one of the founding fathers of the United States constitution, wrote long ago that 'the judiciary, from the nature of its functions, will always be the least dangerous' branch of government.[1] The same is true in New Zealand. Not only is the judicial branch of our government the least dangerous, it is likely to be the most reliable in its adherence to principle, neutrality, and rationality.

Most people, when they think of the courts, think of important criminal trials that are conducted before a jury. The criminal trial, of course, remains central to our system of justice. It provides fundamental protections for the accused person against the might of the state. The accused person has the right to be represented by counsel. He or she has the right to have the evidence against him or her heard in open court and tested by cross-examination. The case against the accused person must be proved by the Crown to a high level: beyond a reasonable doubt. The nature of the charge must be clear—it must be an offence against the law as written down in a statute. Upon conviction the person will be sentenced in accordance with the law. There is a right of appeal against both conviction and sentence.

---

1 A. Hamilton, *The Federalist: a commentary on the Constitution of the United States being a collection of essays written in support of the Constitution agreed upon September 17, 1787*, No. 78, Modern Library, 1941.

The courts also carry out a wide range of other duties. They hear civil cases, which are disputes usually involving money, between one citizen and another, or between a citizen and the government. A great many important matters come before the civil courts: questions relating to taxation; business contracts; a wide range of commercial affairs; questions about wills, trusts, and inheritance; family disputes over divorce, custody, separation, and matrimonial property; cases where negligent conduct has caused another to suffer a loss; disputes over land and other property. This chapter is not concerned with these matters, but focuses on the constitutional role of the courts as a check upon abuse of power by government. The courts go a considerable distance towards checking government excesses and preventing arbitrary and unfair decisions. The New Zealand courts have shown themselves able, in some situations, to strike lethal blows at abuse of power by government.

COURT STRUCTURE AND THE PRIVY COUNCIL

New Zealand's court structure at present can be represented in a figure as follows, although this looks set to change.

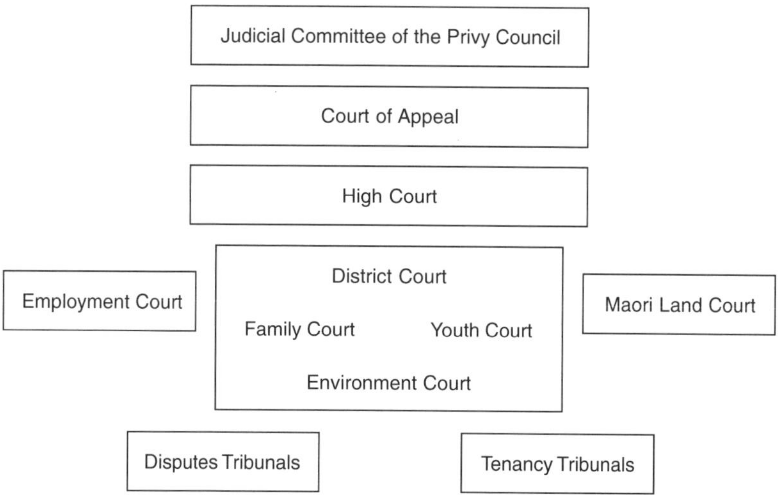

Figure 14.1: New Zealand's court structure

At the moment, for all but a tiny number of cases, the New Zealand Court of Appeal is the final court of appeal for all civil and criminal matters. It comprises seven permanent judges who usually sit three to a case, although in important cases five will sit. Below the Court of Appeal is the High Court, which has around thirty judges and the Chief Justice. The High Court judges usually sit one to a case. The High Court is New Zealand's only court of unlimited jurisdiction. High Court judges preside over the most serious jury trials and civil cases as well as many administrative law cases. Most of the judicial work in New Zealand takes place in the District Court. There are over 100 District Court judges, including the Chief District Court Judge. They deal with most of the crime, a large number of civil cases, they sit in the Family Court, conduct jury trials, and generally have responsibility for the bulk of the nation's judicial business. Most of the disputes resolved in the court system are handled by the Disputes Tribunals and Residential Tenancy Tribunals, which are designed to provide cheap and easy access to a (usually non-legally trained) authority to resolve disputes involving small amounts of money.

In 1996, the Privy Council, which sits in London and comprises mainly United Kingdom judges, is still the highest court for New Zealand. It usually deals with five or six cases a year from New Zealand. It is doubtful how long its jurisdiction will remain. Most other Commonwealth countries, including Australia and Canada, have abandoned the Privy Council. One barrier to removal so far in New Zealand has been the recognition that the Privy Council has served New Zealand well, and its jurisdiction cannot be removed until the structure for New Zealand to handle its own appeals is devised.

In May 1996, the National Government introduced the New Zealand Courts Structure Bill to abolish the right of appeal to the Privy Council. This long overdue announcement followed the recommendations made in the Solicitor-General's report on the subject to the Cabinet Strategy Committee in March 1995. Constitutionally, New Zealand has been able to abolish the appeal to the Privy Council since enacting the Statute of Westminster (Adoption Act) 1947.

Four options were outlined in the Solicitor-General's report.[2] The legislation as introduced by the government was based on option two, whereby cases appealed to the Court of Appeal would go either to the Civil or Criminal Division of the Court of Appeal or, if of significant importance, would go to the full bench of the Court of Appeal. The divisions would be composed of three judges (the Chief Justice and/or a permanent member of the Court of Appeal and one or two High Court judges). The full Court of Appeal would generally comprise five judges and would comprise only permanent judges of the Court of Appeal and the Chief Justice. The criteria and process for deciding whether a case goes to a division or the full bench would be determined by the Court of Appeal and would have to be published. Interestingly, in a 1996 speech, the President of the Court of Appeal, Sir Ivor Richardson, says that the court's planning for operating a three-judge

---

2 *Appeals to the Privy Council*, Report of the Solicitor-General to the Cabinet Strategy Committee on Issues of Termination and Court Structure, 10 March 1995, Wellington, 1995, pp.21–7.

civil division in 1997 as well as the existing criminal division of the Court of Appeal does not depend on the passage of the government's legislation. Existing legislation allows this structure to be established anyway (although the right of appeal to the Privy Council can be abolished only by legislation).[3]

This legislation, if passed, would mean there would be no further right of appeal beyond the Court of Appeal and, if a case originates in the High Court, there would be only one right of appeal. This has been the major cause of concern among those who oppose abolition of the Privy Council. Although it would provide earlier finality in deciding a dispute, some argue that it is important for a third look by a court to be available in difficult cases. But, for most New Zealanders who become subject to judicial processes, appeal to the Privy Council is just not realistic. It is expensive. Very few cases each year are taken to London from this country, but in 1995, 606 criminal and 181 civil appeals were heard by the Court of Appeal in New Zealand. Of the thirty-nine cases from New Zealand heard by the Privy Council in the period from 1989 to 1994, only fifteen appeals were allowed in full.[4] Furthermore, one can appeal a civil decision as of right where the final judgment given in the Court of Appeal amounts to $5000 or more. In criminal proceedings, appeals to the Privy Council are available only at the discretion of the council itself, which has happened just five times in the legal history of this country; only once was the appellant successful.

Some Maori believe that abolishing the Privy Council could have some effect on their rights under the Treaty of Waitangi. The government has stated that there is no logical connection between the abolition of the right to appeal to the Privy Council and the availability of treaty rights. It is understandable that Maori who are concerned with the constitutional status of the treaty would take every opportunity to raise it. Court of Appeal decisions, however, have had more influence than Privy Council decisions in elevating the legal status of the treaty. With respect, it seems to us that the two issues are quite distinct.

Those favouring retention also argue that being able to appeal to judges removed from the local scene allows for some form of objectivity and greater impartiality. The counter-argument to this is equally convincing. By involving overseas judges in decisions about New Zealand law, we run the risk of judgments being made by judges who are not in touch with the conditions of New Zealand society. In a recent case to be appealed to the Privy Council, namely *Invercargill City Council* v. *Hamlin*,[5] (a case involving the negligence of a building inspector), the Privy Council applied New Zealand legal principles, which differ from those in England, and dismissed the appeal. In so doing, the Law Lords conceded that such matters

---

3 Sir Ivor Richardson, 'Court of Appeal Reforms', Address to the New Zealand Bar Association Conference, 27 July 1996.

4 *Appeals to the Privy Council*, 1995, Appendix G.

5 [1996] 1 All ER 756.

should be decided by New Zealand judges in New Zealand in the light of New Zealand community standards and expectations.[6]

Some elements of the commercial and business community have argued that the Privy Council decides law as it should be decided on the basis of precedent, whereas the Court of Appeal has been shown to make value judgments that depart from established legal principles. They allude to the battle over negligence that raged between the two courts before the above case. But whatever decisions a court makes is likely to involve some value judgment. There is value in both the certainty of the law and in fairness of result. The balance struck by particular courts tends to ebb and flow over time and usually reflects (sometimes with some delay) the ebb and flow of social, economic, cultural, and political views in a society. The Privy Council and the Court of Appeal reflect different states of the tide in different societies. The government's legislation would ensure that New Zealand's highest court is located in the South Pacific rather than the North Atlantic.

ROYAL COMMISSIONS AND COMMISSIONS OF INQUIRY

Royal commissions and commissions of inquiry are governed by the Commissions of Inquiry Act 1908, which provides such inquiries with coercive powers. Commissions really exist as distinct entities as they do not technically belong to the legislature, the executive or the judiciary.[7] They do not decide questions put before them as a court does; rather they are set up by government to inquire into and report on all kinds of matters.

A commission decision can be subjected to judicial review by a court if it is made outside of the commission's terms of reference. Sir Ivor Richardson, the President of the Court of Appeal, has commented on courts' role in this context:

> Where a searching inquiry is held into events or rumours which have given rise to public concern with the object of ascertaining the truth and attributing blame if blame is due, individuals may be very tarnished in the process. It is a matter of balancing the public interest in the search for truth in issues of national concern on the one hand, the public interest in the protection of privacy and reputation on the other. That is because, while findings of commissions are in the end expressions of opinion only and do not affect the legal rights of the persons to whom they refer, nevertheless they may greatly influence public and government opinion and have a devastating effect on personal reputations. The courts perform a balancing role in exercising as they do a review function in determining whether the commission has kept within its terms of reference and has acted throughout in accordance with any applicable principles of natural justice.[8]

---

6 *Ibid.* at 766–7.
7 E.J. Haughey & E.J.L. Fairway, *Royal Commissions and Commissions of Inquiry*, Government Printer, Wellington, 1974, p.5.
8 Sir Ivor Richardson, 'Commissions of Inquiry', 7 *Otago Law Review*, 1989, pp.1, 4.

In accordance with section 2 of the Commissions of Inquiry Act, they may be set up to inquire into questions arising out of or concerning the administration of government, the working of any existing law, the necessity or expediency of any legislation, the conduct of any Crown servant, any disaster or accident involving members of the public, and (since 1970) any other matter of public importance.

Royal commissions are set up by the Governor-General in the name of the Sovereign pursuant to clause VII of the Letters Patent. They are usually established to inquire into matters of greater national importance than those dealt with by other commissions of inquiry.

The Commissions of Inquiry Act gives commissions powers to summon witnesses, hear evidence (including that which might not be admissible in a court of law), conduct investigations, and award costs. Where a judge or a former judge of the High Court is appointed as a commissioner, the commission is granted the same powers, privileges, and immunities as a High Court judge in the exercise of civil jurisdiction. Otherwise, members of a commission enjoy immunity only in so far as they stay within their terms of reference and comply with the requirements of natural justice. Once the commission has made its report, the government is free to accept it all, to accept part of it, to reject it all or even to ignore it.

A current example of a commission of inquiry is the controversial investigation into the 'winebox' transactions: the Commission of Inquiry into Certain Matters Relating to Taxation established in September 1994 and still running at the end of 1996. A winebox full of documents belonging to the European Pacific group of companies and allegedly implicating various well-known New Zealand companies in income tax evasion by the use of the Cook Islands tax haven, had been tabled in the House of Representatives by the Hon. Winston Peters MP.

Retired Chief Justice, the Rt Hon. Sir Ronald Davison, was appointed the sole commissioner of inquiry and his terms of reference were to inquire into and report on:

a. Whether the Commissioner of Inland Revenue and his staff and the Director of the Serious Fraud Office and his staff acted, in the course of their official duties, in a lawful, proper, and competent manner in dealing with the transactions referred to in the *Papers presented, by leave, to the House of Representatives by the member for Tauranga, the Honourable Winston Peters, on 16 March 1994* (A6, Volumes 1 to 2):

b. Whether, having regard to the kinds of transactions referred to in the papers so presented, any changes to the criminal law or the tax law should, in your opinion, be made for the purpose of protecting New Zealand's income tax base from the effects of fraud, evasion, and avoidance, and, if so, what:

Somewhat inevitably, Sir Ronald has been plagued by an unwillingness by witnesses to cooperate in the inquiry. A 1995 amendment to the Commissions of Inquiry

Act 1908 now allows a commissioner who is a High Court or former High Court judge to impose sanctions, including detention in custody, upon any witness who without just excuse refuses to answer questions or produce documents.[9] Although the immediate purpose of this amendment was to aid the winebox commissioner in his task, the provision exists to be used by future commissions, and demonstrates their importance in investigating matters of national importance.

Commissions, however, need to be used with considerable circumspection. Their findings can inflict damage upon individuals without those individuals being afforded the protection of a criminal trial. Commissions must adhere to the rules of natural justice including acting reasonably and without bias or predetermination, and giving individuals the opportunity to respond to allegations prejudicial to them.

JUDICIAL INDEPENDENCE

The complaint is often made that the judiciary does not adequately reflect the true make-up and diversity of New Zealand society. Maori, in particular, are noticeably lacking on the bench, particularly in the High Court. This increases calls for accountability of judges, because of the suspicion attached to decisions made by judges who are not representative of society. There have been regular calls for a more transparent system of judicial appointments.

Constitutionally, the present position is clear. It is a function of the executive, and not the judiciary, to appoint judges. Judicial appointments to the High Court and the Court of Appeal are made by the Governor-General on behalf of the Queen, following the recommendation of the Attorney-General. The Attorney-General will not have discussions with Cabinet, but will consult with the Solicitor-General, the President of the Law Society, the Chief Justice, and the President of the Court of Appeal. For District Court judges, the Minister of Justice makes the recommendations. Consultation aside, it is an executive decision. Accountability for the appointments is through the system of ministerial responsibility to Parliament by questioning, debating, and even holding the Minister to account. Select committees may examine the appointments and policies.

Looking at the above process, it would be easy to conclude that party politics play a role in appointments, but they do not. Non-partisan judicial appointments are a powerful constitutional convention. Judicial appointments in New Zealand have so far been free from political entanglements.

In their 1978 report, the Royal Commission on the Courts recommended that a Judicial Commission should be established in New Zealand which would

9 Ss. 13A, B Commissions of Inquiry Act 1908.

administer the courts, recommend appointments, and deal with complaints.[10] It was envisaged that this commission would consist of the Chief Justice, a judge of the Supreme Court (as the High Court was then called), the Chief District Court judge, the Solicitor-General, the Secretary for Justice, and two members appointed by the Governor-General on the recommendation of the New Zealand Law Society. As far as the appointment process was concerned, it was believed that such a commission would reinforce notions of judicial independence by showing more clearly that no political considerations were involved.

In 1995 the Attorney-General, Hon. Paul East, addressed this idea of a commission, as well as judicial appointments in general, in a speech to the New Zealand Bar Association.[11] Although he accepted that the judiciary needed to reflect society as a whole, he dismissed the idea of the commission for some valid reasons. Perhaps the most convincing is that, since the commission would be made up of a number of judges, the range of candidates considered for appointment might be restricted because incumbent judges would choose who were to join their ranks and would deal with any complaints about judges. This would be a direct affront to the notion of an independent judiciary. It would also substitute for ministerial responsibility for appointments.

The process could, however, be made more transparent. In his speech, the Attorney-General outlined a new procedure to be followed for appointments, with a greater focus on consultation. The procedure is:

a) The Attorney-General will consult specified groups and people including the judiciary, parliamentary and professional groups, and invite them to suggest suitable candidates.
b) The wider community will have access to the system in order to make suggestions.
c) Once there is a shortlist, it will be addressed individually and in confidence.
d) The New Zealand Law Society and the New Zealand Bar Association will then be consulted with.
e) A vetting process of the background of potential appointees will then be carried out to avoid any embarrassment after appointment.
f) The offer of appointment will be made and Cabinet will be advised.

The process is administered by an independent unit in the Crown Law Office which is also responsible for maintaining records of factual biographical material

---

10 *Report of the Royal Commission on the Courts*, Wellington, H.2 *Appendices to the Journal of the House of Representatives*, Wellington, 1978, para 654.

11 Attorney-General's Speech to the New Zealand Bar Association Seminar, Centra Hotel, Auckland, 18 March 1995.

on people. The Attorney-General's final comment in this speech is worth reproducing:

> This debate gained some momentum in the last few years, yet I have seen or heard nothing that convinces me the present system is wrong. It is a system shrouded in mystery and subject to gossip and conjecture. But that is a matter of appearance and can be improved upon. It is free of party politics. It has worked well. There is no case for dismantling it.

Part IV of the Constitution Act 1986 recognises the constitutional importance of the judiciary. Section 23 provides that a judge of the High Court (which includes the judges of the Court of Appeal) 'shall not be removed from the office except by the Sovereign or the Governor-General, acting upon an address of the House of Representatives, which address may be moved only on the grounds of that Judge's misbehaviour or of that Judge's incapacity to discharge the functions of the Judge's office'. And a further provision, section 24, provides that 'the salary of a Judge of the High Court shall not be reduced during the continuance of the Judge's commission'.

These provisions, which were formerly in the Judicature Act 1908, came to us as part of English constitutional law, at least since the Act of Settlement in 1700, which was designed to protect the judges by removing the Crown's unfettered discretion to dismiss them. The procedure and grounds for dismissing District Court judges is similar, although the Minister of Justice is involved.

Judges are sworn to be impartial. The oath they take on assuming office says they will 'do right to all manner of people after the laws and usages of New Zealand without fear or favour, affection or ill will'.

The independence of the judiciary is a core principle of the New Zealand constitution. The Royal Commission on the Courts went so far as to say in its report that the independence of the judiciary was, at that time, 'the only real bulwark against the arbitrary exercise of power'.[12] That seems to be claiming too much but the principle is certainly important. Those who make the laws do not interpret them; they do not apply them in disputed cases. It is the function of the judges to say what the law is in particular cases.

The important principle at stake is that the government should not exert any form of pressure on the judges to make decisions in a particular way. Political attacks on the judiciary would weaken the authority and standing of the courts, especially their reputation for impartiality. There is another side to this constitutional convention. Judges must refrain from politically partisan activities; in matters of political controversy, they must avoid taking public sides.

12 *Report of the Royal Commission on the Courts*, Wellington, 1978, p.196.

When judges make decisions they must not be beholden to ministers and MPs. Since the government is often a litigant in the courts, the need for independence is vital. These principles have occasionally appeared to be under attack in New Zealand. Clearly justice must be dispensed even-handedly and the general public must feel confidence in the integrity and impartiality of the courts. This is why the judiciary must be secure from undue political influence, particularly from ministers. Judges must never be seen to be acting as mouthpieces of the executive. If the courts increase their sentences at the invitation of politicians who speak to them through the media, the appearance of independence is imperilled. What is worse, the next offender who comes before the courts for sentence may wonder at the influences at work upon his or her sentence.

There are also powerful laws of contempt of court whereby people can be punished severely for making scandalous statements about judges or making public statements calculated to influence the outcome of a trial. The law of contempt is a strong instrument for protecting the independence of the judiciary and ensuring fair trials.

The 1996 *Cabinet Office Manual*, which establishes guidelines for ministerial conduct, calls for ministers to exercise restraint and care when dealing with judicial decisions within their portfolios.

> 5.141 The separation of the executive and the judiciary under New Zealand's system of Government means that Ministers must exercise prudent judgment before commenting on judicial decisions—either generally, or in relation to a specific sentence. Ministers, following a long-established principle, do not involve themselves in deciding whether a person should be prosecuted, or on what charge. Therefore, they should not express comment on the results of particular cases. Sentencing is a complex process. Ministers must avoid commenting on any sentences within the appeal period, and should avoid at all times any comment which could be construed as being intended to influence the courts in subsequent cases.
>
> 5.142 Ministers should not express any views which are likely to be publicised where they could be regarded as reflecting adversely on the impartiality, personal views or ability of any judge. If a Minister feels he or she has grounds for concern over a sentencing decision, the Attorney-General should be informed.
>
> 5.143 It is, however, proper for Ministers to comment on the effectiveness of the law, or about policies on punishment, ie on those matters where the executive has a proper involvement but not where the performance of the courts is brought into question.

These guidelines have been breached. Furthermore, MPs are not subject to the same restrictions as ministers, but they are constrained only by Standing Order

117, which prevents the use of 'offensive words against . . . any member of the Judiciary'. Restraints on debate in Parliament are imposed by the *sub judice* rule that prevents reference to 'matters awaiting or under adjudication in any court of record' (Standing Order 115).

Politicians are not the only ones to misunderstand the independence of the judiciary. Members of the public often complain about judicial decisions and may consider asking ministers to intervene and set things right. Ministers cannot intervene in court cases. This fact is one of the basic principles of our democratic government. Regrettably, a great many people appear to be ignorant of it.

ADMINISTERING THE COURTS SYSTEM: EXECUTIVE V. JUDICIARY

The constitutional relationship between the executive and the judiciary is characterised by tension. Were it not for the principles of self-restraint that traditionally govern both branches, matters could break into open warfare. Two instances involving judges' superannuation provide pertinent examples of how the interests and decisions of these separate branches of government can clash.

In February 1988, Cabinet received a recommendation from the Higher Salaries Commission that judicial superannuation should be increased. Cabinet decided to query this report with the commission, and the response said basically that if the recommendation was not followed, the commission would simply make a *determination* (for which it enjoyed exclusive jurisdiction) that judicial salaries should be increased. Cabinet felt this might attract more public scrutiny, so the recommendation was passed.

In 1987, the government had announced that the tax treatment of superannuation was to be moved onto the same basis as other forms of savings and investments. Thus, the earnings of the contributor would be taxed, the earnings of the funds would be taxed, but the benefits would not be taxed. The judges were consulted and they objected. They argued that their superannuation entitlements were part of a package, and could not be reduced unilaterally. The Solicitor-General advised the government that the scheme did not breach the constitutional rule. The judges persisted and there were further discussions. In March 1990, the Solicitor-General wrote a further opinion that affirmed his earlier advice. He stated that the measure was part of an overall fiscal restructuring. The judges received their own advice, which was that what was being proposed was contrary to constitutional convention. The government decided to tell the judges that they could sue if they wished to have the matter determined. The judges decided against this option and the legislation went through.

The new government elected in 1990 wanted to close off the government superannuation scheme, including judicial superannuation. The Solicitor-General wrote another opinion reminding them about the constitutional situation and advising that any changes could therefore not apply to sitting judges. So the government dealt with the matter by preserving the existing rights of sitting judges, and by putting new appointees onto a fresh scheme.

These tensions arose in relation to the direct remuneration of judges. But the administration of the court system in general requires a delicate partnership between the executive, the judiciary, and Parliament. Since 1995 the Department for Courts is the organisation that provides administrative services for the courts and tribunals. The department, which is accountable to the Minister for Courts according to ordinary principles of ministerial responsibility, must maintain a close relationship with the judiciary in order to carry out its functions effectively and with full information.

COURTS AND THE CONSTITUTION

In general, the first and most important check upon executive power in New Zealand comes from the law. The executive must act in accordance with the law. In a fundamental manner, the judicial branch of our government does control actions of the executive. Proof of the proposition goes back to a celebrated English case decided by Lord Chief Justice Camden in 1765. In *Entick* v. *Carrington* messengers of the King, under a warrant issued by the Secretary of State, entered the plaintiff's premises and searched and seized papers. The plaintiff brought an action for trespass and breaking and entering. He succeeded and was awarded £300 in damages. Many ingenious arguments were advanced to justify the seizure under the warrant, but none of them was accepted. In particular, it was argued that the issuing and execution of such warrants was necessary for the ends of government. But Lord Camden said that the common law of England did not understand the reasoning about state necessity. Neither could the warrant be justified on any argument of utility. He came to the conclusion that unless the warrant could be shown to be legal, either by a statutory provision or by a rule of the common law, then the action must succeed. 'If it is the law it will be found in our books. If it is not to be found there, it is not the law.'[13]

That case and its subsequent reception by our constitutional history, has established that government must act according to law in everything that it does. The proposition is fundamental. As Professor A.V. Dicey put it in his book *Introduction to the Study of the Law of the Constitution*: 'A man may with us be punished for a breach of the law, but he can be punished for nothing else.'[14]

[13] *Entick* v. *Carrington* (1765) 19 *State Trials* 1029 (1558–1774) *All England Reports* 41, 11 *Digest* (Repl.) 437.

[14] A.V. Dicey, *Introduction to the Study of the Law of the Constitution*, 10th ed., Macmillan, London, 1959, p.202.

Although it is a salutary thought that public authority must point to some specific rule authorising any action that affects a person's rights, it must be observed that the court is not concerned with the content of the rules but with their existence. To meet the test in *Entick* v. *Carrington* it is necessary only that a statutory provision or common law rule which justifies the action taken should be shown to exist. It is not the court's central concern that the provision may be arbitrary, unfair or oppressive. Under our constitutional arrangements, the general understanding is that the court cannot strike down an enacted rule, however bad. There must be rules, but the quality and content of the rules, at least of those made by the legislature, are determined by the political process.

Entick v. *Carrington* is not a dead letter today. Mr Justice Woodhouse relied upon it in a judgment delivered in the New Zealand Court of Appeal in 1977 and it was referred to by Gault J in the landmark Bill of Rights Act case *Simpson* v. *Attorney-General (Baigent's Case).*[15]

Courts in other nations have even greater power to wield against the other branches of government. In the United States and Canada, for instance, the courts can strike down legislation as being against the constitution and the Charter of Rights respectively. As discussed in Chapter 15, section 4 of the New Zealand Bill of Rights Act 1990 does not allow courts to judge legislation and strike it down as being inconsistent with the act's principles. New Zealand has no federal system, which would require the courts to act as umpire between federal government on the one hand and state governments on the other. The basic legal rule of our constitution is that Parliament is supreme. When it passes legislation, that is the law. There is no higher law.

It has usually been thought that there can be no argument that any statute Parliament passes is unconstitutional. Although there have been some statements by judges implying the contrary, the usual understanding is that New Zealand courts cannot strike down as invalid statutes enacted by Parliament.[16] But they have considerable power in interpreting the words of a statute and applying them to cases: a statute means what the courts say it means, not what the executive say it means. In addition, section 6 of the Bill of Rights Act instructs the courts to apply, wherever possible, the interpretation consistent with the act. But Parliament's law is supreme and the judges must apply it.

For these reasons the courts in our system of government do not often have the opportunity of deciding cases that involve the fundamental relationships between the elements of our government. Such a case did occur, however, in 1976. The

---

15 [1994] 3 *NZLR* 667, 710.

16 *L* v. *M* [1979] 2 *NZLR* 519 at 527; *Brader* v. *Ministry of Transport* [1981] 1 *NZLR* 73, 78; *New Zealand Drivers Association* v. *New Zealand Road Carriers* [1982] 1 *NZLR* 374, 390; *Fraser* v. *State Services Commission* [1984] 1 *NZLR* 116, 121; *Taylor* v. *New Zealand Poultry Board* [1984] 1 *NZLR* 394, 398.

decision that year of the Chief Justice Sir Richard Wild in *Fitzgerald* v. *Muldoon* demonstrated that the courts can be bold in checking the excesses of executive power. It was an example of how the courts can uphold fundamental principles.

Three days after the Prime Minister, Robert Muldoon, was sworn in, he issued a press statement (15 December 1975) purporting to give effect to the National Party's election policy of abolishing the New Zealand Superannuation Scheme and refunding all contributions to employees. The offending paragraph of the statement was:[17]

> The compulsory requirements for employee deductions to the New Zealand Scheme will cease for pay periods ending after this date. Mr Muldoon said that he recognised that because of arrangements made for payment of wages and salaries in advance through computer systems or by other means, deductions would in some cases continue for limited periods. All deductions and contributions, including any which may be made from now until 31 March 1976, will be returned to employees through the income tax refund system or could be transferred to another scheme. Similarly, the compulsory requirement for employer contributions will cease as from today in respect of salaries or wages paid from now on.

In a further statement on 23 December 1975 the Prime Minister said:[18]

> The government had already made it clear that the superannuation scheme finished on 15 December and the compulsory requirement for employee deductions and employer contributions ceased for pay periods ending after that date. Empowering legislation, with retrospective effect, would be introduced early in the 1976 Parliamentary session.

At the time the proceedings were issued and the case was decided, Parliament had not been called together so no legislation implementing the government's policy had been passed. Parliament had been summoned for 22 June 1976, ten days after the date of the court decision.

The plaintiff sued the Prime Minister, the New Zealand Superannuation Board, the Attorney-General, the Controller and Auditor-General, and sought various remedies.

The Chief Justice vindicated principle by declaring that the Prime Minister's 15 December 1975 announcement was illegal as being in breach of article 1 of the Bill of Rights 1688, an English provision that is part of New Zealand law and that states: 'That the pretended power of suspending of laws or the execution of laws by regall authority without consent of Parlyament is illegal.'[19] He issued a declaration to that effect, holding that, by making the statements he did, the

---

17 *Fitzgerald* v. *Muldoon* [1976] 2 *NZLR* 616–17.

18 *Ibid.*, p.617.

19 *Halsbury's Statutes*, 4th ed., Vol. 10, Butterworths, London, 1985, p.37.

Prime Minister was purporting to suspend the law without the consent of Parliament. After the declaration was issued all other matters were adjourned for six months because 'it would be an altogether unwarranted step to require the machinery of the New Zealand Superannuation Act 1974 now to be set in motion again, when the high probabilities are that all would have to be undone again within a few months.'[20]

Sir Richard Wild's disposition of this potentially embarrassing case resolved neatly the tension between principle and expediency. On the one hand he stared in the face a frontal attack upon Parliament's power to legislate, and upon the rule of law. Without compromise, he branded the occasion for what it was. On the other side, he faced the practical problem of potential administrative chaos in setting the Superannuation Act going again when everyone knew not only that the government intended to abolish the scheme but that they had the numbers in Parliament to do it. He avoided that problem by the common-sense solution of adjourning for six months the part of the proceedings calling for coercive relief. Although the Chief Justice did not need to base his judgment on the 1688 Bill of Rights, he did so, and followed it with a sustained statement of rhetorical power:[21]

> It is a graphic illustration of the depth of our legal heritage and the strength of our constitutional law that a statute passed by the English Parliament nearly three centuries ago to extirpate the abuses of the Stuart Kings should be available on the other side of the earth to a citizen of this country which was then virtually unknown in Europe and on which no Englishman was to set foot for almost another hundred years. And yet it is not disputed that the Bill of Rights is part of our law. The fact that no modern instance of its application was cited in argument may be due to the fact that it is rarely that a litigant takes up such a cause as the present, or it may be because governments usually follow established constitutional procedure. But it is not a reason for declining to apply the Bill of Rights where it is invoked and a litigant makes out his case.

The Chief Justice went on to rely upon Dicey's dictum that, under the English constitution, Parliament 'has the right to make or unmake any law whatever, and further, that no person or body is recognised by the law of England as having a right to override or set aside the legislation of Parliament'.[22]

In the broadest sense, the case of *Fitzgerald* v. *Muldoon* demonstrates, perhaps more than any case ever decided in New Zealand, the division of governmental powers between the three great components of the constitution: Parliament, the executive, and the judiciary. Each has its role to play. To preserve balance in the

---

20 [1976] 2 *NZLR* 623.
21 *Ibid.*, p.622.
22 A.V. Dicey, *Introduction to the Study of the Law of the Constitution*, 10th ed., Macmillan, London, 1959, p. 39.

system, the activities of each in relation to the others must remain within proper boundaries. In the final analysis, the courts will say what those boundaries are.

The Prime Minister did not take the decision in good grace. He suggested that the Chief Justice had 'misunderstood' the position, although it is significant that no appeal was taken. The Prime Minister accused counsel for the plaintiff of having taken the initiative in instituting the action, rather than acting as mere professional adviser. That accusation was refuted in open court when the Chief Justice awarded $2500 in costs to the plaintiff against the Prime Minister.

ADMINISTRATIVE LAW

Lay people know little about the courts' activity in what is called administrative law. Broadly, this deals with legal checks on the exercise of power by ministers, officials, and government generally. Legislation gives the executive wide discretionary powers in many different areas of activity. As we have seen, numerous tribunals exist to decide specialised questions of licensing and registration.

When ministers, public servants, local authorities or tribunals act in a manner that is outside their powers or according to a process that is unfair, their decision can be quashed by a court. This is known as judicial review of a decision. Courts carry out judicial review of the exercise or refusal to exercise a statutory power under section 4(1) of the Judicature Amendment Act 1972. This is to ensure that an administrative action is within its authority. If it is not, it will be *ultra vires*. Both statutes and the common law provide requirements for administrative action. An administrative action must, therefore, take into account all relevant considerations and no irrelevant ones, it must be reasonable, it must not be biased or predetermined, and it must comply with the principles of natural justice. If these requirements are not satisfied, an individual may apply for judicial review, which creates additional rights for an individual that would not be available in private law.

Judicial review deals with the *legality* of the decision and needs to be contrasted with the hearing of an appeal, which deals with its *merits*. In recent years, however, courts have been more prepared to investigate the reasonableness of administrative decisions so that the merits of decisions are becoming more subjected to scrutiny. Sir Owen Woodhouse, while President of the Court of Appeal, said in a public lecture:[23]

> . . . the Judiciary has extended the ambit of its review of administrative action. In this regard it can be said that the Courts are beginning to find it necessary to approach if not actually enter upon areas which touch upon policy and which the purist would

[23] Rt Hon. Sir Owen Woodhouse, *Government Under the Law*, The J.C. Beaglehole Memorial Lecture, Price Milburn for the New Zealand Council for Civil Liberties, Wellington, 1979, p.7.

> probably consider to be outside their conventional responsibilities. It is a process which I believe will need to be taken further during the next decade or so if a fair balance is to be maintained between the citizen and the executive government, left as it so frequently is by Parliament to exercise wide and even critical delegated discretions.

Other judges, however, have argued that judicial review of administrative action is concerned with the decision-making process rather than the merits of the decision. Otherwise, Lord Brightman said, the court will 'under the guise of preventing the abuse of power, be itself guilty of usurping power'.[24] Nevertheless, administrative law is a complex area that is rapidly changing. In order to explain some of its capacities to act as a check on official action, some New Zealand examples are useful.

A female school-teacher, married and living with her husband, was promoted to a position at a school away from the town in which she was then living. In those circumstances, a teacher was entitled 'to actual and reasonable expenses of his removal to the other position'. The relevant regulations also said that 'The Minister shall lay down from time to time the general conditions governing payment of removal expenses . . .' The Department of Education followed a practice (which had been laid down by the minister on the department's recommendation) of not paying full removal expenses to a married female teacher unless her husband was an invalid or dependent on her financially. In other cases, only the wife's own fares for travelling, the cost of shifting her own personal effects, and hotel expenses had been paid.

The then Supreme Court held that the Department of Education could not lawfully interpret the regulation to discriminate against women in that way and the minister could not validly lay down any such condition. The Court of Appeal upheld the Supreme Court's decision.[25]

In the second example, a former employee of a law firm faced criminal charges involving conspiracy to defraud. He applied for legal aid for the trial pursuant to the Legal Services Act 1991. Legal aid was granted by the Registrar of the High Court, who referred the matter to the relevant subcommittee in order to fix the total remuneration to be paid under section 11 of the act. A memorandum was sent by the employee's counsel setting out the usual costs and suggesting a meeting for discussion. This offer was not taken up and the remuneration was set. Counsel reached an agreement with the plaintiff's former firm whereby the firm would supplement the legal aid grant. It was argued that this decision was outside the act and was *ultra vires*, that it was unfair, and that no subcommittee, acting reasonably and taking into account all relevant considerations, would come to such a decision.

---

24 *Chief Constable* v. *Evans*, quoted in 'The Courts and the Constitution', K.J. Keith, 15 *Victoria University of Wellington Law Review*, 1985, pp.38–9.

25 *Van Gorkom* v. *Attorney-General* [1977] 1 *NZLR* 535.

The High Court judge held that it was a clear breach of natural justice to reduce the amount of legal aid to the plaintiff without warning and without allowing for submissions to be made. The reduced grant was set aside, the original grant reinstituted, and the additional payment from the law firm approved.[26]

There are a number of important limitations on the courts' capacity to quash and review government action. Sometimes, although less often than in the past, the government will try to limit the courts' capacity to interfere or review by express statutory language. The courts have shown a tendency not to be put off by these efforts, but there are areas where it will be difficult to get a court to intervene for that reason.

The courts usually intervene where the authority concerned has acted without legal power, and that may include situations where the authority acts in bad faith or for a wrong purpose. They must ensure that the rules of natural justice are followed. This is affirmed in section 27(1) of the New Zealand Bill of Rights Act. Broadly, this means the courts will ensure that administrators act fairly and reasonably. The rules set the minimum level for decision-making. For example, under these rules no one can be a judge in one's own cause; likelihood of bias is prevented. Contesting parties are entitled to a fair hearing. A person who stands to be penalised must receive fair notice of the charge and be given an opportunity to answer the case.

The cases discussed in this chapter concerned government actions that were held to be illegal for one reason or another. It was the courts' duty to ensure that:

- There is a legal rule under which government has acted.
- The rule has been correctly interpreted and applied.
- The action is not contrary to the rules of natural justice.

In essence, the courts are concerned to protect the fairness and integrity of the administrative process from abuse by the coercive powers of government. Administrative law remedies are discretionary; a great many technical matters have been left out of the foregoing account.

GOVERNMENT REVERSAL OF COURT DECISIONS

A fundamental limitation on the courts' power to check executive decisions results from the government's influence over the legislative machinery of government. The government can change any regulation at will and, by promoting legislative change through Parliament, statutes can be amended. It is reasonably frequent in New Zealand for governments to react swiftly and decisively against judicial decisions that are unacceptable to them.

[26] *Darvell* v. *Auckland District Legal Services Subcommittee* [1993] 1 *NZLR* 111.

A well-known example concerns the Clyde dam. In 1977 the National Government decided that it wanted to build a high dam at Clyde; it would be the biggest concrete dam in the history of the country. The previous Labour Government had decided on another scheme of dams that involved a low dam at Clyde and other dams elsewhere, and did not flood nearly as much land as the proposed high dam. The landowners affected did not object to a low dam at Clyde.

Under the National Government the following steps were taken:

1. On 10 June 1977 the minister applied for water rights relating to construction of a high dam at Clyde to enable electricity to be generated. Those applications were sent to the Otago Regional Water Board for its report and recommendation. The board recommended that the application for a high dam be declined but that a right for a low dam be granted.

2. On 6 December 1977 the National Water and Soil Conservation Authority decided to grant the right for a high dam. The landowners and others appealed to the Planning Tribunal.

3. The judgment of the Planning Tribunal on the appeals was given on 16 December 1980. By a majority of four to two, the appeal against the granting of the application was dismissed. The dissenters were the two District Court judges who sat. The other members were not legally qualified.

4. As they were entitled to do, the objectors appealed on a point of law to the High Court by way of case stated. In a judgment on 13 May 1982 the High Court held that the Planning Tribunal had made an error of law in refusing to consider the end use of the power that the Minister of Energy sought to generate. This use was, of course, the proposed aluminium smelter at Aramoana. The likelihood of the smelter proceeding could be highly relevant, Mr Justice Casey said. This was because the need for the high dam and the inundation of so much more land than the low dam caused was found to be due solely to the smelter's need for power by 1985–86.

So the tribunal had misdirected itself. It had to consider itself free to look at the end use of the power. This did not mean that the minister must lose. Under such a procedure, the question goes back to the tribunal so that it can decide whether the evidence on end use was in fact relevant and if so what weight should be given it. The decision was no fine point of law. It was basic to the integrity of the whole proceedings before the tribunal.

5. On 27 May 1982 the government announced that it was seeking special legislation to overcome the problem. Then it discovered that, owing to a defection in its own ranks, it did not have the numbers to carry the bill through the House.

6. On 14 July 1982 the government entered into an agreement with the two members of the Social Credit Political League in Parliament. Social Credit would support special legislation granting a water right subject to certain conditions. The agreement said: 'The Government undertakes not to introduce a bill for the

purpose of intervening in the process of objection and appeal in regard to the water rights for the Clyde high dam. If the final decision is adverse to the water rights for the Crown then Parliament . . .' would enable the water rights for a high dam to be obtained. The agreement also provided for the actual and reasonable legal costs of the appellants to be met, including 'their actual and reasonable legal costs to date'.

7. On 19 August 1982 after the Crown had finally returned to the Planning Tribunal, the tribunal unanimously ruled against granting the water right. The essence of the decision was simple: no smelter, no dam. The government, said the tribunal, presented 'a paucity of information' on why it needed to generate the electricity. The judgment says: 'The Tribunal has no evidence before it from which it can find that a smelter will be built or is likely to be built.' The decision was also significant for the award of costs to the appellants; the order would reimburse them in full for all their expenses. This very unusual ruling indicated the tribunal's distaste for the government's decision to deprive a litigant of the fruits of the litigation.

Another aspect of the decision exploded a myth long propounded by the government. The government had said repeatedly that it had been granted a water right by the National Water and Soil Conservation Authority after the first appeal was dealt with by the tribunal. Therefore, the government argued, it was quite acceptable to go on with the work. The tribunal ruled that there was no jurisdiction to issue a water right while an appeal on a point of law was pending. The right that had been issued was a nullity. It had never existed.

The whole episode raised important questions about the rule of law. The government had embarked on litigation voluntarily in order to get a water right. When it failed to secure one, it abandoned the proceedings and legislated. Having failed to prove its case on the facts, the government passed legislation to say that it possessed a water right which had been denied to it by the ordinary processes of law. The values of the rule of law were not assisted when Mr Justice Casey's decision was greeted with open hostility by a number of ministers.

Several problems were posed:

(a) The special legislation retrospectively and adversely affected the rights of citizens, who were given those rights by Parliament and who relied upon them.
(b) The government voluntarily submitted itself to the legal process when there were other avenues open to it.
(c) To interfere with the legal process was high-handed and gave the impression that government is above the law when it finds the legal process inconvenient.
(d) To sweep away rights and procedures established by an Act of Parliament requires something in the nature of an emergency.

(e) It makes a mockery of the legal procedures to allow them to continue for five years at considerable cost to the objectors and then announce that the government never intended to accept an impartial examination of the merits anyway.
(f) The special legislation effectively repealed the Water and Soil Conservation Act 1967 in respect to New Zealand's greatest water resource—the Clutha River.
(g) Such a course undermined the rule of law.

Court decisions are not infrequently altered or reversed by Parliament in legislation. Frequently there can be no objection. New policies are made and require new law, or court decisions disclose policy defects of which no one was previously aware.[27] But it is most unusual to legislate retrospectively to deprive litigants of the fruit of their successful litigation, and it is a most undesirable precedent.

Judges' existing capacity to protect people against governmental exercise of excessive and arbitrary power depends upon important fundamental concepts. In the event of dispute, the courts interpret acts and regulations. Although the executive branch has scope for much interpretation in order to run the government on a day-to-day basis, the authoritative and binding interpretations come from the judiciary. It is up to the judges to say what the law is in any given case. We have seen examples where the courts, in providing authoritative interpretation, have curbed the executive. Sometimes the response has been to legislate away the court's interpretation, a dubious practice. The courts, however, do not give in without a struggle.

Apart from the power of statutory interpretation, the courts can give judgments against the government, occasionally in constitutional block-busting cases such as *Fitzgerald* v. *Muldoon*, but more usually, as we have seen, in applying the growing remedies in the field of administrative law. The increasingly bold manner in which these powers are being exercised suggests that our judges are not blind to the growth of executive power in New Zealand and that they are prepared to act when appropriate cases come before them.

The courts have a vital role to play in prodding government to be fair, and in checking it when it is not. To the extent that we have trusted the courts in the past, they have not let us down.

ACCESS TO THE COURTS

There are some problems with the courts, particularly for disadvantaged people. To whom legal services are delivered, at what cost, and by what method are

[27] An example is the Citizenship (Western Samoa) Act 1982 and the case of *Lesa* v. *Attorney-General.*

important questions. Access to justice should not depend on wealth. The Legal Services Act 1991 was enacted so that legal assistance and access to justice were more easily available to the disadvantaged. Under Part IV, the act set up the Legal Services Board, whose responsibilities include administering the criminal and civil legal aid schemes, ensuring that the operation of these is inexpensive, expeditious, and efficient, funding community law centres throughout New Zealand, and providing advice and help to the public.

Criminal legal aid may be granted for proceedings where a person is charged with or convicted of any offence. It is granted if the registrar is satisfied that the grant is desirable in the interests of justice and if it appears that the applicant does not have sufficient means to obtain legal assistance.

Civil legal aid may be granted in most civil proceedings except a few such as the dissolution of marriage. Incorporated and unincorporated societies are not eligible for civil legal aid. Eligibility for civil legal aid depends on disposable income. It is not granted unless it can be shown that the person applying has reasonable grounds for taking or defending the proceedings. The board may have the benefit of a charge on property belonging to the applicant.

A recent review of the act by the Board recorded that the act has improved matters.[28] There are, however, still a number of transitional problems associated with implementation and administration, and further review has been called for.[29] A large percentage of Justice funds is now appropriated to Legal Services. For the 1996/97 year, the estimates record that $73.8 million or 56.2 per cent of the total amount allocated to Vote:Justice will be spent on purchasing services (relating to the administration, provision of, and access to legal services) from the Legal Services Board.

The legal aid scheme goes a step towards ensuring that access to justice is a realistic option for all New Zealanders, independent of financial status. It needs, however, to be seen in the context of other influences on the access to justice, including not only cost but also such factors as the cultural and gender sensitivity of the court system. New Zealanders' perceptions of the ease of access to the courts is a key part of our confidence in the judiciary and the legitimacy of our constitutional arrangements in general.[30]

---

28 *Review of the Legal Services Act 1991*, Wellington, 1995.

29 *Ibid.*, p.2.

30 B.V. Harris, 'Equal Access to Justice: A Constitutional Principle in Need of a Higher Profile', *New Zealand Law Review*, 1995, p.282.

15 The New Zealand Bill of Rights Act

INTRODUCTION

The New Zealand Bill of Rights Act 1990 was passed by the New Zealand Parliament after a considerable period of debate about what its nature should be. It had begun life as a constitutional sledge-hammer, but in its final form it did not give to the courts power to strike down legislation inconsistent with it. In a relatively short time, however, it has established itself an one of the basic building blocks of New Zealand's constitutional arrangements.

The Bill of Rights is designed to protect a number of fundamental rights and liberties from encroachment by government.[1] Although it is not a form of higher law—it is embodied in an ordinary statute that can be changed by a simple majority of Parliament—it is an important brake on Parliament itself. The Attorney-General is obliged to report when a bill introduced to the Parliament is in breach of the Bill of Rights. The Bill of Rights has binding force on the actions of the executive government upon which it acts as an important restraint. Furthermore, the Bill of Rights must be followed by the courts when they are interpreting and applying other laws, as has occurred in several hundred decisions.

The Bill of Rights Act applies to:

- acts done by the legislative branch of government;
- acts done by the executive branch of government;
- acts done by the judicial branch of government; and
- acts done by bodies that perform public functions.

So the range of state action this act opens up to review by the courts is wide, though not unlimited. It is not restricted to the obvious cases of police powers,

---

[1] The Bill of Rights as used in this chapter refers to the New Zealand Bill of Rights Act 1990. It is not to be confused with the United Kingdom's Bill of Rights 1688, which is also part of New Zealand law. On the New Zealand law, see, generally, G. Huscroft & P. Rishworth, eds, *Rights and Freedoms: The New Zealand Bill of Rights Act 1990 and the Human Rights Act 1993*, Brookers, Wellington, 1995.

where many of the cases have arisen so far. It could include a wide range of conduct by state agencies and officials towards even commercial enterprises. Indeed, it could include any citizen with whom agents of the state come into contact. Acts and omissions are covered. The exercise of statutory discretions may well have to meet the standards of the Bill of Rights Act. Common law rules have to meet those standards, at least in some circumstances.

The range of civil and political rights protected by the Bill of Rights Act is considerable and includes:

- the right not to be deprived of life;
- the right not to be subjected to torture or cruel treatment;
- the right not to be subjected to medical or scientific experimentation;
- the right to refuse to undergo medical treatment;
- electoral rights, including the right to vote;
- freedom of thought, conscience, and religion;
- freedom of expression;
- freedom of peaceful assembly;
- freedom of association;
- freedom of movement;
- freedom from discrimination;
- rights of minorities;
- protection against unreasonable search and seizure;
- the right not to be arbitrarily arrested or detained;
- a definition of the rights of persons who are arrested or detained;
- rights of persons charged with an offence;
- defined minimum standards of criminal procedure;
- protection against retroactive penalties and double jeopardy; and
- a right to justice in respect to the procedures of public authorities.[2]

Many people will have difficulty distinguishing the New Zealand Bill of Rights Act 1990 from the Human Rights Act 1993. The latter act defines a number of grounds of discrimination that it outlaws in both the public and private sector of the economy. The first Human Rights Act in New Zealand was passed in 1977 but the 1993 legislation added to the grounds of discrimination. The Human Rights Act is discussed in more detail in Chapter 13.

THE DEBATE ABOUT ENACTING A BILL OF RIGHTS

Like the Constitution Act 1986, the Bill of Rights Act was enacted as an ordinary statute. It was not protected against alteration by a simple majority in Parliament.

[2] New Zealand Bill of Rights Act 1990, ss 8–27.

One issue that arose in the debate over its enactment, however, was whether it should be enshrined in some basic New Zealand constitutional documents as part of a higher constitutional law, immune from alteration by the same processes as ordinary acts of Parliament. Many of the important provisions of the Electoral Act 1993 can be altered only by a 75 per cent majority in Parliament or by a majority of voters at a referendum. Should there be formal restraints on the powers of the executive and Parliament? This notion has been debated in a desultory fashion over the years. If New Zealand is ever to have a formal written constitution, this issue has to be settled. The difficulty with New Zealand's present system has been that small erosions in rights, resulting from some plausible argument at the time, often reduce liberty to an unjustified extent.

The point was well made in the government's White Paper on the Bill of Rights for New Zealand in 1985 (before the decision to introduce MMP):[3]

> The power of the government, alone and through Parliament, without the restraint or even the delay which would come from a second chamber, is enormous. In some senses it can be compared with the power, claimed as well as actual, of the Stuart Kings before the revolution of the seventeenth century. The basic difference between then and now is of course the electorate. But the electorate's role cannot, in the usual case, be focussed on a precise issue. A general election is a blunt instrument. It cannot give judgment on particular issues.

The white paper went on to point out how the New Zealand system of government could ride roughshod over minority interests and that discrimination and oppression could easily result from majority views on such matters. The idea that New Zealand should have a Bill of Rights limiting the power of government and guaranteeing the protection of fundamental values and freedoms was set out in Labour's 1984 election manifesto.[4] It was a policy that had been well advertised, even if it was not well understood. The journey between that announcement and the enactment of the New Zealand Bill of Rights Act 1990 was a long and tortuous one. For many years, the notion of a Bill of Rights that gave the courts the power to strike down legislation inconsistent with it was stoutly resisted. It will be an interesting aspect of the New Zealand experience with MMP to see what attitudes develop towards more formal constitutional arrangements, including an entrenched Bill of Rights.

The fears expressed in the mid-1980s were that an entrenched Bill of Rights would transform our courts into political institutions by empowering them to

---

3 *A Bill of Rights for New Zealand: A White Paper,* A.6 *Appendices to the Journal of the House of Representatives,* Wellington, 1985. p.27.

4 'Open Government Policy 1984' set out in G. Palmer, *Unbridled Power,* 2nd ed., Oxford University Press, Auckland, 1987, pp.281, 282.

overrule Parliament or government action and that this involved substantial risk. The idea of judicial review of a constitutional document contains anti-majoritarian elements. The judges would be a bevy of platonic guardians elected by no one and accountable only to themselves. Government's main function was to establish economic prosperity for all, our political culture did not generate much conflict, and therefore civil liberties were not in jeopardy in New Zealand. The introduction of an entrenched Bill of Rights would be contrary to our pragmatist political traditions. It was not clear that there was any need for it in our small and sensitive political system.

Yet even then, and certainly now, New Zealand was becoming a more pluralistic society. There are more minorities and they are more vocal. The Maori population has significant problems flowing from pronounced social and economic inequality. Increasing immigration from non-traditional sources has added to the diversity of the country; Maori and Pacific Islanders together comprise about 17 per cent of the population. Protecting the interests of 'discrete and insular minorities' is difficult and becomes increasingly so the more a society relies on majority rule.[5] It can be argued that the fabric of society requires that the special interest of minorities be protected from, among other things, a legislature exhibiting the prejudice of a majority.

The argument for a Bill of Rights was put forward before the 1984 election campaign in a series of speeches. Although Labour MPs showed no great enthusiasm for the concept then or later, there was a political market for it. There was a distinct feeling that the Muldoon government had been constitutionally high-handed and repressive. The aftermath of the Springbok tour had produced in the New Zealand middle class a distinct feeling of unease about the powers of executive government and the purposes for which they could be exercised. The 1985 White Paper stated that:[6]

> A Bill of Rights for New Zealand is based on the idea that New Zealand's system of government is in need of improvement. We have no second House of Parliament. And we have a small parliament. We are lacking in most of the safeguards which many other countries take for granted. A Bill of Rights will provide greater protection for the fundamental rights and freedoms vital to the survival of New Zealand's democratic and multi-cultural society. The adoption of a Bill of Rights in New Zealand will place new limits on the powers of Government. It will guarantee the protection of fundamental values and freedoms. It will restrain the abuse of power by the Executive branch of Government and Parliament itself. It will provide a source of education and inspiration about the importance of fundamental freedoms in a democratic society. It will provide

5 The phrase first appeared in the celebrated footnote 4 penned by Chief Justice Stone in *United States* v. *Carolene Products Co* 304 US 144 (1938).

6 *A Bill of Rights for New Zealand*, p.5.

> a remedy to those individuals who have suffered under a law or conduct which breaches the standards laid down in the Bill of Rights. It will provide a set of minimum standards to which public decision making must conform. In that sense a Bill of Rights is a mechanism by which governments are made more accountable by being held to a set of standards.

The Bill of Rights had two features that attracted particular opposition. The first was that it was to be entrenched. To alter it would have required the support of 75 per cent of MPs or a majority at a referendum of electors. This limited the sovereignty of the New Zealand Parliament. To use an argument beloved of constitutional lawyers, Parliament could no longer declare that all blue-eyed babies should be murdered. To do so would be contrary to the Bill of Rights Act and the statute enacting it would be held unconstitutional. Thus Parliament could no longer assume all of its decisions were beyond question in the courts. Many people felt that elected representatives were more sensitive to the democratic will and more accountable than the judiciary. It was argued that judges should not be entrusted with such powers.

The second significant feature of the proposed Bill of Rights was its incorporation of the Treaty of Waitangi; it entrenched the treaty as part of the fundamental law of New Zealand. That caused a great deal of difficulty, not least among segments of the Maori community themselves. Some Maori opposed that step. It should be remembered, however, that this was before Maori won a famous victory in the Court of Appeal in the state-owned enterprises case,[7] which gave real weight and substance to the principles of the Treaty of Waitangi. Had the timing been otherwise, Maori attitudes to giving the court power may have been different.

When the white paper was published it was referred to the Justice and Law Reform select committee of Parliament, which began extensive hearings that took two years. Four hundred and thirty-one submissions were received and the committee published an interim report of 246 pages. This analysed what the submissions said and the policy arguments made in front of the committee. It was clear from that report that the central idea of a Bill of Rights was unacceptable to many: that there would be judicial review of acts of Parliament and that courts could declare unconstitutional acts that did not comply with the provisions of the Bill of Rights Act. Extensive submissions from fundamentalist Christian groups did not help. There were twenty-five submissions saying that the bill should acknowledge God because God is the source of rights and New Zealand is a Christian country. Such sentiments were summed up in the submissions of Matthew J. Jenkinson: 'The government needs to realise that there is a higher authority than its own, and that civil law should be an extension of that law

7 *New Zealand Maori Council* v. *Attorney-General* [1987] 1 *NZLR* 641.

revealed in the Holy Scriptures.'[8] The right to life supporters also contributed a large number of submissions concentrating on whether the right to life in Article 14 should extend to the foetus.

Although the Bill of Rights debate stimulated interest in the way New Zealand is governed, it also exposed lamentable ignorance of how that process is presently carried out. In a thoughtful submission to the Select Committee, the National Council of Women observed what they had found in dealing with their branches:[9]

> A small but not insubstantial number of replies were of doubtful value because of evident ignorance of how the New Zealand system of government works beyond the legislature. This was particularly, but not exclusively, in relationship to the proposed function of the courts; many seem unaware of the whole field of administrative law. We consider that before effective consent can be given to the Bill of Rights, steps must be taken to educate the electorate on the processes of government.

The arguments for and against an entrenched Bill of Rights for New Zealand emerged before the select committee in a comprehensive fashion, despite the prominence of those determined to argue the merits of their single-issue campaigns. Opponents of the measure advanced these arguments:

(a) the measure gave power to the judiciary, who were not elected, not accountable, and unrepresentative of the community;
(b) the bill was required to be enforced through the judicial process to which people, especially the poor, did not have equal access;[10]
(c) because some acts of Parliament could be repugnant to the Bill of Rights, and it was not readily predictable which laws these would be, there would be considerable uncertainty about what the law is;
(d) there would be increased litigation as a result of the bill;
(e) if more checks and balances were needed, better ones were available (thirty-nine submissions thought an upper House would be better);
(f) it would be premature to adopt a Bill of Rights, more time was needed to study the implications, and it was not necessary, as there were no threats to human rights in New Zealand;
(g) a Bill of Rights would freeze New Zealand's constitutional development and not allow for social change in the future;
(h) the bill emphasised individual and not collective rights.

---

8 Submission by Matthew Jenkinson, p.16 (1985).

9 Justice and Law Reform Committee, *Interim Report on the Inquiry into the White Paper—A Bill of Rights for New Zealand,* 8A *Appendices to the Journal of the House of Representatives,* Wellington, 1986, p.22.

10 On this issue, see B.V. Harris, 'Equal Access to Justice: A Constitutional Principle in Need of a Higher Profile', *New Zealand Law Review*, 1995, p.282.

A number of somewhat grotesque arguments were put forward against the Bill of Rights—that it did not guarantee New Zealand's sovereignty, or protect the flag, that it linked New Zealand with the United Nations, that it was communist inspired, and that it would take rights away. Unfortunately, extremely eccentric people seem to gravitate to constitutional issues and lavish their attention upon them.

Those submissions supporting a Bill of Rights argued from what were basically constitutional grounds:

(a) New Zealand lacked constitutional safeguards and a Bill of Rights would be a check on the executive;
(b) the Bill of Rights would protect the interests of minorities and disadvantaged groups, which democratic elections do not and cannot protect;
(c) the Bill of Rights would educate New Zealanders about human rights and raise their level of awareness in this area;
(d) the Bill of Rights would be a necessary safeguard against the erosion of fundamental rights;
(e) the Bill of Rights would advance New Zealand's compliance with its international obligations to respect human rights, especially the International Covenant on Civil and Political Rights.

As a result of these debates, the National Party decided that it was opposed to an entrenched Bill of Rights. It also opposed, in the House of Representatives, the bill that was enacted. That opposition in itself made the conduct of the enterprise much more difficult. Basic constitutional change really does need widespread political support if it is to succeed. Constitutional change is different from other reform. It binds everyone and it cannot be rammed through on the basis of the preferences of one group. But there has been no move to repeal the Bill of Rights. As one commentator has sagely noted, 'No government would want to go down in history as the government which repealed the Bill of Rights . . .'[11]

In the end a compromise emerged—the measure was converted from one that enacted a higher law to an ordinary statute that preserved Parliament's capacity to enact measures inconsistent with it. The Treaty of Waitangi was removed. Parliament could disobey the Bill of Rights if it chose to, but it would have to do so knowing that it was breaching a fundamental principle. The Attorney-General would certify when bills introduced into Parliament contained provisions contrary to the Bill of Rights, so that the select committee considering the bill, and the public, would know that was the case.

11 P. Rishworth, 'The Birth and Rebirth of the Bill of Rights', in *Rights and Freedoms: The New Zealand Bill of Rights Act 1990 and the Human Rights Act 1993*, eds G. Huscroft & P. Rishworth, Brookers, Wellington, 1995, p.29.

The Bill of Rights Act contains a long title that is significant:

An Act—

(a) To affirm, protect, and promote human rights and fundamental freedoms in New Zealand; and

(b) To affirm New Zealand's commitment to the International Covenant on Civil and Political Rights.

It is important to realise that New Zealand's international obligations, solemnly undertaken, require it to observe in its domestic law certain fundamental guarantees and protections. These are set out in the International Covenant on Civil and Political Rights, which was ratified by the National Government as long ago as 1978. The Human Rights Committee of the United Nations can check whether New Zealand is actually providing those protections. As part of its obligations under the covenant, New Zealand is obliged to report to the Human Rights Committee every four years about its compliance. In addition, in 1989 New Zealand ratified the Optional Protocol to the covenant, which means that individuals may complain to the Human Rights Committee that the New Zealand Government has breached their covenant rights.

New Zealand likes to hold its head high on the international stage when it comes to human rights issues, but if it is to do so with credibility it must enforce those standards rigorously through a domestic law that is consistent with the international norms. In reporting periodically to the Human Rights Committee of the United Nations, New Zealand has difficulty from time to time explaining some features of our law; not the least of which was, in the last report, the fact that the Bill of Rights Act could be easily amended and could be overridden by Parliament.[12]

THE PRACTICAL EFFECTS OF THE BILL OF RIGHTS

The New Zealand Bill of Rights Act 1990 has turned out to be a great deal more important than the legal profession and political commentators understood at the time it was enacted. It is a very important addition to our constitutional laws. The manner in which the courts have gone about interpreting it in the hundreds of cases indicates that it has already become an important plank in our constitutional jurisprudence.

But the Bill of Rights is not important only in the courts. One of the most

12 *Third Periodic Report of State Parties Due in 1990: Addendum: New Zealand*, UN Doc CCPR/C/64/Add 10 (1994); *Consideration of Reports Submitted by States Parties under Article 40 of the Covenant—Comments of the Human Rights Committee*, UN Doc CCPR/C/79/Add 47, para 11.

fundamental of its effects is upon the government itself. People outside government misunderstand how necessary it is to have certain obstacles in place so that enthusiastic but misguided people cannot do things that should not be done. This message was spelt out in the introduction to the 1985 White Paper:[13]

> In practical terms the Bill of Rights is a most important set of messages to the machinery of Government itself. It points to the fact that certain sorts of laws should not be passed, that certain actions should not be engaged in by Government. In that way a Bill of Rights provides a set of navigation lights for the whole process of Government to observe.

The New Zealand Bill of Rights now provides that protection. Earnest and careful analysis has to be carried out in government before legislation is introduced to ensure that it does not breach any of the principles enacted in the Bill of Rights Act. This, in itself, is a considerable hurdle to those within government who wish to promote legislation that has, tucked away within it, objectionable provisions.

The Attorney-General is obliged by section 7 of the act to 'bring to the attention of the House of Representatives any provision in the Bill that appears to be inconsistent with any of the rights and freedoms contained in this Bill of Rights'. Ministers have to have the matter drawn to their attention by officials. As required by the *Cabinet Office Manual*, the Ministry of Justice vets all bills for compliance with the Bill of Rights, except those promoted by the Minister of Justice, which are vetted by the Crown Law Office. The Attorney-General's power to certify can be a potent weapon. It must be done on proper professional legal advice; it is not a matter of political judgement, but of law. There will be considerable hesitation about bringing to Parliament measures that require a certificate.

The procedures for the Attorney-General's certification have been tightened up in the 1995 revisions to the standing orders. The Standing Orders Committee found that the previous procedure was 'not satisfactorily specific about how the procedure was to be followed. It has concluded that the best way in which the Attorney-General's obligation can be fulfilled is by the presentation of a report that is published by order of the House as a parliamentary paper.'[14] These recommendations have been followed through in new Standing Order 258, which requires that the statement of inconsistency must be made 'before a motion for the bill's second reading is moved'.

Certificates have been made by the Attorney-General on a number of occasions. For example, the Kumeu District Agricultural and Horticultural Bill attracted such a report,[15] with the result that the select committee deleted the provisions

---

13 *A Bill of Rights for New Zealand*, p.6.

14 New Zealand House of Representatives, *Report of the Standing Orders Committee on the Review of the Standing Orders*, Wellington, 1995, p.51.

15 *Report on the Kumeu District Agricultural and Horticultural Society Bill*, tabled in Parliament by the Attorney-General, 23 July 1991, 517, *New Zealand Parliamentary Debates*, p.3035.

involved. The Napier City Council Skateboards Empowering Bill attracted a certificate and did not proceed.[16] The Transport Safety Bill provision about random breath testing drew a certificate but was eventually passed nonetheless.[17] A certificate has also stopped at least one proposal from being introduced—the first version of a bail bill in 1992.

Some complain that the values embodied in the Bill of Rights Act inhibit effective law enforcement practices, but people have different views of how effective these should be, depending on whether they expect to be subjected to them. The Bill of Rights is designed to be a safeguard for individuals and groups of individuals against the coercive power of the state. It is already clear that the requirement to test legislative proposals against a clear set of principles has a beneficial effect in protecting the values embodied in the Bill of Rights Act. There is a question about whether it could be made even more effective. In an MMP environment, significant and substantive amendments to bills are likely to be proposed as they are going through the House. There is no formal process for vetting such amendments against the Bill of Rights Act nor any established relationship between the Attorney-General's certificate and select committee consideration of bills.

THE BILL OF RIGHTS IN THE COURTS

The large number of cases that have come before the courts on the Bill of Rights cannot be canvassed in detail here, but we will outline some of the more important ones.

In 1990 Robert Lee Flickinger appeared before the Auckland District Court when the Hong Kong Government sought his extradition for offences of commercial fraud allegedly committed there. The court allowed the application under the Fugitive Offenders Act 1881, a United Kingdom statute in force in New Zealand. The hearing took eight weeks. The High Court turned down an application for a writ of habeas corpus and the matter went to the Court of Appeal. It had been held in a previous case that the Judicature Act 1908 did not confer a right of appeal in a criminal matter, and this was a criminal matter. The court said that this could not continue to be the legal position because of section 6 of the New Zealand Bill of Rights Act 1990, which provides: 'Whenever an enactment can be given a meaning that is consistent with the rights and freedoms contained in this Bill of Rights, that meaning shall be preferred to any other meaning.'

So the court said that if section 66 of the Judicature Act could be given a

16 *Report on the Napier City Council (Control of Skateboards) Empowering Bill,* tabled in Parliament by the Attorney-General, 15 August 1991, Vol. 518 *New Zealand Parliamentary Debates,* p.4095.

17 *Report on the Transport Safety Bill,* tabled in Parliament by the Attorney-General, *New Zealand Parliamentary Debates,* pp.6367–8 (17 December 1991).

meaning consistent with the rights and freedoms contained in the Bill of Rights Act, that meaning must be preferred. Furthermore, section 23(1)(c) of the Bill of Rights Act provided that everyone who is arrested has the right to have the validity of the arrest determined without delay by way of habeas corpus.[18]

The Court of Appeal said that the Judicature Act should now receive a wider interpretation. The judges assumed this to be the case, without deciding it. They went on to find that nothing had occurred in the proceedings contrary to the Bill of Rights Act and Flickinger had to go back to Hong Kong to face eight fraud trials. The case is a good illustration of how the New Zealand Bill of Rights Act will influence the courts in interpreting the language of acts of Parliament. Interpretation of statutes is a vital function in the protection of liberty.

Important as statutory interpretation is, the substantive application of the Bill of Rights Act is likely to be even more striking. Consider the case of an Auckland man detained by the police at 12.20 a.m. and not formally arrested or charged until 3.38 a.m. He had been chased by a constable, handcuffed to a fence, and then put in a police car and taken to three police stations without being told of his right to consult a lawyer until almost the end of an interview, in which he made damaging admissions. The Court of Appeal ruled that the confession he made in those circumstances could not be used against him because the police had breached the right in section 23 of the Bill of Rights Act.[19] That section provides:

> 23. Rights of persons arrested or detained—(1) Everyone who is arrested or who is detained under any enactment— . . .
>
> (b) Shall have the right to consult and instruct a lawyer without delay and to be informed of that right.

A rule similar to the one above has been accepted in New Zealand for many years and is found in administrative practices and instructions to law enforcement authorities. But when elevated to a plain statement of principle of general application, and put in the law, it can have important consequences, as a 1992 decision of the New Zealand Court of Appeal demonstrated. In an important decision under the Bill of Rights Act, the court held by a majority of four to one that the provision quoted above required the law enforcement authorities to inform two people of their right to consult and instruct a lawyer when required to go to a testing station for an evidential breath or blood test. (This is *not* a decision which holds that people have the right to a lawyer before undergoing roadside breath testing.) The Transport Act, which created the offence, was silent on the question of whether a person required to undergo a test should be told of the right. Sir Ivor Richardson put it this way in his judgment:

---

[18] *Flickinger* v. *Crown Colony of Hong Kong* [1991] 1 *NZLR* 439.

[19] *R* v. *Kirifi* (1991) 7 *Criminal Reports of New Zealand* 427, 431.

> The right to consult a lawyer is part of our basic constitutional inheritance. Not surprisingly it is also a central feature of contemporary international statements of human rights. The right is pivotal in assuring so far as possible that both those detained and those detaining them act in accordance with the law. It recognises the reality that an individual who is arrested or detained is ordinarily at a significant disadvantage in relation to the informed and coercive powers available to the State. Access to counsel is a means of reducing that imbalance and of ensuring that anyone arrested or detained is treated fairly in the criminal process. In that regard the right to a lawyer facilitates access to knowledge and also allows for representation by an independent intermediary.[20]

In practical terms, there must now be reasonable opportunity for telephone consultation with a lawyer before taking the test. It was clear from the evidence in the case that, given the metabolism of alcohol in the human body, allowing time for the consultation would not prejudice the test. The judgment was an important one because the judges went to great trouble to establish the principles that would be applied to interpreting its provisions. They clearly regarded the act as one having a special character. It has been suggested that, since the rights in the act are those which New Zealand has an international obligation to uphold, they will be scrupulously protected by the courts.

Perhaps the most important Bill of Rights case yet decided by the New Zealand courts was the decision of the Court of Appeal in some complex litigation that has become known as *Baigent's Case*.[21] In *Baigent* the plaintiffs alleged that police officers has persisted, unreasonably, in bad faith, and maliciously, with a search of the late Mrs Baigent's house when they knew, or ought reasonably to have known, that her property had been mistakenly named in a search warrant issued in respect of a suspected drug dealer. The plaintiffs sued on a number of common law grounds such as negligence, trespass to land, and trespass to goods. But they also sued in respect of a breach of section 21 of the Bill of Rights, which refers to the right to be secure against unreasonable search and seizure. The Crown relied, among other things, on section 6(5) of the Crown Proceedings Act 1950, which said that no proceedings could lie against the Crown for anything done by any person discharging responsibilities of a judicial nature or in connection with the execution of judicial process. Four of the five Court of Appeal judges held (without finding whether the allegations were justified) that a cause of action lay directly against the Crown for breach of the Bill of Rights, which was unaffected by any of the statutory immunities pleaded, and that damages could be awarded against the Crown. Although Parliament had not provided a new remedy for breaching the

---

20 *Ministry of Transport* v. *Noort* [1992] 3 *NZLR* 360.

21 *Simpson* v. *Attorney-General* (*Baigent's Case*) [1994] 3 *NZLR* 667. For a somewhat more critical perspective of *Baigent* see: J.A. Smillie, 'The Allure of "Rights Talk": *Baigent's Case* in the Court of Appeal', 8 *Otago Law Review*, 1994, p.188.

Bill of Rights Act (and the issue had been considered in formulating the act), the Court of Appeal found one anyway.

The majority reached their conclusion by the following process of reasoning:

- the fact that the Bill of Rights did not include any express remedies provision did not mean that Parliament had intended to exclude a right to compensation;
- in interpreting the Bill of Rights, considerable weight must be given to New Zealand's obligations under the International Covenant on Civil and Political Rights to ensure that the victim's rights' violation have an effective remedy;
- it follows that the courts must have jurisdiction to grant an effective remedy, including damages where appropriate, for breaches of the Bill of Rights;
- the liability for breaches of the Bill of Rights is a direct liability of the state as guarantor of the rights and freedoms contained in the Bill of Rights. The liability is in public law, not the private law of torts;
- the Bill of Rights cause of action lies independently against the Crown and is not caught by the bar in section 6 of the Crown Proceedings Act.

The Court of Appeal judgment goes on to point out that the award of damages is not available as of right; it is discretionary and the court will determine what is an adequate remedy in the circumstances. Juries will not be used. There is no doubt that the broad swathe cut by the judgment of the court was of deep concern to the Crown. The Law Commission was asked to examine whether something should be done to reduce the Crown's exposure as a result of the case.

The Court of Appeal decisions on the Bill of Rights to date affirm the importance of the basic rights of individuals and groups of individuals against the coercive power of the state in a civilised society. It is the application of such standards, and not arbitrary power, which advances the humane use of power. The state must set a high standard and follow it. Abuse of power is easy if the full might and resources of the state are available to those who transgress. As Sir Owen Woodhouse has observed: 'The mere presence of constitutional safeguards to which ordinary people could appeal at any future time of crisis would act in times that were normal as a sensible brake upon the Executive and encourage revival of the true functions of Parliament.'[22]

It is not easy to judge when the language of the act may apply, but it certainly provides a flexible and creative means of protecting the rights of New Zealanders. It does that by holding the state to certain fundamental standards defined by the law. That was the original intention of the legislation and it has been efficiently translated into action. There is now a set of rules that is binding on the government. The question is not whether the New Zealand Bill of Rights Act is a beneficial

22 Rt Hon. Sir Owen Woodhouse, *Government Under the Law,* Price Milburn for the Council of Civil Liberties, Wellington, 1979, p.17.

constitutional reform, but whether it goes far enough. Should the standards it defines be put beyond alteration by a simple majority in Parliament?

In 1960 the Canadians enacted a Bill of Rights similar to our own. In 1982 they replaced it with the Canadian Charter of Rights and Freedoms, a full-blown constitutional document taking away the sovereignty of Parliament and providing limits on the power of government in Canada at both federal and provincial levels. It is quite conceivable that we will follow the same path.

16 The Treaty of Waitangi

INTRODUCTION

Maori came to Aotearoa before Pakeha. The legitimacy of the system of government we have in New Zealand today owes much to the Treaty of Waitangi entered into between the Crown and Maori in 1840. Although a short document, the treaty symbolises the rights of Maori and the undertakings that were given to them when the Crown assumed authority. In one sense, New Zealand's right as a nation to make laws, to govern, and to dispense justice can be said to spring from that 1840 compact between the Crown and the Maori.

Many Maori feel that, over the years, the government has failed to honour the undertakings given in the treaty. There are many claims that the treaty has been breached by the Crown and the last twenty years have seen much controversy over the way in which the Crown has dealt with these claims.[1] In the last few years, this controversy has been accompanied by two other particularly significant developments: growing attention among Maori to the constitutional place of the treaty, and growing awareness of the social and economic disadvantage of Maori in New Zealand.

WHAT IS THE TREATY OF WAITANGI?

Maori and English versions of the treaty were signed at Waitangi on 6 February 1840 and, over the next several months, in many different places in New Zealand by the Crown and over 200 Maori chiefs.[2] The treaty itself is set out in the

1 See, generally, 'Treaty Issues: The Unfinished Business: Proceedings of a Conference held in Wellington, February 1995', 25 *Victoria University of Wellington Law Review*, 1995, pp.91–248; A. Sharp, *Justice and the Maori: Maori Claims in New Zealand Political Argument in the 1980s*, Oxford University Press, Auckland, 1990; I. H. Kawharu (ed.), *Waitangi: Maori and Pakeha Perspectives of the Treaty of Waitangi*, Oxford University Press, Auckland, 1989.

2 See C. Orange, *The Treaty of Waitangi*, Allen & Unwin/Port Nicholson Press, Wellington, 1987.

illustrative New Zealand constitution in Appendix I of this book. Its most immediately striking aspect is its length: it has only three articles and each is reasonably short and uncomplicated. Its conciseness is matched by its ambiguity of meaning.

The first article expresses the cession of 'sovereignty' or 'kawanatanga' (which may be translated as 'governorship') by Maori to the Crown. The second article expresses the guarantee by the Crown to Maori of 'full, exclusive and undisturbed possession' or 'te tino rangatiratanga' (which may be translated as full chieftainship, but *Reed Dictionary of Modern Maori* [3] gives as 'kingdom, principality, sovereignty, realm') of their 'lands, estates, forests, fisheries, and other properties', and their 'taonga' ('treasures'). The third article expresses the legal equality between Maori and other New Zealand citizens.

Some hint of the difficulties hidden with the treaty is given by comparing the substance of articles 1 and 2. How is the balance to be struck between the sovereignty/kawanatanga of the Crown and te tino rangatiratanga/chieftainship of Maori? Most debates concerning the treaty's meaning involve the application of this question. In 1983, the Waitangi Tribunal stated:

> The Treaty represents the gift [by Maori] of the right to make laws in return for the promise to do so so as to acknowledge and protect the interest of the indigenous inhabitants . . . That then was the exchange of gifts that the Treaty represented. The gift of the right to make laws, and the promise to do so so as to accord the Maori interest an appropriate priority.[4]

In the same report, the tribunal also said:

> The Treaty was also more than an affirmation of existing rights. It was not intended to merely fossilise a status quo, but to provide a direction for future growth and development. The broad and general nature of its words indicates that it was not intended as a finite contract but as the foundation for a developing social contract.[5]

In its 1988 Muriwhenua Fishing Report, the tribunal said: 'Tino rangatiratanga refers not to separate sovereignty but to tribal self-management over their own resources, on lines similar to what we understand by local government.'[6] The rhetoric of 'sovereignty' or 'rangatiratanga' is symbolic and abstract. A confrontational battle between the two could go on for years without the participants being sure whether they disagree. What people mean by these abstract concepts becomes apparent only when they start using examples in particular contexts. In some ways it is easier, and more constructive, to debate how the

3 P. M. Ryan, *The Reed Dictionary of Modern Maori*, Reed, Auckland, 1995.

4 Report Findings and Recommendations of the Waitangi Tribunal on an application by Aila Taylor for and on behalf of Te Atiawa tribe in relation to fishing grounds in the Waitara District—*Motunui-Waitara Report*, Wellington, 1983, pp.55, 65, 61.

5 *Ibid.*, p.52.

6 *Report of the Muriwhenua Fisheries Claim* (Wai 22), Waitangi Tribunal, Wellington, 1988.

Department of Conservation and the local tangata whenua can work together in caring for an ecologically and commercially important wetland. On the other hand, it seems to make sense to have some idea of what principles should inform the evolution of such particular arrangements.

In 1989, the Labour Government set out five principles by which it would act in dealing with issues arising from the Treaty of Waitangi. Although these have been neither explicitly confirmed nor rejected by subsequent governments, they remain useful in demonstrating the sort of principles that can be derived from the treaty to guide government action. The five principles are:

1 The Principle of Government: The Government has the right to govern and to make laws.

2 The Principle of Self Management: The iwi have the right to organise as iwi and, under the law, to control the resources they own.

3 The Principle of Equality: All New Zealanders are equal under the law.

4 The Principle of Reasonable Cooperation: Both the Government and the iwi are obliged to accord each other reasonable cooperation on major issues of common concern.

5 The Principle of Redress: The Government is responsible for providing effective processes for the resolution of grievances in the expectation that reconciliation can occur.

At a somewhat similar level of generality, Professor Mason Durie has proposed to the Maori Congress Executive three principles to guide tino rangatiratanga in a modern society:[7]

- *nga matatini Maori* (Maori diversity: in 1995 Maori live in a diversity of everyday realities);
- *whakakotahi* (Maori unity: the potential for Maori solidarity based on a shared sense of belonging and a common destiny);
- *mana motuhake Maori* (Maori autonomy and control: Maori should be able to determine their own futures, control their own resources, and develop their own political structures).

Professor Durie also identifies four fundamental foundations of tino rangatiratanga:[8]

7 M.H. Durie, 'Tino Rangatiratanga: A discussion paper', in *Report for the Congress Executive*, 13 May 1995, Maori Congress, Wellington.

8 M.H. Durie, 'Tino Rangatiratanga: Maori Self-Determination', *He Pukenga Korero* Vol. 1, No. 1, 1996, pp.44–53.

- *mana wairua*: a spiritual dimension relevant to all aspects of Maori life and organisation;
- *mana whenua*: the security of relationships with land and other physical resources and the authority of tribes to exercise control over their resources;
- *mana tangata*: individual well-being, citizenship rights and freedom from financial dependence on governments; and
- *mana ariki*: the authority of ariki to lead and guide their own and other peoples.

THE WAITANGI TRIBUNAL AND TREATY CLAIMS

Most of the public controversy about the treaty over the last twenty years has been related in some way to claims by Maori that the Crown has breached the treaty in many different ways since 1840 and questions about what should be done to resolve these.

The Treaty of Waitangi Act 1975 established the Waitangi Tribunal to hear grievances arising under the treaty and to make recommendations to government about them.[9] The tribunal, with its three part-time members, was not formally established until 1977 and had few matters to consider until the mid-1980s. The Waitangi Tribunal is chaired by the Chief Judge of the Maori Land Court and now comprises two to sixteen members appointed by the Governor-General on the recommendation of the Minister of Maori Affairs after consultation with the Minister of Justice. But through a succession of reports in the mid-1980s (*Te Atiawa* Report 1983, *Kaituna* Report 1984, *Manukau* Report 1985, *Te Reo* Report 1986), the Waitangi Tribunal gained considerable mana and status. Until 1985, however, its jurisdiction was limited to grievances occuring after the Tribunal's establishment.

In 1985 the tribunal's jurisdiction was extended by act of Parliament to deal with grievances going right back to 1840. Any Maori may claim that he or she (or a group to which he or she belongs) has been prejudicially affected by any legislation, regulations, policy, practice or act of the Crown since 6 February 1840. This represented a substantial increase in the claims the tribunal could hear and created a forum for historical breaches of the treaty, especially those in the nineteenth century, to be examined anew. Nineteen eighty-five also marked the beginning of a process of rationalisation, corporatisation, and privatisation of government assets. The first major step along that path was the passage of the State-Owned Enterprises Act 1986 which contained, in section 9, a provision

9 See P. Temm, *The Waitangi Tribunal: The Conscience of the Nation,* Random Century, Auckland, 1990; and W.H. Oliver, *Claims to the Waitangi Tribunal,* Waitangi Tribunal & Daphne Brasell Associates Press, Wellington, 1991; and, more generally, regarding legal developments in the 1980s, G. Palmer, *New Zealand's Constitution in Crisis: Reforming Our Political System,* John McIndoe, Dunedin, 1992, Ch. 4.

that 'Nothing in this Act shall permit the Crown to act in a manner that is inconsistent with the principles of the Treaty of Waitangi.' This reference has been followed by many other legislative references to the principles of the treaty, which means that, in interpreting such legislation in a particular case, courts have to interpret what those principles are. As at May 1995, the State Services Commission identifies twenty-nine acts containing a reference to the Treaty of Waitangi, and twenty-six containing a reference to the aims and aspirations of Maori.[10]

In the first modern landmark case in treaty jurisprudence, *NZ Maori Council* v. *Attorney-General,*[11] the Court of Appeal concluded, in the words of its then President Cooke: 'First that the principles of the Treaty of Waitangi override everything else in the State-Owned Enterprises Act. Second that those principles require the Pakeha and Maori Treaty partners to act towards each other reasonably and with the utmost good faith.' In the same case Lord Cooke's successor, Sir Ivor Richardson, stated that:

> I have mentioned these matters in this way in part because of the wide-ranging arguments in the present case and in part because much of the popular discussion of the Treaty seems to assume that the answers to these questions are simple and straightforward. Unfortunately this is not so. The way ahead calls for careful research, for rational positive dialogue and, above all, for a generosity of spirit. Perhaps too much has at times been made of some of these differences and too little emphasis given to the positive and enduring role of the Treaty. Whatever legal route is followed the Treaty must be interpreted according to its principles suitable to its particular character. Its history, its form and its place in our social order clearly require a broad interpretation and one which recognises that the Treaty must be capable of adaptation to new and changing circumstances as they arise.

The court found that section 9 of the State-Owned Enterprises Act obliged the Crown to work out a system to safeguard Maori claims under the treaty before transferring land to SOEs. Following that decision, the Crown and the Maori Council negotiated a regime, implemented in the Treaty of Waitangi (State Enterprises) Act 1988 to allow lands and other assets transferred to SOEs from the Crown to continue to be used as redress in settling treaty claims relating to them. Most notably, this legislation gave the Waitangi Tribunal a binding power to order those particular pieces of land to be compulsorily acquired from whoever owns them (for compensation) and returned to claimants. In a subsequent court case, this regime was also found by the Court of Appeal to apply to coal.[12] The Crown Forests Assets Act 1990 followed this example by giving the tribunal similar

10 State Services Commission, *The Public Service and the Treaty of Waitangi,* Appendices 4 and 5, Wellington, 1995.

11 [1987] 1 *NZLR* 641.

12 *Tainui Maori Trust Board* v. *Attorney-General* [1989] 2 *NZLR* 513.

powers over commercial forest land and the value of the tree crop on it and the Education Amendment Act 1990 applied the regime to land transferred to tertiary education institutes. Land transferred to Crown health enterprises (CHEs) or Crown research institutes (CRIs) are not subject to the same legislative regime, but the sale and purchase agreements by which these lands are transferred often contain a similar power of compulsory acquisition at the discretion of the Crown and land onsold by CRIs is subject to treaty considerations.

The legislation and court cases mentioned have raised the public and political profile of treaty claims, but have also increased public misunderstanding and unjustified fears. The Waitangi Tribunal has the power to order land that has been transferred to some institutions to be returned to claimants (although it has not yet done so) but that power is explicitly noted on the title to those lands so that whoever buys the land knows the situation, and is compensated. The tribunal has never had any compulsory power over private land, but there was so much public fear about this that a legislative amendment was passed in 1993 explicitly preventing the Tribunal from recommending that any private land be returned to Maori ownership or acquired by the Crown.

It should be remembered that the legislation and court cases mentioned above concern the ability of the Crown to return land or other assets to Maori claimants *in the event* that that is required under an agreed settlement of a treaty claim. The actual settlement of treaty claims is still gathering momentum. As at 30 June 1995, 522 claims were registered with the Waitangi Tribunal.[13] Of these, 105 had been reported on, withdrawn or further inquiry had been closed, 107 were in preparation, and sixty-two were proceeding. Land claims by major iwi stand out: Waikato-Tainui, Ngai Tahu, and Taranaki. But the nature of the claims before the tribunal varies widely. Many are about historical breaches by the Crown, such as raupatu or unjustified confiscation of lands, but some are about alleged contemporary breaches, involving issues such as health or education, or regulation of natural resources such as telecommunication airwaves or of industries such as kiwifruit production.

As with any dispute, there are three basic elements to resolving treaty claims:

- finding out what happened (establishing the facts);
- comparing that with what the treaty says should have happened (applying the rule); and
- deciding on what should be done about it now (deciding on redress).

The resolution of these three elements of treaty claims tend to follow two basic tracks, which are also similar to ordinary disputes:

---

[13] Department of Justice, *Annual Report for the Year Ended 30 June 1995*, p.146.

- hearings by the Waitangi Tribunal of both sides' arguments, resulting in a report by the tribunal; or
- negotiating between both sides to reach agreement.

A mixture of the two tracks can be followed. For example, the Waitangi Tribunal has held hearings and produced interim recommendations on the claims of both Ngai Tahu and, in 1996, Taranaki. This established what happened and whether that was consistent with the treaty, but largely left it to the parties to negotiate further on what should be done about it now—at least until the tribunal holds further hearings on redress for each claim. The fact that the tribunal is able to order the compulsory acquisition of some billions of dollars worth of SOE land and Crown forests compensation, if it is related to a claim, means that both the Crown and treaty claimants are bargaining in the shadow of that possibility—just as parties to a court battle can agree to settle in the shadow of a potential court decision. At the time of writing that power has not yet been exercised, but there are signs that it may be soon in relation to a particular property, given the tribunal's increasing impatience at the progress of negotiations between the Crown and individual claimants.

Two major binding settlements of historical treaty claims have been reached at the time of writing: a generic settlement of Maori claims to commercial fisheries and settlement of the raupatu claim of the Waikato-Tainui. There are also media reports of progress in negotiations on the two outstanding major claims: by Ngai Tahu and Taranaki.

The Sealords commercial fisheries settlement of 1992 is interesting. The Crown negotiated this deal with Maori leaders on a national basis, leading to some $170 million worth of fishing quota and cash being transferred to the Maori Fisheries Commission, Te Ohu Kaimoana. That organisation, directed primarily by Maori appointed by the Minister of Maori Affairs, has the task of managing those assets and of allocating the benefits to Maori throughout New Zealand. These tasks have attracted ongoing controversy and even litigation among Maori over the basis of allocation.

The settlement between the Crown and Waikato-Tainui in 1995 was the result of direct negotiation on all elements of the claim. The deed of settlement, signed by the Prime Minister, Jim Bolger, and the Maori Queen, Dame Te Atairangikaahu, was given effect by the Waikato Raupatu Claims Settlement Act 1995, which received the royal assent by the Queen of New Zealand, Elizabeth II. The act:

- recites in its preamble an account of historical facts regarding the confiscation in the 1860s of 1.2 million acres of land from Waikato-Tainui and the process by which settlement was reached;
- records an apology by the Crown to Waikato;
- enables the implementation of the deed of settlement (in particular: the transfer

and valuation of lands from the Crown, and from several Crown entities, up to the value of $170 million; the future exercise of a right of first refusal to buy other Crown lands that become available in the Waikato; the removal of the Waitangi Tribunal's compulsory jurisdiction in respect of Waikato's raupatu claims).

The last few years have seen a shift in emphasis from the Waitangi Tribunal towards direct negotiations between the Crown (through the Office of Treaty Settlements) and Maori claimants. In 1990, the National Government made a commitment to resolve all the major claims under the Treaty of Waitangi by the year 2000. The government also decided that it needed to be clearer about the guidelines the Crown would follow in conducting its side of treaty negotiations. In December 1994 the government released the *Crown Proposals for the Settlement of Treaty of Waitangi Claims* for public consideration and debate, including hui held around the country and written submissions. This package of policies became known as the fiscal envelope, because a key part of it was that the Crown had decided to set aside $1 billion for the settlement of historical treaty claims. The *Crown Proposals* also set out the way in which the Crown intended to approach other aspects of the resolution of grievances and breaches of the treaty, including its proposed approach to:

- guiding principles;
- the use of conservation lands in settlements;
- natural resources in relation to settlements;
- lands gifted to the Crown by Maori;
- the process of negotiations, claimant representation, and the finality of settlements; and
- the mechanism for protecting claimants' potential interest in lands being sold by the Crown.

The fiscal envelope proposals caused intense anger and controversy during 1995. The government was heavily criticised and faced many demonstrations by Maori at regional hui at a time of several Maori occupations of claimed land.[14] The government received and summarised 2077 submissions as the basis for further consideration and analysis of how the Crown should approach treaty settlements.[15] The submissions illustrate the strength and divergence of views about the treaty in New Zealand. The following illustrative quotes are from the *Report of Submissions*:

> Any payment of money outright will never be a solution to a problem such as this. The problem is both spiritual and economic and therefore the answer has to embody both

[14] W. Gardiner, *Return to Sender: What really happened at the fiscal envelope hui,* Reed, Auckland, 1996.

[15] *Report of Submissions: Crown Proposals for the Treaty of Waitangi Claims,* Wellington, 1995.

> of these elements, along with being acceptable to both parties—the Maori and non-Maori people of New Zealand. (page 41)
>
> Clearly it would not be acceptable to wider New Zealand for a thief to steal a new car and say 150 years later that he will not return the car to its rightful owner since it has gained vintage status with special qualities to be appreciated by all. (p.56)
>
> The Kakapo is such a unique NZ, and indeed a world, taonga, that under no circumstances . . . [should] its potential survival . . . be further placed at risk by the introduction of split management regimes. (p.64)
>
> . . . when I am on the land it feels like my father mother and tupunas are enfolding me in aroha and a sense of belonging. No other piece of land will give me this feeling. If this land was taken off me it would be like losing my parents all over again . . . From a Maori perspective money can never make up for the loss of land. Land is priceless because of how Maori feel about it.' '(p.109)
>
> [The] . . . whole practice of 'Treaty handouts' is racist, inflammatory, and not in the spirit of fairness to ALL New Zealanders . . . there is a ground swell of anger and frustration on the part of most New Zealanders who see Treaty claims as the first step in minority rule. Government action over Treaty claims has only inflamed these fears. (p.111)
>
> . . . in many educational programmes rarely do we encounter non-Maori who once informed of the issues are opposed to restitution of treaty rights to Maori or the just redress of claims. (p.119)

The specific results of this process are not clear at the time of writing, but one important effect is clear. The fiscal envelope proposals have provided a unifying impetus for Maori as few other events in New Zealand history have done. Sir Hepi Te Heu Heu, paramount chief of Ngati Tuwharetoa, called three national hui of Maori at Hirangi in 1995 and 1996. The first, of over 1000 people in January 1995, was called in reaction to the Crown's proposals and was successful in staking out a position that was reemphasised by individual iwi and hapu.[16] The second and third Hirangi hui, in September 1995 and April 1996, built on that momentum but became oriented not to treaty settlements but to wider issues of tribal organisation, governance, autonomy, education on treaty-related issues, the recognition of tino rangitiratanga, and the constitutional place of the Treaty of Waitangi.

16 M.H. Durie, 'Proceedings of a Hui held at Hirangi Marae, Turangi', 25 *Victoria University of Wellington Law Review*, 1995, p.109.

THE CONSTITUTIONAL PLACE OF THE TREATY

It is clear that the Treaty of Waitangi is an integral part of New Zealand's constitutional arrangements. What is not clear is the nature and extent of that integral part. The Treaty of Waitangi is not an ordinary law. It is not given general effect by a statute. The courts do not use it directly to rule actions or legislation unlawful. The treaty is not part of a basic constitutional document with overriding effect; New Zealand has no such document. Yet the treaty is a key source of the New Zealand government's moral and political claim to legitimacy in governing the country. It may have some formal status in international law. It is referred to, and given specific legal effect, in a number of specific pieces of legislation. It is used by courts as an aid to interpretation of statutes. It is the basis on which the Waitangi Tribunal recommends, and in some cases can order, action by government. The Crown proclaims its intention to abide by the treaty and to settle past breaches of it.

This book stresses the dynamic and constantly evolving nature of a constitution. Perhaps the best way of viewing the constitutional significance of the Treaty of Waitangi is through the evolution of attitudes to it.

In 1996, the Treaty of Waitangi is an important influence on decision-making in the executive branch of government. Cabinet papers identify the implications of proposed policy recommendations in terms of the treaty, and all executive proposals for legislation have to report on consistency with its principles. An officials committee composed of senior chief executives coordinates work across government departments concerning treaty policy. There is a specific Cabinet committee concerned with treaty issues and some of the most sensitive and significant papers on the agenda of the key Cabinet Strategy Committee concern treaty issues. Operationally, chief executives are required to ensure that their departments act consistently with the treaty.

The treaty is often relevant to the legislative process, whether through legislation implementing specific settlements, provisions in general legislation referring to the treaty, or Parliamentary questions, petitions, select committee investigations regarding some aspect of treaty settlements or treaty policy. The advent of MMP seems destined only to increase the political salience of the treaty. There is one more Maori seat in the first MMP Parliament than previously and most political parties have responded to the increased importance of all votes to increase the representation of Maori in high places on their party lists.

Judicial attitudes to the Treaty of Waitangi have undergone a remarkable transformation in New Zealand in 100 years. Thirty-four years after the signing of the treaty, the Chief Justice of New Zealand found that the Treaty of Waitangi was a 'simple nullity'.[17] One hundred and fifty-six years after the signing of the

[17] *Wi Parata* v. *Bishop of Wellington* (1877) 3 N. Z. Jur. (N.S.) 72.

treaty, the President of the Court of Appeal in 1996 stated, 'It is simply the most important document in New Zealand's history.'[18] Apart from possibilities that future courts might find direct legal effect in the treaty, the sleeping giant of legal implications lies in the common law doctrines of aboriginal title—irrespective of the treaty. Paul McHugh and others have argued that aboriginal rights to use land and other resources are recognised by the common law of England and inherited by New Zealand's legal system and expire only when explicitly extinguished by legislation.[19] In 1986, the High Court gave credence to this in *Te Weehi* v. *Regional Fisheries Officer*.[20] The Australian High Court decision in *Mabo* (1992)[21] adds weight to the potential relevance of that view in New Zealand.

Maori attitudes to the treaty also seem to have undergone an important evolution. The land marches of the 1970s denounced the treaty as a sham and a fraud. Yet in the 1980s this attitude changed, through litigation and political activity by the Maori Council and through two important hui in 1984 and 1985, to invoke legal effect in the treaty. Further legal and political activity in the 1990s seems to be focusing increasingly on pushing for more formal constitutional recognition of the treaty.

Interestingly, many Maori reacted negatively to the Labour Government's 1986 White Paper proposal on the Bill of Rights. The proposed Bill of Rights would have recognised the Treaty of Waitangi as part of the supreme law of New Zealand by incorporating it into an enforceable bill of rights. It would have provided that 'The rights of the Maori people under the Treaty of Waitangi are hereby recognised and affirmed' and 'The Treaty of Waitangi shall be regarded as always speaking and shall be applied to circumstances as they arise so that effect may be given to its spirit and true intent.' It is not clear that Maori would reject such a proposal today. Nor is it clear that a government would be so ready to propose it.

The constitutional place of the treaty must also be seen in the context of other developments in domestic and international law.[22] The operation of the Race Relations Conciliator and Human Rights Commission, and other such bodies as canvassed in Chapter 13, is based on a view of the rights of individuals in New Zealand society. The Treaty of Waitangi can be seen as also governing the rights and obligations of collective groups. Are these differences important? How do they relate to the various international instruments regarding human rights to which New Zealand is a signatory, such as the International Covenant on Civil

18 Sir Robin Cooke, 'Introduction', *New Zealand University Law Review,* 1990, p.1.

19 P. McHugh, *The Maori Magna Carta: New Zealand law and the Treaty of Waitangi*, Oxford University Press, Auckland, 1991.

20 *Te Weehi* v. *Regional Fisheries Officer* [1986] 1 *NZLR* 680.

21 66 *ALJR* 408.

22 See W. Renwick (ed.), *Sovereignty and Indigenous Rights: The Treaty of Waitangi in International Contexts,* Victoria University Press, Wellington, 1991.

and Political Rights that allows complaints to be taken to the United Nations? And the tension between kawanatanga and tino rangatiratanga that lies at the heart of the Treaty of Waitangi is similar to the tension in the concept of self-determination advanced by indigenous peoples internationally. This is referred to in the draft Declaration of the Rights of Indigenous Peoples now being debated by governments internationally through the United Nations.

The constitutional position of the Treaty of Waitangi deserves considered and extensive debate and dialogue throughout New Zealand. Debate and dialogue themselves contribute to the clearer definition of that constitutional position. The issues need to be addressed systematically. This is why the Royal Commission on the Electoral System recommended, in 1986, that 'Parliament and Government should enter into consultation and discussion with a wide range of representatives of the Maori people about the definition and protection of the rights of the Maori people and the recognition of their constitutional position under the Treaty of Waitangi.'[23]

[23] Report of the Royal Commission on the Electoral System, *Towards a Better Democracy*, Wellington, December 1986, p.112.

17 International Law

INTRODUCTION

Hugo de Groot, known as Grotius, was born in Holland in 1583. He wrote several famous books and in one of them he sought to distinguish between 'just' and 'unjust' wars, to establish a means of deciding when a war was lawful and when it was not. International relations have not become any easier since the time of Grotius, who is often regarded as the father of modern international law, but the distinctions he made find echoes in the Charter of the United Nations. The charter attempts, in Chapter VII, to regulate the use of force by nations and to provide for action to be taken over threats to the peace, breaches of the peace, and acts of aggression.

The law of nations, as international law is sometimes called, dates from only about the time of Grotius, when the states of Europe emerged in something resembling their modern form. Defining international law is by no means easy. The best effort is that of Professor J.L. Brierly who wrote: 'The Law of Nations, or International law, may be defined as the body of rules and principles of actions which are binding upon civilized states in their relations with another.'[1]

THE NATURE OF INTERNATIONAL LAW

It is hardly surprising that nations need rules to govern their dealings with one another. It is sometimes said that international law governs only relations between independent states. Indeed, one influential theory, expressed by the Permanent Court of International Justice in 1927, says that the source of these rules flows from the free will of states.[2] But it is generally accepted now that international organisations, such as the United Nations itself, and myriads of others, are the subject of international law as well as nation states.

1 J.L. Brierly, *The Law of Nations*, 6th ed., Oxford University Press, Oxford, 1963, p.1.

2 *Case of the SS Lotus* 1927 P.C.I.J. ser.A, No. 10, at 18.

Some analysts go further and make wider claims for international law. Dr C.W. Jenks wrote in 1958:

> International law can no longer be adequately or reasonably defined or described as the law governing the mutual relations of States, even if such a basic definition is accompanied by qualifications or exceptions designed to allow for modern developments; it represents the common law of mankind in an early stage of development, of which the law governing the relations between States is one, but only one, major division.
>
> By the common law of mankind is meant the law of any organized world community, constituted on the basis of States, but discharging its community functions increasingly through a complex of international and regional institutions, guaranteeing rights to, and placing obligations upon, the individual citizen, and confronted with a wide range of economic, social and technological problems calling for uniform regulations on an international basis which represent a growing proportion of the subject-matter of the law. The imperfect development and precarious nature of the organized world community is reflected in the early stage of development of the law, but does not invalidate the basic conception.[3]

Much international law is intensely practical. Nations send ambassadors from one country to another; the rules under which they are received, and how they must be treated, are the subject of much international law, which becomes reflected in domestic law. For example, every time an ambassador from a foreign country breaks the law in New Zealand, there are calls to charge the ambassador with an offence before the New Zealand courts. That cannot usually be accomplished because of an international treaty called the Vienna Convention on Diplomatic Relations signed in 1961 (although there had been similar rules for centuries before). New Zealand has ratified that treaty; it has agreed to be bound by it. New Zealand wants protection for its diplomats overseas, so, as so often happens in international law, there is a powerful reciprocal interest operating. So New Zealand domestic law reflects the international treaty to which New Zealand has agreed. That is another important point to keep in mind. Even if New Zealand has ratified a treaty, for it to be effective in New Zealand domestic law, the treaty's obligations must be converted into a domestic New Zealand legal obligation, usually by an act of Parliament.

A great quantity of international law is of such importance that nations go along with it, even if they do not like some of the details. For example, a lot of New Zealanders like to fly overseas. International aviation is governed by a complex series of treaties and rules that regulate international aviation. The International Civil Aviation Organisation (ICAO) carries out a range of important responsibilities to ensure that international aviation is safe. The ICAO Council, which has thirty-

---

3 C.W. Jenks, *The Common Law of Mankind,* Praeger, New York, 1958, p.58.

three members, adopts international standards and recommended practices covering a wide range of matters. Standards become effective when adopted by two-thirds of the council, unless, in the meantime, a majority of member states disapprove. Although, in theory, individual nations who do not agree may opt out, in practice, the advantages to them and their citizens of being in the organisation are too great. So they remain and follow standards with which they may disagree.

It is obvious enough from the examples given that nations have powerful incentives to follow the rules of international law most of the time. As Professor Louis Henkin has written: 'It is probably the case that almost all nations observe almost all principles of international law and almost all of their obligations almost all of the time.'[4] Spectacular events occur when they do not; France was in gross violation of international law when its agents bombed the *Rainbow Warrior* in Auckland Harbour on 10 July 1985.

Such notorious examples have led some to argue that international law does not really exist. The theory of *realpolitik* suggests that international law, and even international organisations, are essentially irrelevant to a proper understanding of international affairs and the relations between states. What matters is power. The constraints upon nations flow not from law, but from power. According to this view, law might have some instrumental justification as a means of defending what was done, but generally Machiavelli's teachings explain more about what occurs between states than do the rules of international law.

The main argument levelled against international law tends to be that it is not law because it lacks characteristics of domestic legal systems. First, there is no legislature at international law. New Zealand has a Parliament, which makes laws. There is no institution with such authority at the international level, not even the United Nations. Most international law comes from treaty obligations. Treaties are, in many ways, like contracts; if you do not like the terms, you do not sign up. Nations who do not like a particular treaty will not ratify it and unless they ratify it they cannot be bound by it. To be bound, a nation must consent. When the New Zealand Parliament passes a law it is binding upon everyone in New Zealand, whether they agree with it or not.

Notwithstanding the absence of a legislature, a wide range of norms, or commonly followed practices, are binding on nations, whether they flow from treaty or have become customary international law. Legal obligations can exist without a legislature. The fact that international law differs from domestic law in this regard does not invalidate its claim to be considered as law.

The second argument against international law is that there is no enforcement of the rules because there is no organised international policing force with that responsibility, and there is no centrally organised system of sanctions for non-

---

4 L. Henkin, *How Nations Behave—Law and Foreign Policy*, 2nd ed., Columbia University Press, New York, 1979, p.47.

compliance. Not only that, but there are no courts with compulsory jurisdiction before which nations can be compelled to come and account for their actions. If a New Zealander commits an offence in New Zealand, he or she does not need to consent to be tried before a court; there is no choice in the matter. At international law, things are different. There is no compulsory adjudication, which does tend to make international law seem 'unlawlike'. But it all depends on what you mean by law. If law is conceived of as a system that produces order backed by threats if its commands are not followed, the international law may not pass.[5] But that is not necessarily the best way to look at law.

The best evidence for the real existence of international law is that every state recognises that it does exist and that it is under an obligation to observe it. All nations have legal advisers in their foreign ministries. Most governments will pay attention to their international obligations, even if they sometimes decide to breach them.

There is an international community or society. International law deals with the nature and structure of that society and the obligations that arise within it. Nations and other international actors make demands and claims on each other all the time in terms of the rules and principles of international law. In many areas there is a large measure of consensus about what these obligations are, and there are costs to nations in not complying. Nations accept that they are not at liberty to disregard the rules. After all, France was ordered by the Secretary-General of the United Nations to pay New Zealand $US7 million compensation for the damage New Zealand suffered by the sinking of the *Rainbow Warrior* and to make an unqualified apology for the attack, which was ruled to be contrary to international law.[6]

THE SOURCES OF INTERNATIONAL LAW

Since the nature of international law is different from domestic law, its sources are different too. The most authoritative statement of the sources of international law is to be found in Article 38 of the Statute of the International Court of Justice, which states that the court is to apply international law to the disputes submitted to it, and goes on to define the sources of those rules.[7] These are:

---

5 For an extended discussion of these issues see H.L.A. Hart, *The Concept of Law*, Oxford University Press, Oxford, 1961, pp.89–95, 212–15.

6 Ruling Pertaining to the Differences between France and New Zealand arising from the *Rainbow Warrior* Affair, Secretary-General of the United Nations (1987) 26 *International Legal Materials* 1346; (1987) 74 *International Law Reports* 256.

7 For a comprehensive examination of international law as it affects New Zealand law, see Law Commission, *Report 34: A New Zealand Guide to International Law and its Sources*, Wellington, 1996. For those who want detailed accounts of the content of international law, the best book is probably I. Brownlie, *Principles of Public International Law*, 4th ed., Oxford University Press, Oxford,1990.

- international treaties or conventions, whether general or particular, establishing rules expressly recognised by the contesting states;
- international custom, as evidence of a general practice accepted as law;
- the general principles of law recognised by civilised nations;
- judicial decisions and the teachings of the most highly qualified publicists of the various nations, as subsidiary means for the determination of rules of law; and
- to these should be added declarations, statements, and other material called 'soft' international law.

International Treaties or Conventions

Treaties, or conventions, are the most important source of international law. They are the main instruments by which the norms and rules are developed and international matters are regulated. Changes are made by new treaties and conventions. The sheer volume of conventions and treaties is remarkable; there are more than 160 conventions concerning the environment alone. The entire text of the operative treaties in the world takes many volumes. There are many different types. Some have more than 100 nations of the world as parties; many are between two nations only. They go under a variety of names—convention, treaty, protocol, agreement, arrangement, statute, exchange of notes, final act, and others. Some treaties establish undertakings that are contractual in nature; others make new law and establish the norms of complete legal regimes.

One of the fundamental rules of international law relates to treaties—the principle of *pacta sunt servanda*; treaties must be observed, they have binding force. Treaties establish norms which are binding on the nations that are parties to the treaty. It is quite an undertaking for any country to keep track of all the treaties to which it is a party and to ensure that it keeps all its undertakings. The consequences of being in breach can be serious and embarrassing.

The negotiation of treaties can be a difficult business. Multilateral conventions are usually negotiated in complicated international conferences, often several conferences over a number of years, with steering committees and drafting committees, plenary sessions, and rapporteurs. At such meetings, informal negotiations are often as important as the formal sessions in hammering out compromises and language. When there are many nations involved, there is often a tendency to use language in the treaty that covers issues in an ambiguous manner because there is a measure of disagreement. There is an element of the lowest common denominator in treaty negotiations because of the principle of unanimous consent—a nation that does not agree and will not ratify cannot be bound by the treaty.

Conventional international law takes time to develop and it is often cumbersome. Treaties have first to be negotiated, then ratified, and this process can sometimes be so slow and time-consuming that events overtake the convention. Such was the fate of the Convention on the Regulation of Antarctic Mineral Resource Activities, which was agreed to in 1988 but will not enter into force because of the widespread conviction that its provisions do not sufficiently protect the Antarctic environment.[8] Negotiations on the convention began in about 1982, and in the end were outstripped by public opinion. Now a different protocol has been negotiated.[9] Yet only the Antarctic Treaty partners, a small segment of the international community, were involved in the negotiating.[10] The difficulties are greatly multiplied when virtually every country in the world is involved; multilateral conventions require extensive multilateral diplomacy.

There is a complicated series of rules for interpreting treaties, and concerning their suspension, termination or withdrawal from them. One interesting example involving New Zealand was the decision by the United States, under the ANZUS Treaty, to suspend its security obligation to New Zealand because of the latter's anti-nuclear policy.

The dispute with the United States over ANZUS involved a treaty and an alliance. New Zealand took the view that the ANZUS Treaty did not oblige New Zealand to accept nuclear weapons in our ports; the Americans said they could no longer be bound by the provisions of the treaty to come to New Zealand's aid in the event of an armed attack if we did not accept their vessels on a 'neither confirm nor deny' basis. In response, New Zealand said it was happy to have ship visits so long as the non-nuclear policy was met. The New Zealand government was prepared to make the judgement without disclosure from the Americans. The Americans said that was not acceptable and suspended their obligation under the treaty, but they did not argue that New Zealand was in breach of the ANZUS Treaty, which is silent on nuclear matters.

Customary International Law

Customary international law is entirely different from treaty law. As treaties have proliferated, customary international law is perhaps not as important as it once was, but in many ways it is the bedrock of the system, what is relied upon when there is no treaty. And it can be used in creative ways. Sometimes, where they have been very widely adopted and followed by nations, treaties can influence the content

---

8 Convention on the Regulation of Antarctic Mineral Resource Activities, 2 June 1988, reprinted in (1988) 27 I.L.M. 860.

9 Protocol on Environmental Protection to the Antarctic Treaty, 21 June 1991, reprinted in (1991) 30 I.L.M. 1461, reprinted in L.D. Guruswamy, G. Palmer & B. Weston, *Supplement of Basic Documents to International Environmental Law,* West Pub. Co., St Paul, Minnesota, 1994, p.321.

10 The original members of the treaty were Argentina, Australia, Belgium, Chile, France, Japan, New Zealand, Norway, South Africa, Poland, the Federal Republic of Germany, Brazil, India, the People's Republic of China, Uruguay, the former German Democratic Republic, and Italy.

of customary law. Not all custom in the international arena amounts to customary international law. For a custom to give rise to legal obligations a number of elements are necessary:

- the same practice by a number of states in regard to a particular situation;
- continuation of the practice over time;
- a belief that the practice is required by the prevailing international law; and
- general acquiescence in the practice by other states.

In other words, the search is for a general recognition among states that a certain practice is obligatory.

Custom allows international law to evolve over time, to respond to new challenges. Sometimes, the main obstacle in deciding that a concordant state practice amounts to customary international law is the requirement of what is known as *opinio juris*—a belief that the practice is obligatory as a matter of law.

One of the oldest branches of international law concerns the law of the sea. This law was entirely customary for centuries, although it has been heavily modified in recent years and is now virtually all taken over by treaty in the form of the 1982 United Nations Convention on the Law of Sea, which entered into force in 1994 and to which New Zealand is a party. In the famous *Corfu Channel* case,[11] the United Kingdom sought to hold Albania responsible for damage caused to British warships that were travelling through the channel when they hit mines moored there. Albania, for its part, sought satisfaction for conduct by the British authorities who had passed through the channel without the permission of the Albanian authorities. In deciding the case, the court relied upon customary international law in deciding that the Corfu channel was international waters through which ships of all nations could make innocent passage.

> It is, in the opinion of the Court, generally recognized and in accordance with international custom that States in time of peace have right to send their warships through straits used for international navigation between two parts of the high seas without previous authorization of a coastal State, provided that the passage is innocent. Unless otherwise prescribed in an international convention, there is no right for a coastal State to prohibit such passage through straits in time of peace.

Recognised general principles of law

The 'general principles of law recognised by civilised nations' are most usually accessed through the domestic legal decisions of those nations. Given the variety of legal systems in the world, the search may not be an easy one. In federal systems,

---

11 *Corfu Channel* (UK v. Albania) (1949) ICJ Reports 4 (April 9).

cases between states and between states and federal government may provide cases for consideration under this head. There is, however, considerable controversy about what is meant about this source of international law. Some of the newer countries are suspicious that 'civilised' is designed to discriminate against them and that the existence of customary international law does so as well since those nations were not in existence when the principles were established.

Judicial decisions and teachings

Little needs to be said here about this source of international law: judicial decisions and the teachings of the most highly qualified publicists. These are only subsidiary means for determining the rules of international law. But it should be said that there is a vast quantity of ruling on international law in many languages and it is of greater influence in the international system than is scholarly commentary in our own legal system, where decided cases have much greater authority.

Also, this final source is thought to have no binding force except between the parties and in respect of that particular case. In other words, the system of precedent that is so important in a common law domestic legal system such as New Zealand's has no place in international law. But, in practice, cases are of considerable value to later cases in the international system.

'Soft' international law

There is also an emerging course of international law known as 'soft' law. 'Hard' law in the international arena comes mainly from custom or treaties. Custom takes time and, often, a lot of state practice before it hardens into a legally enforceable rule. Treaties take a long time to negotiate and nations tend to shy away from the specificity they often involve. A much more politically attractive approach is the soft law option.[12] We believe that this phenomenon is increasingly used because it is so politically convenient.

Resort to soft law leaves large amounts of discretion to states. The standards are often so vague that third-party adjudication would be impossible even if it were provided for. Often the standards themselves are discretionary. What is important about these instruments is not so much the form in which they appear as the manner in which the obligations, if any, created by them are expressed. Frequently, what is expressed is a series of political statements or values. The Stockholm and Rio declarations on the environment are good examples. The use of soft law has substantial advantages and is particularly helpful in creating a climate that can, eventually, produce a hard law instrument.

---

[12] See generally C.M. Chinkin, 'The Challenge of Soft Law: Development and Change in International Law', (1989) 38 *International & Comp. Law Quarterly* 850; J. Carlson, 'Hunger, Agricultural Trade Liberalization, and Soft International Law: Addressing the Legal Dimensions of a Political Problem', 70 *Iowa Law Review,* 1995 p.1187.

All politicians know the value of ambiguity. It can serve to secure agreement where it might not otherwise be achieved. International instruments are frequently drafted with studied ambiguity. Such an approach may have deceptive elements and may create wrong impressions, but it promotes very valuable feelings of international comity and cooperation. Since political leaders and countries must continue dealing with one another, it is better that those dealings be based on agreement than on disagreement—and soft law solutions produce agreement.

More important, soft law solutions change the political thinking on an issue. They alter the circumstances in which an issue is considered; they cause opinion to coalesce. These changes can be a very important catalyst in later securing an agreement with a harder edge. Soft law solutions can, therefore, be useful steps on a longer journey. Soft law is where international law and international politics combine to build new norms. The Helsinki Declaration on the Protection of the Ozone Layer is such an instrument.[13] Its purpose was to ensure that the London meeting in 1990 could agree on hard amendments to the Montreal Protocol;[14] the consensus expressed at Helsinki was undoubtedly helpful in that respect.

MECHANISMS FOR SETTLING INTERNATIONAL DISPUTES

The most common means of settling an international dispute is for the nations concerned to negotiate about it. Diplomatic practice and protocol are well-established methods that allow governments to communicate with one another in a variety of ways. Where a dispute is just too contentious for negotiations to succeed, third-party nations may intervene and offer their good offices to help settle the dispute. This is what happened in the *Rainbow Warrior* dispute between France and New Zealand. The Prime Minister of the Netherlands, a nation on good terms with both countries, offered to mediate. He suggested that the dispute be handed over to the Secretary-General of the United Nations for rulings on outstanding questions. Both nations agreed to do this.

International arbitration is a common method of settling international disputes; many treaties provide for disputes to be dealt with in this way. Usually each country in a bilateral dispute will nominate a highly qualified international lawyer as its arbitrator and those two will choose an independent third arbitrator, who will chair the panel of three. This is what occurred when France breached the rulings of the United Nations Secretary-General in the *Rainbow Warrior* affair. The Secretary-General's ruling had included a provision concerning compulsory arbitration in the event that there was a dispute on the interpretation or implementation

---

13 Helsinki Declaration, 2 May 1989, reprinted 28 I.L.M. 1335 (1989).

14 London Amendments to the Montreal Protocol 29 June 1990, reprinted in Guruswamy, Palmer & Weston, *Supplement of Basic Documents to International Environmental Law*, p.471.

of the ruling. The provision required each nation to designate a member of an arbitral tribunal and those two would choose the third. The tribunal was given power of binding decision. When the dispute arose, New Zealand designated Sir Kenneth Keith, France designated M. Jean-Denis Bredin, and they chose Eduardo Jiminez de Arechaga, a Uruguayan and former judge and president of the International Court of Justice. France was again found to have committed material breaches of international law and in 1990 the tribunal told France to make a contribution of $US2 million to set up a fund to promote close and friendly relations between France and New Zealand. Arbitral tribunals are usually created specially for a particular dispute. There is, however, a standing body that can be used to arbitrate international disputes: the International Court of Justice (ICJ). This has also been the forum for international disputes between New Zealand and France.

In 1973 Australia and New Zealand had launched separate cases against France at the ICJ that were heard one after the other. In those days, France was engaged in atmospheric nuclear testing at Moruroa atoll in the Pacific. France was most upset at these proceedings being taken. It refused to turn up at the ICJ or to take part in the proceedings and it renounced its acceptance of the ICJ's compulsory jurisdiction as a result of the case. But while the case was still before the ICJ, the French government announced that it was abandoning atmospheric testing and would henceforth only test underground. The ICJ then, in effect, said the case was moot: there was nothing left for it to decide. The ICJ attributed legal effect to France's press statement that it was ceasing atmospheric testing. That, it said, was all the litigants wanted, the statement was binding on France, and so the case was at an end. In essence, the ICJ ducked the issue as to whether it had jurisdiction in the case and, if it did, whether nuclear testing was lawful under international law. New Zealand's case was heavily tied to the damage to the environment from nuclear testing.

The ICJ's 1974 judgment contained a curious paragraph. Referring to France's commitment not to test in the atmosphere, it said:

> Once the Court has found that a State has entered into a commitment concerning its future conduct it is not the Court's function to contemplate that it will not comply with it. However, the Court observes that if the basis of this Judgment were to be affected, the Applicant could request an examination of the situation in accordance with the provisions of the Statute; the denunciation by France, by letter dated 2 January 1974, of the General Act for the Pacific Settlement of International Disputes, which is relied upon as a basis of jurisdiction in the present case cannot itself constitute an obstacle to such a request.

In 1995, on the strength of this paragraph, New Zealand returned to the ICJ and requested an examination of the situation in light of the fact that France had detonated over 100 underground nuclear explosions on Moruroa and was proposing a new series. New Zealand argued that there was a question as to how many more explosions the atoll could stand without major structural damage, which might release nuclear contamination into the sea. This, it said, was the same sort of environmental damage it had complained about earlier in relation to French atmospheric testing.

By a majority of twelve to three the ICJ rejected New Zealand's request (Geoffrey Palmer being in the minority). The majority of the court reached the conclusion that the previous judgment dealt exclusively with atmospheric testing and it could not consider issues relating to underground tests. The wider environmental risks could not be looked at. Although its case did not succeed, New Zealand forced France to defend its actions in the full glare of international publicity in the Peace Palace at the Hague where the ICJ sits. On this occasion, the French Government did appear and argue the case.

This example underlines the relatively weak position the ICJ occupies compared with domestic courts. Essentially, the ICJ requires consent from the litigants before it can entertain a case. That consent might be contained in an international convention to which a nation has signed up that gives the ICJ jurisdiction to decide disputes arising under the convention or it may be consent given under article 36(2) of the court's statute, which provides:

> 2. The states parties of the present Statute may at any time declare that they recognize as compulsory ipso facto and without special agreement, in relation to any other state accepting the same obligation, the jurisdiction of the Court in all legal disputes concerning:
>
> a. the interpretation of a treaty;
>
> b. any question of international law;
>
> c. the existence of any fact which, if established, would constitute a breach of international obligation;
>
> d. the nature or extent of the reparation to be made for the breach of an international obligation.
>
> 3. The declarations referred to above may be made unconditionally or on condition of reciprocity on the part of several or certain states, or for a certain time.

This is called the optional clause. Those nations who do make declarations under it often hedge them around with a variety of qualifications that render enforcement unlikely. The majority of nations in the world do not accept the court's jurisdiction under this clause at all. Of the permanent members of the United Nations Security Council, only the United Kingdom does so. France withdrew as a result of the nuclear test cases just discussed, and the United States withdrew in response to the ICJ's 1988 decision where the United States had mined the harbours of Nicaragua.

It is a sad and regrettable fact of international law that the compulsory adjudication of the ICJ is not widely accepted.[15] Indeed, the number of nations that accept it has declined in recent years. There may be a number of reasons for this, but the main one is political. Nations do not relish the prospect of having their conduct passed upon or possibly labelled unlawful by an independent court. They prefer negotiation on their own terms. Even when third-party adjudication is required, there is a preference for arbitral tribunals established specially for the particular dispute.

Nations prefer negotiation partly because they can keep the dispute under more predictable political control. They can stand by their respective versions of the dispute and ignore the law when they wish to. In this way cherished political flexibility is preserved, which could be lost if the ICJ looks at a matter.

Notions of state sovereignty underlie the ICJ jurisdictional requirement of express consent. Obviously, consent can be indicated in a number of ways, including ratification of a treaty that gives the court jurisdiction to decide disputes, and by special agreement in a particular case.[16] Professor Brownlie reported that, between 1946 and 1988, the ICJ dealt with only sixty contentious cases and twenty requests for advisory opinions.[17] When the ICJ was being established in the aftermath of the Second World War, New Zealand argued that its jurisdiction should be compulsory, but this has not happened. New Zealand does, however, accept the optional clause of the ICJ statute and has done so for the court's entire history.

INTERNATIONAL LAW AND NEW ZEALAND LAW

We live in an international and global age that touches every aspect of our life. Standards in New Zealand on a wide range of issues must take into account, and sometimes be bound by, a relevant international standard or obligation. To a degree unheard of fifty years ago, New Zealand cannot please itself as to what policies it pursues. In the four years to June 1995, 109 treaties were tabled in the New Zealand Parliament. In total, well over 30,000 treaties are registered with the

---

15 Statute of the International Court of Justice, *Basic Documents, supra* note 9, *International Court of Justice at a Crossroads*, Lori F. Damrosch (ed.), Transnational Pub., Dobbs Ferry, New York, 1987; V. Lowe & M. Fitzmaurice (eds), *Fifty Years of the International Court of Justice*, Cambridge, 1996.

16 Statute of the International Court of Justice, art. 36(1), reprinted in Guruswamy, Palmer & Weston, *Supplement of Basic Documents to International Law*, p.32.

17 See I. Brownlie, *Principles of Public International Law*, 4th ed., Oxford University Press, Oxford, 1990, p.733.

United Nations. It has been calculated that two new treaties are made every day worldwide. According to the Legislation Advisory Committee, New Zealand has been or is party to about 1500 treaties.[18]

In our relations with other nations there are the practical everyday rules of cooperation that cover a wide range of matters—postage, civil aviation, weather information, communications, customs, diplomatic and consular relations, visas, trade rules, banking obligations, money exchange, the movement of people, refugees, extradition, and many others. Many of these matters are regulated through international treaties and conventions and some have international organisations to look after them. All those obligations place substantial restraint upon the New Zealand Government's freedom of action. Even our relations with Australia are the subject of many agreements, the most important of which is the Closer Economic Relations Agreement, which has changed greatly the relations between the two economies and brought them closer together.

Many of New Zealand's policies are the result of international agreements and treaties from which we derive great benefit. In formulating these agreements, New Zealand's voice is heard to a greater extent than its population really warrants. It is important to realise that, on many issues, New Zealand cannot be a decisive voice in international forums, yet we must live in the world and interact with it. Our national independence has been reduced and it cannot be regained. As Sir Kenneth Keith has said, the international legal context is 'critical to the health of our legal system and our wider economy, society and identity . . .'[19] In the same address he isolated a number of critical areas where international obligations effectively drive the domestic policy:

- international peace and security through the United Nations;
- the General Agreement on Tariffs and Trade (GATT) and the law administered by the World Trade Organisation as well as the United Nations Commission in International Trade Law;
- international communications by sea, air, and through telecommunications and post covered by a growing body of complex technical law;
- movement of people and immigration law, refugees and abduction of children subject to a large number of internationally agreed obligations;
- a whole host of international environmental requirements;
- standards laid down by the International Labour Organisation;
- standards defined in the International Human Rights instruments to which New Zealand is a party, particularly the International Covenant on Civil and

---

[18] Report No. 6 by the Legislation Advisory Committee, *Legislative Change—Guidelines on Process and Content*, rev. ed., December 1991, p.78.

[19] Sir Kenneth Keith, Address to the New Zealand Bar Association Conference, Queenstown, 21–22 July 1995.

Political Rights which was affirmed in the New Zealand Bill of Rights Act 1990.

There is little awareness of the effects of the last of these in New Zealand. Because New Zealand is a party to the first Optional Protocol of the International Covenant on Civil and Political Rights, the Human Rights Committee of the United Nations monitors New Zealand's performance in relation to the covenant and the government has to report periodically on what has occurred. The most recent report of the Human Rights Committee argues for greater protection for these rights.

The Optional Protocol also enables individual New Zealand citizens to make complaints to the Human Rights Committee of the United Nations if they believe their rights under the covenant are being breached by the New Zealand Government and they have exhausted their remedies under New Zealand law. Until April 1996, 694 comunications had been received by the Human Rights Committee in respect to fifty-one countries (of the eighty-seven that are party to the Optional Protocol). Of the 555 concluded cases, the committee found that 168 'disclosed a violation'. In that period, five such complaints had been made against New Zealand, involving issues ranging from prison conditions to the validity of the Sealords Treaty of Waitangi settlement.

It has been estimated by the Legislation Advisory Committee that about a quarter of all the statutes passed by the New Zealand Parliament raise issues relating to international treaties.[20] The committee prepared a list of eighty-seven New Zealand statutes that had possible implications for New Zealand treaties. A large number of regulations would also have treaty implications.

In recent years, the New Zealand courts have increasingly referred to the international treaties and their obligations where they are interpreting a statute relevant to the international obligation New Zealand has undertaken. In particular, in 1994 the New Zealand Court of Appeal indicated that the Minister of Immigration should have had regard to the International Convention on the Rights of the Child in exercising a statutory discretion relating to a deportation order.[21]

The legal rule in New Zealand in relation to treaties is that the making of a treaty is an executive act. The performance of the treaty obligations, if they entail alteration of the existing New Zealand domestic law, requires legislation action by Parliament. That is the usual rule.[22] In Australia, where they have the same rule, it has given rise to contention because the government of the Commonwealth of Australia can enter into international agreements that might change the law of

---

[20] Report No. 6 by the Legislation Advisory Committee, *Legislative Change—Guidelines on Process and Content,* Rev. ed., Wellington, 1991, p.15.

[21] *Tavita* v. *Minister of Immigration* [1994] 2 *NZLR* 257.

[22] *Attorney-General for Canada* v. *Attorney-General for Ontario* [1937] AC 326.

the state governments, who, under the Australian Constitution Act, have no part in the conduct of external affairs. Furthermore, in a case *Minister of Immigration* v. *Teoh* in 1995, the High Court of Australia ruled that an international convention that had been ratified by the Commonwealth Government affected the latitude for executive discretion in an immigration matter, even though the International Convention on the Rights of the Child had not been legislated for domestically.[23] This led to legislative initiatives to require treaties to be tabled in Parliament before ratification with a 'treaty impact statement', and to establish a Joint Parliamentary Committee on Treaties. For the time being, the Australian Government has adopted a new arrangement to allow treaties to be tabled in the Parliament and scrutinised before binding action is taken by the executive.

It is possible that, under MMP, similar tensions may emerge in New Zealand. In 1996 the Standing Orders Committee discussed this issue without reaching a conclusion. The executive government may sometimes find it wise to consult the Parliament before entering into binding international obligations. It would be most unsatisfactory if the government entered into an agreement only to find that the Parliament would not pass the resulting legislation to change New Zealand's domestic law. What notice, then, should courts take of the obligation? This could easily happen under MMP and it is urgent that steps be taken to deal with it. Democratic procedures require that the executive should give Parliament ample notice about the progress in treaty negotiations. There may be cases where that is inappropriate, but they are unlikely to be many.

The Law Commission in New Zealand examined these issues in a 1995 paper,[24] which recommended 'the need for and practices of notification and consultation at the negotiating stage be assessed'. The commission found there was an issue as to whether legislative consultation requirements for treaties should be imposed, and also recommended that, as far as possible, legislation implementing treaties in New Zealand should give direct effect to the actual text of the treaty. The commission found that, in order to avoid breaching its international obligations, New Zealand needed a more systematic practice for giving effect to its treaty obligations. To us, it seems inevitable that, under MMP, the Parliament will demand a greater say in the international obligations that New Zealand undertakes.

The importance of international issues and international obligations within New Zealand's sytem of government will only increase in the years ahead. The

---

23 *Minister of Immigration* v. *Teoh* (1995) ALR 353. See Parliament of the Commonwealth of Australia, *Trick or Treaty? Commonwealth Power to Make and Implement Treaties: Report by the Senate Legal and Constitutional References Committee*, Government Printer, Canberra, 1995.

24 Sir Kenneth Keith, *The Making, Acceptance and Implementation of Treaties: Three Issues for Consideration,* Law Commission, Wellington, June 1995; and Law Commision, *Report 34: A New Zealand Guide to International Law and its Sources*, Wellington, 1996.

Law Commission conclusion to the paper quoted above can serve as a useful conclusion to this chapter: 'To conclude, the Law Commission emphasises the need for all those involved in the making, application, interpretation, review, development and especially the teaching of the law, to be increasingly aware of the international or global context in which much law operates and from which it arises.'[25]

---

25 *Ibid.*, p.21.

part five
future government

18 Where Next?

ASSESSING MMP

The predominant theme of this book has been the changes to New Zealand's system of government wrought by the introduction of the new electoral system, MMP. How far MMP will change the system can be judged only after we have had some experience with it. Many reforms can produce effects that are unexpected and surprising. It may be so with MMP.

In summary, we have suggested that the following key changes may occur as a result of the move to minority and coalition governments under MMP:

- Parliament and opposition parties will determine the continued existence of a minority government;
- Parliament and opposition parties will determine whether particular minority government policies will be implemented through legislation and possibly whether particular individual ministers will resign;
- there will be more pressure on Cabinet ministers of different parties to disagree publicly with coalition Cabinet decisions;
- the role of the Prime Minister and senior officials in coordinating ministers and officials in a coalition government will be more difficult;
- ministers may tend to make decisions within their individual portfolios without reference to a coalition Cabinet;
- minority governments will tend to use regulations to avoid the need for legislation;
- legislation that is not supported by a minority government may still be passed;
- select committees of Parliament will be more important to the passage of legislation and to the scrutiny of minority governments;
- there may be more meaningful public debate over government policy;
- public servants will face more direct pressure from opposition politicians;

- there will be pressure to increase the resources available to Parliament, compared with the executive; and
- the judiciary may take up an increased policy-making role.

The Electoral Act 1993 requires a parliamentary select committee to report to Parliament by 1 June 2002 on whether there should be:

- changes to the system for determining the number of general seats on the electoral system;
- changes to the system of Maori representation; and
- a further referendum on changes to the electoral system and, if so, the nature of the proposals and the timing of the referendum.

This review of the new system may be rather too soon after its introduction to make definitive judgements about it; only two MMP elections are required by then, although there may turn out to be more.

There was significant opposition from some sections of the community to the introduction of MMP. There have been expressions of concern in the run-up to the first MMP election as a result of the development of new political parties and problems in some of the old ones, often due to the impact of MMP on the prospects of sitting MPs. These concerns are unlikely to disappear. Similarly, MMP will not be a cure-all for New Zealand's constitutional problems, as its proponents have sometimes claimed. This may also lead to some disillusionment with the new system as people realise that politicians will still argue with each other and policies will still be implemented in the face of opposition.

Despite these factors, we do not believe it is likely that New Zealand will reverse MMP later on. The reason is that the new system is essentially more democratic than the old one. There is no perfect system of government. In general, there is a trade-off between efficiency and representativeness. In our view, New Zealand's old first-past-the-post electoral system, combined with its single, small house of Parliament, absence of an entrenched Bill of Rights or federal system, and doctrine of parliamentary sovereignty, meant that the whole constitution was skewed more towards efficiency than representativeness. Indeed, New Zealand's old constitution was cited internationally as the most streamlined Westminster democracy in the world. MMP redresses the balance in a fundamental way, and that is the reason for the new title to this book. Through encouraging government by more than one political party, MMP is likely to lead to more debate, more consensus, and more national dialogue about government policies before they are enacted. The transition to the new system is unlikely to be too difficult—after all, the fundamental procedures and structures of Westminster government evolved in an era of decentralised political negotiations before the advent of mass political parties.

This is not to say that constitutional changes are likely to cease. The pace of change in New Zealand's constitutional development has accelerated in recent years. Every chapter of this book has required substantial revision (and several are completely new) since the second edition was published in 1987. MMP has been the biggest change but it is by no means the only one. There is a growing sense of confidence that we can reach out and find our own solutions to problems. Although it will take some time yet before we find it, we have started to search seriously for our own constitutional destiny.

CONSTITUTIONAL CHANGES SINCE 1979

Since the first edition of this book was published in 1979 a remarkable number of changes have occurred. No area has been immune from alteration.

The Constitution Act 1986 has given a more consolidated, accessible, and clearer base to our constitution. It has removed most of the remnants of our British colonial heritage. Changes to the office of Governor-General have also brought that office up to date and removed other vestiges of colonialism.

There has been a developing interest in the intersection of Maori issues and the constitution. The Treaty of Waitangi, and the Waitangi Tribunal that hears grievances arising out of it, have made some stirring contributions to our national consciousness. The course of those developments is far from over; the issue remains of exactly how to recognise the appropriate place of the treaty and how to complete the process of reconciliation.

The New Zealand Bill of Rights Act 1990 has connected New Zealand's international obligations in the human rights arena to our domestic law. The act as it has been interpreted by the courts is proving to be a significant check on the excesses of governmental power, even to the extent of providing remedies in damages against the government when its standards have been flagrantly breached.

Profound changes have been made both to the structure of the public service and the way that it works by the State-Owned Enterprises Act 1986, the State Sector Act 1988, the Public Finance Act 1989, and the Fiscal Responsibility Act 1993. Accountability is sharpened and relocated. There is much more discipline and rigour over the spending of public money. Fiscal and economic policy and its effects have to be more transparent and surprises are made more difficult.

Government by regulation is being subjected to increased scrutiny. New protections against regulations have been put in place and the power to make regulations with a broad policy content has been cut back by repealing a number of key statutes. The power of the executive has thereby been restricted and contained.

Official information is now more readily available, lifting the veil of secrecy on government and making it possible for people to participate more effectively in the policy development process. The same principles apply to local government. And the protections against maladministration and bad decisions have been increased, first by the Ombudsmen and then by a variety of other agencies that allow complaints to be examined impartially and cheaply by high-ranking officers of state who owe no allegiance to the government of the day.

Better parliamentary methods of scrutinising legislation have been put in place. Almost all bills now go to select committees of Parliament for scrutiny and public submissions put before those committees often lead to drastic alteration of proposed legislation. And Parliament now has a system of committees that can examine every department, government entity, and issue within the public realm thoroughly and professionally in terms of policy, administration, and expenditure. Parliament is freer of ministerial control. MPs are now better provided with support services than ever before. The legislative process of Parliament has been thoroughly overhauled and considerably improved as a result of the new standing orders that came into effect in 1996.

WHAT LIES AHEAD?

It is always risky to speculate about the future. In the last edition of this book the case for the introduction of MMP and the introduction of a Bill of Rights were described as unclimbed peaks of constitutional reform. They have now been scaled. In the next decade a number of issues are likely to come onto the agenda for constitutional reform.

Local government has been reformed in important ways in the last few years. As pressure continues for services to communities to be managed by communities, the constitutional place of local government may develop considerably.

The place of international developments, international law, and the international obligations that New Zealand has assumed is better appreciated now than when this book was first written. These influences will deepen and intensify in the future. Although it is a small and relatively isolated nation, New Zealand is nevertheless vitally affected in its trading and political relationships by other nations and the growing measure of international interdependence. As they already do, those international influences will continue to influence markedly the content of our domestic law, and they will also alter our constitution.

The courts, as this book has argued, have served the nation well over the years. The Privy Council, as the apex of the New Zealand court system and its final court of appeal, is likely to go. Its going will hardly be noticed by ordinary New Zealanders, who will probably continue to be more concerned about whether the justice system, and the court system in particular, is easily accessible, regardless of wealth, race, gender, and other distinctions.

We also consider it likely that moves towards New Zealand becoming a republic will be discussed in the next decade and may come to pass within that time, especially if Australia becomes a republic. In the view of one prominent New Zealand constitutional scholar, 'New Zealand, like Australia, though a constitutional monarchy in form, is a de facto republic with the Governor-General functioning virtually as a President appointed by an elected Prime Minister.'[1] To change the situation formally is not so simple. Becoming a republic is a big legal change that would require a lot of preparation. To remove the sovereign is a fundamental change to our existing constitutional arrangements and would require the most careful preparation.

The Treaty of Waitangi's place in Aotearoa's constitutional and legal system is not yet defined. It is half out and half in the legal system, depending on the degree to which the principles of the treaty are contained in statutes passed by Parliament. The present stage is not likely to be sustainable and there will be further development in the next decade. That is likely to take the shape of different ways of addressing breaches of the treaty and may include the exploration by many different groups of new methods of making the treaty part of fundamental constitutional law.

It is possible that all the forces that we have outlined here will combine into the demand for a new constitutional settlement in New Zealand. Almost every other nation in the world has a basic written constitution that constitutes the basic law of the country and cannot be easily altered by a simple majority in Parliament. New Zealand does not have a constitution in that sense. It may be that, in the next decade, the question will be whether New Zealand should have such a law and, if so, what form it should take.

Ever since the abolition of the upper house of the New Zealand Parliament on 1 January 1951, there have been spasmodic demands for a written constitution. During the 1950s and 1960s the Constitutional Society for the Promotion of Economic Freedom and Justice in New Zealand (Inc.) devoted considerable effort to promoting a written constitution. The society also advocated the reintroduction of a second chamber for Parliament and a Bill of Rights within a written constitution. In a 1961 petition to Parliament the Constitutional Society advocated all three in a draft document.

A written constitution, without a Bill of Rights, would bring together the various elements of our existing arrangements. Some existing elements are in acts of Parliament; others are not written down in any law. Indeed, some of the most important points in our Constitution depend upon customs known as conventions. In 1977 Dr D.E. Paterson prepared a draft written constitution for consideration

1 F.M. Brookfield, 'Republican New Zealand: Legal Aspects and Consequences', *New Zealand Law Review*, 1995, p.310.

by the New Zealand Section of the International Commission of Jurists. Dr Paterson's draft illustrates the sort of matters a written constitution could cover:

- the territory of New Zealand—the boundaries;
- the Sovereign, including the royal style and titles and setting out the powers, privileges and obligations of the Sovereign. In particular the 'reserve' powers of the Sovereign are defined, particularly the occasions when the Sovereign is not obliged to act on the advice of the ministers;
- the role and functions of the Governor-General are defined and the instances in which the Governor-General could, in exceptional situations, act other than in accordance with the advice of the executive council are set out as above;
- where the Governor-General cannot act, provision is made for an administrator to act as a substitute; provision is also made for the office of Deputy Governor-General;
- the composition of the executive council is defined and the functions of that body set out;
- the office of Prime Minister is dealt with, the method of appointment and the broad constitutional functions of the office;
- Cabinet composition and the powers and duties of ministers of the Crown are set out. Ministers shall 'determine and formulate policy, and secure the implementation of that policy . . .';
- departments of state, public corporations, commissions and councils, the armed forces, and the police force are briefly described;
- the most basic rules governing elections are put in the constitution—secret ballot, drawing up of electorates by the Representation Commission, the Maori seats, and the qualifications and disqualifications for being a member of Parliament;
- the functions of Parliament are briefly mentioned;
- the court structure is set out;
- the basic functions of tribunals and the Ombudsmen are defined;
- the constitution is expressed to be the supreme law of New Zealand and all other law must be subject to it and void if there is any inconsistency;
- amendments can be made by two methods—by a majority of two-thirds of all members of the House of Representatives or by an act of Parliament passed by a simple majority of MPs and endorsed by a simple majority of electors.

Dr Paterson's aim seems to have been to put down exactly in writing the best understanding of our existing arrangements, including the constitutional conventions; no great changes were contemplated. The proposed functions of the branches of government were almost identical to what they then were. At present we have no supreme law. With limited exceptions, and some judicial doubts at the margin, the usual understanding is that Parliament can pass any law without being subject to any higher law enshrined in a constitution.

There are arguments against a written constitution. If it were too prescriptive it would reduce government's capacity to evolve. Once the basic powers of the branches of government are written down, disputes could arise over whether each branch has acted within its proper sphere. Those disputes could result in litigation and, in that sense, the courts would play a greater role in determining our constitutional arrangements. The courts would simply be deciding what the supreme law in the constitution means, but it would involve them in a new function and it is as well to recognise the fact.

Codifying the fundamentals of a parliamentary democracy might appear to be a protection against an easy road to dictatorship. Certainly it seems likely such a document may help prevent New Zealand slipping unconsciously from one pattern of government to another, but its capacity ought not to be exaggerated. Such a document would not prevent our democracy breaking down if conditions were propitious for its collapse. And the courts could not save us if we were determined to travel to the edges of anarchy.

With the passing of the Constitution Act 1986 we are closer than we have been before to a written constitution. As the report upon which the act is based put it, 'we have brought together the principal pieces of statutory constitutional law applicable to New Zealand as a fairly coherent whole containing much of what a "written" constitution would provide'.[2] That development, agreed to on all sides in Parliament in 1986, put to an end for the immediate future the question of a written constitution for New Zealand. The basic elements of our constitutional arrangement in statutory form are now accessible. But the pressures already mentioned are likely to cause those judgements to be re-examined in the ten years after 1996.

For that reason, for illustrative purposes, we have taken the existing elements of our constitutional arrangements and combined them into a written constitution of the type used by many other countries, but using only tried and tested New Zealand ingredients in the recipe. We have taken the existing elements of the New Zealand Constitution Act 1986, together with the two other most important constitutional documents, the New Zealand Bill of Rights Act 1990 and the Treaty of Waitangi, and combined them into a draft model constitution that would be superior law. According to this, all other law, both statute law and common law, would be subject to the overarching authority of the constitution. Laws that were incompatible with it would be struck down. Such a constitution does not abolish the monarchy. To do so raises fundamental issues about the bedrock elements of the system and we have not thought our way through those issues.

---

2 First and Second Reports of an Officials Committee, *Constitutional Reform*, Wellington, February 1986, p.27.

We offer this constitution simply as a means of stimulating and focusing public debate. It contains neither a number of important elements of the New Zealand system of government, nor many of the elements recommended by Dr Paterson. In many ways this constitution is quite a conservative document—it attempts just to bring together, and give added force to, those constitutional elements that we have now. What is radical is the whole notion of having an entrenched written constitution. That would be a big change to the New Zealand system.

New Zealand's constitution-makers will have to address some difficult issues if it is decided to introduce a new type of constitution:

- whether to try to write down a number of the important conventions of the constitution, such as the existence and functioning of Cabinet;
- whether to entrench some institutions or procedures beyond the reach of a simple majority in Parliament, such as the independence of the judiciary or officers of Parliament;
- how to define the meaning of the Treaty of Waitangi;
- whether to reserve or define a constitutional role for local government; and
- many other issues of significant complexity.

Despite the problems, there would also be advantages in a written constitution in New Zealand. It ought not to be so immutable that change would be very difficult, but change ought not to be so easy that it could be done in a single parliamentary evening with a compliant majority. With MMP here and the prospect of republicanism, coupled with the need to resolve the position of the Treaty of Waitangi, it seems to us that the big constitutional issue in the next decade will be whether New Zealand should take a further step in its constitutional development and adopt a written constitution as a form of higher law.

Already some New Zealand scholars have called for such a move.[3] Others are likely to resist it stoutly. In essence, moving to a written constitution would change the flexibility of the rules of power and, at the margins, its location. The issues have been raised in a 1996 High Court decision of Justice Baragwanath. The plaintiffs were fishers, aggrieved by the Quota Appeal Authority, which had held that they were not entitled to some quota in circumstances where others had been granted it. Parliament had changed the law. The fishers argued that the amendment to the law deprived them of access to the courts to secure a declaration as to the legal position. The Attorney-General had told Parliament, before it was passed, that the legislation would breach the New Zealand Bill of Rights Act 1990. The fishers argued, following a line of suggestions in earlier cases by Lord Cooke of Thorndon and in academic writings, that this was an instance where the courts should reserve the right to decide that some fundamental rights were so deep that

[3] Brookfield, 'Republican New Zealand', p.323.

Parliament could not override them and that the legislation that did so should not be followed.

The argument failed. Justice Baragwanath found that the purpose of the amendment was not so much to deprive the fishers of access to the courts to enforce their rights, as it was to deprive them of legal rights in the matter altogether. The judge said:[4]

> The settled rule of law that the Courts will give effect to an Act of Parliament according to its terms provides the answer to these cases. They also illustrate why both Parliament and the Courts observe, and must be clearly seen to observe, the conventions whose acceptance in New Zealand has substantially avoided the constitutional friction that is a feature of the arrangements of other societies.
>
> Our small society has to date found it unnecessary to equip itself with techniques of judicial challenge to Parliament and its work. Whereas other larger societies have done so [USA, Canada, Australia, United Kingdom] . . . and in constitutions of the new Commonwealth such provisions are the rule, in New Zealand both Parliament and the judiciary recognise that constitutional peace and good order are better maintained by adherence to conventions rather than judicial decision.

It is not clear that this orthodoxy will continue unchallenged. We think there are likely to be serious challenges over the next decade to the orthodox understanding of the relationship between the judiciary and Parliament. We do not attempt to predict the outcome of such a classic constitutional debate. We simply draw attention to it, in the belief that this constitutional issue, like all others, vitally affects the exercise of power in New Zealand society and is worthy of general public discussion and debate.

In offering a stimulus to public debate, this book emphasises the importance of dialogue among individuals and groups in New Zealand. It is social, economic, cultural, and political debate that underlies any constitution. In the decade following 1996, New Zealand will come face to face with its own constitutional destiny. We should seek a uniquely New Zealand identity for our system of democratic government. What form that will take will depend, ultimately, on what sort of society we think we are.

---

4 *Cooper* v. *Attorney-General*, unreported 7 May 1996, CP 1400/92, Auckland Registry, Baragwanath J, p.3, 6–7.

Appendix

CONSTITUTION ACT OF NEW ZEALAND

Analysis

Parliament

CONSTITUTION ACT OF NEW ZEALAND

An Act to institute a Constitution as the supreme law of New Zealand

WHEREAS

(1) New Zealand is a democratic society based on the rule of law and on principles of freedom, equality and the dignity and worth of the human person;

(2) New Zealand does not have a Constitution enjoying the status of Supreme Law and it is desirable to change that situation and adopt a Constitution;

(3) The Maori, as tangata whenua o Aotearoa, and the Crown entered in 1840 into a solemn contract known as Te Tiriti o Waitangi or the Treaty of Waitangi, and it is desirable to recognise and affirm the Treaty as Part of the Supreme Law of New Zealand;

(4) New Zealand in 1978 ratified the International Covenant on Civil and Political Rights;

(5) It is desirable to guarantee the human rights and fundamental freedoms of all the people of New Zealand without discrimination;

BE IT ENACTED by the Parliament of New Zealand as follows:

1. Short title and commencement—(1) This Act may be cited as the Constitution of New Zealand.

(2) This Act shall come into force on 1 January 2000.

PART I

GENERAL PROVISIONS

2. Entrenchment—No provision of this Constitution shall be repealed or amended unless the proposal for the repeal or amendment—

(a) Is passed by a majority of 75 percent of all the members of the House of Representatives; or

(b) Has been carried by a majority of the valid votes cast at a poll of all electors eligible to vote in New Zealand.

Cf Electoral Act 1993 No 87, s268

3. Legal effect of Constitution—(1) Wherever a law can be given a meaning that is consistent with the Constitution, that meaning must be preferred to any other meaning.

(2) Where there is an inconsistency between any law and the Constitution, the Constitution must prevail.

Cf 1990 No 109, s6

PART II

The Treaty of Waitangi/Te Tiriti o Waitangi

4. The Treaty of Waitangi / Te Tiriti o Waitangi—(1) The rights of the Maori people under the Treaty of Waitangi / Te Tiriti o Waitangi are hereby recognised and affirmed.

(2) The Treaty of Waitangi / Te Tiriti o Waitangi shall be considered as always speaking and shall be applied to circumstances as they arise so that effect may be given to its spirit and intent.

(3) The Treaty of Waitangi / Te Tiriti o Waitangi means the Treaty as set out in Maori and English in the Schedule to this Act.

Cf Treaty of Waitangi Act 1975, No 114

5. Court appointment of *amicus curiae*—In any proceedings in which the question of consistency with the Treaty of Waitangi / Te Tiriti o Waitangi is in issue, the court may appoint an *amicus curiae* to represent any party who, in the opinion of the court, should be represented and who, but for the appointment of the *amicus curiae*, would be unrepresented.

PART III

The Sovereign

6. Head of State—(1) The Sovereign in right of New Zealand is the head of State of New Zealand, and shall be known by the royal style and titles proclaimed from time to time.

(2) The Governor-General appointed by the Sovereign is the Sovereign's representative in New Zealand.

Cf 1986 No 114, s2

7. Exercise of royal powers by the Sovereign or the Governor-General—(1) Every power conferred on the Governor-General by or under any Act is a royal power which is exercisable by the Governor-General on behalf of the Sovereign, and may accordingly be exercised either by the Sovereign in person or by the Governor-General.

(2) Every reference in any Act to the Governor-General in Council or any other like expression includes a reference to the Sovereign acting by and with the advice and consent of the Executive Council.

Cf 1986 No 114, s3

8. Regency—(1) Where, under the law of the United Kingdom, the royal functions are being performed in the name and on behalf of the Sovereign by a Regent, the royal functions of the Sovereign in right of New Zealand shall be performed in the name and on behalf of the Sovereign by that Regent.

(2) Nothing in subsection (1) of this section limits, in relation to any power of the Sovereign in right of New Zealand, the authority of the Governor-General to exercise that power.

Cf 1986, No 114, 4

9. Demise of the Crown—(1) The death of the Sovereign shall have the effect of transferring all the functions, duties, powers, authorities, rights, privileges, and dignities belonging to the Crown to the Sovereign's successor, as determined in accordance with the enactment of the Parliament of England entitled The Act of Settlement (12 & 13 Will. 3, c. 2) and any other law relating to the succession to the Throne, but shall otherwise have no effect in law for any purpose.

(2) Every reference to the Sovereign in any document or instrument in force on or after the commencement of this Act shall, unless the context otherwise requires, be deemed to include a reference to the Sovereign's heirs and successors.

Cf 1986 No 114, s5

The Executive

10. Ministers of Crown to be members of Parliament—(1) A person may be appointed and may hold office as a member of the Executive Council or as a

Minister of the Crown only if that person is a member of Parliament.

(2) Notwithstanding subsection (1) of this section,—

(a) A person who is not a member of Parliament may be appointed and may hold office as a member of the Executive Council or as a Minister of the Crown if that person was a candidate for election at the general election of members of the House of Representatives held immediately preceding that person's appointment as a member of the Executive Council or as a Minister of the Crown but shall vacate office at the expiration of the period of 40 days beginning with the date of the appointment unless, within that period, that person becomes a member of Parliament; and

(b) Where a person who holds office both as a member of Parliament and as a member of the Executive Council or as a Minister of the Crown ceases to be a member of Parliament, that person may continue to hold office as a member of the Executive Council or as a Minister of the Crown until the expiration of the 28th day after the day on which that person ceases to be a member of Parliament.

Cf 1986 No 114, s6

11. Power of member of Executive Council to exercise Minister's powers— Any function, duty, or power exercisable by or conferred on any Minister of the Crown (by whatever designation that Minister is known) may, unless the context otherwise requires, be exercised or performed by any member of the Executive Council.

Cf 1986 No 114, s7

12. Appointment of Parliamentary Under-Secretaries—(1) The Governor-General may from time to time, by warrant under the Governor-General's hand, appoint any member of Parliament to be a Parliamentary Under-Secretary in relation to such Ministerial office or offices as are specified in that behalf in the warrant of appointment.

(2) A Parliamentary Under-Secretary shall hold office as such during the pleasure of the Governor-General, but shall in every case vacate that office within 28 days of ceasing to be a member of Parliament.

Cf 1986 No 114, s8

13. Functions of Parliamentary Under-Secretaries—(1) A Parliamentary Under-Secretary holding office as such in respect of any Ministerial office shall have and may exercise or perform under the direction of the Minister concerned such of the functions, duties, and powers of the Minister of the Crown for the time being holding that office as may from time to time be assigned to the Parliamentary Under-Secretary by that Minister.

(2) Nothing in subsection (1) of this section limits the authority of any

minister of the Crown to exercise or perform personally any function, duty, or power.

(3) The fact that any person holding office as a Parliamentary Under-Secretary in respect of any Ministerial office purports to exercise or perform any function, duty, or power of the Minister concerned shall be conclusive evidence of that person's authority to do so.

Cf 1986 No 114, s9

The Legislature

14. House of Representatives—(1) There shall continue to be a House of Representatives for New Zealand.

(2) The House of Representatives is the same body as the House of Representatives referred to in section 10 of the Constitution Act 1986.

(3) The House of Representatives shall be regarded as always in existence, notwithstanding that Parliament has been dissolved or has expired.

(4) The House of Representatives shall have as its members those persons who are elected from time to time in accordance with the provisions of the Electoral Act 1993, and who shall be known as 'members of Parliament'.

Cf 1986 No 114, s10

15. Oath of allegiance to be taken by members of Parliament—(1) A member of Parliament shall not be permitted to sit or vote in the House of Representatives until that member has taken the Oath of Allegiance in the form prescribed in section 17 of the Oaths and Declarations Act 1957.

(2) The oath to be taken under this section shall be administered by the Governor-General or a person authorised by the Governor-General to administer that oath.

Cf 1986 No 114, s11

16. Election of Speaker—The House of Representatives shall, at its first meeting after any general election of its members, and immediately on its first meeting after any vacancy occurs in the office of Speaker, choose one of its members as its Speaker, and every such choice shall be effective on being confirmed by the Governor-General.

Cf 1986 No 114, s12

17. Speaker to continue in office notwithstanding dissolution or expiration of Parliament—A person who is in office as Speaker immediately before the dissolution or expiration of Parliament shall, notwithstanding that dissolution or expiration, continue in office until the close of polling day at the next general election unless that person sooner vacates office as Speaker.

Cf 1986 No 114, s13

Parliament

18. Parliament—(1) There shall continue to be a Parliament of New Zealand, which consists of the Sovereign in right of New Zealand and the House of Representatives.

(2) The Parliament of New Zealand is the same body as that which was established by section 14 of the Constitution Act 1986.

Cf 1986 No 114, s14

19. Power of Parliament to make laws—Subject to this Constitution the Parliament of New Zealand continues to have full power to make laws.

Cf 1986 No 114, s15

20. Royal assent to Bills—A Bill passed by the House of Representatives shall become law when the Sovereign or the Governor-General assents to it and signs it in token of such assent.

Cf 1986 No 114, s16

21. Term of Parliament—The term of Parliament shall, unless Parliament is sooner dissolved, be 3 years from the day fixed for the return of writs issued for the last preceding general election of members of the House of Representatives, and no longer.

Cf 1986 No 114, s17

22. Summoning, proroguing, and dissolution of Parliament—(1) The Governor-General may by Proclamation summon Parliament to meet at such place and time as may be appointed therein, notwithstanding that when the Proclamation is signed or when it takes effect Parliament stands prorogued to a particular date.

(2) The Governor-General may by Proclamation prorogue or dissolve Parliament.

(3) A Proclamation summoning, proroguing, or dissolving Parliament shall be effective—

(a) On being gazetted; or

(b) On being publicly read, by some person authorised to do so by the Governor-General, in the presence of the Clerk of the House of Representatives and 2 other persons,—

whichever occurs first.

(4) Every Proclamation that takes effect pursuant to subsection (3)(b) of this section shall be gazetted as soon as practicable after it is publicly read.

Cf 1986 No 114, s18

23. First meeting of Parliament after general election—After any general election of members of Parliament, Parliament shall meet not later than 6 weeks

after the day fixed for the return of the writs for that election.
Cf 1986 No 114, s19

24. Carrying over of Parliamentary business—Where the House of Representatives resolves that any Bill, petition, or other business before it or any of its committees be carried over to the next session of Parliament (whether the same Parliament or not), that Bill, petition, or other business shall not lapse upon the prorogation or dissolution or expiration of the Parliament in being when that resolution is passed but shall be carried over accordingly.
Cf 1986 No 114, s20

Parliament and Public Finance

25. Bills appropriating public money—The House of Representatives shall not pass any Bill providing for the appropriation of public money or for the imposition of any charge upon the public revenue unless the making of that appropriation or the imposition of that charge has been recommended to the House of Representatives by the Crown.
Cf 1986 No 114, s21

26. Parliamentary control of public finance—It shall not be lawful for the Crown, except by or under an Act of Parliament—

(a) To levy a tax; or
(b) To raise a loan or to receive any money as a loan from any person; or
(c) To spend any public money.

Cf 1986 No 114, s22

The Judiciary

27. Protection of Judges against removal from office—A Judge of the High Court shall not be removed from office except by the Sovereign or the Governor-General, acting upon an address of the House of Representatives, which address may be moved only on the grounds of that Judge's misbehaviour or of that Judge's incapacity to discharge the functions of that Judge's office.
Cf 1986 No 114, s23

28. Salaries of Judges not to be reduced—The salary of a Judge of the High Court shall not be reduced during the continuance of the Judge's commission.
Cf 1986 No 114, s24

PART IV

BILL OF RIGHTS

General Provisions

29. Bill of Rights—(1) The rights and freedoms contained in this Bill of Rights are guaranteed.

(2) The provisions of this Part of this Act shall be known as the Bill of Rights.

30. Application—This Bill of Rights applies only to acts done—

(a) By the legislative, executive, or judicial branches of the government of New Zealand; or

(b) By any person or body in the performance of any public function, power, or duty conferred or imposed on that person or body by or pursuant to law.

Cf 1990 No 109, s2

31. Justified limitations—The rights and freedoms contained in this Bill of Rights may be subject only to such reasonable limits prescribed by law as can be demonstrably justified in a free and democratic society.

Cf 1990 No 109, s5

32. Other rights and freedoms not affected—An existing right or freedom shall not be held to be abrogated or restricted by reason only that the right or freedom is not included in this Bill of Rights or is included only in part.

Cf 1990 No 109, s28

33. Application to legal persons—Except where the provisions of this Bill of Rights otherwise provide, the provisions of this Bill of Rights apply, so far as practicable, for the benefit of all legal persons as well as for the benefit of all natural persons.

Cf 1990 No 109, s29

Life and Security of the Person

34. Right not to be deprived of life—No one shall be deprived of life except on such grounds as are established by law and are consistent with the principles of fundamental justice.

Cf 1990 No 109, s8

35. Right not to be subjected to torture or cruel treatment—Everyone has the right not to be subjected to torture or to cruel, degrading, or disproportionately severe treatment or punishment.

Cf 1990 No 109, s9

36. Right not to be subjected to medical or scientific experimentation—Every person has the right not to be subjected to medical or scientific experimentation without that person's consent.

Cf 1990 No 109, s10

37. Right to refuse to undergo medical treatment—Everyone has the right to refuse to undergo any medical treatment.

Cf 1990 No 109, s11

Democratic and Civil Rights

38. Electoral rights—Every New Zealand citizen who is of or over the age of 18 years—

(a) Has the right to vote in genuine periodic elections of members of the House of Representatives, which elections shall be by equal suffrage and by secret ballot; and

(b) Is qualified for membership of the House of Representatives.

Cf 1990 No 109, s12

39. Freedom of thought, conscience, and religion—Everyone has the right to freedom of thought, conscience, religion, and belief, including the right to adopt and to hold opinions without interference.

Cf 1990 No 109, s13

40. Freedom of expression—Everyone has the right to freedom of expression, including the freedom to seek, receive, and impart information and opinions of any kind in any form.

Cf 1990 No 109, s14

41. Manifestation of religion and belief—Every person has the right to manifest that person's religion or belief in worship, observance, practice, or teaching, either individually or in community with others, and either in public or in private.

Cf 1990 No 109, s15

42. Freedom of peaceful assembly—Everyone has the right to freedom of peaceful assembly.

Cf 1990 No 109, s16

43. Freedom of association—Everyone has the right to freedom of association.

Cf 1990, No 109, s17

44. Freedom of movement—(1) Everyone lawfully in New Zealand has the right to freedom of movement and residence in New Zealand.

(2) Every New Zealand citizen has the right to enter New Zealand.

(3) Everyone has the right to leave New Zealand.

(4) No one who is not a New Zealand citizen and who is lawfully in New Zealand shall be required to leave New Zealand except under a decision taken on grounds prescribed by law.

Cf 1990 No 109, s18

Non-Discrimination and Minority Rights

45. Freedom from discrimination—(1) Everyone has the right to freedom from discrimination on the grounds of colour, race, ethnic or national origins, sex, marital status, religious or ethical belief, disability, age, political opinion, employment status, family status or sexual orientation.

(2) Measures taken in good faith for the purpose of assisting or advancing persons or groups of persons disadvantaged because of colour, race, ethnic or national origins, sex, marital status, religious or ethical belief, disability, age, political opinion, employment status, family status or sexual orientation do not constitute discrimination.

Cf 1990 No 109, s19; 1993 No 82, s21

46. Rights of minorities—A person who belongs to an ethnic, religious, or linguistic minority in New Zealand shall not be denied the right, in community with other members of that minority, to enjoy the culture, or profess and practice the religion, or to use the language, of that minority.

Cf 1990 No 109, s20

Search, Arrest, and Detention

47. Unreasonable search and seizure—Everyone has the right to be secure against unreasonable search or seizure, whether of the person, property, or correspondence or otherwise.

Cf 1990 No 109, s21

48. Liberty of the person—Everyone has the right not to be arbitrarily arrested or detained.

Cf 1990 No 109, s22

49. Rights of persons arrested or detained—(1) Everyone who is arrested or who is detained under any enactment—

(a) Shall be informed at the time of the arrest or detention of the reason for it; and

(b) Shall have the right to consult and instruct a lawyer without delay and to be informed of that right; and

(c) Shall have the right to have the validity of the arrest or detention determined without delay by way of habeas corpus and to be released if the arrest or detention is not lawful.

(2) Everyone who is arrested for an offence has the right to be charged promptly or to be released.

(3) Everyone who is arrested for an offence and is not released shall be brought as soon as possible before a court or competent tribunal.

(4) Everyone who is—

(a) Arrested; or

(b) Detained under any enactment—

for any offence or suspected offence shall have the right to refrain from making any statement and to be informed of that right.

(5) Everyone deprived of liberty shall be treated with humanity and with respect for the inherent dignity of that person.

Cf 1990 No 109, s23

50. Rights of person charged—Everyone who is charged with an offence—

(a) Shall be informed promptly and in detail of the nature and cause of the charge; and

(b) Shall be released on reasonable terms and conditions unless there is just cause for continued detention; and

(c) Shall have the right to consult and instruct a lawyer; and

(d) Shall have the right to adequate time and facilities to prepare a defence; and

(e) Shall have the right, except in the case of an offence under military law tried before a military tribunal, to the benefit of a trial by jury when the penalty for the offence is or includes imprisonment for more than 3 months; and

(f) Shall have the right to receive legal assistance without cost if the interests of justice so require and the person does not have sufficient means to provide for that assistance; and

(g) Shall have the right to have the free assistance of an interpreter if the person cannot understand or speak the language used in court.

Cf 1990 No 109, s24

51. Minimum standards of criminal procedure—Everyone who is charged with an offence has, in relation to the determination of the charge, the following minimum rights:

(a) The right to a fair and public hearing by an independent and impartial court;

(b) The right to be tried without undue delay;

(c) The right to be presumed innocent until proved guilty according to law;

(d) The right not to be compelled to be a witness or to confess guilt;

(e) The right to be present at the trial and to present a defence;

(f) The right to examine the witnesses for the prosecution and to obtain the attendance and examination of witnesses for the defence under the under the same conditions as the prosecution;

(g) The right, if convicted of an offence in respect of which the penalty has been varied between the commission of the offence and sentencing, to the benefit of the lesser penalty;

(h) The right, if convicted of the offence, to appeal according to law to a higher court against the conviction or against the sentence or against both;

(i) The right, in the case of a child, to be dealt with in a manner that takes account of the child's age.

Cf 1990 No 109, s25

52. Retroactive penalties and double jeopardy—(1) No one shall be liable to conviction of any offence on account of any act or omission which did not constitute an offence by such person under the law of New Zealand at the time it occurred.

(2) No one who has been finally acquitted or convicted of, or pardoned for, an offence shall be tried or punished for it again.

Cf 1990 No 109, s26

53. Right to justice—(1) Every person has the right to the observance of the principles of natural justice by any tribunal or other public authority which has the power to make a determination in respect of that person's rights, obligations, or interests protected or recognised by law.

(2) Every person whose rights, obligations, or interests protected or recognised by law have been affected by a determination of any tribunal or other public authority has the right to apply, in accordance with law, for judicial review of that determination.

(3) Every person has the right to bring civil proceedings against, and to defend civil proceedings brought by, the Crown, and to have those proceedings heard, according to law, in the same way as civil proceedings between individuals.

Cf 1990 No 109, s27

PART V

Miscellaneous Provisions

54. Enforcement of Constitution—(1) Any person may seek a declaration in the High Court that any of the following are inconsistent with the Constitution —

(a) Any law;

(b) Any action by the sovereign, legislative, executive or judicial branches of the government of New Zealand;

(c) Any action by a person or body in the performance of any public function, power, or duty conferred or imposed on that person or body by or pursuant to law.

(2) Where any law or action has been held by any court to be inconsistent with the Constitution, the court may make such orders as are fair and reasonable in the circumstances in order to remedy any person adversely affected by the action.

55. Involvement of Attorney-General in proceedings—In any proceedings in which the question of consistency with any part of the Constitution is raised, the Attorney-General may be joined as a party, and if not joined may intervene.

56. Interpretation—In this Act, unless the context otherwise requires,—

'Constitution' means the provisions of this Act.

'Law' means any enactment in force at the commencement of this Act, any enactment made after the commencement of this Act, and any rule of common law.

57. Repeals—(1) The Constitution Act 1986 is repealed.

(2) The New Zealand Bill of Rights Act 1990 is repealed.

SCHEDULE

Te Tiriti o Waitangi

(THE TEXT IN MAORI)

Ko Wikitoria, te Kuini o Ingarani, i tana mahara atawai ki nga Rangatira me nga Hapu o Nu Tirani i tana hiahia hoki kia tohungia ki a ratou o ratou rangatiratanga, me to ratou wenua, a kia mau tonu hoki te Rongo ki a ratou me te Atanoho hoki kua wakaaro ia he mea tika kia tukua mai tetahi Rangatira hei kai wakarite ki nga Tangata maori o Nu Tirani-kia wakaaetia e nga Rangatira Maori te Kawanatanga o te Kuini ki nga wahikatoa o te Wenua nei me nga Motu-na te mea hoki he tokomaha ke nga tangata o tona Iwi Kua noho ki tenei wenua, a e haere mai nei.

Na ko te Kuini e hiahia ana kia wakaritea te Kawanatanga kia kaua ai nga kino e puta mai ki te tangata Maori ki te Pakeha e noho ture kore ana.

Na, kua pai te Kuini kia tukua a hau a Wiremu Hopihona he Kapitana i t e Roiara Nawi hei Kawana mo nga wahi katoa o Nu Tirani e tukua aianei, amua atu ki te Kuini e mea atu ana ia ki nga Rangatira o te wakaminenga o nga hapu o Nu Tirani me era Rangatira atu enei ture ka korerotia nei.

Ko te Tuatahi

Ko nga Rangatira o te Wakaminenga me nga Rangatira katoa hoki ki hai i uru ki taua wakaminenga ka tuku rawa atu ki te Kuini o Ingarani ake tonu atu-te Kawanatanga katoa o o ratou wenua.

Ko te Tuarua

Ko te Kuini o Ingarani ka wakarite ka wakaae ki nga Rangatira ki nga hapu-ki tangata katoa o Nu Tirani te tino rangatiratanga o o ratou wenua o ratou kainga me o ratou taonga katoa. Otiia ko nga Rangatira o te Wakaminenga me nga

Rangatira katoa atu ka tuku ki te Kuini te hokonga o era wahi wenua e pai ai te tangata nona te Wenua-ki te ritenga o te utu e wakaritea ai e ratou ko te kai hoko e meatia nei e te Kuini hei kai hoko mona.

Ko te Tuatoru

Hei wakaritenga mai hoki tenei mo te wakaaetanga ki te Kawanatanga o te Kuini-Ka tiakina e te Kuini o Ingarani nga tangata Maori katoa o Nu Tirani ka tukua ki a ratou nga tikanga katoa rite tahi ki ana mea ki nga tangata o Ingarani.

(Signed) WILLIAM HOBSON
Consul and Lieutenant-Governor

Na ko matou ko nga Rangatira o te Wakaminenga o nga hapu o Nu Tirani ka huihui nei ki Waitangi ko matou hoki ko nga Rangatira o Nu Tirani ka kite nei i te ritenga o enei kupu, ka tangohia ka wakaaetia katoatia e matou, koia ka tohungia ai o matou ingoa o matou tohu.

Ka meatia tenei ki Waitangi i te ono o nga ra o Pepueri i te tau kotahi mano, e waru rau e wa te kau o to tatou Ariki.

Ko nga Rangatira o te wakaminenga.

Treaty of Waitangi

(THE TEXT IN ENGLISH)

HER MAJESTY VICTORIA Queen of the United Kingdom of Great Britain and Ireland regarding with Her Royal Favour the Native Chiefs and Tribes of New Zealand and anxious to protect their just Rights and Property and to secure to them the enjoyment of Peace and Good Order has deemed it necessary in consequence of the great number of Her Majesty's Subjects who have already settled in New Zealand and the rapid extension of Emigration both from Europe and Australia which is still in progress to constitute and appoint a functionary properly authorised to treat with the Aborigines of New Zealand for the recognition of Her Majesty's Sovereign authority over the whole or any part of those islands—Her Majesty therefore being desirous to establish a settled form of Civil Government with a view to avert the evil consequences which must result from the absence of the necessary Laws and Institutions alike to the native population and to Her subjects has been graciously pleased to empower and to authorise me William Hobson a Captain in Her Majesty's Royal Navy Consul and Lieutenant Governor of such parts of New Zealand as may be or hereafter shall be ceded to her Majesty to invite the confederated and independent Chiefs of New Zealand to concur in the following Articles and Conditions.

ARTICLE THE FIRST

The Chiefs of the Confederation of the United Tribes of New Zealand and the separate and independent Chiefs who have not become members of the Confederation cede to Her Majesty the Queen of England absolutely and without reservation all the rights and powers of Sovereignty which the said Confederation or Individual Chiefs respectively exercise or possess, or may be supposed to exercise or to possess over their respective Territories as the sole Sovereigns thereof.

ARTICLE THE SECOND

Her Majesty the Queen of England confirms and guarantees to the Chiefs and Tribes of New Zealand and to the respective families and individuals thereof the full exclusive and undisturbed possession of their Lands and Estates Forests Fisheries and other properties which they may collectively or individually possess so long as it is their wish and desire to retain the same in their possession; but the Chiefs of the United Tribes and the individual Chiefs yield to Her Majesty the exclusive right of Preemption over such lands as the proprietors thereof may be disposed to alienate at such prices as may be agreed upon between the respective Proprietors and persons appointed by Her Majesty to treat with them in that behalf.

ARTICLE THE THIRD

In consideration thereof Her Majesty the Queen of England extends to the Natives of New Zealand Her royal protection and imparts to them all the Rights and Privileges of British Subjects.

W. HOBSON Lieutenant Governor

Now therefore We the Chiefs of the Confederation of the United Tribes of New Zealand being assembled in Congress at Victoria in Waitangi and We the Separate and Independent Chiefs of New Zealand claiming authority over the Tribes and Territories which are specified after our respective names, having been made fully to understand the Provisions of the foregoing Treaty, accept and enter into the same in the full spirit and meaning thereof: in witness of which we have attached our signatures or marks at the places and the dates respectively specified.

Done at Waitangi this Sixth day of February in the year of Our Lord One thousand eight hundred and forty.

[Here follow signatures, dates, etc.]

Index